D1634146

FIGHT FOR THE TIGER

FIGHT FOR THE TIGER

One Man's Fight to Save the
Wild Tiger from Extinction

Michael Day

Founder of The Tiger Trust

HEADLINE

Copyright © 1995 Michael Day

The right of Michael Day to be identified as the Author of
the Work has been asserted by him in accordance with the
Copyright, Designs and Patents Act 1988.

First published in 1995
by HEADLINE BOOK PUBLISHING

10 9 8 7 6 5 4 3 2 1

All rights reserved. No part of this publication may be
reproduced, stored in a retrieval system, or transmitted,
in any form or by any means without the prior written
permission of the publisher, nor be otherwise circulated
in any form of binding or cover other than that in which
it is published and without a similar condition being
imposed on the subsequent purchaser.

British Library Cataloguing in Publication Data

Day, Michael
Fight For The Tiger
I. Title
001.95

ISBN 0-7472-1548-0

Typeset by
Letterpart Limited, Reigate, Surrey

Printed and bound in Great Britain by
Mackays of Chatham PLC, Chatham, Kent

HEADLINE BOOK PUBLISHING
A division of Hodder Headline PLC
338 Euston Road
London NW1 3BH

To Sophy, without whose generous love and support,
none of this would have been possible.

CONTENTS

ACKNOWLEDGEMENTS

A great many people have entered my life over the past five years and played a significant role in my endeavours to fight for the survival of the world's last remaining wild tigers. To each and every one of them, I owe a great debt of gratitude. Some were there at the very beginning, others have seemingly popped up out of nowhere more recently and been of invaluable assistance in the ongoing international campaign. To name some and omit others is a business fraught with complexity and one which I would prefer not to even attempt. Nevertheless, there are a number of very key individuals that fully deserve the modest public recognition that I can offer them on this page. There remain a few that I dare not mention for fear of endangering their lives.

In Thailand: Dwaila Armstrong, Phil Watkins, Aroon Srisuwan and Sorut Kanket opened my eyes to the tiger crisis and helped me not to walk away. In Hong Kong: Martin Williams pointed the way and Wong Kwok Hung believed in my mission and trusted me like an old friend. Caroline Harper, Peter Kirrage, Tom Hartje and Stephanie Cross-Wilson helped establish the solid base for much of my work in the Far East. In Taiwan, Keith and Suzie Highley provided sound advice and a stout shoulder of support and I am in debt to Wu Hung Bhiksu for his patience and wise counsel. In Russia, Valentin Ilyashenko, Vladimir Shetinin and Sergei Shaitarov have become invaluable allies in the war against the poachers and in the United States, Sam LaBudde deserves special recognition for his financial and moral support. Don Watson for his technological brilliance and sense of humour, John Fitzgerald for his legal expertise and Marshall Jones and Sue Lieberman at the US Fish and Wildlife Service for their guts in the face of adversity. In this country, Ian MacPhail's wisdom and friendship have been of great comfort, Nick Gray's skill behind the camera helped launch the plight of the tiger into the hearts of millions, Sean Ryan encouraged me to write it all down and helped get me started, while Mike Shaw coached the concept to fruition with extraordinary patience and skill. To everyone else, including Peter Jackson, Dr Bill Clark, Harald Mertes, Patrick Gotoking, Kate Pearce, Diane MacEachern, Tim Redford, Martha Benson, and Peter Knights, I say thank you once again. To Rebecca Chen and Steve Galster, two of the most courageous people it has ever been my privilege to know and work with, no humble words of mine could ever thank you enough and finally to Boonlerd Angsirijinda, I miss you more than I can say.

PROLOGUE

Harbin, People's Republic of China, July 1993

The battle-scarred Bakelite telephone rattled angrily on the bedside table. It was 11 p.m. No-one would normally ring at this hour. Unless it was him again.

The man had phoned earlier that night demanding to know where I had been all weekend. It was none of his business. I fed him an elaborate saga involving a beautiful maiden and a hideaway love-nest in the mountains. His vile and wheezing voice had chortled salaciously into my ear. Reassured now, he arranged to meet me early the following morning in the downstairs lobby. I had no intention of being there. After that call, I went directly to the bar and swallowed a large scotch. Fifteen minutes later, having settled my account with the hotel cashier, I returned to the room to purge the evil of the past three days from my skin.

Turning off the bath taps, I stared impatiently at the steaming water. Damn the phone!

'Yes,' I growled, recognising the pidgin English of the late-night caller. 'Have you any idea what time it is?'

The wheezing voice was menacing now. 'Mister Mike, what are you playing at, why you check out of hotel?'

My brain catapulted into gear, searching for clues. Was he alone and *where* was he? How did he find out, and what the hell could I tell him?

'Oh, yes, but of course, I should have mentioned it before,' I struggled to sound convincing. 'My father-in-law is flying in from Taipei tomorrow and wants me to stay with him at the Excelsior.'

'Don't believe!' he bellowed. 'I think you are spy. People coming now to your room. We find out truth!'

My hackles stood on end as he spat out the words.

1

The leather holdall lay open on the bed, and buried deep inside a hidden pocket was the incriminating video tape. If I could only get this vital evidence safely out of the country, the world would finally know the truth. Counting seconds, I carefully turned on the bedside radio.

'Just a second, I think my bath water is overflowing, won't be a minute,' I stammered, setting the receiver down gently, an inch from the loudspeaker.

Stripping the towel from my waist, I made a frenzied dash for the bathroom and grabbed my clothes. Dressing in seconds, I threw the tiny cameras and video equipment from the bed unceremoniously into the bag and hurled myself toward the door. Outside, mercifully, the corridor was empty. I double-locked the room and fled.

I hid in the shadows of the stairwell, my pulse thundering inside my head. In the hall I heard the elevator stop and the sound of heavy feet running down the passage.

Slowly, one by one, I crept up the stairs away from the angry shouts and the loud banging at my door. Somehow I had to find a way out. If they found me, there would be no mercy . . .

PART ONE
THE AWAKENING

*'Faith is permitting ourselves to be seized
by the things we cannot see.'*

Martin Luther

CHAPTER ONE

Southern Thailand, January 1990

I awoke very early, too early. Something was out there, and that *something* had just summoned me from my befuddled dreams and cast me back into the land of the living with an uneasy jolt.

There was still not enough light to read the time from my battered wristwatch and yet I knew, even at this hour, the jungle should be alive with the noise of some creature or other, if only the beating wings of the nocturnal scurrying home through the trees, like vampires before the dawn. But there was nothing. I had been woken by the sudden sound of silence.

Sleep clogged my eyes. I rubbed them with the heels of my hands, forcing my swollen fingers harshly through tangled hair. I focused hard on the snagging pain on my scalp, forcing the sensation deep into my brain, desperately trying to sharpen my dulled senses.

All was strangely quiet, the air still, yet charged with the presence of the unseen. I had no idea what it was. Instinctive fear helped drive the adrenaline through my veins. My heart began thumping, and it was hard to swallow the bile as my stomach tightened. Slowly my senses came alive.

Straining hard now, with head held rigidly still, my eyes began to focus in the half light of early dawn. I peered anxiously through the grey mesh of the mosquito net, not wishing to move or get too close to the sheer gossamer that separated me from whatever was out there.

A twig cracked away to the right of the camp, sending a deep shudder down my spine. Fifty feet away, or was it closer? Impossible to tell. There was no doubt now, but could it see me? Could it smell my fear? Was *it* afraid too?

Inside the makeshift bamboo shelter that housed our bed, I

looked across at my three companions. The gentle rise and fall of their sleeping-bags did not falter, they were still asleep. No point in waking them, I thought. Foolish, what would I say? 'Can you hear that? Yes, *that*, you know . . . nothing!'

And so I waited, long seconds turning into minutes, ears straining for the next sound. But there was only the faint whisper of measured breathing as my racing pulse gradually returned to normal.

Last evening, as the others drank warm beer and Mekong whisky by the glowing embers of the camp fire, I had slipped quietly away, a half bottle of Sang Thip rum in the pocket of my jungle fatigues, and watched the moon dancing in the silver water of a forest stream. The liquid was harsh and warm, and I prayed that its potent strength would protect me from the nightmares I knew would surely come. The crackling fire sent sparks of orange light high into the canopy behind me and as the tree frogs croaked their nightly chorus all around, a persistent memory began to slowly emerge like some ghoulish corpse drifting menacingly downstream from the shadows into the pale moonlight before me . . .

Gothenburg, Sweden, March 1984

Wednesday morning was much like any late winter morning in that part of town. Blackened snow still lined the streets, and damp air and cold north-easterly winds ensured that the dawning of spring was still on a very distant horizon. I had not expected to, and yet I awoke refreshed from an untroubled sleep, my mind suddenly clear and disentangled despite the relentless torment of the previous weeks. During the night I had moved on to a different plateau. Somewhere in the depths of my subconscious a decision had been made. I now knew exactly what I had to do, and I was being given the strength and courage to see it through. Dressing in yesterday's clothes, I padded barefoot into the kitchen. From the small balcony, I watched the silent people trudging through the street below, people that I would never meet. I quietly wished them well, knowing that wherever they were going, I could not join them.

Peter and Katarina lived in a small apartment on the outskirts of town and I knew that they would be at home. They would not be surprised at my arriving uninvited to join them for a late breakfast. They had been good friends, especially Peter. He seemed to know, unlike most men, the pain and turmoil of depression, and although

I was quite sure that he had never experienced such despair himself, he was always able to find the time to listen to my unremitting self-pity.

I wondered if I were letting him down, but reasoned that somewhere in his huge heart he would be able to understand and forgive. Returning to my own apartment later that day, I was convinced that there had been no hint of suspicion. We had talked endlessly about how I should rebuild my life, snap out of my melancholy; start again. But the pain that burned inside me was just too intense. His soothing words simply evaporated all around me. My carefully made plans remained intact.

At four o'clock I left the building. I needed to buy a few things; especially a bottle of good gin. It was already quite dark by the time I got back. I ignored the messages on the answer-phone. Only habit had made me switch it on before I went out, and I was in no mood to talk to anybody. Fierce determination had begun to possess me, and the confidence that came with it might all too easily be dented by idle chatter.

From the sparc room I retrieved two large suitcases, and carried them into the bedroom. With one sweep I gathered an armful of clothes from the wardrobe. Shirts, jackets, trousers, woollens and underwear, somehow I managed to fit them all in. I looked at the empty space that I had made. It didn't move me at all.

I needed a drink, and poured an extremely large gin into a tumbler and splashed the dregs of a forgotten tonic water over the top. I took the bottle with me from the kitchen and sat on the edge of the bed. I unwrapped a small package that I had bought and laid it out on the bedside table. It felt hard and cold. I swallowed the gin in two gulps, as if it were water. From a side drawer I took out an envelope and quickly scribbled an address, then, putting a spare key inside, I taped down the flap.

The suitcases were heavy, but I didn't have to go far. Outside, the temperature had dropped to below freezing, but the fire of the gin kept me warm as I marched purposefully through the snow toward the Oxfam charity shop. A large metal door positioned on the side of the building pivoted inwards. I heaved both cases into the opening and watched with satisfaction as they hurtled down the chute into the darkness below.

Across the street I could see the letter-box that I had planned to use. The small metal plaque advised me that the last collection was at seven forty-five each evening. It was already nine-fifteen, perfect.

I dropped the letter carefully inside and returned home.

I showered away the city grime, carefully brushed my hair and, taking two small bottles from the bathroom cabinet, retreated to the sanctuary of my bedroom. I shook the entire contents of both bottles into my left hand, and with my right took firm hold of the bottle of gin. With several enormous gulps of the ferocious liquid, I finished the bottle, washing the last of the white tablets down my throat. The crumpled paper package lay waiting on the bedside table. With steady fingers I took out the gleaming scalpel and got slowly into bed. There was no pain as the sharp metal sank deep into my wrists, only blessed relief. I was going to sleep for the last time . . .

I look back now and remember all too vividly the power of the subconscious mind that overtook all reasonable and rational thought. The subliminal power that made it seem so easy to ruthlessly and quite callously dispose of my own life. I had known at the time of the intolerable distress that I would cause others; I knew that I was saying goodbye to all the things that most people look forward to in life, the joy of marriage and parenthood, family holidays, successful careers and healthy bank balances, even the simple everyday wonder of the sunrise, and yet I didn't care. The depression that consumed me at the time was so great and so painful that my subconscious had taken over. It had shown me a way out, a way to end all the pain and misery, and it made it blissfully easy, arming me with a cunning and a calculating fortitude – and the ultimate power to take my own life.

Only a series of strange coincidences saved my life that night. By a curious quirk of fate, the post-box on Vallgatan had not been emptied until very late and my letter arrived safely at its destination early the next morning; one full day ahead of schedule. My lawyer had reacted with lightning-speed efficiency and I was found in the nick of time. It was the torment of the closeness of that escape, the hospital and, later, the institution, that now kept me from my sleep. Remorse mixed with fear as I fought my inner turmoil. For six long years I had battled on, and I knew that I was slowly winning. The healing process took time, and alcohol helped me to be patient.

It was as if I now saw my life as two completely separate segments: pre-March 1984 was a time of great self-indulgence, fast money, fast cars, fast women, and all the trappings of a successful career in advertising; post-March 1984 had mostly been a time of

8

humility, of giving thanks for the wonder of living and all living things. Gone were the ambitions of luxury cars, Caribbean holidays, money to burn, life in the fast lane. In its place had developed a greater understanding of the natural world. Perhaps there was even an emerging appreciation that somewhere, in the great scheme of things, I had a role to play, things to do. It was probably that latent urge that had brought me to Thailand in the first place, in the wake of those forces, far beyond my control, that had conspired six years earlier to keep me alive. And yet now, deep inside the tropical rainforest, I was still searching to find out just exactly what that purpose might be . . .

There was more light now and that first quick intake of breath which had sent blood thundering through my veins and beads of sweat on to my brow now seemed distant and unreal. I blinked as the first ray of sunlight filtered through the dense canopy of the jungle, and with it came the first birdsong.

Whatever had been out there had by now slipped gently away into the shadows, stopping only momentarily to mark an ancient rock. As the early breeze carried the acrid smell to my nostrils, I knew all at once what had awoken me.

I lay awake watching the day break and listening to the sounds slowly return to the forest as the birdsong built up to the climax of the jungle dawn chorus. I heard Bun, one of our trackers, moving about outside and decided it was safe to get up. I whistled quietly to attract his attention and, as he caught my eye, I pointed to my ear in a questioning gesture. Had he heard anything, I wondered?

Bun instantly put his index finger to his lips and beckoned me with that casual underhand flick of the hand so typical of the Thai to quietly join him. He looked nervous as he watched me laboriously pulling on my jungle boots. For serious jungle treks Bun wore only flip-flops and couldn't understand the *farang's* (westerner's) need for stout leather foot protection. Particularly the sort that made so much noise even as I tiptoed gently over to meet him. He winced in displeasure at the crunch of broken twigs and crackle of leaves underfoot, although I did my best to move silently.

Whatever it was that had aroused me from my sleep, Bun had felt it too. Years of tracking along the smuggling routes of the opium barons in the rainforests of The Golden Triangle had finely honed his survival skills. He sensed rather than knew that whatever had been out there had now left the camp area. Nevertheless we both continued to scout around for clues. Suddenly I heard the sound of a

9

sharp whistle of air through clenched teeth as Bun, gesticulating wildly, urged me to join him. Squatting low to the ground, he showed me a small patch of earth, clearly still depressed from the weight of a large footprint. As I watched, small blades of grass sprang back intermittently bolt upright.

Bun swept the area lightly with his hand.

'*Siah*,' he said, the Thai word for tiger!

I took a couple of cautious steps forward, and yes, there and there, clearly visible now, were the paw-prints of a very large cat. He had come into the camp that night, his presence had stirred me from my rest, he had stayed long enough to know that I had awoken, long enough to know that I had felt his very being, and then departed as silently as he came. But why had he come? With all the millions of acres available, why this particular spot? What possible motive was there? We could have had guns and yet the king of the jungle was not afraid. I wanted to find out more about this bold and primal creature, and I smiled at Bun, who looked gravely back at me, clearly disturbed by the arrogant intrusion of this great beast. I walked back to wake the others, counting quietly to myself as I went. The 'intruder' had passed less than thirty feet from my bed!

Dwaila, our experienced team leader, was by now awake. She listened intently as, interspersed by frantic gabbling from Bun, I told her what we'd found. She was clearly flabbergasted. A tiger had never come this close before, she said. We decided to eat quickly and follow the tracks.

Our Dutch companions elected to guard the camp while we were gone, despite Dwaila's assurance that there was little risk of actually seeing the tiger, let alone being attacked by it. She was most curious to discover where he was lying up, since this was clearly his territory. Each armed with nothing more than a machete and a large stick, we set off. We followed the tracks down to the stream and it was easy to see where he had crossed. Bun wrinkled his nose as he caught the pungent aroma of the animal's urine, which had been sprayed as a final parting gesture against a large rock on the far side of the water.

It had been less than an hour since he'd passed by.

I looked over at Bun and Dwaila. Their faces were distorted as they strained their senses and searched for vital clues, clearly anxious that the tiger *might* attack. And yet, for some reason, I knew that he wouldn't. He'd had the chance whilst we were

10

sleeping, but hadn't taken it; this tiger was no man-eater. The creature we were tracking had no need to interfere with us, he was merely being inquisitive. All cats are curious but this one had aroused in me a sense of kinship. There was an unmistakable curiosity, and now it was mutual. It was almost as if he wanted me to follow him; but why? What on earth for? I was being drawn closer toward him as if by some unseen thread that had been tied between us during the night. And that thread was getting shorter by the minute.

The trail was quite visible through the trees and down to the old lumber road, where we followed it for a mile, back towards Dwaila's river camp, until it veered off sharply into the undergrowth. We hacked our way through some dense foliage and on to a well-trodden game path, the sort frequently used by deer and *gaur*, the large wild oxen of the region. We were moving quickly, almost too quickly, I thought at one stage. What if we caught up?

We slid down a steep bank on our backsides and into a tight gully at the bottom. The overhanging rocks on both sides would have made a perfect ambush point for a tiger up to no good. However, this was the entrance to something much more sinister.

This was the only way to reach 'the communists' cave', the home of guerrilla fighters during the insurgent 1970s, and where they had hidden their cache of weapons. They had all gone but who lived here now, I wondered? I knew almost nothing about tigers, their habits, habitat, etc. Bears lived in caves, I had read somewhere, so did the mountain lions in the American wild-west adventures of my youth. But did tigers?

Bun almost blundered straight into the mouth of the cave as he came to an abrupt and grinding halt, frantically throwing up his hands for us to stop as, too late, we concertina'd into the back of him. The reality of the situation seemed to hit us all simultaneously. The tiger's tracks went in but didn't come out.

The tiger was still *inside* the cave.

It was high time for us to beat a swift and silent retreat, although we almost fell over each other tiptoeing backwards away from the entrance. It was not until we were several hundred feet away that we collapsed in a fit of laughter as the reality of that close call finally hit us.

'Bun was going to just walk right in,' I said, imitating the bold and confident stride of our most experienced tracker.

Dwaila translated, and we all started laughing again. Neung, the

11

youngest boy, threw up his hands in mock surprise and perfectly mimed poor Bun's look of horror as he started to tiptoe backwards. He finally fell to the ground, seized by another fit of hysterics. We were letting off steam, and venting the sort of relief that only comes after looking sheer terror in the face.

'This is the sort of camp-fire story that will certainly improve with the telling!' said Dwaila, and we all laughed again.

Eventually we all quietened down, the tension relieved, and left the tiger in peace. As we returned to camp, each of us was mentally preparing our own version of events for the hapless Dutchmen.

And yet my mind was racing, turning over and over again the events of the past two days. Fate was showing me a new direction; a door had been opened in my subconscious, and I had taken the first few steps into the corridor beyond. And as I lay in my bed that night, high above the ground in the tree-top house, I felt as contented as I had been for a long, long time. And the nightmares didn't come.

CHAPTER TWO

England, December 1989

Although the events of 1984 had left permanent scars, both physically and mentally, I was determined somehow not to let the past haunt me forever. If there was to be some plausible explanation as to just why exactly I had been allowed to survive, then I knew I had to seek it out. It surely wouldn't come to me. Life is never that simple.

To both friends and family alike, I had developed into something of an enigma. Often moody, switching from abject melancholy to blind euphoria without warning and impossible to anticipate, I would launch myself into all sorts of wild hare-brained schemes, throwing everyone around me into complete and utter confusion. My desperate search for some rational answers produced only the inevitable series of disappointments, each ultimately doused and then forgotten by a binge on the bottle.

Frequently inebriated and frivolous, sometimes drunk and obnoxious, at times an alcoholic in all but name, I drifted from year to year. I wasn't so much a ship without a rudder, but one lacking in both destination, purpose and, perhaps more poignantly, a mate.

The latter half of the eighties had been years of both feast and famine, a never-ending series of ups and downs. Try as I might, they held no quick solutions and as the decade ended, I resolved to bury the past once and for all. Or rather, I drowned it, in a magnum of vintage Bollinger.

Christmas had been spent getting to know the family of my 'sometimes' girlfriend Sophy, at their farmhouse home in Norfolk. It had been a pleasant round of drinks parties, lunches and dinners. It all felt dangerously comfortable. I found it tantalisingly tempting, but it was an all-too-easy way out, and had I embraced this new family and responded in kind with the same affection that they showed me, I felt that the relationship would not have lasted very long.

Instead, I endeavoured to keep my distance, not too aloof, I hoped, but sufficiently reserved to maintain a modicum of independence.

And on New Year's Eve, Sophy and I returned to London. Seeing out the old year together seemed a logical way of ensuring that we'd start the new decade in each others' arms. I made only one New Year's resolution, which I was quite determined to keep. I resolved to enter the new decade with a completely new outlook on life, free of personal commitments, responsibilities and hang-ups. Free as never before to control my own destiny. I needed to purge my soul once and for all if I was ever to find true happiness and contentment. Harmony with others would only come if I laid to rest the ghosts of the past. It was going to be tough on both myself and Sophy, but it had to be done.

For the past few months I had been ducking the relationship. The reality that it required conviction and commitment had been creeping up on me, and I simply wasn't ready to commit. Cruel, inconsiderate and selfish as I was, I couldn't shake Sophy off. My drunken antics didn't impress her at all. To her they were totally transparent and although her friends said, 'Ditch this guy, you're wasting your time', her instincts told her otherwise, and she patiently watched and waited.

One night in early December, I had almost gone too far and although I probably didn't realise it at the time, my destiny was sealed from that night on. I had been at a favourite watering hole, imbibing first an excellent bottle of Australian Chardonnay, and then the best part of a bottle of late vintage port, with only a snack in between. A taxi would have cost less than a fiver but I chose to drive, and as I crossed the New King's Road, I noticed in the rear-view mirror that I had picked up a tail. The sort with blue flashing lights.

On December 20th, 1989, at West Hammersmith Magistrates Court, I was banned from driving for eighteen months and fined £250.

It was fortunate that I had taken one or two precautions. At the end of the proceedings I dutifully surrendered my green British driving licence to the court bailiff, although both my pink Swedish licence and my brand new, dark-grey international licence stayed firmly tucked away inside my wallet.

The die was now cast. England was no place for a man without the freedom to drive as he pleased, and particularly for one currently lacking in the bourgeois virtues of moderation and caution. It was time to leave, but where should I go?

I had been to Thailand a number of times before, and had always found the people friendly, the food excellent, the weather marvellous and the scenery stunning. My father had been a prisoner of war for almost four years up on the Thai/Burmese border, forced like so many tens of thousands of young soldiers to construct a railway at the behest of their Japanese captors. His youth had been buried in the jungles of Siam, as Thailand then was, along with the bodies of his friends and colleagues who died of ill-treatment, malnutrition or disease. Perhaps if I could unearth his lost spirit, then somehow I would liberate my own. A fanciful notion indeed, but nonetheless one with more than a grain of purpose to it. And so, two weeks into the new decade, I said my collective goodbyes, some tearful, others thankful, and set off with a one-way ticket to Bangkok.

The culture shock of the big city was worse than I had expected, and I didn't stay long. Within days of my arrival I had secured a flight south to the beautiful island of Phuket and found a blissfully quiet coastal village called Kata Noi.

The tropical beaches of Southern Thailand are scattered with bare, bronzing (but not always beautiful) bodies throughout most of our winter months, and I was not embarrassed to peel off and join them. The sun and I had hitherto always enjoyed a lasting and harmless relationship whenever we met up around the world. I was always quick to tan, but why a few days later, two large burns had appeared in exactly the same place on each arm, I shall probably never know. It was as if I had been ceremonially branded.

Further sunbathing was quite out of the question. On local doctor's orders, the sea and the beach were designated out of bounds and for days, huddled over a book in the shadows of a large parasol in the hotel garden, sipping rice whisky to kill the pain, I would wonder quietly, why me?

In desperation I travelled to Phuket Town to fax a friend, a very dear friend of whom I had been thinking more and more just recently. 'What,' I asked, 'was man to do? Should I stay or should I

15

return? Perhaps, darling, you'd like to fly out to join me and help ease this malaise?'

Sophy's response was, I suppose, typical, and to be expected. 'Perhaps!'

As I stepped out into the late afternoon air, I still clutched Sophy's one-page communiqué. Wondering if I should quietly go and crawl inside a bottle of Mekong whisky at some roadside noodle shop, I was distracted by the sight of two rather voluptuous-looking creatures on the far side of the street. They appeared deeply engrossed in a highly animated discussion, wafer-thin cigarettes clutched tightly between carefully manicured fingers, their bottoms, tightly squeezed into pants, hot to the point of scalding, leaning against the bonnet of my rented jeep.

'Lady-boys,' I thought, the local colloquialism for transvestites. I simply had to have a closer look! Trying not to be too conspicuous, I meandered slowly down the opposite side of the street, looking for a suitable gap in the stream of one-way traffic. Taking my life in my hands, I slipped uneventfully across the path of a swerving taxi and into the front entrance of a small souvenir shop about five doors down from my quarry.

'The boys' had not moved. If anything, they now looked even more firmly glued to the garishly painted bodywork of my Suzuki four-wheel-drive vehicle. I decided to keep watch on them through their reflections in the shop windows as I casually made my way up the street, homing in with every step. Quite what I expected to do when finally I encountered the duo I hadn't yet worked out, so engrossed was I in the fun of the stalk.

It must have been about then that fate stepped in, because instead of seeing the reflected images of the transvestites, I found myself looking through the glass at a figure leaning back in a chair behind a desk, spewing files, papers, contracts and other obscure items of clerical paraphernalia through the window in front of me.

He was a rather striking, white-haired gentleman, in the colonial style, and was busily talking into the receiver of a well-abused telephone. Could he be English, I wondered? He obviously worked here, so must surely know the town and the surrounding area. He must know of some meaningful diversion to keep me away from the beach? As the sun was almost over the yardarm, he might like a drink, so I pushed open the door. He glanced over and, smiling warmly, motioned for me to sit down in the vacant chair opposite him. If nothing else, I thought, we can have a pleasant chat,

16

perhaps a cocktail or two, something to pass the time.

Phil Watkins eventually finished his call, slowly spun round in his ancient swivel-chair, and fixed me with one of the most genuinely friendly smiles I'd seen in a long time. Although Thailand is often known as the 'land of smiles', all too frequently Thai smiles are shallow and without sincerity. Given the nature of some of the pleasure-seekers that frequent their shores, perhaps that's not so surprising.

We exchanged the usual niceties, and spoke briefly about the weather, as Englishmen away from home tend to do. Before long, though, we were far away, talking about his adventures in the various jungles of the world where he'd spent the best part of the last twenty-five years collecting snakes. He'd worked for zoos, universities, research institutes, and the film business.

It had never occurred to me before that all those film scenes – of rattlesnakes in westerns and massive boa constrictors in Tarzan epics – had to be choreographed by someone. There was always a snake handler, and Phil was one of the best known in the industry. He had retired a few years earlier, and moved to Phuket with his Thai wife. Ill-health had largely contributed to the curtailment of his globetrotting, which, by all accounts, he was missing desperately.

He now ran a small travel and tour service and, as we talked, he tried to kindle deep inside me an interest for the jungle. It didn't take long. I was born on a farm in East Anglia, and grew up loving the woods and meadows, the river banks and summer cornfields, all fabulous playgrounds for a boy, full of adventure and imaginary wild jungle animals. Life in Sweden had taught me a deeper love of forests, but the jungle, the real jungle, was something completely new to me. Phil's tales of real tigers and monkeys were just too tempting to resist, and he suggested that I should travel up to a place he knew of outstanding natural beauty: a 'Shangri-La' with a massive lake, out of which limestone mountains jutted proudly like enormous tree-clad spinning tops. I should, he said, meet an old friend of his who was running very small but very exclusive three-day treks deep into the rainforest.

As I listened, he told me a tale of the last party of stalwarts that had taken this excursion. They had used a young elephant to carry supplies, and late one afternoon, as they were approaching camp, it had been startled by a tiger, bolted into the undergrowth and hadn't been seen since!

I was hooked. By the time I left his office it was quite dark, and

17

the 'lady-boys' had vanished. All I could think about was the majesty of the rainforest that, by sheer luck, I was about to experience at first hand.

The following morning I checked out of my beach-side hotel in Kata Noi, left the keys of my jeep with the porter at the front desk, and caught a bus heading north out of Phuket island, across the southern peninsula and bound for the east-coast town of Surat Thani, a favourite hopping-off point for travellers to the islands of Kho Samui. Although the distance was less than 250 km, the bus seemed to stop at every available town and village along the way. It wasn't until late afternoon that I found myself walking the last two and a half miles down a dusty pot-holed track through coffee and rubber plantations. The distant drone of traffic on the road gradually disappeared, to be replaced by the sound of wild gibbons calling in the early evening from the spectacular cliff face beyond the tree line to my right.

So this was the 'Shangri-La' where Dwaila Armstrong had chosen to make her home. It was one of the most staggeringly beautiful places that I had ever seen.

Dwaila was now more Thai than her native American. Born and raised in Idaho, she had been sent to Thailand by the Peace Corps some twenty years earlier. Over an excellent dinner of local Thai specialities, washed down with ice-cold Singha beer, she told me something of her life in her adopted country and how she eventually came to stay.

She quite candidly confessed to having always been a bit of an oddball, and her square-peg-in-a-round-hole nature ensured that she was constantly shunted around Thailand from one posting to another, most of which ended in tatters. She simply tried too hard, she said.

Finally, and in some desperation by her superiors as to what to try next, she was given a baby elephant to look after. It was rumoured to be a white elephant but nobody was really sure. It wasn't expected to live long anyway.

However, nobody had really counted on the tenacity of young Miss Armstrong. She simply resolved that *no way* was this 'cute little sucker' going to die, so she promptly moved her sleeping-bag and mosquito net into the young creature's cage and nursed him back to life.

As the elephant recovered, it became completely devoted and followed her everywhere. Finally, when it was officially recognised as a white elephant (a most elaborate process involving hair follicle analysis, hide scrubbing and seventy-one other white-elephant defining tests), Dwaila was assigned the honour of presenting it to the King. And her future in Thailand was secured from that moment on.

Although she had become a minor celebrity and the toast of the red-neck bars in the quiet backwaters of Idaho, she quietly vowed never to return.

Foreigners came and went and were generally tolerated by the moderate Buddhist nature of most Thai people. Dwaila had stayed and made friends. Her house she had built herself, she was that kind of woman. It had taken over seven years, but the result was an outstanding achievement. She had also mastered the Thai language and the local dialect, and was both loved and hated with equal passion by the surrounding villagers, many of whom had provided the vital building skills necessary to erect the five spectacular tree-houses, two hundred yards from her front porch, at the base of a thousand foot almost perpendicular limestone rock face.

It was in one of these tree-houses that I stayed that night. Studying the construction, I could see that the walls and windows had been cleverly designed. The tree-house was in fact octagonal with eight supporting struts under the floor angled down at forty-five degrees and lashed tightly to the trunk. The bathroom section had a long blue pipe stretching rather incongruously down through the floor and buried deep into the ground below. There was a large fifty-gallon water barrel, filled daily by an ingenious bucket and pulley arrangement fed by a long hose-pipe from the well. The engineering had obviously been carefully thought out; the water alone must have weighed a quarter of a tonne. The floor was made of bamboo, the wood with a thousand uses, the walls made from its weave. The conical thatched roof was of woven coconut palm leaves, light, yet strong and effective. But perhaps the most remarkable thing about my tree-house was the feeling of equanimity it gave. As I lay under my mosquito net, sixty feet above the ground, and listened to the unfamiliar night sounds all around me, I began to realise that this was truly a wondrous place, and possibly somewhere that I might look for some real answers to the mystery of life.

There were two new faces at breakfast the next morning, a father and son team from Holland who had heard of Dwaila through

19

university contacts. They didn't look quite the intrepid explorer type in their matching shell-suits and squeaky white trainers. I shot a glance at Dwaila, who winked back knowingly.

As was her way, and with little ceremony, we all set off before first light, hanging on to the back of a decrepit old pick-up, back down the dusty road and then east through the Khao Sok National Park.

Khao Sok is a stunning kaleidoscope taken from the most fertile imaginations of Walt Disney illustrators and the most exotic travel brochures imaginable. Nothing could have prepared me for the sheer drama of the limestone mountains that appear, thrust skyward from the very bowels of the earth, straight through the canopy of the rainforest like great monolithic fingers. Each magnificent rock seemed covered in dense vegetation and surrounded by soaring birds against a backdrop of the most perfect blue skies. Standing in the back of the old pick-up, I wanted this drive to last forever. I still do, every time I see it, even now.

We stopped at a small village to buy provisions and soon were off again, this time turning north, into the mighty rainforest that lay before us. As we twisted our way down the mountain road, turning corners into new vistas, each more beautiful than the last, our driver finally pulled over. Dwaila, jumping down from the back of the truck, beckoned us over to a small hillock and we scrambled up behind her. When we approached the top I caught sight of the lake on the other side, several hundred feet below us, and my heart skipped a beat.

'That sure is some view, ain't it?' asked Dwaila.

There was nothing more to be said. I stood in awe looking out over what must be one of the most beautiful expanses of water anywhere in the world.

'Fancy a boat ride?' she asked finally. 'My river camp is across the other side.'

Crossing the lake in a fisherman's long-tail boat was even more spectacular than the drive. Here the great fingers of rock actually jutted out from the water, and we were able to manoeuvre the boat up close to examine the texture of the rock, and the stalactite-like globules of petrified stone. Creepers and buttress roots wound their way in and out of these bizarre formations like enormous drips of candle wax, inching down in search of water. We were also able to get very close to the gibbons and dusky leaf monkeys living on these peculiar mountains, and to witness their aerobatic antics as they swung from tree to tree, high above us, defying the several hundred foot drop into the lake below.

Reluctantly, we left the monkeys behind and journeyed on until, about two hours later, we approached Dwaila's river camp. There, nestled in the shallow waters of a hidden tributary was a group of tiny, one-roomed shacks, made from bamboo, lashed together across the narrow river basin. Precariously floating and yet never in danger of sinking. From the most submerged of the group, a single plume of smoke rose vertically. It was the cookhouse, I later discovered.

As we approached, three smiling faces greeted us, young, well-scrubbed faces covered in 'prickly heat' powder. These were to be our trackers and companions for the next three days. The oldest of the boys began excitedly talking to Dwaila. She'd been gone for almost a week; much had happened, and all had to be reported verbally, and in meticulous detail.

Over dinner that evening, of freshly caught and deliciously deep-fried fish, we learned of the events of the preceding few days: of the mating porcupine, the discarded king cobra skin, the newly discovered nest of hornbills, and the fresh tracks of a Malayan sun bear, all within walking distance of the camp.

It was going to be an exciting few days, I thought, as I lay that night on the bamboo floor of my hut and allowed myself to be lulled gently to sleep by the croaking chorus of tree frogs all around me.

The following day we rose before sunrise, ate a light breakfast of fruit, rice and the previous evening's leftovers and trekked slowly along a disused lumber path, looking out for tracks of animals that had been that way during the previous night. It wasn't long before we caught sight of the unmistakable pug marks of a large male tiger.

'That's the big boy,' said Dwaila, as if he were an old friend. She seemed so matter-of-fact, almost as if finding fresh tiger tracks were a daily occurrence. I recalled Phil Watkins' story about one of her elephants being spooked by a tiger and bolting into the under-growth. And yet here we all were, casually walking along the same path that quite obviously had been used by a large tiger only a few hours earlier. I couldn't help but feel nervous and walked on in silence, wondering just how far away the big boy was now.

By early afternoon we had travelled more than five kilometres deeper into the jungle, and were as far away from civilisation as I'd ever been in my entire life.

Through a narrow clearing I eventually spotted Dwaila's remote jungle camp. It was spartan to say he least, but I didn't care. There was a solitary bamboo construction, built on stilts two feet off the ground, about ten feet wide and seven feet deep. It was open along one side and was to be our only shelter for the night. The Dutch seemed unimpressed, but it looked marvellous to me.

We swam in the stream at the edge of camp that evening and watched a thousand butterflies drinking salt close to the roots of a fallen fig tree.

Dwaila read quietly in her hammock before dinner and I chatted politely with the mathematics professor from Utrecht. Mostly I just wanted to drink in the intoxicating jungle atmosphere. Greystoke was obviously no fool.

By nightfall, the boys had bivouacked themselves in trees around the camp and the four of us remained chatting idly by the fireside until some haunting shadow flashed briefly behind my eyes and I knew that I had to be alone. That was when, with only the warm rum for company, I walked down to the moonlit stream to face the ghosts of my past.

Later, as I snapped out of my sordid reverie, it was as though a dark cloud had vaporised into the night sky. My mind seemed clearer, purged for the time being of those haunting memories. I weaved my way gently through the camp and retired to the mattress of banana leaves, with only the gossamer-thin wall of the mosquito net separating me from the jungle beyond. I was blissfully tired and sleep came easily.

CHAPTER THREE

Khao Sok National Park, January 1990

We had left the jungle camp shortly after two o'clock, the worst of the midday heat behind us. Lunch had been a fry-up of the previous night's leftovers, made all the more tasty by the delicious thrill of that morning's brush with the tiger. The Dutch professor and his son were unimpressed with the food, and anxious to get going. His hyperactive brain had already calculated the walking time to our destination, and had obviously allowed plenty of time for rest and relaxation along the way.

It seemed that both Dwaila and I, and the trackers Bun and Neung who had accompanied us that morning, had become somewhat alienated from the rest of the group, as if our earlier private adventure had set us apart from our companions. It was not our fault, the jungle was there to be enjoyed and explored. The third Thai boy, Bun's cousin, simply felt left out, an exciting experience missed. He'd picked the short straw and had to stay behind. The Dutch had had quite enough, they just wanted to go home. We left the camp in silence.

Determined not to allow this to spoil our afternoon, I joked and made light of our 'morning stroll', painting ourselves as reckless adventurers. Hadn't the Dutch also ventured out on to uncharted waters three centuries ago, I enquired, in search of new land and answers to the mysteries of the world? It was no use, these Dutchmen were of a different ilk and of passive persuasion. They merely wanted the briefest *soupçon* of the primitive world, a modest pandering to their heroic ancestors, and the chance to embroider a good yarn over a jar of Heineken back home.

I walked alone for a while, Dwaila and Neung up ahead jabbering incessantly. Bun and his cousin had fallen back, keeping a few paces behind the Dutch. I counted species of birds: kingfishers, coucals, barbets, various jungle babblers, a tiny blue-winged leafbird. Suddenly we all stopped as Dwaila raised her hand to signal the heavy beating wings of a small flock of hornbills just before they broke through a clearing ahead of us. We zigzagged our way across the stream, until the flow became a small river and we had to cross again. This time the water came up to our knees and, using our sticks to form a human chain spanning the river, we waded to the far bank for the last time.

We stopped for a first break and Bun was sent off upstream, ostensibly to check in case some rotting cadaver might be polluting the river.

Dwaila came over and said to me, 'Walk with me a while. You know, when you're ready.'

Bun returned carrying a huge banana leaf above his head like a parasol. Always smiling he called, '*Mai mee pen ha!*' (No problem!)

Gratefully we filled our water-bottles from the crystal-clear water and, dousing my lucky silk scarf, I tied the soaking fabric around my neck in a loose knot. Cool drops ran down my spine. It felt delicious.

'Where did you learn that trick?' asked Dwaila as we began to set off on the next leg of our journey.

'Oh, I don't know,' I replied, 'I think I saw it in an old western a hundred years ago. At least it feels like that. Here in the jungle one loses all sense of time and perspective.'

'Ain't that the truth,' she said, with her customary economy. Then, 'What's your story, Mike?' she asked, in that blunt way so typical of the Thai.

In Thailand every lost soul had a story. I'd seen it myself in the expatriate community in Phuket: so many sad and lonely people, and an awful lot of dead-beats, full of spit and wind, with the odd eccentric artist and entrepreneur thrown in for good measure. Dwaila's probing antenna had detected my inner turmoil, and after more than twenty years in Thailand she had opted for the direct approach.

'What do you see?' I tried.

'A wife back home somewhere, possibly a girlfriend. Figure you need some time to sort things around in your head. And a lot more b'sides.'

'How much more?'

'That's what I can't quite figure out yet. Last night, when you

24

went off all alone, abrupt like. You got your troubles, that's for sure!'

'Ain't that the truth,' I replied.

Dwaila laughed so loud that I thought she might implode. She cupped her hand over her eyes, shielding them from the sun, squinting at me with a faint quizzical look that accentuated the deeply tanned lines around her face.

'Dwaila,' I said, 'mind if I stick around for a few days?'

'Thought you'd never ask,' she replied, and we both laughed.

As we walked on past wild banana plants, each with a flower like some enormous phallus pointing to the earth, and through lianas suspended from the sky, waiting only for Tarzan to come swinging through the trees, Dwaila became suddenly more introspective as if for every step she was seeing things for the last time.

'I guess you've seen a lot of change around here in the last twenty years,' I ventured. She looked at me again, probingly, as if gauging the depth of my interest. And just how much of the truth I could handle.

'When Bun went off back there, you think he really went looking only for some rotting carcass upstream? Now where'd you think a cadaver like that would come from anyhow?' Her words suddenly hit me like a thunderbolt.

Poachers, I thought, but this is a national park. *Take nothing but pictures, leave nothing but footprints* and all that. As if reading my mind, Dwaila went on. She was on a roll, there was no stopping her now.

'You don't really believe all that bullshit you read back at the park headquarters, do you now? Six hundred and fifty square kilometres of untouched, pristine, *virgin* rainforest? The way this place has been *fucked* in the last twenty years makes the word *rape* seem positively serene.'

There was both anger and hatred in her sudden outburst, a blunt statement of fact delivered with scathing contempt. The kind that comes only with first-hand experience. Perhaps that's why I wasn't so much shocked by how she said it, but *what* she had said. I'd heard coarse language like this from a woman before. Profanity was usually the last resort of the inarticulate or the inebriate, but for Dwaila it was a momentary unveiling of a darker, more sinister side, a chink in the armour of someone who had done battle with the most evil of men.

'Back up the stream aways,' she went on, 'there's another camp and the people that use it don't ought to be there. They've been trapping and snaring just about everything that either flies or walks in these parts, cutting down rattan and stuff for as long as I can remember. And, in case you're thinking about asking, the folks down in them fancy park offices knows all about it. 'Cept they're just too damn idle and corrupt to give a shit.'

My God, I thought, as I felt the fragile walls of this Shangri-La begin to crumble all around me. Even here, in this fabulous wilderness, nothing was as it seemed.

'Why?' I spluttered hopelessly.

'When you was in Phuket, did you ever go down to Patong Beach, 'specially at night, to them *girlie* bars?'

'Sure, I've been there,' I confessed, and then it clicked. 'The gibbons?'

'You got it. Hunters come up here to get the young ones and kill the mothers, and if she's still lactating, so much the better. Baby gibbons is easy to bottle-feed, dress them up in diapers and folks thinks that looks cute too. The fat-arsed perverts from Germany and the likes that *frequent* those bars seem to think it's kind-a-quaint. Dumb mother-fuckers. I'd like to herd them all up into a ditch and pull the plug on the lot of them.'

'Yeah,' I said hopelessly. Then, 'Tell me more about the poachers, what else do they take?'

'You name it, wild boar, hog and barking deer, gaur. The army chiefs and police commissioners come up here on weekends, get drunk and shoot the shit out of anything that moves, 'specially the gaur. The horns is big face. If they can, they drag the kill back to their camp and butcher it there. What they don't eat or carry out gets thrown in the river when they're done.'

We walked on for a while in silence. Bun had found some foliage to gnaw on, and came trotting up to push a sprig of leaves into my hand. He pointed to his glistening white teeth, chomping furiously, smiling as always. His look said 'Try some', so I did. Anything once, I thought. The leaves tasted surprisingly good, with a faint trace of liquorice. I smiled back at him in thanks, grateful for his timely intrusion. He skipped off back to join the others, stopping to offer some leaves to the Dutch. He seemed not the least surprised when they wrinkled their noses in unified disapproval. Bun was the personification of the Thai expression 'Sabai, sabai'. Take it easy!

I could tell somehow that Dwaila was waiting for an opportunity to continue her conversation, and yet the more she spoke and the more she confided in me, the more entangled I was to become in the sinister intrigue that surrounded Khao Sok National Park.

This place wasn't just an enigma waiting to be unravelled, I thought, there is something here much more serious. A profoundly entrenched evil possessed part of this beautiful land, and its force was subliminal and pervasive, touching anyone and anything that might stop long enough to care.

'Tigers?' I asked, suddenly fearful for the life of the early morning intruder.

'King of the jungle as far as the poachers are concerned. Top dollar. There ain't no part of the tiger that don't have some value or other for these people.' She spat the words out in disgust. 'Time was, not so long ago, when there were maybe two dozen or more in these parts. Now you'd be lucky to find half a dozen, and they ain't long for this world the way things are going.'

'And the park guards, the rangers, don't they try to protect them?' I asked.

'Don't make me laugh,' she said angrily. 'Those that do care are far outnumbered by those that are on the take. Let's face it, pal, the tiger's doomed; it's only a matter of time now. Be thankful for your brief encounter this morning; in a few years' time, they'll all be gone!'

'Not if I can help it,' I said suddenly.

'What was that?'

'Oh, nothing. What about the Buddhist reverence for life and all living things?' I tried, knowing that ninety-five per cent of the Thai were supposedly Buddhist.

'And what exactly do you know about the precepts of Buddhism?'

'No more than most visitors, I shouldn't wonder,' I said, somewhat put out, 'except that there are eight principles and sanctity of life is one of them.'

'Well, my friend, I'll tell you the others. Apart from forbidding killing, which you so rightly pointed out, the Buddhist precepts also advise against: stealing, adultery, telling lies, intoxicants, eating after midday, indulging in dancing and other forms of musical entertainment, *and* pre-marital sex. And I'll tell you another thing; I've been around these parts for long enough to know that most folks indulge in several of them and I could even name one or two that have indulged in *all* of them!'

'What about the monks, aren't they at least supposed to demonstrate some sort of example?'

'The monks maybe, but I don't trust all of them neither. As for the rest, the only thing they truly revere is the green-back and the more the better. Did you see all them TV aerials poking out of the roofs of them floating hooches on the lake? Those were for colour TVs. Most of them remote control too. Big face. In the villages around the park it's the same. TVs, fancy refrigerators, mobile phones, pick-up trucks with alloy wheels, you name it. Now where'd you think they get that kinda money?'

'Isn't anybody doing anything?'

'Those of us that know have tried. I've been shot at twice, my dog's been poisoned, truck sabotaged. One day I took off and some bastard had cut the brake lines. After a while you learn to keep your mouth shut. One thing's for sure and that is as long as that son-of-a-bitch Panas is in charge of things – and he's stomped on every young ranger that's ever dared have a go – it's just a matter of time before the only wildlife you'll see around here is leeches and red-ants!'

'Who's Panas?'

'He's the park superintendent, except he superintends Bangkok most of the time. According to the rules he should have only been here three years before he was rotated someplace else. Supposed to stop bribery and corruption. He's been here almost eleven years, that should tell you something about the system.'

'You mean he's still here because of connections, bribery, or both?'

'I'll let you work that one out.'

Her diatribe was over, and I was left feeling like a voyeur in her private world. I began to wonder if anyone *could* make a difference; the rot appeared to go all the way to the top. Then I began to think about seriously filming the natural splendour of the park and trying to capture its most spectacular inhabitant, the tiger, on film. Would the 'big boy' allow me to get close enough? If not, I would have to try and outwit him. But how on earth would I go about doing anything, let alone filming, in the middle of the jungle, miles away from human settlement and all the amenities like electricity, hot water and telephones? Although I understood about cameras, I certainly didn't possess the knowledge or experience to mount a full-scale documentary project of the size that was buzzing around inside my head at the time. And yet if only I could capture *some* of it on film so that I could show people the sheer magnificence of the place, then surely it would be protected. Fanciful notions perhaps, but real enough to me at the time, and I resolved to record as much material as I could on video and then try and convince the professionals back home in England to back the project. Slowly an idea began to take shape in my mind. It would take a great deal of ingenuity and hard work, not to mention good luck, and would probably wipe out my savings into the bargain, but it might just work.

'Has anyone ever filmed the tigers in Khao Sok?' I asked Dwaila.

'Nope, not to my knowledge,' she replied. ''Course, anyone that could get close enough with a camera would also be close enough with a gun, and in the minds of most folks around here, bullets is cheaper.'

White-handed gibbons whooped and babbled from the limestone cliffs a stone's throw away from my tree. A dog barked below, a challenging, playful bark. Recognising this, and in mock torment, the gibbons seemed to call even louder, and then the cicadas joined in. First a sentinel, then ten thousand responded to a cacophony of grinding legs, piercing the early dawn with their tumultuous clatter.

Wake-up call, jungle style!

Remembering Dwaila's words, I pulled my blanket tightly around my shoulders as a shiver ran up my spine. This is their country, their wildlife, their future, I thought. Didn't they realise what they were doing, were they too blinkered or too blind to see? Would my plan work? I had to find Dwaila and talk to her. If anyone could help me, it would be her.

I re-read the letter written to Sophy the previous evening. Nothing's changed, I thought, if anything I'm even more determined now.

I padded barefoot over to the cramped washing area of my circular living platform high above the ground. Splashing water on to my face and washing away the last cobwebs of sleep, I noticed that I had disturbed a column of tree-ants on their march up the trunk, across the cracked mirror, over my last tube of toothpaste and out into the early morning sunrise. They looked harmless enough as I made a grab for the Colgate, but they didn't seem to mind and made a detour around the untouched razor instead.

Dressing quickly in the only clean trousers and last shirt that I'd got left, I found my silk scarf had dried perfectly during the night and, tying it loosely around my neck for good luck, I stepped out on to the landing in search of my shoes. Newly acquired knowledge had taught me to always check inside first before putting them on. The dark interior made a wonderful nest for scorpions, Dwaila said! Tapping them on the wooden balustrade of the steep stairway nothing emerged, just a few stones and a crumpled leaf. Satisfied that my toes were safe, at least for the time being, I put them on and ventured cautiously down the stairs.

Lai, Dwaila's maid, came out of the kitchen to welcome me down to breakfast.

'Morn-ing,' she said cheerfully.

Lai was thirty-something, always difficult to tell with Thai women, her round and well-scrubbed face slightly pock-marked, the legacy of adolescent acne. Her long, jet-black hair was tied severely into a ponytail, revealing a high and distinguished forehead. Like most Thai, her nose was almost flat across her face; beneath it, full lips and a vast expanse of shining teeth shone in their early morning greeting. She'd learned English Idaho-style from Dwaila who, in turn, owed her masterly command of Thai to her charismatic companion. They'd been a team for as long as they both cared to remember.

'Where's Pee-mem?' I enquired, using Dwaila's Thai epithet.

'She gone first to bus-stop, then to mar-ket,' responded Lai, keeping her English as typically monosyllabic as her native Thai. 'Old man, he want go back to Phu-ket, no like here, too qui-et. He have prob-lem with his sto-mach al-so. Have to sit on bus long time,' she giggled.

Poor sod, I thought, a queasy tummy is bad enough at the best of times but to have to sit on a Thai bus for five hours must be agony. Built-in loos hadn't yet made it to Thailand's cross-country bus fleet. He was in for an uncomfortable ride.

'When she come back?' I asked, falling into the pidgin English trap.

'Not long-time now,' she replied. 'Sit down please, I make you break-fast.'

There was little concept of time or distance in Thailand, I reflected. Things were invariably either long or short, with very little in between. 'Short-time' was a term used when negotiating with a prostitute and had to be used with extreme caution; perhaps 'long-time' was too, although I didn't know!

'Long-time' might mean several days or even years; it was generally up to one's own interpretation, depending on the subject in question. 'Not long-time' skilfully avoided the pitfall of using 'short-time' and was intended to mean before sunset, although you could never be sure. One seldom saw Thais biting their nails in impatience. They weren't at all bothered by punctuality, or lack of it. Local wisdom dictated that the best thing to do when there was time to kill was to pass the time either: sleeping (always a solid choice), eating (second best because it invariably precipitated the first option), gossiping (always about friends and neighbours), getting drunk (at *any* hour of the day), or a combination of all four. If one was alone that was just hard luck. The Thai seldom read books but understood that *farangs* found them convenient to pass the time, although could never appreciate quite why we found them so enthralling, particularly when there were so few pictures!

Lai appeared with freshly cut pineapple. '*Sap-a-lot*,' she said proudly, and almost dropped it in my lap.

'*Sap-a-lot*,' I replied, trying to sound enthusiastic at what might turn into a blow-by-blow, inaugural Thai language lesson around the breakfast table.

'Flied egg?' she enquired.

'No, thank you,' I said, at which Lai looked mortified. 'I like Thai break-fast!' She beamed, and scurried off back into the kitchen.

From behind the thin walls I heard shrieks of laughter as Lai obviously relayed my order to the kitchen staff. I recognised the word *farang* several times, followed by fits of hysterical giggles. I began to wonder just what they were preparing in the way of my get-up-and-go meal. Perhaps they were putting something inside it to make sure that I did! Perhaps that's what happened to the poor Dutch professor!

Perhaps I could just sneak away now, while the going was good, but too late. The babble in the kitchen abruptly stopped, and I caught sight of Lai emerging from the bowels of the cookhouse with a steaming bowl in her hand. And, as she put it down in front of me with a triumphant flourish, I noticed with horror the raw egg descending to the bottom of the dish with a final, defiant 'plop'!

The dish was actually very good, the egg obviously an o vital ingredient. I'd had something similar before in Hong Kong, but the egg was normally whisked up by the chef before serving with chopsticks. Here the locals preferred to eat with fork and spoon and, quite apparently, whisk up their own eggs. 'When in Rome,' I thought. The broth was piping hot and the egg cooked quickly as I added some spicy vinegar sauce from the condiments on the table.

I decided to explore Dwaila's home after breakfast. It was essentially a two-tier residence, the ground floor of which consisted

31

mainly of highly polished hardwoods. The feeling was open-plan, with brightly coloured scatter cushions dotted around and a more formalised western style, three-piece suite arrangement in one corner, the centrepiece of which was a large, ornately carved, glass-topped mahogany coffee-table. Sandwiched between the glass and the wood, and partially bleached by the sun, was an old newspaper clipping from the Thai English language daily, *The Bangkok Post*. I recognised the face smiling up from the page at me: it was Dwaila, and the centre-fold feature article was about her presentation to the King and the extraordinary life she had carved out for herself at Tree-Tops ever since.

Remarkable lady, I thought. I was now more convinced than ever that she had the strength and depth of character to help. But where *was* she?

My watch read nine forty-five, and it was the tenth of February. I'd been in Thailand just under a month. It seemed much longer than that. Much had happened, but I knew that there was much left to discover, especially about Khao Sok. I needed a guide, someone who knew its secrets, someone who spoke my language. Where the hell was she?

Outside I heard first one dog bark, then another. 'Ah! Pee-mem com-ing,' called Lai from the kitchen.

And sure enough, spluttering and coughing in a cloud of dust, Dwaila's ancient and rusted pick-up appeared far away on the dirt road that cut straight through the rambutan plantation. Three dogs of uncertain pedigree danced around it, one snapping rather over-enthusiastically at the wheels which groaned and rasped against the sagging undercarriage of an abundantly overloaded axle. Bun, cousin-of-Bun, Newt the boat-boy and Neung stood in the back, holding on for dear life to the roof like charioteers from some epic biblical movie. Behind them, piled on top of miscellaneous engine parts, spare wheels, rocks and other paraphernalia were brightly coloured shopping bags, booty from the early-morning forage at the local town market. The procession turned into the drive and Dwaila honked the horn by way of a combined greeting/warning. She obviously didn't trust the brakes!

'Whooo!' breathed Dwaila, as the truck offered a penultimate rebellious wheeze. 'How'dey!'

'And good morning to you,' I smiled. 'Looks like you've been busy. Need a hand?'

'No, its OK, the boys'll get it. I needed some coffee. Lai-eeeee!'

'I think she's ahead of you,' I said, pointing to the pot of 'freshly brewed' Nescafé on the table. 'Mind if I join you?'

'Help yourself, pull up a chair. Tell me what you've been up to.'

'Not much really, thinking mostly,' I said.

'Yeah, I figured you for the thinking type. Where'd them thoughts take you now, Mike?'

'Well, that's what I wanted to discuss with you, actually. You see, I really have been doing some very serious thinking. You gave me a lot of food for thought yesterday and what it boils down to is basically this . . .'

CHAPTER FOUR

Tree-Tops, February 1990

For two days there had been a helter-skelter of discussion and debate, at times erupting into heated exchanges as I battled with Dwaila's erratic and totally unpredictable mood swings. At first she had listened, then her impatience had got the better of her and she'd cut me off mid-sentence.

'Colour me dumb, make that stupid, but where in the hell did you get a half-assed notion like that from?'

'Hear me out,' I said, 'please.'

On that first day we'd sat for over two hours at the weatherbeaten wooden table in her conservatory overlooking the mango and papaya trees in the fields at the base of the escarpment. Carefully I laid out, piece by piece, what I had in mind.

'You been watching too many of them Tarzan movies,' she said, 'you're about as addle-brained as a hound-dog howling at the moon.'

'Look,' I said finally, 'it's my life and my money. You said so yourself. It's never been done before. No one's ever filmed a wild tiger in Thailand. All I'll need is a permit.'

'Hell, you're madder than a rabid jack-rabbit in a cabbage patch. But if you think you can do it, why shit, I'll help ya!' And with that she was off into the kitchen.

'Wait there,' she yelled. 'This calls for a beer!'

And so we sat there most of the afternoon. We discussed the practicalities of life in the jungle: the isolation, the loneliness, the possible dangers. She offered me the use of her river camp as a living base, and I began to jot down some of the things that I thought I would need. It quickly developed into a very long list, and most of the items on it would have to come from abroad. Lai appeared with the most wonderful meal I'd ever had in Thailand: a fabulous green chicken

35

curry, hot and spicy with a dash of coconut milk; *tom yam kheung*, a delicious prawn soup flavoured with coriander and lemongrass; a thick clam chowder; deep-fried squid with a tangy ginger and lime sauce; wafer-thin slices of tender beef in oyster sauce; savoury seafood salad with a mouthwatering dill and tarragon vinaigrette; freshly steamed rice and gallons of ice-cold Singha beer to wash it all down.

'What a feast,' I said finally, and belched quietly in the time-honoured tradition.

'Frog,' said a new voice from behind me.

'Frog?' I said, puzzled.

'Frog,' he repeated, and belched loudly by way of explanation.

We all burst out laughing.

'Mike,' said Dwaila, 'I'd like you to meet Thao. Thao, say hello to my new friend Mike here.'

'Good after-noon,' said Thao, 'you enjoy your meal?'

His English was measured and spoken with great gusto, as if he'd practised for hours alone in front of a mirror. I guessed him to be in his late teens and he seemed blessed with that blissful innocence that comes only with a slightly below average IQ. He had a shock of black hair that kept falling across his left eye that he constantly flicked back with a smile and a flourish. I liked him instantly and knew that we were going to be good friends.

'Good afternoon to you too, Mr Thao,' I said. 'Pleased to meet you.'

'You too,' said Thao, and laughed.

Thao had been off for a few days visiting his family up north, explained Dwaila. He was her sometime house-boy, sometime tracker, apparently depending on how well he behaved. He was always full of mischief, playing practical jokes on everyone, and more often than not in the doghouse for one reason or another. Mostly he's fine, Dwaila told me later, he keeps us all well entertained with his pranks, but sometimes I do think he's one short of a six-pack and he'll do something and hurt himself. She obviously cared very deeply for this young rascal, it was easy to see why.

Thao helped Lai clear away the debris from our phenomenal lunch, and the atmosphere subsided into that relaxed, vaguely melancholic mood that comes in the aftermath of a momentous decision made and then sealed with excellent food, booze and good company . . .

Shadowless waves swept through the paddy-fields in the early morning breeze. Vast oceans of green. Water-buffalo stood waist

36

high in mud pools, their tails swishing incessantly back and forth. A flock of egrets alighted by the filthy water; one bold male landed on the back of an old bull, and began pecking savagely at the blow-flies on his back. The stunning contrast of the pure white plumage of the bird against the background of stagnant black earth and slime beguiled the subtlety of nature at work.

Beauty and the beast.

Small children splashed one another with naked innocence in the tiny stream that fed the mud pools, and an aged woman dozed in a threadbare hammock nearby, oblivious to the whining gearbox of the bus as it sped through the valley south toward Phuket.

I sat well back from the driver watching as he thrashed the engine to within an inch of its life. The door was kept wide open and a youth, his eyes dilated with speed, hung precariously by one hand flagging furiously at the traffic with a tattered rag as the bus all but bull-dozed it off the road. The Thai, I thought, always in a frantic rush to go nowhere.

The Surat Thani to Phuket route, like most in Thailand, was fiercely competitive, and rival bus firms vociferously fought for passengers at the down-town terminals with the only weapon left at their disposal after price. Speed.

'I can get you to Phuket faster than Blue-Bus Company,' a huckster would shout. 'Come with me. You save time and money!'

And so it went on. In Bangkok the competition was ferocious and at times violent as rival gangs accosted passengers for the highly lucrative southern overnight route. Several years ago I had made the mistake of taking the Bangkok-Phuket sleeper. It was one of the worst nights of my life. A freak tropical rainstorm hit around midnight, sending torrents of water across the road. The sky erupted time after time in brilliant white light as massive bolts of lightning hammered into the ground all around us. And yet the driver didn't slow down. It was as if his right foot was somehow welded to the accelerator. Twice I felt the back tyres lose their fragile grip on the pot-holed tarmac beneath us, and twice he managed to counterbalance the skid as oncoming headlights swerved violently out of his path.

On through the night, this madman at the wheel defied anyone and anything that dared challenge his chosen position in the centre of the road. Only divine fortune prevented some other demented idiot taking him on and sending us all careering over the mountainside to oblivion. We eventually arrived in Phuket two minutes ahead of schedule, and I vowed that if I could prevent myself strangling this crazed imbecile with my bare hands, I would never do that journey ever again as long as I lived. Three weeks later I read that an overnight express had gone off the road, killing all thirty-nine people on board, four of them young students from Europe. Now where Thai bus drivers are concerned, if I detect the slightest trace of alcohol on the breath, the remotest dilation of the pupils, I take the next one. Whenever it comes.

That morning, as Dwaila dropped me off at the end of her long drive, young Thao frantically waving good-bye, she'd spotted two other people waiting at the bus-stop.

'Thought we might have missed it there,' she said. 'The next one ain't until just before noon.'

It was seven o'clock and I thought then that a five-hour wait in this fabulous part of the world wouldn't be so bad if the bus driver didn't pass muster. In the event he turned out to be late middle-aged, always a positive sign, and reeked of nothing more sinister than stale coffee and cigarette smoke.

I heaved my bag aboard and waved farewell to Dwaila, shouting back over my shoulder, 'See you in about a week. Give me a call if you need anything from Singapore.'

'Sure,' she said. And I was on my way.

I'd dozed on and off for the first hour or so, mischievously thinking about the Dutch professor who had taken this very same journey two days before. I was surprised when we stopped for a coffee break in the small town of Takua Pa on the other side of the great mountain range, smiling to myself as I imagined the old man bent over, clutching his stomach and running for the filthy loos at the back of the roadside truck-stop.

The road now cut through the wonderful fertile valley that stretched for the next eighty kilometres down toward Phang-Na Bay. Once there we would turn west and head for the Andaman Sea until we reached the Sarasin bridge that separates the island of Phuket from the peninsula. I was sad to be leaving Khao Sok behind, and was hating the prospect of the glitzy Phuket by comparison.

Out of the right-hand windows of the bus I could now see the lush blue-green waters of the Andaman Sea. The sun was approaching its zenith as we crossed the narrow bridge, sped past the police barrier and on to the island. There was much to do. Inside my pocket was the letter that I'd written to Sophy two nights before. My plans hadn't changed, but would she understand? Silently I prayed that she would, knowing that from somewhere deep inside she would find the strength to be patient and let me work things out in my own time. It would be Valentine's Day soon, I thought. I must remember to send her a card.

The bus was now hurtling through the outskirts of Phuket town, hooting at everything as the driver's thinly disguised impatience drew him ever closer to the down-town terminus. With a final lurch to the left and right, we swept in through the narrow gates, and with a whoosh of the air-brakes we pulled to a halt. Inadvertently I glanced at my watch. It was eleven thirty-nine, one minute ahead of schedule.

Stepping down from the bus and into the blinding light of the cloudless sky, I weaved my way through the thronging mass of bodies that descended on the bus like vultures from the heavens.

'Where you go, you want *tuk-tuk*?'

'Hey you! You want massage?'

'Live-show mister, beauty-foon Thai lady?'

'Jesus,' I said, 'at this hour of the morning?'

I was bombarded from every angle – cab-drivers, hawkers, hucksters, hustlers, pimps, dopers, beggars. In Marrakesh or Calcutta perhaps, but here in Phuket?

Out of the corner of my eye I noticed a baby elephant being led past the queues of people waiting to buy tickets and out toward the open market. On his back was a bright red blanket with garishly embroidered gold lettering: 'Kurt's Beer Stube, Patong.'

Welcome to Sleaze-ville, I thought, forcing my way through the crowd. A hapless *tuk-tuk* driver decided to give chase and pursued me up the road as I strode out on to the main drag into town.

'Where you go?' he ventured.

'Chiang Mai,' I responded, 'now bugger off!'

'Chiang Mai?' he exclaimed, 'Chiang Mai, ah-ha, hee-hee-hee,' and he was gone.

I needed a drink and I needed to see Phil Watkins, in that order. The first was easy: Phil on the other hand was nowhere to be found.

'Mr Phil-ip, he gone fish-ing, no come back long-time,' said a tiny face in his office.

'Damn,' I thought, 'that's all I need. Never mind, he's not the

39

only agent in town,' and with a faint smile I left his office, closing the door behind me.

Hungry-time I thought, and headed toward the Pearl Hotel where Phil and I had eaten our last meal together. Their lunch buffet was modest but adequate.

After that, it was time to go. I slipped quietly out into the car-park, and darted across the road into the modest offices of Tradewinds Airlines, the short-haul subsidiary of Singapore Airlines. Fifteen minutes later, with a round-trip air-ticket to Singapore in my pocket, I set off back to the beach-side hotel in Kata Noi, where I'd stayed before. And as the *tuk-tuk* stopped outside the Mansion Hotel, I looked at the white-washed façade that I'd left only five days before, and thought that it seemed a lifetime away.

The sleek Boeing 737-300 touched down shortly before ten in the evening. The runway was in flood, and great sheets of torrential rain lashed the side of the aircraft as it taxied slowly toward the locking gate. Two men in bright orange sou'westers hung tightly to one another as they fought against the tempestuous gale, wading ankle deep across the rain-swept tarmac. As the plane slid to a halt, they slipped the anchor chocks carefully under each wheel until finally, their duties completed for the night, they battled their way back across the tide to shelter.

I stood up, stretching slightly, and reached for my modest possessions in the overhead locker. The flight was not busy, mostly Thai and Singaporean businessmen in crumpled, dull grey suits, clutching monogrammed imitation leather briefcases and duty-free plastic carrier bags bursting at the seams with cheap booze. The flight-crew however, by stark comparison, were stunning. An exotic blend of the most beautiful and alluring in the Orient. Some with large dark doe-like eyes that shone through perfect smiles with intoxicating sensuality.

I presented myself to the immigration clerk, overnight bag held tightly in one hand, passport and arrival documents in the other. Many years before I had visited this former Colonial outpost, when my hair was much longer than it was now. At one time President Lee Kuan Yew forbade entry to any man with longer than shoulder-length hair. Those unwilling to pay the $10 fee for a short-back-and-sides on the spot were promptly refused a visa and unceremoniously put on the first flight out again. The elderly clerk before me was

40

obviously a disciple of that draconian era. He shot me a condescending glance that appeared not only to absorb the comparison between my face with the snapshot on my passport, but also to take in the back of my hair as well.

With a final perfunctory look, he rubber-stamped my visa with regimental precision and nodded for me to get out of his sight. I made a mental note to always wear a clean shirt and tie whenever I flew into Changi Airport in future. Customs, on the other hand, were singularly unconcerned with the contents of my bag, and waved me through with mechanical indifference.

'Singapore has a superfluity of mid to upper-class hotels,' I had read recently: 'quality is high, of international standard, and inexpensive.' Armed with that newly acquired snippet of globe-trotting knowledge, I had felt it unnecessary to pre-book my overnight accommodation from Thailand and therefore headed straight across the airport arrivals concourse toward the sign for hotel information. After the Mansion, I was in the mood for some modest indulgence.

Raffles Hotel had always had a wonderful ring to it, and a Singapore Sling at the famous Long Bar with a punkah-wallah at my side was just what I had in mind. But as I found the desk six deep in voucher-waving pandemonium, I knew that something was terribly wrong.

'I'm *terribly* sorry, sir,' said a tired voice, obviously not for the first time that evening, 'everywhere is booked solid.'

'But I have a reservation docket,' screamed an irate Taiwanese in a polyester shell-suit. 'So have I.' 'And me.' 'Look here, miss.' A chorus of impatient voices bellowed out, all demanding to be heard at the same time.

I stood for a while at the back of the queue, listening to the chaos in front of me. Dozens of furious people, shaming both humanity and themselves, hurled a unified litany of abuse at the poor girl behind the counter as if it were singularly her fault that their hotels had double-booked. This is common practice in the Far East and generally allows for last-minute cancellations to be filled from the reserve allowance that each hotelier has carefully calculated into his occupancy projections. Today, however, the glut of hotel rooms that I had so confidently read about were now filled by visitors from all around the globe who had descended en masse for the world's 'Second International Aero-Space Convention'.

'What a monumental screw-up,' I said under my breath.

41

'First time in Singapore?' asked a friendly voice beside me.

'No, not exactly,' I replied, looking up at the familiar blue-green uniform and radiant smile of the chief stewardess from my flight.

'You might try the Metropole,' she said. And with a cheerful wave she was off.

It was time to leave this manic crowd, time to strike out on my own. There was nothing to be gained by waiting around and so, scooping up my bag, I ventured out into the stormy night and clambered aboard the first shuttle bus that I could find with the words 'Down-town. Orchard Road' blazoned across its front.

It was 11.30 p.m., February 14th, Saint Valentine's Day.

The public-transit system in Singapore is efficient, cheap and invariably spotlessly clean, and this bus was no exception. A one-dollar transfer from the out-of-town airport to the centre of the bustling metropolis was an amazing deal in any currency. The torrential rain had subsided to a steady drizzle and the rhythmic drone of the windscreen-wipers kept my mind focused on the task ahead. Somewhere, somehow, I had to find a room for the night.

The problem now before me required a certain amount of applied intuitive resourcefulness coupled with a bold, forthright and confident approach, spiced with a dash of bullshit for good measure. And as the first skyscrapers appeared in the distance, I resolved with some trepidation to start at one end of town and work my way through to the other, trying every hotel if necessary.

Despite my boldest endeavours, however, I was unsuccessful.

I began to roam aimlessly from one hotel to another, trying it on, but always with the same response. Singapore was full to the gunwales.

I seemed to be walking round in circles. I began to recognise the same buildings and street signs and getting nowhere. The odd thing that struck me though, as I propped myself against a lamp-post to study my map, was that I hadn't found the famous Raffles Hotel.

My sodden and badly creased map offered few clues. Eventually, however, I spotted it, 'Raffles' in tiny, almost illegible script. From the map, it appeared to be fewer than half a dozen streets away. With a jaunty step, and defying the incessant drizzle, I set off.

There was no brightly lit neon sign as I crossed the Bras Basah Road toward the point that I had marked on the map. In fact there was no Raffles, only an ancient façade with crumbling pillars and expansive open verandahs in that classic and magnificent colonial style. Raffles looked like a bomb site as I peered through the perimeter wall of builder's screen.

The rain was more persistent now, and with a heavy heart I turned my back and trudged away, kicking puddles in defiant contempt for the modern world.

I turned into a narrow street of battered awnings and porticos, seeking shelter from the downpour. Miserably, I dragged myself along until, finally, I dropped my bag in a shop doorway, too tired to go on. I needed sleep.

As my drooping eyelids, still stinging from driving rain, began to shut out the night, I heard a faint crackling sound above me. I cocked my head to one side, straining to detect its source. Ahead of me and in a puddle of filthy brown rainwater, a green light flickered on and off. I watched it, mesmerised for some time until I understood the correlation between sight and sound. Curious now, I stood up on damp and shaky limbs, holding tight on to a pillar until the blood flowed back into my veins and the feeling returned to my weary legs. I staggered out into the road like some punch-drunk street-fighter, and looked up at the neon light, a cable dangled precariously from one side, spitting sparks and blue smoke into the wind. Half the letters appeared to have been blown out by a short circuit. It coughed again, brighter now as if in one final desperate signal to my exhausted brain. 'Metropole Hotel.'

Well, I'll be damned, I thought, as new energy pumped through my flagging frame. Picking up my bag, I jumped out into the street laughing to myself. The bloody Metropole Hotel!

The front door was unlocked as I stepped in from the rain. From behind a battered reception counter a stern but sympathetic face looked down at me over the top of silver-framed bifocals, taped on one side with Elastoplast.

'And how can I help you?' it enquired.

'Well, I'm sure you're not going to believe this,' I lied, 'and I'm absolutely positive that nobody has ever asked you this before, especially tonight, so here goes . . . Have you possibly got a vacant room?'

Patrick Gotoking laughed as his broad features broke first into a smile and then resounded with a deep chesty bellow. 'Now what makes you think that I can help you in that department?' he enquired with a devilish grin.

'Oh, I don't know,' I replied. 'It's just that I met this incredible angel about a hundred years ago who said that if I ever found myself in Singapore, I simply had to stay at the Metropole.'

'How wise she must have been,' he said. 'Well, you're here now, and if I'm not too much mistaken, in about forty-five minutes' time, a rather bedraggled banker is going to be running down those steps on his way to catch the first and only flight to Bangladesh. Do you think you can wait that long?'

'Are you kidding?' I asked, unable to believe my luck.

'Sit down over there on the couch,' said Patrick. 'Can I get you a cup of cocoa?'

'That would be splendid,' I replied. 'And you wouldn't have a phone that I could use, would you please? You see it's *still* Valentine's Day back home in London, and I would really love to call my girlfriend.'

The cocoa was sweet and good. From under the counter Patrick poured in a splash of Captain Morgan rum and I felt the warmth as the chocolate cocktail gushed into my stomach.

After the banker left for his flight, Patrick made me temporary night-clerk while he rushed upstairs to change the sheets in the spartan single room. The phones were silent, it was still early. Then he came back and graciously handed me the key to room 501, and wished me goodnight. It was five o'clock when my head hit the pillow. I was dog-tired and slept solidly until noon.

Hunger kept me from sleeping all day. Hunger for food and for the quest that had compelled me to travel all this way. I needed to explore this town, and I needed to get my bearings.

As I walked out of the hotel lobby into the fierce sunshine of a cloudless day, I took out my notebook to jot down the name of the street where I lived. I glanced up at the enamel sign, its rusted screws holding it firmly on to the yellowing concrete wall. And for the second time in less than twelve hours, my heart skipped not one beat, but several.

I was living on Seah Street and 'seah' is the Thai word for tiger!

CHAPTER FIVE

Kata Noi, Phuket, February 1990

A distant head bobbed rhythmically far beyond the shoreline. Athletic arms cut through the glistening water with ease as powerful legs kicked backward in a vigorous confident stroke. Swiftlets dived and weaved, their eyes scanning the early morning sky for tiny insects. From around the bay, an ancient wooden fishing boat chugged lazily into view, decks stacked high with tangled nets that hid the meagre spoils of their nightly catch. Years of illicit dynamiting had already devastated much of this coastline's once bountiful marine life. Tourists expected prime Phuket lobster. And the tourists had to be fed!

The lone swimmer quickened his pace, more determined now. He turned for the beach and in a frantic dash broke through the surf as a gigantic wave crashed on to his back and deposited him in a crumpled, gasping heap on to the shimmering sand. He lay there for several minutes fighting for breath, as he had done every morning at this hour for many weeks. Slowly he rose to his feet, and I watched him jog confidently away into the sunrise, quietly admiring his discipline. There was a time in Sweden when I had run at least fifty kilometres every week, many of those as a mere warm-up to a punishing and arduous session in the gym. With more than a tinge of regret, I thought just how quickly the body regresses to a more sedentary way of life. I was lean and fit, but not that fit. It was high time to get back in shape and I made a mental note to use my new running shoes later that day.

It was not yet eight o'clock, but the sun was already beginning to burn the back of my neck as I stood on the tiled balcony gazing out to sea. Retreating into the fan-cooled room, I decided to put a call into Tree-Tops. Dwaila would be up and about, and it would be a

45

good time to catch her. The receptionist explained that it might take some time to get through as the call would have to be relayed by short-wave radio from the local town of Takua Pa.

Aware of the problem, I sprawled on the bed to wait. Stretching, as if in a silent tribute of solidarity with the unknown athlete jogging up the beach, I let my mind wander over the events of the past three days . . .

Singapore had been everything that I had expected, a dynamic and vibrant, if not somewhat repressive, contrast to the laid-back lethargy of Phuket. The spotless streets and carefully manicured parks that separated the city blocks bore witness to a people who were proud to share their tiny nation with the millions of visitors that arrived each year in an endless search for wealth and bargains from the duty-free stores. Millions of dollars changed hands every day as covetous visitors took advantage of the glittering array of goods on offer: gold and gemstones from the Orient; chic designer goods from Paris; Rolex and Cartier watches from Switzerland; electronic wizardry and cameras from Japan.

I had found the first items on my expansive list with relative ease that very first afternoon. In fact, so astonished was I to find myself living on Tiger Street that I resolved to explore its every nook and cranny.

The narrow thoroughfare was essentially a loosely connected row of small food shops and ethnic restaurants, interspersed here and there with an archaic tailor's shop, two hairdressing salons and a decrepit watchmender's which was more or less a hole in the wall.

On the other side of the street was Raffles Hotel. At least, what was left of it. The old place was undergoing a complete overhaul, involving cavernous excavation of the original foundations and a total re-structuring of the building itself. The only section preserved for posterity was the crumbling façade. Although I imagined that even this would undergo a major face-lift, before the famous establishment ever re-opened its doors.

At the opposite corner of the street from my hotel, I made a quite remarkable discovery. For there, nestled away under an extensive yet anonymous awning, was an Aladdin's cave of army surplus and survival gear. Later, I was to discover that it was the only one of its kind in the entire city. And yet it was right there on my doorstep and

46

contained just about everything I would need to keep myself alive in the weeks ahead.

Taking voluminous notes and jotting down the prices of the most important items of kit on display, I politely declined the offer of help from the gregarious assistant who ambled up to my side.

'You American?' he enquired affably.

'No, English,' I said, trying not to sound discourteous.

'I was in Florida last year,' he persisted, 'Disneyworld, far out!'

I knew that he was just being convivial and doing his job, but I always felt ill at ease when pursued, however cordially, around a shop. Especially when I had yet to make up my own mind about a particular purchase. Sensing this, he backed away and busied himself unpacking a large cardboard box in the corner.

'Well, you please let me know when you need some help,' he called cheerfully.

I noticed the subtle use of the word 'when' and not 'if'. Was it deliberate, I wondered? Was a subliminal seed being surreptitiously sown in my subconscious by this smooth-talking salesman? I made a mental note to tread carefully from then on.

This was to be my exploratory day, and I had made the conscious decision to buy nothing more than food and drink, and possibly some clothes. Price comparison and finely honed bargaining skills were absolutely vital when shopping anywhere in the Far East, as were patience, prudence and procrastination, invaluable tools to fend off the seductive urge to spend, spend, spend. It was easy to see how a fool and his money could be easily parted in this town!

By early evening I'd had enough. The culture shock, the thronging masses of people everywhere, the dazzling array of merchandise alluringly set out in every window of every shop for countless miles on end were hypnotic and confusing. It seemed that I had half a dozen different quotations for the same piece of equipment from six different stores. At one, the price was so unbelievably cheap that I was convinced I was being made the victim of the old monkey scam, Singapore style.

An experienced storekeeper could always tell when someone was simply doing the rounds comparing prices. It was not difficult to understand why they should resent their profit margins being analysed and set against competitors. When all else failed, the unscrupulous were not averse to the use of a little cunning to make a sale once a suitable 'monkey' had been identified. Quite simply, a price would be quoted for a particular item of merchandise that was so impossibly low as to make it unbeatable. Tired and weary after countless abortive attempts to beat the deal, the hapless shopper would eventually return, worn out and ready to make his purchase.

Only to be told in the most apologetic manner imaginable, 'I'm terribly sorry sir, the last one has just been sold. If only you had let me know earlier, I would have kept one back for you especially. Would you like a cup of tea, you look exhausted?'

Sooner or later, the tired and despondent monkey would let down his guard, and the jackal would move in for the kill. 'Of course, this model is far superior in my view,' a soothing voice would quietly say as an inferior and much more expensive version appeared as if a phoenix from the ashes of the victim's shattered dreams. 'You might not know the name, but it is the very latest, everybody is buying them these days . . .'

And before he realised what had happened, the sacrificial monkey was thanking the storekeeper profusely for his wise counsel and blindly counting money into his hands.

Some other poor mugs returned home only to find that their 'Panasonic' compact disc-player contained anything but 'Panasonic' parts and had in fact been shoddily thrown together in a counterfeiter's sweat-shop in Southern China.

Patrick became a trusted adviser and a veritable fountain of information as we sat together on that evening of my first day, sipping ice-cold beer on the verandah.

Patiently he charted a course for me through the hazardous minefield that some of his more spurious countrymen had lain to catch the unsuspecting foreign devil. He went out of his way to be courteous, and arranged introductions for me to traders that he felt could be trusted, whilst making doubly sure that I avoided those whom he knew to be less than honest. He was fascinated by my plans and showed not the slightest indication if he felt they were reckless or ill-advised.

'Why would someone like you, so obviously in love with your sweetheart back home, want to go chasing off into the jungle to film tigers?' he had asked, clearly baffled by my impetuosity.

'You know, Patrick, the short answer to that is that I really just don't know. And that's the truth,' I replied rather lamely.

'Have you thought about the dangers, the discomforts, the risk?' he persisted.

'I'll need to be more careful about *who* rather than *what* I might meet in the jungle,' I said. 'And if and when I do meet up with someone, then I'm just a crazy foreigner making a natural history programme.'

'But even if you do succeed in filming the tiger and proving your theory about the poaching, do you really believe that anyone will care enough to actually do anything constructive to help?' he asked.

'At the risk of sounding repetitious, Patrick, I really don't know. All I do know is that *something* is making me do this. Don't ask me to explain what it is, because I don't know; but it *feels* right. And I have to believe in that and I have to believe that I will succeed.'

'The world would be a better place if there were more around like you,' he said finally. 'Alas, I won't be around to see if you succeed.'

'Oh come, come,' I replied uncomfortably, alarmed by his sudden fatalistic tone. 'There must be millions like me. I'm just very fortunate to have the opportunity to try and test some of my crack-pot ideas. And besides, what's all this nonsense about "not being around"? You look to me as though there's plenty of life in you yet.'

'If only that were true,' he said with hopeless resignation. 'Now, if you'll excuse me, I must attend to my duties.' Putting his hand on my shoulder, he pulled himself up from his chair. A shadow of pain flashed across his eyes as he fought to steady his stance. He was a proud man, clearly distressed at the deterioration in his physical bearing.

'I do apologise,' he murmured.

'Is there anything that I can do?' I enquired gently.

'No, no, young man, thank you, I don't think there's very much left that anyone can do. Now you get some rest, you have a busy day tomorrow.' And with that he shuffled wearily off down the corridor to begin his all-night vigil behind the reception desk.

The next morning, after a troubled night's sleep, I went downstairs early expecting to find him still at his post. In Patrick's place was an elderly turbanned gentleman called Billy whom I had met the previous afternoon.

'Where is Mr Patrick?' I enquired delicately.

'Oh, Mr Patrick is going home, sir. Mr Patrick is very sick man. Very sick man indeed. Not long to live now, very sad. Yes, very sad indeed,' intoned Billy with obvious sincerity.

'But I don't understand,' I spluttered. 'What's wrong with him? Why?'

'Oh, my goodness me. The very same that took Mr Patrick's wife

49

and she pass away only last year, sir,' explained Billy gently. 'You see, Mr Patrick has the cancer.'

I was unused to the directness of the Asian mind, and Billy's words hit me in the stomach like a thunderbolt.

'Mr Patrick cannot sleep sir, this is why he is working at the night-time,' persisted Billy.

'Yes, yes, thank you, I understand.' I cut him off.

With a heavy heart I turned and retreated up the stairs to the sanctuary of my room thinking, not for the first time in recent weeks, just what a shitty world we live in at times.

The Nike running shoes that I had bought the previous day lay still boxed and untouched on the floor of my wardrobe. I needed some air, and I needed to run and clear my thoughts. Changing quickly into an old sweatshirt and shorts, I bolted out from my room and down the stairs four at a time.

It was seven o'clock, and the street was still empty. The air was light, but all too soon exhaust fumes would combine with the effects of the sun to produce an atmosphere unsuitable for strenuous exercise. I pounded the streets of Singapore for thirty-five minutes before staggering breathless back up the front steps of the Metropole and up to my room for a hot shower.

My appetite had returned, so I took a quick breakfast of ham and scrambled eggs in the downstairs coffee-shop before returning to my room to plan the day. On the doormat was a white hotel envelope with a single folded sheet of headed notepaper. It was a message from Patrick. '*Dear Mike. Hope you slept well. I'm feeling much better now. You have an appointment with Mr Shah at 10 a.m. and my good friend Danny Chew will expect you at 2 p.m. Good luck! Patrick.*'

I ordered a taxi to arrive at nine-thirty and was grateful that he was punctual and that the air-conditioning had been running for some time, full blast. A thick blanket of translucent smog seemed to have descended over the city, precipitating almost one hundred per cent humidity. The air was foul and clammy and my shirt clung to my skin even in the three steps it took to reach the car door.

'Rain later, I shouldn't wonder,' said the driver enthusiastically. 'Where would you like to go?'

I gave him the small slip of paper Patrick had written for me and sat back to enjoy the ride in the comfort of my own thoughts. He drove confidently and with an almost pious regard for the strange chiming sound that emanated from his dashboard every time he exceeded thirty miles per hour. Obediently, he would reduce his speed and the wretched thing fell silent. The device was new to me and I imagined the sort of abuse it would receive if foisted on an unsuspecting London cabby. However the Singaporeans appeared, at least on the face of it, to be a law-abiding bunch and I was grateful that my driver knew his way around. We arrived with five minutes to spare and I asked if he would wait until after I had concluded my business.

'Oh yes, Sahib, very happy to oblige,' he chirped agreeably.

Taxis were inexpensive and efficient in Singapore and, above all, invariably honest. There was rumoured to be a department that kept tabs on them, with staff posing as tourists in an attempt to catch them out. Occasionally, an inspector would deliberately leave a wallet or camera on the back seat to see what the driver would do. These items were unfailingly handed in later with few exceptions, as a taxi-licence was worth its weight in gold and, once revoked, could never be reinstated. Most cabbies would therefore cast a cursory glance over their shoulder to *make sure* that their fare did not leave any valuables behind.

Mr Shah greeted me warmly on the steps of his modest showroom and ushered me inside. We exchanged polite pleasantries and he insisted that I pass on his sincerest personal regards to Mr Patrick. That done, he summoned a young assistant and together we inspected the gleaming and well-polished merchandise that was his firm's speciality. At length, he enquired as to whether I would like a demonstration of any particular model. I settled upon a shining red and black example in the middle of my price range.

Duly satisfied with its exemplary performance, I studied in more detail the technical specification and operation manual whilst Mr Shah busied himself with a pile of paperwork. I interrupted him only briefly for clarification of one or two minor details. At ease now, we discussed the question of price, and agreed upon a figure that was acceptable to us both. All that remained was for me to leave a small deposit, collect a receipt and make arrangements for collection.

As this was being done, I recalled a powerful red and black tug that I had seen, labouring into the port of Gothenburg, towing a vast container vessel a hundred times its size. The name on the side in sprawling white letters was Hugo. I looked down at the sturdy generator that I had just agreed to buy and thought, I shall call you Hugo. But how in hell will I get you back to Thailand?

Outside, patiently waiting, was my faithful chauffeur. It was beginning to rain, just as he had predicted.

'Where to now, Sahib?' he asked in his staccato tone.

'Back to town,' I said, as I shook hands with Mr Shah.

It was approaching midday, and the rain was falling faster now. Large heavy drops of tropical rain beat down on to the car roof, cascading over the side windows. As we reached Orchard Road the storm struck with a violent clash of thunder directly overhead. A sudden sharp gust of turbulent wind bent the palm trees lining the boulevard at almost right angles, and vast surges of water swept down from the sky. The traffic ground to a virtual halt; buses and lorries pulled off the road, unable to see through the deluge, knowing that the flood would soon subside.

And then, as if some mighty sprinkler in the sky was slowly being turned off, the torrent became a shower, then turned to drizzle and then the sun broke through. The storm had passed.

'I'm glad that's out of the way,' said my driver, suddenly buoyant again. 'Do you mind if I drop you off at the Hilton Hotel. I'm having to change shift now.'

'No, not at all,' I replied, 'I enjoy a walk after the rain.' Handing him a hundred dollar bill with a nod that meant 'keep the change' I said goodbye to this cheerful soul and ducked inside the Hilton for some lunch.

The afternoon sun was blistering as I stepped back out on to the street. The last of the rain rose in small clouds of steam underfoot in the distance, although the pavement and tarmac appeared perfectly dry. Dank vapour still hung in the air. If I had walked, within minutes my shirt would have been soaking wet. Forgoing the stroll, I opted for the comfort of a cab. It was one forty-five in the afternoon.

The shopping plaza was thankfully cool as I stepped out of the elevator on the third floor. My taxi had dropped me down in the basement car-park as instructed and the lift was a convenient way of avoiding the herds of shopaholics on the floors and moving stairways above me. I silently thanked Patrick for his excellent suggestion: multitudes of people in confined spaces made me feel claustrophobic.

The small map that Patrick had drawn for me was both detailed and accurate. I found the shop of Mr Danny Chew without difficulty. It stocked an extensive range of goods, all of the best quality. Inside, one long wall was given over to rows of glass shelves, each carefully presenting a selection from around the

52

world. Two customers sat at the expansive counter on circular, chromium-finished revolving stools, occasionally pointing up to the display requesting to inspect a particular item of merchandise and studying each part in turn with genuine absorption.

One chap briefly looked up at me as I walked into the store. Taking spectacles out of the breast pocket of a large checked shirt, he scrutinised me momentarily and then, as if in failed recognition, returned his concentration to the obviously expensive item before him. I stared at his profile for several moments, his bristly features vaguely familiar, troubled that I had seen him somewhere before, and equally convinced that it had been very recently.

A chubby and ebullient man in his early forties squeezed his way behind the counter. His oval head was balding and thick horn-rimmed glasses perched precariously on top. He extended a fleshy hand in welcome and ushered me to a vacant seat in front of him with a warm smile.

'You must be Mr Michael,' he said with self-assured directness. 'I have been expecting you.'

'Danny Chew, I presume. Your reputation precedes you,' I acknowledged, with extravagant aplomb.

The chap in the checked shirt looked askance, puzzled by this sudden and companionable banter.

'Now tell me, what can I do for you?' enquired Mr Chew graciously, ignoring him.

I took a folded scrap of hotel notepaper and smoothed it carefully out on the glass counter before me. There were many items on the list, most of which I was confident that Mr Chew could supply. Patrick had said that he could be trusted, and that his prices were reasonable. And whilst there was every possibility that some minor savings might be made on certain elements elsewhere, I felt no compelling urge to hunt around the sweaty streets until I found them. And so we went to work.

For almost two hours I sat there examining one camera after another, listening patiently to the various pros and cons of each one in turn. Chew was extremely knowledgeable and knew his chosen profession well. Refreshments were served in a continuous stream from a small refrigerator at the back of the shop, and whilst many new customers came in and out of the store during my visit, only myself and the checked shirt remained steadfastly glued to our seats.

From time to time, Danny would dive underneath the counter or disappear into a back room only to reappear again triumphantly, holding a missing piece of my jigsaw puzzle.

On one such occasion, when he had been gone longer than usual, I was suddenly struck by a mysterious urge to talk to the stranger in the next chair.

'Excuse me, but haven't I seen you somewhere before?' I ventured after a while, unable to control my curiosity any longer. 'I'm sure I recognise you from somewhere.'

Don Watson straightened and turned to face me. He slouched rather than sat on the plastic stool. Unshaven for more than a week, his crumpled lumberjack's shirt must have been at least three days past its wash-by date. His eyes seemed disproportionately large behind heavy spectacles, and his unkempt hair was tied loosely in a shaggy ponytail. The overall appearance was one of a saddle-weary back-packer down on his luck, but there was something deeper in those alert green eyes, a penetrating intelligence that was subdued and yet disarming.

He fixed me with an analytical gaze and then, turning his head ever so slightly to one side, allowed his face to erupt into one of the warmest and most original smiles I'd seen for weeks.

'Sure, I've seen you too back there, when was it now? Yeah, must have been yesterday.' His accent was smooth and Californian. 'Seems like you and me, we're on the same circuit!'

Danny Chew resurfaced looking flustered, unable to find what he was looking for. We agreed to call it a day and meet again in the morning when, he assured me, he would have everything neatly assembled and ready. He was very grateful for the business, and I thanked him for his diligence and prepared to leave.

At the door and for some inexplicable reason, I turned to the young Californian and called, 'Fancy a beer?'

'Sure,' he said, 'why not, I'm just about done here anyhow.'

We sat in a secluded beer garden just off Orchard Road. The air was much lighter now as the sun moved slowly toward the horizon, and the bar began to fill with early evening drinkers, some tired from the office, others simply parched from the vagaries of shopping. The beer was cold and good. Don insisted on buying the first round and vanished swiftly upon arrival, returning with two large bottles on a circular wooden tray and a pair of frosted tankards steaming as the icy vapour condensed on the glass.

'Have you tried this one?' he asked. 'It's just the best. My favourite beer in all the world.'

54

A butchered Siberian tiger lies in the snow; a victim of the Chinese medicine trade (*Steve Galster*)

A large selection of tiger bone products still widely available in Chinese communities around the world (*Michael Day*)

Daybreak on the lake at Khao Sok National Park, Thailand (*Sophy Day*)

These young tigers were orphaned when their mother was killed by poachers in Thailand (*Michael Day*)

The hotel room workshop in Kata-Noi, Thailand (*Michael Day*)

Mr Prasit, poacher and convicted murderer, Khao Sok, Thailand
(*Yorkshire Television*)

Dwaila, Newt the boat-boy, and I shortly after our fuel pipe was slashed by poachers (*Sophy Day*)

Tiger skins for sale in Burma. Many of these will be smuggled into Thailand and sold in Bangkok (*T. J. Redford*)

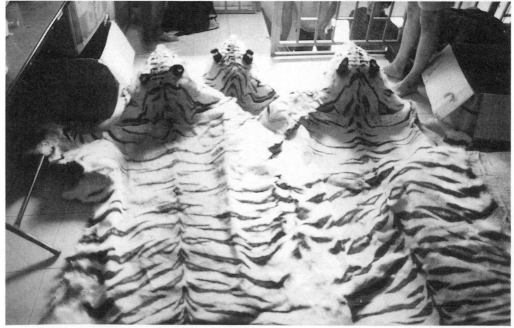

One of Dr Manette's clouded leopards; a front paw has been severed in a poacher's trap (*Michael Day*)

A tiger skull for sale in a Taipei shop; clear evidence of the illegal trade (*Michael Day*)

The hat-camera I used to expose the illegal tiger trade in Taiwan (*Michael Day*)

When Rebecca showed me these photographs from a Taiwanese magazine I couldn't believe my eyes (*Ren Jian*)

Hard evidence. A Taiwanese waitress explains how to make tiger penis soup (*Michael Day*)

Yorkshire Television director, Nick Gray, suspects Sorasit is covering up for the poachers (*Sophy Day*)

'No, I don't think so, the label doesn't look familiar,' I said. 'What's it called?'

'They only make it here in Singapore,' he replied. 'Here, take one, it's called Tiger beer.'

I had told him nothing of my plans up to that point and yet for some truly mysterious reason he'd chosen a beer named after the very species that had brought me to Singapore in the first place. It was as if a pattern were gradually emerging. Something singularly undefined and yet prophetic was unfolding, and I was trapped helplessly in the middle.

We talked for a long time. Don had a remarkable intellect, with a quick-witted, sharp and rational uptake. We joked about everything from hang-dog Irishmen to Chinese table manners. For a time we talked about our respective girlfriends, temporarily abandoned on the other side of the planet, and then we put the world to rights with a round or two of tequila.

After a while the conversation became more subdued, and he told me a little about himself, about his work in Hollywood and his experiences working on the set of the hit film *Total Recall*. What he couldn't have known at the time was that he had just the skills I was looking for.

Somewhere in the back of my mind I had this crazy notion that if only I could film a wild tiger close up and at ground level, then the professional wildlife documentary film-makers would have to take me seriously. The only way to achieve that would be through the use of modern technology and adapting a video camera to somehow operate more or less by remote control; knowledge that I certainly didn't possess. I needed a technician to put my theory to the test, and here I was, chatting happily away with perhaps the greatest expert in the field, who had simply popped up out of nowhere right on cue. Fate was obviously dealing me another card in the form of Mr Don Watson, and one which I would have to play very carefully if I was to persuade him to help me in my implausible mission. I asked him more about his work, hoping to find the right moment to ask him; he could only say no, I thought, praying that he wouldn't.

It turned out that Don was an electronics wizard, employed at great expense by the big-name studios to animate anything from severed hands to extra-terrestrials. His specialist field was robotics, and his last contract had paid a handsome $500 per day plus expenses for a total of thirteen weeks. Don was certainly not down on his financial luck, although he'd only just escaped a potentially life-threatening encounter with a late-night mugger a few days before.

He had been staggering home a little worse for wear, when a gang of thugs had appeared from the shadows and pushed a knife to his throat. They took his passport, credit cards and several hundred dollars in cash. He was lucky: when violence strikes in Singapore it often ends in bloodshed. American Express were doing all they could, he explained, but not fast enough and he had already missed his connecting flight on to Bali and the Philippines.

With a shrug he dismissed the problem. As if a deeper philosophy within him dictated that it had all probably happened for some pre-ordained reason . . .

The phone jangled harshly beside my bed, shattering my reverie and sending me thundering back to earth with a start. Grabbing the receiver, its plastic surface scarred for life by a careless cigarette burn, I shouted, 'Hello, Dwaila, is that you?'

'Just a moment, caller, we're putting you through now,' intoned the operator.

'Mike, how you doing? How the hell are you? When did you get back? Over,' came the familiar voice, accustomed to the long-winded communications system and used to firing several questions off at once.

'I'm fine, thank you. The trip was successful. Got back to Phuket late last night, over,' I replied with the zeal of a seasoned radio ham.

'Hey, when you coming up? Thao's been missing you. Over,' came the crackling drawl.

'Well, that's why I'm calling actually. You see my plans are somewhat delayed. I've still got one or two things to pick up, and I'll need a jeep to carry them. In fact I'm driving back to Singapore tomorrow. I'm trying to persuade a new friend to join me, you'll like him. Over,' I said, wondering desperately if Don and Dwaila would really hit it off.

'You're *driving* back to Singapore! Have you gone stir crazy or . . .' And then the line went dead.

CHAPTER SIX

Singapore, February 1990

Fax to: Sophy Pilkington
From: Michael Day
Metropole Hotel, Singapore
February 19th, 1990

Dearest Sophy

Well, I've done some insane drives in my time, but this one takes some beating! Phuket to Singapore via Phang Nga, Krabi, Trang, Hat Yai, Saboa, Butterworth, Ipoh, Kuala Lumpur and Johor Bahru. Just over 1600 kms in 23 hours . . . That should amuse the Fulham Road plod (temporary custodians of my driving licence)! This trip had everything; it was fun, exhilarating, exciting but at times somewhat lonesome. Fog, rain, clear blue skies and sun. Pitch darkness, wide open highways and one stretch with a long (80 km) diversion through southern Malay jungle on what can only be described as a farm track, complete with ruts and pot-holes with only the thinnest veneer of tarmac! Huge lorries thrashing along forcing me off the road on to the dirt verge to avoid collision. Wow! Gruelling but fun; now, quite understandably I'm shagged (oops!) and checked back into the Metropole, room 903, for some well-earned shut-eye before I continue my search for that which has brought me hither. Needless to say, they don't have any in Thailand, their most recent imports are 20 years out of date, so I rented a four-wheel-drive and returned to civilisation. The petrol bill? Would you believe 35 pounds. Fuel is cheap and I mean cheap! So I'm contactable by phone (yes please!) or fax here until Friday or maybe Saturday before I begin the long trek back. Looking forward to some company on the return leg as John Denver, Fleetwood Mac and Fine Young Cannibals tend to lose their charm after a while! Trust all is well with you. Will now retire to dream of you and burning tigers. What did Blake mean by that anyway? Love and miss you, Mike. P.S. Will you join me?

Patrick smiled as I gave him the fax. He was used to my late arrivals and erratic hours. He referred to Sophy rather quaintly as my 'sweetheart', remembering the long call that I had made to her on Valentine's Day.

'I've asked her again to join me,' I said to him with buoyant optimism.

'And she's keeping you guessing, am I right?' he asked in his warm, avuncular manner.

'I don't know what to think, perhaps it's unwise after all,' I said. 'Life in the jungle isn't everyone's cup of tea.'

'From what you've told me, she sounds like a very special young lady,' continued Patrick. 'Be patient, let her work it out in her own time. If she faxes back, I promise not to read it first!' We both laughed.

There was a marvellous message waiting from Don confirming that he now had his new passport and was looking forward to the trip. It was too late to call, and I was tired after the long drive, so, saying goodnight to Patrick, I crawled upstairs to bed. It was 3 a.m.

The next day I met Don for breakfast. He was excited and had been very busy. He brought with him a small box containing an extraordinary collection of micro-electronics, none of which I understood, but all essential for the purpose, he assured me.

Later I told him of my plan to smuggle 'Hugo' back with us. 'We could do with a couple of passengers,' I explained.

'Whatever for?' he asked, clearly perplexed.

I told him that it would look much better if we travelled as a group of four. Two might look suspicious, and I reasoned the more we were, the more we would look just like any other gang of easygoing tourists strolling about on an Asian safari.

He thought I was mad. My kind of insouciance appealed to him, but there was more to it than that. Don was a deeply religious guy, and totally in harmony with his spiritual self. He admitted to me later that he considered our chance meeting to be divine providence, as if

58

some mysterious unseen force had contrived to ensure that our two paths crossed. His statement troubled me for a long time, my spiritual side being somewhat underdeveloped. And yet there *had* been so many strange coincidences over recent weeks.

The single-page advertisement looking for extra passengers that I pinned up on the notice-board of the YMCA brought a deluge of calls. Most backpackers took the rickety bus from Singapore to Butterworth; an air-conditioned Jeep that could stop anywhere along the same route was too good an opportunity to miss. In the end we settled for Hansel and Gretel, as we called them, Kurt and Ilse from Munich. They were mid-twenties, clean, respectable and amusing company. Don thought Ilse was a 'babe'. When he explained to me what that meant, I thought so too.

We spent the afternoon doing the rounds of the various stores, jumping in and out of taxis, consolidating everything under one roof in my room. At four o'clock, I went off to collect 'Hugo', paying the balance of my account to Mr Shah.

Everything had gone perfectly to plan. Upon arrival over the causeway from Singapore into Johor Bahru the jeep was ignored by Customs, blending perfectly into the night-time stream of vehicles crossing the border heading for the superb Malayan food and a tankful of cheap petrol. We had crossed peninsular Malaysia quietly during the night; traffic was light. We ate an excellent breakfast of satay and sickly-sweet doughnuts at a road-side café before we made the final break for the border.

The neck brace was beginning to feel distinctly uncomfortable, but it was not yet time to take it off. The rigid polycarbonate frame was digging relentlessly under my jawbone, chafing away continuously at my skin. My head began to throb and my spine was aching in defiance at this bandaged imposter clamped around my throat. Small beads of sweat broke out on my brow as I gripped the steering wheel more tightly.

Not that much farther to go now, I thought. Keep calm.

Up ahead in the distance I could see the shimmering light of the noon-day sun bounce off the dirt road as an endless stream of pick-up trucks and lorries headed for the border. Clouds of dust rose violently from the track, swirling upward together with great plumes of thick black exhaust as engines lurched closer to the rcd and white barrier.

In the agonising crawl forward, engine never out of first gear, the temperature gauge on the dashboard slowly began to rise. Damn, I thought. Incongruously the only quick way to reduce the heat was to turn off the air-conditioning. It was going to be stifling with four of us and our luggage in the cramped interior of the rented jeep.

Don sat beside me in the passenger seat, clutching the vehicle registration papers and our passports. Buried in the glove-compartment among the breakdown manual and John Denver tapes was a dirty white envelope containing various receipts and other bills of sale from our shopping spree the day before. Silently I prayed that we wouldn't need them.

Behind us, sandwiched together on the back seat, were Hansel and Gretel. Behind them, hidden under their rucksacks, our luggage and covered with an old ground sheet, was 'Hugo' along with several thousand dollars' worth of other contraband.

We inched forward, bumper to bumper with the rest of the herd. The jeep was filthy: I had deliberately driven through every muddy pot-hole and blackened puddle that I could find. The Germans were puzzled at first, then I told them it was a game. They didn't push it, so I didn't have to lie to them.

In a seaside town in Mexico, some years before, I had made the grave error of parking a newly rented, gleaming white Willy's Jeep right outside a bank whilst I changed travellers' cheques inside. Big mistake! Five minutes later, my business concluded, I left the bank only to find a traffic cop officiously scribbling down my registration number in his notebook. I walked straight into a trap. The other cars both in front and behind me had not moved, there was no yellow line and yet, according to him, I was illegally parked. A tow-away truck was on its way and that would be expensive, explained the policeman menacingly. Such inconveniences could be waived, however, with a modest allurement, and with a crisp ten-dollar bill in his back pocket he deftly took out his whistle, held up the traffic and saluted smartly as I sped off into the distance. Never again, I thought; muddy jeeps from then on.

The truck behind was blaring his horn impatiently. A six-foot gap had grown now to the car in front and I was expected to fill it, and quickly! It was getting unbearably hot in the cab and I wound down the window, resting my elbow nonchalantly on the door sill, resisting the temptation to retaliate.

My neck was stiff, I felt ridiculous, and I was beginning to have my doubts that the subterfuge would, in fact, work. Years before, after being ill on a Philippine island and inadvertently extending my visa by ten days, I had tried the same deception, pretending I was crippled by injury. It had worked, and now it was time to put my theory on human kindness to the test once again.

Don was fascinated by my nonconformist, irreverent approach. 'You have absolutely no regard for decent middle-class values like moderation and caution,' he had said. 'There is something of the cavalier about you and they were always more fun than the roundheads.' One of Don's many hobbies was taking part in medieval costume pageants back in California. In his heart, I suspected, Don was very much the cavalier as well.

Cavalier or not, there was a limit as to how far to go. I had singularly refused to involve our young travelling companions in the deception. As far as they knew I had twisted my neck in the whiplash of an emergency braking situation on the way to pick them up from their hostel the previous evening. They had no idea what was stashed away out of sight in the back. In the event that I was caught, the less they knew the better.

I could see the portly Customs guard quite clearly now, busying himself with documents and occasionally opening car boots for inspection. Many of the trucks were empty, returning to Thailand having done the early morning run from the Thai border town of Hat Yai over to the Malaysian markets of Butterworth and Penang. There were few Malaysian cars. They normally travelled much later, under the cover of darkness, on their way to the flesh-pots and brothels dotted all across the border.

The engine temperature had cooled and I flicked the air-conditioning back on. The engine choked as the device kicked in.

The pale blue Mazda pick-up in front was waved through with a cursory nod from the sweating, overweight official. He took out his filthy white handkerchief as I had seen him do a hundred times that morning to mop the perspiration from his brow as I pulled the car to a halt beside him.

I swivelled my face laboriously to greet him with a feigned smile. And, nodding graciously with strained and contorted features, twisted my head slowly so that Don could let me have our passports.

'Show time,' he said softly as he pushed them carefully into my hand.

'Good morning, officer,' I said politely to the bulbous head, handing him our papers with a slight wince.

'Where you go?' he snapped.

'Oh, Phuket,' I said. 'Beautiful Thai lady!' I offered with a much constricted, knowing wink.

He leaned forward closer into the window, to look at each of our faces in turn. His breath smelled of garlic and stale tobacco. I tilted my head slightly to one side in acquiescence, flinching impressively at the imagined pain.

'OK,' he mumbled finally, 'you can go.' As he handed back our passports, his expression seemed to say, 'in your state, they'll eat you alive, pal!'

And we were off, we'd made it!

Hansel and Gretel were content to get off just inside the Thai border, as they wanted to explore every inch of Thailand, they said. Wiping an imaginary tear from his eye, Don kissed her hand in an outrageous display of Hollywood dramatics and benign chivalry. With a final wave, I lost sight of them in the rear-view mirror. After a couple of miles we pulled up on to the grass verge.

'Just a moment,' I said to Don. 'I've got to get this damn thing off.' And with a sharp wrench at the velcro straps, I dropped the wretched thing into my lap, rubbing the back of my neck.

'Whoopee!' yelled Don, in his best cowboy holler, and then more quietly, 'Fancy a beer?' We both laughed.

We took the side roads for a while. My companion was an excellent navigator and soon we were back on the main highway with the border crossing fifty kilometres behind us. Out of reach now, we stopped at a small wayside grocery store and bought an ice-cold six-pack of Singha beer; it tasted delicious.

'How did you know it would be that easy?' asked Don, wiping the froth of his second can of beer from his lips.

'I didn't,' I replied honestly.

'Of course, if we had been caught, you'd got enough cash left to pay the duties and stuff, hadn't you?' he asked confidently.

'Nope!' I admitted.

'You mean to tell me, we went through all that with no downside limitation?' he demanded with a wry smile, and in his Los Angeles gobbledygook.

'Matter of fact, I'm down to my last hundred bucks, and if Sophy hasn't managed to sell my car in the last week, I'm in shit-street,' I said soberly.

'Dwaila was right, you are some crazy son-of-a-bitch. Cheers to you.'

'Don't worry,' I said matter-of-factly. 'It is a good car, some clown will buy it. I did, didn't I?'

And with that we clashed our beer cans together, the spell broken. Paying for the next stage of the operation was tomorrow's problem. For the time being at least, we both had good reason to feel happy.

CHAPTER SEVEN

Phuket, March 1990

The back road out of Phuket, the scenic route, was no more congested than normal at this time in the late afternoon. Except it all just felt terribly wrong. Ever since I'd left Theo's cluttered blacksmith's yard, there had been this nagging feeling in the back of my mind that something awful was about to happen. Over and over again I told myself to be rational. But the dark foreboding that was beginning to engulf me would not disappear.

We had now been back in Phuket for over three weeks and had acquired two bedrooms at the Mansion Hotel in Kata Noi: one for living and sleeping, and another that looked like a bomb-site. The staff had accepted us as two eccentric *farangs*, and for the most part left us in peace. With one minor exception.

Every morning, at least at some hour before noon, we would phone room service to order breakfast: hot coffee, toast and marmalade, orange juice and bacon and eggs. And every morning there would be a gentle tap at the door as the same waitress brought our humble sustenance on a battered metal tray. Both Don and I were serious coffee drinkers, an idiosyncrasy seemingly lost on the Thai. Each day, and without fail, room service would pass our order to the kitchen who would make the coffee first, Nescafé granules, then the toast, then cook the eggs and bacon so that by the time everything was ready and carried to our room, the coffee was stone cold!

Every morning we complained, but to no avail. In desperation we bought a thermos flask and presented it to the waitress. The subtlety of our approach was totally lost on her, but her colleagues in the kitchen got the message and she was teased relentlessly from then on. Tired of her new nickname, 'Hot-coffee', she never came to our room again and would glare at us whenever we saw her. And try as we might to placate her crumpled ego, she never forgave us.

Don had built a work-bench for himself from the frame of an upturned bed and on this unlikely operation table, he performed his wizardry with surgical precision.

In Singapore, I had casually asked him on that first evening if it was possible to modify a broadcast-quality VHS video camera so that it could be completely remote-controlled. What I wanted, I explained, was the ability to film eyeball to eyeball with a wild tiger, but from the safety of a platform thirty feet off the ground. The camera would have to tilt and pan, zoom and focus and switch itself on and off at the flick of a switch.

'Sure. It's never been done before, but yes, as long as you can get me the circuit diagrams,' he said, after some thought. 'Do you want me to make it walk as well?'

We had bought two Panasonic MS1 Super VHS models which were the best that I could afford. Now one of them lay on Don's work-bench stripped to the core, tiny multi-coloured wires protruding from every orifice. Scattered around were dozens of carefully labelled perspex boxes, each the size of a cigarette pack, inside which were hundreds of electronic component parts I couldn't even begin to comprehend. He was truly a master of his trade. Despite the apparent chaos and the ungainly look of the once imposing camera, it was difficult not to marvel at the way he made everything appear so prosaic.

I had once shared a flat in London with two Cambridge graduates who used to play mental chess with one another. I would be the hapless referee and follow their moves on a pocket-size companion set, unable to fathom the complexities of minds that could play the game without a board. When I mentioned this to Don, he admitted without sentiment to having mastered the technique by the age of eleven, advancing to three-tier mental chess by his fourteenth birthday. It was not a boast, it was a cold statement of fact, delivered in a manner not designed to impress, but merely to obliquely hint at the child prodigy that he once had been.

I forgave him this uncharacteristic self-indulgence; he had no need to convince me of his extraordinary genius. I only hoped that he didn't find his prevailing challenge too mundane.

Whilst Don beavered away with his soldering iron and precision screwdrivers, I would work on the complicated lighting rigs that I hoped would turn night into day in the depths of the jungle. At the time, I knew very little about tigers other than that they were carnivorous, largely nocturnal and not to be hit on the nose with a stick! If I was to succeed in filming them, then more likely than not it would be achieved by subterfuge and most probably at night. Should I succeed in luring them to a particular spot I reasoned, and then gradually illuminate the area, Don's camera might possibly do the rest.

I had assembled an instrument panel that was largely reminiscent of the dashboard of the De Lorean automobile in the film *Back to the Future*. There were glass dials indicating electrical output and current, a joystick that operated a marine flashlight and a profusion of levers, knobs and switches of various colours and sizes. I had installed a dimmer board bought from a discotheque supplier in Singapore that would independently deliver a measured amount of power to any lamp in turn and, sitting proudly in the centre, a six-inch colour TV monitor from which I could steer Don's incredible innovation. None of which could possibly work without a power source. And that's where Hugo came in.

Electrical generators in Thailand were largely of the diesel-in-one-end, black-smoke-out-of-the-other variety, with an erratic and totally unpredictable flow of electricity from somewhere in between. If you were lucky. By contrast, in Singapore, Mr Shah stocked the very latest in air- and water-cooled petrol-driven models from around the world that were both remote controlled and quiet. But not *that* quiet.

Sound travels over great distances at night in the forest and Hugo, with his 4,500 watts of power just raring to go, needed to undergo some minor surgery designed to reduce his unpretentious gurgle to a fine whisper. Thereafter he would be entombed in a shallow grave under a specially constructed sound-proofed mausoleum, imaginatively referred to as Hugo's House, one hundred metres away from the control panel.

La maison d'Hugo, as it was also known, resembled more of a dog kennel than a house. It was built of marine plywood over a box metal frame and lined with ten inches of polystyrene foam covered with a padding of egg boxes – a trick Don knew about from a friend in Los Angeles who had built a recording studio in his cellar. One trick that Don didn't know quite so much about, however, was how to obtain that all-important balance between air extraction and noise emission. If the generator got too hot it would cut out at best or explode at worst. Maintaining a cool operating temperature involved, for practical purposes, extraction of the hot air whilst simultaneously stifling the sound. More a question of trial and error really. Hugo was now on trial and Theo was the judge.

Theo was busy pummelling away on the foot-bellows when I arrived, boosting the incredible heat in the ancient furnace to the critical melting point so vital to his work.

He was a great ox of a man, with powerful forearms, a bull neck and wide muscular shoulders. The Thai word for blacksmith is *chang lek*, which, slightly mispronounced, translates to *small elephant*, an eminently suitable nickname for this unlikely artisan. His huge barrel chest was adorned with a primitive tattoo depicting a spread-eagle with four lines of wavy Sanskrit lettering underneath. He had a massive head and his thinning black hair was kept close-cropped by his 'second wife' who worked in a nearby barber shop. Theo wore only shorts and flip-flops but despite his imposing physique greeted all his customers with a warm and toothy smile. He was a giant among men, a gentle giant.

The cherry Titan had finished welding the silencer by the time I returned, and together we heaved the cumbersome machine on to the tailgate of the jeep. I lashed the door tightly to the roll-bars with an elaborate series of nautical knots. The flimsy canvas hood remained folded and untouched under the back seat. It was March, there would be no rain for at least two months, and the open-top jeep gave a great perspective on the outside world.

Theo assured me that the new silencer was as good as possible and after a brief demonstration to prove his point, invited me into the shade of his kitchen for a drink.

Old newspapers and *Time* magazines stood in neat piles on the terracotta floor, well-polished pots and pans hung from the ceiling, and there seemed to be a cat on every available warm surface around the large black stove. We sat and drank ice-cold Cokes and talked of his adventures working on the many and varied feature films that had been made in this part of the world.

He proudly showed me a sun-bleached photo of himself shaking hands with James Bond, as he called him, during the filming of *The Man with the Golden Gun*. He'd met Robin Williams and Mel Gibson, and spoke of them as one might of old school chums. He was excellent and very amusing company, and it would have been easy to have stayed with him all evening listening to anecdotes. But alas, I had other things to do and, with a wave of farewell, set off on the twenty-mile drive back to the Mansion Hotel in Kata Noi.

The first part of the journey was uneventful enough except for the usual mindless kamikaze motor-cyclists speeding on to the road from the left without a cautionary look behind, in typically hare-brained fashion.

I'd read once in a local 'Tips for Travellers' guide, written by some expatriate wag, that there were possibly three explanations for this singularly Thai and suicidal manoeuvre:

1) If the motor-cyclist was hit, he/she could claim it wasn't his/her fault because he/she hadn't seen the other vehicle!
2) That looking over the shoulder could cause him/her to lose balance, so therefore it was much better not to.
3) That if he/she was hit, it was all in his/her karma and therefore predestined and unavoidable.

All perfectly logical to the Thai intellect and therefore to be respected and understood by the unwashed foreign devil, whose own detestable ways and filthy habits had to be endured by the natives regardless. Driving in this extraordinary land was indeed an experience! Nevertheless, with lashings of patience and good humour, seemingly inevitable accidents could somehow be miraculously averted.

The traffic lights on the main airport road were taking a long time to change, and a decrepit push cart, overladen with ripe watermelons, was meandering slowly along the slip road making it impossible to pass. For some unknown reason I began tapping my fingers on the steering wheel impatiently. Come on, I thought, get a move on!

Eventually the lights changed. Billows of putrid black smoke belched from all around me as engines were gunned remorselessly to life. I indicated to turn left and followed a garishly painted minibus for a while until he lost patience with the *tuk-tuk* in front of him, overtook dangerously, and sped away into the distance. There was no great rush, I thought incongruously, except to find the answer to whatever it was that was nagging at me.

The road had narrowed now, and the light was fading fast. On and on I drove, at first through a rubber plantation, its regimented columns of trees stretching far into the periphery of my vision. I tried to count the rows but I couldn't concentrate. The harrying feeling in the back of my mind persisted. In fact it was getting worse.

I passed an old hand-pump petrol station. A young girl in aviator sunglasses had stopped her moped for some two-stroke mixture and the aged female attendant in a raggedy gingham sarong cranked furiously on the handle. Her husband lounged idly by, propped up in a hammock, one foot resting lazily on a stool, his lice-ridden mutt snoozing in the dirt at his feet.

There was a bus-stop up ahead, deserted. Later, long after the last bus had passed by, people would gather here under the high-pitched corrugated-iron roof to drink Mekong whisky before wandering aimlessly back into the darkness from whence they came.

Beyond was a stretch of open land, cleared for building, with a lone coconut palm swaying gently in the breeze. Dotted around the site were small bonfires that blackened the grass, sending up curls of blue smoke to disappear into thin air. Was this the precursor to the ill-wind that was haunting me? Get a hold of yourself, I muttered, as the tenuous grip on my sanity began to evaporate.

Music, I thought, and I reached into the glove compartment for a cassette. I rummaged around blindly among the mosquito spray and bits of string until I found a tape and pushed it abruptly into the player. Damn! The bloody thing's on the blink again, I cursed, as I twisted the controls impatiently searching for sound. Wrenching the tape out wildly, I hurled it over my shoulder on to the back seat.

What *was* that old *King and I*, Rogers and Hammerstein number? 'Whenever I feel afraid, I whistle a happy tune . . . and no-one will suspect I'm afraid.' I tried to whistle, but my lips were too dry. I licked them and tried again; my mouth wouldn't respond.

What's *wrong* with me, I thought, I can't even bloody whistle now!

My mind raced through all the alternatives. Could it be Sophy, I thought, suddenly alarmed? I hadn't heard from her for over a week and still didn't know whether or not she was coming out to join me. Oh no, please God, I hope she's all right. There was a phone box down at the filling station on the Ao Chalong roundabout; I'd stop there and call her.

Was it Don, had he electrocuted himself or blown himself up? No, it wasn't that. What about Dwaila, had there been a shoot-out with poachers, had she been killed? No, don't be ridiculous. That's possible but much too far-fetched, I told myself.

I looked down at my hands. The knuckles had turned white and they felt sweaty and cold. The speedometer reading was a steady fifty kilometres per hour. Slow down, I thought, but why? This was a perfectly safe speed.

And then it came to me. The ropes, yes, of course, the ropes!

Don't be so bloody stupid, I argued with myself, it can't possibly be the ropes, you're an experienced yachtsman, you know how to tie knots. And yet the sinister apprehension that one of the knots had somehow come loose wouldn't leave me. I would just have to pull over and check them.

It can wait, a tiny voice said in my mind. There's nothing wrong with them at all. The generator is not going to fall off the back on to the road and into the path of some unsuspecting motor-cycle.

And so on I drove, past the large yellow road-sign with the thick black snake, thinking that I could check the knots and make the phone-calls at the same time from the petrol station just a few more miles down the road. Then everything would be just fine.

I tried to concentrate on the road, focusing on what was going on around me. A child was chasing chickens around the family's back yard, an old tyre hung by a rope from a tree above their heads. Normally I would have tooted the horn and waved as I drove past, but my hands were glued to the wheel.

A decrepit moped joined the road from a junction up ahead – two adults, two children and a dog were sandwiched somehow on to the plastic seat, precariously balancing as the overburdened machine gradually built up speed. An old woman pulled a trolley piled high with brightly coloured soft toys, on her way to the night market in Patong, her teeth stained red with betel-nut. A muddy-coloured Isuzu three-ton pick-up overtook me, and at least two dozen building workers waved and taunted me to speed up and catch them, jabbering hysterically as they passed.

Was that a signal? Surely if something was wrong with the jeep they would have warned me? I tried to find every and any plausable reason not to give way to this crazy notion that possessed me. And yet it just wouldn't go away.

On along the windy road I drove, arguing manically with myself. Pull yourself together, God damn it! To my right I saw a convenience store, bright flags and bunting flapping in the wind. Outside, overflowing waste-bins and above the mess and discarded junk a Pepsi-Cola sign and above that in large blue letters 'Lucky Mart'.

There, I told myself, an auspicious omen if ever there was. Be reasonable! But reason was nowhere to be found.

At first the nerves in the top of my back began to twitch, and then a sudden chill sent a violent shudder from my spine up through my neck. Within seconds my head began to shake uncontrollably. Trembling arms locked solidly through to my wrists and I clenched the wheel in a vice-like grip. My back was rigid as I forced myself deep into the seat, bolt upright and shaking with fear.

'It *is* the ropes, God damn it, pull off the road! Pull off the road now!'

I wrenched the wheel hard down to the left, swerving violently on to the grass verge and slammed on the brakes. The jeep skidded in a cloud of dust, throwing me against the wheel. I recoiled in the seat, slamming the engine into fourth gear, stalling it instantly. With a final lurch, it ground violently to a halt.

Wrenching open the side door, I leaped angrily to the ground, half of me furious with myself for giving in, the other anxious that I might have lost control of my mind.

And then I saw them. From around a blind bend less than fifty metres in front of me, two enormous, heavy-duty, gravel-moving lorries were bearing down on me at high speed. Side by side they blocked the road as if locked in some feudal overtaking battle so intense that they were completely oblivious to whatever lay before them.

I stood riveted to the ground as they hurtled toward me. I was still holding on to the open door and staring in disbelief as neither lorry seemed prepared to give way. Oh my God, this is it, I thought, they were going to hit me head on. I slammed the door shut and hurled myself to the back of the jeep in one continuous reflex action as the ten-wheeled trucks, blaring their horns wildly, raced past.

My knees buckled and I sank to the ground in a hopeless, crumpled heap, like some broken rag-doll. I buried my face deep in my shaking hands and wept.

I must have stayed that way for some time, trembling in unashamed relief as my pounding heart slowly relaxed and its beat returned to normal. I stood up finally on wobbly limbs, gripping the rear bumper tightly for support, and stared down impassively at the ropes, somehow knowing already what I'd see. They were fine. I shook the tailgate finally for good measure: it was as solid as a rock.

Looking upward to the heavens, I closed my eyes and thanked the Almighty for my deliverance. Then, slowly and very carefully, I walked around the jeep and, opening the door, slid back in behind the steering wheel. The glove compartment had fallen open and a tape by Chris de Burgh lay on the floor. I picked it up and absent-mindedly pushed it into the player and started the engine. The machine clicked once and his voice sang out from the speakers.

'No borderline . . . No borderline . . .!'

I sat listening to the tape, unable to move. There was a lot of religious sentiment in his songs, the sort of thing that Don could identify with, but I had found difficult to relate to. Until then. I rubbed my face in my hands searching for some rational explanation, some way to explain what had just happened to me.

I thought of Sweden, that fateful night and the bizarre series of events that had saved my life. Now, here in Thailand, thousands of miles away, I had again been snatched from the jaws of death by an unseen hand. Even the cassette player had failed to operate at that critical time, keeping my mind focused on the voices in my head. And now, as if to soothe me, it had come back to life . . .

Don looked up as I walked into the room, the scars of fear and inner turmoil written all over me.

'What's happened, Mike?' he asked, knowing instinctively that something had.

'I can't tell you right now,' I said, 'I have to phone Sophy. Do you fancy a beer later on?'

'Sure, just let me know when you're ready.'

I went next door into the bathroom, and stared at my reflection in the mirror. What's happening to me, I thought, as my eyes suddenly fixed on the salty white tracks across my cheeks. Running the hot tap into the sink I splashed water on to my face and washed away the dried tears.

Grabbing a beer from the minibar I sat heavily on the bed beside the phone and called London. I heard the familiar ringing tone. Come on, I thought, pick up the phone . . . and then the easygoing sound of Sophy's voice . . .

'I'm sorry I'm not in right now, but if you'd like to leave a message . . .' Damn, damn, damn, I thought, about to hang up.

'Sophy, its me,' I stumbled, 'please come. Something's happening, I can't explain, please come. Please!' I hung up slowly, staring impassively at the receiver.

Don helped unfasten the ropes and lift Hugo to the ground. He could see that something was deeply troubling me, and clowned around making light of everything, trying to break the spell and snap me back to life.

'Poison beer?' he asked.

'OK, poison beer,' I replied, and he jumped into the back of the jeep hanging upside down on the roll-bars like a crazed chimpanzee. He stayed that way, scratching his armpits, thumping his chest and whooping madly until I pulled up right outside Hip's Bar.

'Ah, Monkey-Don and Tiger-Mike,' Hip said cheerfully from behind the bar. 'Poison beer?'

'Yep! Two, in frosty glasses please,' called Don, leaping to the ground.

Hip's Bar had become a local favourite of ours. It was handy and served ice-cold draught lager in tankards straight from the ice-box. The owner, a powerfully built Thai named Hip, had an awesome collection of CDs and one of the best sound systems on the island. He also made devilish cocktails.

'You'd better throw a Zombie at me as well, please, Hip,' I said.

This, as the name might suggest, was a lethal concoction of spirits – rum, tequila, vodka – plus fresh fruit punch, coconut milk and God knows what else. It was cunning, like most good drinks, delicious, and had a kick like a mule. After three of those nobody, but nobody could stand up. I settled for just the one.

The 'poison beer' was equally lethal in that the formaldehyde content was such that few brain-cells remained unaffected after a pint or two and the hangover lasted a week! Don't ask me why we drank the stuff. Almost all beer in Asia had some form of preservative thrown in to extend the shelf-life well into the next millennium, and formalin was cheap and effective, but devastating the day after!

Hip's English was excellent, he had been a cocktail barman most of his adult life and had worked mainly in the big resort hotels dotted around the island. Over the years his language skills had improved and every day his savings had grown closer toward his ultimate dream, his own bar, which he now proudly owned.

It was Hip one night who started joking with Don after we had both knocked back a double-Zombie. Don's hair was still long and hung down well over his shoulders; his thick stubble was beginning to resemble a fledgling beard and his lumberjack shirt was unbuttoned to the waist, revealing an expanse of hairy chest.

'You look like big monkey,' said Hip after a while. Don's eyes

74

were beginning to roll with the effects of the cocktail, and Hip thought he was fair game.

'Yeah, watch this,' said Don, and leaped off his bar-stool, grabbing hold of the rafters above his head. Taking hold of a beam firmly, he deftly looped his legs over and hung upside down by his knees, pounding his chest hysterically.

'Hey, Hip, what the hell did you put in that drink,' I laughed.

'Jungle juice,' grinned Hip.

'Jungle, huh?' I said. 'Got any more?'

He reached behind for a bottle and poured a healthy measure into my glass.

'Here,' he said, 'this will make you roar like a tiger!'

I took a long deep drink and roared as loud as I could. The noise reverberated around the bar, and Don gave an almighty monkey-screech in response.

'You're both crazy,' announced Hip. 'Monkey-Don and Tiger-Mike!' and the names just stuck. We had been trying to think of a suitable nickname for him ever since, but nothing seemed to quite fit.

That night, as I sat on the black circular bar-stools with the clever arm-rests that doubled as support to stop one falling off, I noticed a photograph that I hadn't seen before on the expansive collage of pictures of Hip and his friends and customers that he kept proudly on one wall. It was of a man in swimming goggles with a white bathing cap head-on into the camera in what looked like a butterfly stroke.

'Is that you, Hip?' I asked, pointing at the strange figure.

'Yes, long time ago, I want to swim for my country, not good enough,' he said sadly.

'Do you still swim?' I asked.

'Not for competition, only for keep fit. Running too, every morning on the beach.'

'What,' I said incredulously, 'is that you I have seen in the mornings?'

'Sure, I like, before I go to the market,' he replied earnestly.

Don glanced at me with that knowing look that said if you live long enough, all the answers to the mysteries of life will come to you. I wondered how or if I would ever receive a satisfactory explanation to the near fatal crash earlier. All in good time, I thought. And then suddenly a suitable name came to me.

'Butterfly-Hip,' I suddenly announced. 'That's it! Butterfly-Hip.'

He looked horrified. Both Don and I knew that Hip had a reputation with the ladies, but what he didn't know was that we were also aware what the word 'butterfly' meant to them as well. A man that found it impossible to stick to the same blossom!

'No, no. Name no good,' objected Hip. 'Thai lady not like men who are butterfly.'

'Methinks thou dost protest too much,' announced Don, seizing the advantage and determined not to let him off the hook, as Hip fought in vain to shake off his new sobriquet.

'That which is sauce for the goose, shalt be sauce also unto the gander,' he continued in mock-Shakespearian gibberish.

'Guess you're stuck with it, now,' I said solemnly, 'unless of course you want to call the whole nickname thing off.'

'No, no,' protested Hip, 'him *look* like monkey!'

We all laughed, and later, at the Sunset restaurant, I told Don of the near miss, letting the alcohol inside me do most of the talking. He listened patiently as I explained everything in minute detail; from the moment I left Theo's yard, to the time when I felt the hot air of the trucks on my face as they hurtled past me, only inches away from my nose.

He seemed inexplicably unmoved by the entire incident, interrupting me only once or twice for clarification whilst rubbing his hands together deep in thought. Finally he looked up at me and said simply, 'It just wasn't meant to happen, Mike.'

We walked back to the hotel in silence. I was trying to unravel exactly what he was trying to tell me, and he was giving me time to work it out.

Somboon, the night porter who could never stay awake, was sleeping on the sofa as we crawled up the steps. He sprang to his feet as he heard us, and darted behind the reception desk for our keys.

'Ah, Mr Mike, have message for you, just a moment please,' he said rummaging around until he produced a folded scrap of paper.

'Goodnight, sir,' he said, finally handing it to me.

I opened the note. In spidery ballpoint pen were the words: 'Sorry I missed your call. I'm on my way. See you soon. Love Sophy.'

CHAPTER EIGHT

Mansion Hotel, April 1990

It was time for the big tidy-up. But first the big test-run. Scientific advances should always take precedence over mundane housework! And if later we didn't have time for the cleaning before Sophy arrived, then there was always the maid.

Except she had been banished from the workroom weeks earlier having inadvertently vacuumed up a vital capacitor that had fallen to the floor from Don's work-bench. Unfortunately for her, he'd heard the thing rattling its way up the aluminium hose of the vacuum cleaner, and launched an uncharacteristic volley of four-letter abuse at the poor girl. Most of which, thank God, she didn't hear, such was the intolerable noise of the machine. Later, he had patiently sifted his way through the dust-bag until he found it, whilst the young maid sat on the floor, close to tears, unable to fathom the importance of such a tiny piece of plastic. He'd given her a flower after that and a polite caution never to set foot in the room again. One less to clean was of little consequence to her, and the two parted company on relatively good terms.

Nearly a month later, the room looked like an absolute tip. Don was now wondering how to woo her back.

It was well past the hour of darkness, and I carried my control panel out on to the balcony. The flies, moths and hundreds of other bugs and beetles buzzed maniacally around the light. In the trees beyond, the cicadas launched into their nightly chorus. I gently lowered the cables with their tiny plugs over the edge to the ground and, with a wave, Don began to meticulously connect them, one by one, into the camera which he had carefully set up on a specially adapted tripod below.

Somboon came out from behind his desk; it was now April, the hotel was not busy and tourists were thin on the ground. He sat and watched, fascinated by the robot camera that had just mysteriously appeared from one of his rooms above. The staff were always gossiping about the two crazy *farangs*, largely because that was the Thai way, although none of them knew what we were really up to. Until now. He watched, mesmerised, as Don put the machine through its paces, overriding the remote until he was absolutely confident and ready to give me the signal. He asked Somboon patiently not to touch the camera and not let anyone else go near it. The boy nodded gravely.

'Hang on there,' he called. 'I'm coming up.'

Within minutes Don was beside me at the controls looking down. 'Here we go,' he said softly, and flicked the master-switch.

Years ago when I'd learned to fly at Elstree, just outside London, the discipline of check lists had been thoroughly drummed into me – pre-flight check lists, start-up and taxi-ing lists, pre-take-off lists – all of which were essential to both safety and the efficient running of the aircraft. Now, looking down at the notes in front of me, I realised how important that training had been. Each switch and knob was carefully labelled, and the sequence in which they were to be used was critical.

The TV monitor flickered into life providing another target for the moths. Don turned down the brightness control and they lost interest.

'Now for the big one,' he said, taking hold of the camera control box. He depressed a small green perspex button and a miniature LCD lit up on the panel.

'All right!' he said triumphantly, as a shadowy picture slowly began to emerge on the monitor screen. He pushed another button marked 'Light 20w', and the image became brighter.

Below, atop the camera, a flashlight had come on, providing yet another target for the moths.

'Let's see what we can see,' said Don, as he let his fingers dance over the scanning control buttons.

And there, suddenly, was Somboon's befuddled face as the camera zoomed in, capturing his head full frame on the TV.

'Smile, you're on TV,' called Don to the boy below, 'wave to Pappa!'

And his face lit up on the small screen before us.

'Don, you're a bloody genius,' I said to him, and I meant it as he gave me a full demonstration of the incredible machine.

'Just a few minor adjustments,' he said finally, 'and then it's all yours.'

We had done the impossible. Back in Singapore I had asked Danny Chew if he knew of such a camera.

'Not on the market,' he had said confidently, but added with a frown, 'the way technology is advancing, it won't be long, I guess.'

But here, in a remote beach-front hotel in the middle of nowhere, this master technician from Hollywood had already built one with his bare hands! It was an incredible achievement. The only thing he had not developed was the facility to rewind the video tape and play back the recorded material through the monitor by remote control.

'That will always be a manual operation,' he had explained, 'and probably best that way; the fewer things to go wrong, the better. By the way, I'm sorry, but I didn't have time to make it walk.'

'Don,' I said, 'even if you had made it fly, it wouldn't be better than it is now. Thank you, you're a star!'

He went downstairs to collect his masterpiece, and left me to pack up the controls. Back in the room, I looked around at the mass of equipment that we had acquired and accumulated over the previous weeks. There were now seven purpose-built cases, all foam-lined, into which each item of kit could be dismantled and safely stowed away.

In one corner was a pile of supplies that I had eventually bought from the army surplus shop on Siah Street in Singapore: camouflage clothing and stout leather Timberland boots; rucksacks, tents, sleeping-bags and cooking utensils; anti-snake-venom kit and a host of other survival gadgets; an M16, United States military issue bayonet; compass, Mag-Lites, the best torch in the world; a Stanley, remote-controlled, 100watt marine searchlight; two Sony VHF transceivers; and, of course, all the invaluable video, stills camera and sound-recording equipment locked away safely in Pelican waterproof cases. And then there were the books.

On my first visit to Singapore I had discovered the Times Book Store, and bought everything they had on the subject tiger; it wasn't much, but it was a start. Colonel Jim Corbett, Billy Ardjan Singh, Fateh Singh Rathore, Kailash Sankhala, Valmik Thapar, Guy Mountfort and one or two more. I had read each one with deep interest and fascination at least twice. Much of the material was repetitive and I was dismayed to find few original accounts of confrontations with the big cat outside of the Indian sub-continent. Over the weeks my knowledge grew, but it was never slaked, and I desperately wanted to find out more.

On one occasion it occurred to me that perhaps tigers, like their remote and very distant domestic cousins, might be attracted to cat-nip, and so I sent a fax to my old friend Timmy Orchard back home in London.

Tim, bless his heart, was by now well used to me sending him bizarre conundrums to unravel and was quick to respond to my vexing questions as to what cat-nip was! He immediately contacted the curator at Kew Gardens who fed Tim with a lengthy discourse on the species *Nepita cataria*, and back came a fax the following day. It didn't tell me how to grow the plant or where to find it or the seeds for that matter. However, Tim, in his irrepressible manner, did add a minor footnote commenting that if the stuff had the same effect on wild tigers as it did on his own pet moggy, don't be within a sixteen-mile radius at the time!

Ever the mad closet scientist, I bought a case of the stuff from a pet shop on one of my many visits to Singapore, intending to test Timmy's theory and hopefully live to fax him the outcome.

Not all my time was spent in hare-brained speculation, and I endeavoured, over the weeks, to cram my mind with every and any snippet of information about tigers that I could possibly lay my hands on. Then, of course, I would enlighten Don, and anyone else that would listen, with all my newly acquired knowledge and he would question me on bizarre aspects of tiger trivia.

I came to learn the Latin names for each of the eight sub-species, their distribution and approximate numbers in the wild. I was alarmed to discover that three of those sub-species had already gone extinct during my lifetime and that one more seemed to be teetering on the brink. I studied tiger behaviour, mating habits, the gestation period of the tigress, the amount of time she spent training her cubs, the recessive gene factor that precipitated the rare white tiger. All these things became familiar as I pored over the books whenever I had the chance.

But nowhere, however, did I read about the tigers in Thailand or of any calamitous and immediate threat to the species in the wild. It was true that the late Colonel Jim Corbett had written once in 1946 to the then Viceroy of India, Lord Wavell. In this letter he pointed

80

out that due to excessive hunting, in his estimation, only between three and four thousand tigers were left on the sub-continent. He went on to predict that they would be 'practically extinct' within ten to fifteen years.

Wild populations had indeed continued to decline dramatically in India until finally, in 1972, the late Mrs Indira Gandhi launched a pioneering effort to save them. This scheme, known as 'Project Tiger', succeeded in reversing the decline, and wild tiger populations seemed to be recovering. Since that time, very little substantive information had been collected, let alone written about, the touchy subject of tiger poaching. Many of the books appeared to rely largely upon personal anecdotes, historical symbiosis, obsolete, and therefore unreliable, population estimates. To all intents and purposes, the poaching epidemic had disappeared with the swish of a political wand, and an iron fist to back it up.

It was difficult to know what or whom to believe. Dwaila could be one of the most cynical and abrasive individuals on the planet at times, but nevertheless she was living in the middle of it all. Surely her first-hand experience should count for something? There was one thing for certain, however: none of the textbook writers really knew or, if they did, for some reason they weren't telling.

Don had remarked once with lacerating understatement, 'It isn't particularly surprising, given the nature of the beast and man's preoccupation with sex, money and the pursuit of the technologically and morally indefensible.'

That comment made me chuckle at the time, coming as it did from a man who earned his living making severed artificial limbs crawl across the floor and extra-terrestrials fly bicycles to the moon. But he did have a point, and I began to wonder if people actually cared about wildlife any more.

'Well, you seem to,' he had said to me. 'I just hope that you can cope with the truth and that it doesn't freak you out when you find it.'

'All I'm doing is trying to film the bloody things,' I had replied indignantly.

'Yeah, but will it stop there?' he demanded.

'I'll tell you that when I've done it,' I said, trying to end the conversation.

'Hey, wait up,' he said, diving back in. 'So what happens, let's say, when you find out that things aren't exactly all fine and dandy. What makes you think that anyone will give a damn?' He was playing devil's advocate, I knew, testing my resolve.

'Well, I'll just have to cross that bridge when I come to it,' I answered lamely.

'That's not good enough and you know it. If you discover something up there, how do you think you'll make people listen, how is one lonely voice going to change things?' he went on, twisting the knife.

'I simply don't know, Don, and that's the truth. But one thing I do know is this. A couple of years ago there was a guy in your part of the world, California I think, who did find out things that some people didn't want to know about. Answers to what was actually happening to marine wildlife.'

'Oh yeah, and then what happened?'

'Well, he took his evidence to the news media and they *did* listen, big time! You see he was a marine biologist, and like many of his colleagues he had become concerned about the sudden absence of dolphins from his stretch of shoreline. Of course all the antagonists said that it was just a seven-year rotation cycle or some such gibberish, but he *felt* there was something seriously wrong. Anyway he got himself a job on a tuna fishing boat and every morning would shin up the mast with a small rucksack on his back and watch the nets being hauled in. The crew got used to him doing that and ignored him after a while. Then one morning, as they were pulling in their catch and clubbing the dolphins over the head in the process, this guy reaches into his pack, pulls out a camcorder and films them. I remember seeing a documentary about it. I think it was called "Where Have All The Dolphins Gone?" That film had such an impact that canned tuna virtually vanished from the supermarket shelves overnight, such was the outrage of the American public. They put "dolphin friendly stickers" on the stuff now thanks to the legal reforms that guy made possible. Do you know who I mean?'

'Yeah,' said Don, 'his name is Sam LaBudde.'

'Well, he sure as hell did make a difference, Don. I'm not saying that I'll ever be able to do anything like that, but I am saying that it is never too late for change, and all it takes is one tiny push to make that happen.'

He'd looked at me for a long time after that, his chin resting on the bridge of his hands, rocking slowly back and forth. Somehow, it seemed, he had heard the answer that he was looking for and he let the matter drop.

All he said after that was, 'Be careful.'

Don came back into the room holding the camera proudly under his arm, and I started to notice a strange aura of serenity about him. It was as if a burden had been lifted from his shoulders.

With renewed vigour he set about tidying up his work-place as if, I wondered with a sense of unease, he was rehearsing it for the last time. He had expressed no great wish to come with me up to the jungle, although I had always quietly harboured the hope that he would decide to join the expedition. Now, looking at him from across the room, I was filled with the apprehension that he was preparing to leave.

I busied myself with tidying up, trying to dismiss the thought from my mind. There were bits of wire and plastic, sawdust, fragments of wood and all manner of rubbish on the floor, so I went off in search of the maid's vacuum cleaner to help with the work-load and to give myself something else to think about.

I eventually found the machine lurking behind an unconvincingly locked door which wisely surrendered to a judicial twist of my Swiss army knife. I swaggered back to the room, nozzle in one hand, cylinder repository in the other, determined to vanquish my unease. Don stared at the appliance as if confronting an old enemy and promptly picked up a broom and poked it playfully at me.

'*En garde!*' he declared, and he lunged at my chest like some crazed musketeer.

'OK, if that's the way you want it,' I said, wrenching the hose-pipe out of the machine, 'prepare to die!'

What then ensued can only be described as mayhem: a chaotic battle around the room. There was only one rule, and the shout would go up: 'Mind the equipment!' Apart from that, every tenet of the gentle art of swordplay was disregarded and unceremoniously violated. We fought to the point of farcical exhaustion, finally collapsing in an uproarious heap on the unswept floor.

'Poison beer time,' we both said in unison, looking at the havoc we'd just created, and convulsed in another attack of uncontrollable laughter.

'What about the tidying up?' said Don in a hilarious Donald Duck voice.

'The hell with that,' said John Wayne.

'Hey, that's pretty good,' said Don. And we both laughed again.

The spell had been broken and we charged out of the room and down the stairs with Don hurling himself into the back of the jeep, hanging upside down from the roll-bars as usual. We did the normal rounds, calling in to see Hip, terrorising him with his new nickname. From there we drove over the hill into Karon Centre to see Gangi at the New Wave Bar, eat and shoot some pool.

Gangi was an impish rogue, all four feet six of her. I was over six feet tall and Don only a couple of inches shorter and yet she would look up at us with that mischievous twinkle in her eyes that didn't betray for one second where the next prank was coming from. Her English was excellent, the food delicious and she played backgammon faster than anyone I'd ever seen in my life. I never once saw her lose. When she wasn't hiding chillies in Don's ice-cream, hot-wiring the jeep and parking it on the beach, putting beer-mats under one leg of the pool-table or dropping ice-cubes down my back, she would be out on the sea pounding the waves with her wind-surfer at every available opportunity. She was good.

That night she came with us to Patong and played bodyguard, fending off all the groping hands and the lewd calls from the street hucksters . . .

'Hey, you!' one called out to me. 'Wanna see a live show?'

'Get real, man,' said Gangi. 'We've seen all that crap. How about a dead show, my friends here are seriously into necrophilia!'

'Gangi,' said Don in mock alarm, 'I don't believe I heard you say that!'

'Ping-Pong show, mister?' said another.

'Only if I get to hold the paddles,' said Don, getting the idea.

And so it went on late into the night until finally, tired and a tad inebriated, we wended our weary way back over the hill to the Mansion.

The next day I got up early and went for a swim to drown the hangover. Sophy was arriving at the airport around mid-morning and I wanted to look vaguely respectable. Don had ordered breakfast by the time I got back and the coffee, praise the Lord, was piping hot!

Sophy's flight was delayed and I passed the time chatting with a gang of departing Koreans whose flight to Seoul was held over in Bangkok. The tour guide and interpreter had asked me what I was doing in Thailand and for want of a plausible fib, I told him the truth.

'Trying to film tigers,' I had said with a dismissive wave.

There followed a brief but highly animated translation which ended in rumbustious laughter and lots of back slapping that seemed to indicate that I was a jolly good fellow. Wildlife film-making was clearly an honourable profession in Korea, I thought.

Until one of them said: 'Oh yes, Thai *girls* very sexy! Ha ha ha!'

I left them thinking they had met the king of the local pornography film-making business and went in search of a coffee. And, with mixed emotions that ranged from trepidation to euphoria, watched the Thai Airways flight with its extra-special passenger touch down gently on the runway.

Sophy looked lovely as she ran into my arms and we hugged away the weeks that we had been apart. There was much news to catch up on – friends, family, pets, the value of my car – none of which seemed to matter during the slow drive back across the island as Sophy, clearly jet-lagged and exhausted from the long flight, tried desperately to keep her eyes open.

She was seeing Thailand for the first time, and that impression had been favourable. And she knew in her heart that there was no rush, she had come to stay.

Putting her to bed in the spare room, I called in to see Don and explain that she was tired and that we'd all go out for a huge dinner later on. His bench was cleared as I opened the door, and a suitcase lay open on the floor.

'Hey, what's all this?' I asked, suddenly alarmed.

'You don't need me any more now, Mike,' he said. 'Besides, I've got to get back, family problems, you know.'

'For heavens sake, Don, not like this, not without any warning. Stick around for a few days at least. Both you and I deserve some fun, and Sophy's been dying to meet you. She'd feel mortified if she thought she was driving you away,' I said, pleading with him.

'OK,' he said after a moment's thought. 'I could do with some R&R, but only until Saturday, then I've got to get a flight out of here.'

The three of us spent four wonderful carefree days exploring the island, discovering secluded beaches, playing tourist and visiting the pearl farms and scorpion shows, taking boat trips out to the neighbouring islands, and eating excellent food. Most evenings we would drop by and see Hip, and Don would regale us all with his hilarious stories from Hollywood, about what the stars were *really* like, the time he met Woody Allen, and other tinsel-town gossip.

One evening, the conversation turned to pet hates, and Sophy spotted a big hairy one crawling up the wall. She should have known better in such boisterous company, but she was eventually forced to confess a mild dose of arachnophobia. And of course that did it, from then on it was Spider-Sophy, Monkey-Don, Butterfly-Hip and Tiger-Mike. And what a fine quartet we were too.

Saturday came round all too fast and it was time to say goodbye to Don. He'd refused the offer of a ride out to the airport, and a taxi was waiting at the steps to the hotel. It was a sad day, and one that I shall always remember. Neither of us was very good at long farewells, and no words that I could offer were sufficient to convey the deep gratitude and affection I felt for that extraordinary chap who had suddenly popped up out of nowhere like a magical jack-in-the-box and was about to disappear out of my life again, perhaps for ever. We shook hands and embraced in that ungainly way that men do, and then he was gone.

For the next few days Sophy and I busied ourselves with the final preparations for the trip back to Dwaila's camp. Sophy's artistic skills were invaluable as every piece of baggage and kit became camouflaged with spray paint using a clever stencil that she had made. By the end of that week we were ready to go, and with the help of Gangi found a flat-bed truck and driver to transport the equipment up north.

Little did we know on that last night at the Mansion Hotel just what the future had in store. Had we known then the dark secrets of Khao Sok, and where they would lead us, we would have probably taken the first flight out of there and home to England. But life is never that simple.

PART TWO
THE UNDERSTANDING

*'Life is what happens when you're busy
making other plans.'*

John Lennon

CHAPTER NINE

Khao Sok, April 1990

I took little notice at the time of the gangling youth with the gawping eyes who sloped off up the track, hands buried deep in the pockets of tattered jeans, just as we arrived. He had that deranged stare of an imbecile that defies close scrutiny, and his gaunt and demented features haunted me for several minutes long after he had disappeared from view.

Out of the corner of my eye I could see that Sophy was watching Newt the boat boy inspecting the engine. Something was wrong: he kept scratching his head as if puzzled, bending down periodically, peering into some unseen crevice at his feet, and then shaking his head very slowly from side to side. Suddenly he snapped bolt upright and let out a piercing cry. He began shouting and waving frantically at Dwaila who rushed immediately to his side. Newt was pointing down through the inspection hatch and jabbering hysterically. She followed his gaze, staring down in horror.

Then, as if in slow motion, I saw her hands move to her mouth as her head turned slowly upward. Her throat became taut with anger, fingers bunched tightly into fists at her temples. And, when her wrath could be contained no more, she struck out blindly in tempestuous fury and unleashed an almighty blast of obscenities into the empty sky.

We had travelled up from Phuket the day before; it had been a long one, that began two hours ahead of schedule and almost ended in disaster. For some inexplicable reason, Thais are seldom punctual; they are mostly either unbelievably early or incredibly late. Gangi had arranged for the lorry driver to arrive at nine o'clock and, true to form, he was downstairs blaring on his horn shortly after seven.

After Don had left, Sophy and I had moved into the 'work-room', primarily to save money. My car had been sold, but the ravages of the recession in England had dramatically affected the price. The preparations thus far had made a massive dent in my savings, so it was time to tighten our belts. The place was a complete mess: our clothes and equipment were everywhere; trunks and cases stacked high; piles of cables, boxes, bags. That was only a small proportion. The bulk of our gear was downstairs under a tarpaulin in the hall.

Although I recognised the dilapidated truck, the driver was definitely not the man we had met earlier. This chap, poor soul, had a wonky eye and a club foot, and I began to suspect a possible downside to Gangi's formidable bargaining skills.

Determined not to notice the man's obvious disabilities, and under no circumstances to appear uncharitable, I greeted him with a cheery 'Hello', and we set to work loading the flat-bed lorry. The sudden noise of the first section of metal-lighting rig to hit the tailboard woke his young mate who emerged from the cab, rubbing sleep from his eyes in thinly disguised displeasure, and reluctantly joined us. Sophy came down with a procession of hotel staff bearing the contents of our room, and work began in earnest. Hugo's house was the heaviest and most cumbersome piece of kit to haul aboard, but after that was done the rest came easily. Within a couple of hours we were loaded up and ready to go.

Gangi had agreed to come with us up to the Sarasin Bridge and to look out for one last possible extra item on the way. She carefully briefed the driver to take his time and make sure that the lorry was never left unattended. That done, we confidently left him to do the journey at his own pace and eventually lost sight of him crawling up the hill out of Kata Noi, heading approximately north.

The girls talked continuously in the back; they had become good friends. It was good to see Sophy laugh again. Occasionally I would get a tap on the shoulder as they pointed out some amusing sight, but for the most part I was left to my thoughts.

In one of the stories by Colonel Jim Corbett that I had read during the previous weeks, he had written that the sound of a bleating billy goat never failed to attract a wild tiger. In his day, however, the goat would be tethered to a bush with the sportsman and his rifle safely above ground in a *machan* or platform in the trees. The hapless goat was invariably attacked and fatally wounded long before the hunter could react and shoot. Eighty years later, I hoped to test his theory but with the aid of modern technology. Don had helped me adapt a sophisticated, portable stereo sound system so that it now ran perfectly from a twelve-volt car battery. All that remained was to record the woeful bleating of a young goat on cassette tape, and replay the sound in the dead of night in the jungle. Dogs could be fooled by recordings of barking, wildfowlers illegally used tapes to attract ducks, so why not tigers, I reasoned? It was certainly worth a try.

In the small town of Thalang, Gangi helped us buy a young goat. Sophy sat with him on her lap for a while, and we racked our brains to come up with a suitable name. We couldn't think of anything appropriate, so we called him Barney.

With a tearful farewell, we dropped Gangi off and headed north.

The day was beautifully clear and I wanted to show Sophy the park from my favourite vantage point so, just beyond the crest of the mountain, I pulled the jeep over on to the verge and killed the engine. We crossed the road and scrambled up the steep bank on the other side, stones and small rocks skidding down on to the road under our shoes. I watched her eyes as she looked down on the awe-inspiring landscape for the first time.

'It's beautiful,' she had said quietly. And so was she, I thought, with an enormous sense of pride. This intrepid girl had left behind a highly lucrative career in decorative arts back in London so that she could join me on this extraordinary adventure. I thought, not for the first time, what an incredibly lucky man I was to have found such a perfect soul-mate.

We sat there for a long time. There were small billows of pure white cloud in the sky and as they passed the sun, the light change in the valley below us was both stunning and wildly dramatic – as if some enormous giant was walking across the panorama, casting a fleeting shadow across the countryside below. Sophy was seeing everything with an artist's perspective. For her, the view would never be the same: each time the light would paint different hues of green on the trees, and the sky would be another subtle shade of blue. For me, it was one of the most alluring places on earth, and yet I couldn't dismiss the dread that it might also be the hunting ground of some of the most evil men in Thailand.

We arrived at Tree-Tops in a cacophony of barking dogs and whooping gibbons just as the sun was disappearing over the limestone hills and the house was bathed in shadows. Shangri-La revisited. Dwaila appeared from under a tractor covered in oil and grease.

91

'Hi, Mike, and you must be Sophy,' she said, wiping her hand on her shorts. 'Excuse the dirt, but we have to fix up most things ourselves out here. Come inside and have a beer.'

We talked for two hours. Dwaila was anxious to report fresh evidence of 'the big boy' and to hear all our news. Apparently, Bun had heard a small troop of langur monkeys cry out a warning of his presence not far from the river camp several nights earlier. These wily creatures are always vigilant sentinels and can see and hear much of the activity on the forest floor from their vantage points high up in the trees. Their alarm call had been picked up by a hog deer, who barked loudly in defiance as he made his escape. Later in the night, Newt the boat boy was awoken by a piercing shriek far away in the darkness. The following morning, both Bun and Newt set off early to scout for signs of the drama played out around them only hours before, and found fresh tiger tracks and evidence of blood close to the old lumber path. They concluded that 'the big boy' had killed a wild boar and had obviously dined well that night.

Young Thao appeared to light the lanterns as the last of the light vanished into darkness, and he jumped with glee as he recognised my face. It was good to see him again, and he fell in love with Sophy at first sight. We totally forgot about the lorry until Dwaila asked again where all our equipment was. It was seven o'clock.

'Did you say that you had a brand-spanking-new generator on that truck, Mike?' she enquired, less than delicately.

'Yes, and a good deal else besides. Don't tell me you're thinking what I think you're thinking?' I said deliberately, suddenly alarmed.

'How long have you known this guy?' she asked. It was obvious what she meant. The man might well have done a bunk and on the face of it, if that was the case, there wasn't a damn thing we could do about it.

The three of us sat and tried to rationalise the whole thing. Of course, we knew how to find the yard again in Phuket, but what if the owner denied all knowledge of the driver, claiming his lorry had been stolen? No, that was too far-fetched. Our man was hardly inconspicuous and yet, did that matter? Most crimes against foreigners went unsolved in Thailand simply because the vast majority of visitors had only a limited amount of time in the country. And, as far as the police were concerned, the old maxim 'out of sight, out of mind' applied in such cases. If we had been conned, would the police be sympathetic?

We sat in the candlelight for at least another hour, my optimism evaporating by the minute. I was beginning to rehearse my speech to the Thai police for the next day, and how I might explain our predicament, when Dwaila suddenly raised her right hand to her ear. We heard the ridgeback growl first, and then the rest of the dogs began to bark as a faint glimmer of light appeared through the plantation.

'Looks like we've got visitors,' said Dwaila.

'Let's hope it's our man,' I replied earnestly.

And as the glimmer became a beam, and the engine hum became a spluttering diesel cough, we knew it could only be a lorry. With an uproarious cheer we recognised the rusty blue paintwork of the truck, and made out the silhouette of our equipment still piled high on the back.

We greeted our driver as if he were a knight returning from the crusades. The poor man admitted to never having been outside of Phuket in his life, and confessed to having become hopelessly lost. He'd eventually been put on the right road by an obliging traffic cop, having driven nearly ninety kilometres in the wrong direction. He graciously accepted the offer of sustenance and shelter for the night, and by the time Sophy and I emerged from our tree-top hideaway in the morning, all our belongings had been neatly stacked on the ground. We found him waiting impatiently at the breakfast table for his modest remuneration so that he could be off and back to the familiar sanctuary of his beloved Phuket as quickly as possible.

Dwaila had arranged for two local pick-ups to transport our gear, and by eight o'clock we were on the road again, heading east and into the heart of the Khao Sok National Park. We stopped at the village of Ban Tankun and she bought provisions for the next few days. She introduced us in turn to each of the market traders, and told them to take care of us should we decide to shop there in future. She bought fat pork and chickens, eggs, dried noodles and milk, and plenty of rice; fresh vegetables and fruit, herbs, spices and flavouring sauces; kerosene for the lamps; and a host of other bits and pieces. We carried everything to the trunk, made one last stop to collect beer, soft drinks and ice, until finally, loaded down to the gunwales, we left the village heading across country for the Rajjahphrabha Dam and the great man-made lake.

We travelled in convoy until we arrived at the closed barrier to the sprawling EGAT hydro-electric plant. The Electricity Generating Authority of Thailand owned a vast expanse of land bordering the lake, its waters vital to fuel the great turbines that provided power for much for the surrounding region. A uniformed guard begrudgingly got up from behind his empty desk and sauntered over to inspect Dwaila's papers and, after a short delay, waved us nonchalantly through. There was something sinister about his look and the atmosphere around the gatehouse that was hard to define, and I was left with the feeling that, as far as he was concerned, we were all unwelcome intruders.

Beyond the gate, most visitors turned right and continued up over the hill and then down the meandering lane to the tiny ramshackle fishing village. We drove straight on and into the small town that EGAT had built for its staff and their families, then past the shops, houses and school and out to the other side until we could see the fabulous lake stretching for miles into the distance.

We finally meandered down a steep, pot-holed dirt track to a small inlet where EGAT kept their cruiser tied up to a special purpose-built pontoon. The general manager of the plant was a kind and obliging man who allowed Dwaila to use the jetty when she needed. He took no responsibility, however, for the security of her boat whilst it was there . . .

'Fucking son-of-a-bitch, some bastard's cut the fucking fuel pipe! Shit, goddamn it, those fucking assholes!' she screamed. 'I'll kill that pop-eyed, cock-sucking bastard!'

I ran down on to the quayside to see what I could do to help. She was holding the neatly severed end of the main diesel-feeder pipe. There was fuel everywhere.

'Do you know who did this?' I asked.

'Oh yes,' she said, spitting venom. 'I have a pretty good idea.'

'OK, we'll sort him out later,' I said. 'For now let's try and get it mended. Do you have any spare hose?'

'Nope. And this can't be fixed just like that either. It's a reinforced type of tubing. There's too much pressure from the pump to patch it up. We ain't going no place for a while, that's for damn sure.'

We unloaded all the equipment on to the jetty, and Dwaila sent Newt together with one of the drivers to the neighbouring coastal town of Surat Thani in search of a replacement. It was a three-hour round-trip at best.

'Wait here,' said Dwaila. 'I'm going to see if we can rent a boat over in the village.' And with that, she marched off abruptly to her dilapidated pick-up.

She had murder in her eyes. If she found the person that did this, there could be trouble, I thought.

'Hang on a minute, I'm coming too,' I shouted.

She glared at me with scowling eyes, a devastating look designed to make me back off and mind my own business. It didn't work. When she knew that she had lost she mumbled grudgingly, 'Suit yourself.'

I smelt the village long before I actually saw it. The revolting stench of dead and decaying fish that assaulted my senses as we approached was worse than any rotting flesh I had ever known. It was more like a shanty town, a ramshackle collection of bits of wood and bamboo jumbled together in a motley assortment of hovels, huts, lean-tos and sundry shacks masquerading as shops. Naked children with filthy, unscrubbed faces played in the dark puddles blackened by slime and excrement. Featherless chickens scratched frantically amongst the ubiquitous garbage searching for scraps of food. Piglets of uncertain pedigree rooted around in the dust, snorting furtively. And the sky was alive with the constant drone of a thousand blow-flies as they buzzed through the fetid air looking for blood.

How anyone could have the base self-esteem to live in such squalor was beyond my comprehension. It was not simply a question of poverty. I had seen penury before, but here, on the edge of this beautiful and bounteous lake, surrounded by fertile land, surely there was no excuse. The men who slept in the shade of a ragged tarpaulin and the women, teeth stained by betel-nut, who gossiped in the shadows as we approached, must have given up on life. The perceived futility of their humble existence had obviously caught up with them, and now they looked upon the world each day through a consolatory alcoholic haze.

We drove down in silence; there was nothing to say. The squalid scene before us said it all. An infant boy picked up a tiny handful of gravel and threw it at the car. It was a futile gesture, and one which would have had little significance outside of this wretched place, and yet here it seemed to be indicative of the contempt in which we were held and the stories that must have

95

been told about the foreign devil to these innocent children.

'I hadn't wanted you to see this place until I thought you were ready,' Dwaila said finally, parking the jeep. 'There ain't nothin' that goes on around the lake that these folks don't know about, and just about everything comes through here in one form or another. And I do mean everything.'

I looked at her eyes, which were dark with sorrow. She had brought me, although unwittingly, on our first day to this evil den of iniquity. To the place whose very atmosphere reeked of the vile abomination that was being wrought upon the jungles beyond, and she was sad. All at once I understood the supercilious manner of the guard back at the barrier. There was only one way in and out of this place, and that was under his nose.

He and his colleagues, these villagers, the fishermen and probably the park rangers themselves, must all have been part of a silent conspiracy to rape this landscape of its wildlife treasures. The waters of the lake gave access to the most remote corners of this wilderness and, at the same time, provided the perfect means to transport its bounty to the village and the markets beyond.

We got out of the jeep and looked around. Dwaila was trying to find the village headman, and went over to talk with the women. One of them shouted to a small child who went scampering off up a dirt path. Almost immediately a man appeared from the shadows of a hut, he stepped out into the sunshine pulling up his ragged trousers. He had very dark swarthy skin and a full head of grey hair which he covered hastily with a long piece of cloth. He smiled briefly at Dwaila, exposing a mouthful of gold teeth and nodded, holding up six calloused fingers as they spoke. She held up four and he shook his head gravely, holding up five, and the deal was done.

'OK, he's bringing his long-tail around, it'll cost ya 500. Sorry about that, but it's the best I could do,' she said solemnly.

I shrugged, indicating that it didn't matter and we climbed back into the jeep and left the kids, the chickens, the pigs and the conspirators alone to wallow in the decay that was their world. The youth with the hollow eyes stepped out of the shadows as we ground our way slowly back up the hill.

It was almost dark by the time we arrived at our destination across the vast expanse of water, Dwaila's river camp. She had told me that she had built two more floating raft-houses at the base of the tiny inlet, and they looked enchanting as we approached very slowly through the narrow passage that kept them hidden from the lake.

96

There were four of them now, strung together across the thin stretch of water, built almost entirely from bamboo. There was a wooden bridge connecting them to dry land, and in the middle was a large covered platform which served as a communal reception and eating area. To the left was a kitchen, and flying atop a makeshift flagpole was the Thai ensign, flapping in the evening breeze.

Bun was waving and clapping cheerfully as we approached. He'd been alone there for some days, and was quite obviously overjoyed to see us.

'So this is going to be our home for a while,' I said to Sophy. 'What do you think?'

She looked carefully around with her artist's eyes, taking everything in, until she looked at me with that disarming smile and said, 'This is perfect.'

The next day, we awoke early to the sounds and smells of breakfast coming from the cookhouse. Newt had arrived quietly in the night, his repair mission accomplished, and we agreed to go scouting for a suitable place to build a tree-house from which to operate our cameras.

It was an exciting time, full of expectation, and Bun, Newt, Sophy and I set off shortly after we had eaten. As we were leaving, I noticed Dwaila hand Newt something which he promptly stuffed into the belt at the back of his trousers. I'd never liked hand-guns, and felt safe enough with my knife, but she obviously had a good reason to think that Newt should take it with him, so the incident passed without comment.

We followed the river line for a while, skirting around an area of waterfalls as we began to climb away from the lake. The raft-houses looked bewitching and tiny from above, and we soon lost sight of them as we moved deeper into the forest and came upon the old lumber path.

Years ago, when the concept of a new dam and the flooding of the lake were being discussed, an enterprising timber company took out logging concessions for this part of the forest, knowing that when the lake came the logs could be easily floated out and stored close to the main road for onward transportation. Elephants were brought in and a path was cut through the pristine jungle beside the narrow river and down into the valley where Dwaila now had her raft-houses. The felling licence would have stipulated selective cutting only of mature hardwoods, most specifically teak, and that new saplings had to be planted in place of the old.

However Thai lumber firms were notorious for bending the rules and over-indulging in the immediate gratification of their own ends. Perhaps it is something to do with the Buddhist concept of impermanence and transience that has made Thai people live more for the present than for the future. The idea of replacing the old life with something that would take a hundred years to mature must have been inconceivable to them at the time, and twenty years later, the legacy of their rapacious onslaught was in evidence all around us.

In place of the ancient and majestic teak, clumps of bamboo and wild banana trees had sprung up, colonising extensive tracts of once fertile soil. It was easy to imagine the loggers cutting and burning everything that stood in their path in their marauding frenzy, plundering the rich forest of its treasures, and sharing the booty with the venal authorities that were supposedly empowered to control them.

As we walked on away from the lake the signs of past human activity became less obvious. Vast evergreen forest giants towered high into the canopy, the tallest of which were meranti or seraya trees. Beside them stood the majestic ironwood and Burmese sal, its leaves now dyed yellow from the deep red of the colder months. Some of the evergreens had been taken over by strangling figs, their gnarled tendons encompassing the entire trunk like twisted leathery sinews. From the branches above, knotted corkscrews of liana hung down, stems blotched with their characteristic wavy pattern making them look like giant reticulated pythons poised to strike.

We reached the brow of a knoll and looked down. There below us was a small waterhole, and we began to notice some tracks in the ground that led to it.

Bun had brought along a small picture book, and pointed out porcupine, wild boar, civet cat, barking and samba deer and, as we approached, the unmistakable pug mark of the tiger. In one corner of the stream-fed natural pond I noticed a group of strong young trees overhanging the water where three narrow paths converged. These trails had been made by animals coming here to drink. It seemed the perfect place to build our tree-hide.

I signalled to Bun, and Sophy drew a quick diagram in her notebook. He nodded excitedly. Yes, it could be done. We scouted around the water's edge and found more signs. This time bear, gaur and a smaller cat, probably clouded leopard.

The place was perfect. Not more than two kilometres from

Dwaila's river-camp raft-houses, yet far enough away to be unaffected by the human activity there.

We had already decided that we would visit Dwaila's jungle camp where I had had my first encounter with the tiger, and I wanted to show Sophy the communists' cave if we had time, but that was much further on down the trail. For now it was difficult to imagine a more ideal place to set up our base, and I wanted to get started at once. Nevertheless, this was to be the day of exploration and discovery, and so we left the waterhole, although in the back of my mind I had already made my decision.

Langur monkeys crashed around in the trees above as we marched single file into the depths of the jungle. We saw hornbills and hill myna birds, red-throated barbets feasting on the fruits of the fig trees, streak-eared bulbuls, coucals, and we heard the piercing cry of a pheasant. Newt spotted a banded kingfisher and we knew then that we were close to Dwaila's camp and the forest stream.

Bun had gone on ahead, and suddenly we noticed him crouch down on his haunches. Instinctively we did the same. Slowly he beckoned us to join him, putting his finger to his lips to indicate silence. We crept quietly toward him, and he whispered something to Newt who cupped his hand around my ear and said softly, 'People, maybe poachers.'

Now I understood the importance of the hand-gun as he took it from his belt and checked the magazine. Satisfied, he buried it away again, and we spoke quickly to each other.

'We're going in,' I breathed to Sophy.

'No, Mike, please. What if they have guns?' she gasped.

'Don't worry, wait here.'

And the three of us stood up and ran full gallop into the undergrowth and down the steep bank into the camp. There were two men huddled over a steaming saucepan, boiling stew over an open fire. They stood up startled as we rushed to confront them.

'What are you doing here?' demanded Newt. 'This is a restricted area.'

One of the men looked up with bloodshot eyes. Newt was a full head taller than him, and he didn't look capable of putting up a fight. Bun was an experienced bush-fighter and the man must have thought that I looked like Rambo. He sank to his haunches in submission. At ease now, we sat and talked.

I called to Sophy that everything was all right and, obviously

99

much relieved, she clambered down the embankment to join us.

The men explained that they were basket-weavers and were looking for rattan, a type of climbing palm, much over-harvested throughout most of the accessible forest land, and not easily grown in plantations. It prefers to regenerate in its natural jungle habitat, and here in Khao Sok rattan could still be found without difficulty. Close to the stream we could see evidence of their work with several bundles cleaned neatly and stacked, ready to be hauled out.

'You know this is illegal. You do realise this is a national park, and nothing can be taken from this place?' asked Newt.

'We pay money already in the village,' they replied stubbornly, thereby indicating that they had bought all the protection they felt necessary.

Newt remonstrated patiently with them for a time, explaining that the park was the people's property, a national treasure to be preserved for future generations. But these men didn't care. As far as they were concerned, it was a free-for-all and a harvestable resource. They had paid their dues to the local Mafia who would take care of any interference from either the park rangers or meddling *farangs*.

Bun was furious and wanted to burn the rattan there and then. Newt was more pragmatic, and asked me to photograph both the men and their nefarious booty. He delivered them a stern warning that he would be back with police at first light the very next day. There was little more that we could do, and with a final curse from Bun, we left the camp.

The day had been ruined. These men were not alone, they were indicative of an all-pervasive rot that had begun to permeate this beautiful heartland and was systematically plundering anything and everything that had any monetary value. In other similar camps dotted all over the 650 square kilometres of supposedly protected area there would be other poachers. Some specialists like the rattan weavers; others looking for rare herbs, spices and sandalwood. There would be bear-trappers, deer-hunters and those that indiscriminately laid their snares, not much caring what they caught, so long as it fetched a good price in the market.

Female gibbons would be shot from the trees, their infants snatched and taken to the grotesque bars that littered the squalid streets of Kata, Karon and Patong in Phuket. Gaur, its mighty head adorned with magnificent horns, would be stalked so that some powerful official could brag about the new trophy on his wall. Nets would be stretched high up in the trees catching every bird that was unfortunate enough to choose the wrong path, and even the lowly snakes would be taken and stripped of their valuable skin so that some aspiring rhinestone cowboy could show off a new pair of boots.

And the most sickening part was that it appeared as though the very people entrusted with the protection of this wilderness were busily lining their pockets as well. I would have to be very careful indeed if I was to safely gather enough evidence to effect any change in this green and verdant land.

CHAPTER TEN

Khao Sok National Park, May 1990

The tree-hide was built in less than three weeks. Dwaila had somehow managed to arrange through her influential and locally respected partner the granting of a restricted permit that allowed us *'to construct a temporary observation platform for the scientific study of the park's flora and fauna'*.

This document carefully set out preciscly what we were allowed to do and not do, and, more specifically, what natural materials we could use. It was all we needed, and gave us the legitimate right to remain in that area for at least twelve months. The hide was constructed almost entirely of bamboo which was a natural and rapidly renewable resource. Any additional timbers that we needed were especially selected by our experienced work-force and came only from under-developed softwoods in areas where it was unlikely that they would ever have grown to full maturity. We were determined not to upset the delicate balance of the natural ecosystem in any way, and the project probably took considerably longer to construct as a result.

The finished article looked like some bizarre prehistoric ark that had somehow become lodged in the trees after the great flood. However, it was light, practical and camouflaged, fitting perfectly in with its natural surroundings. The only alien substance used was in the manufacture of the roof: this was made out of several plastic tarpaulins sewn together, suspended above the platform like an enormous fly-sheet, and tethered to the ground by powerful nylon guy-ropes.

The entire design, shape, structure, engineering and assembly had proved to be a unique challenge for me. I'd built no end of dens and even a small tree-house on my father's farm as a boy, but never

103

anything quite so ambitious as this! There were no hardware stores deep in the jungle, so each section had to be devised and fabricated individually so that it combined perfectly to produce a finished construction that was weatherproof, strong, robust and, above all, secure. It was a fascinating experience explaining to Bun and Newt what I had in my mind, through the medium of Sophy's detailed diagrams, and then seeing the project slowly take shape. The twenty-five-foot ladder that they made entirely out of bamboo was a masterpiece in itself, and Thao jumped around playfully on each rung separately just to prove to us that it was safe!

Since the incident with the rattan poachers, none of us had returned to Dwaila's old jungle camp, and early one morning I decided to take one of my video cameras for a test run and follow the trail back in that direction and see what I could find. It was still dark as I kissed Sophy lightly, promising to be back before lunch-time. Dressed in full camouflage combat gear, I set out from the raft-house across the rickety bridge into the jungle.

Barney the goat bleated dolefully at me from the darkness. He would normally like to follow us up to the tree-hide site every morning, and couldn't understand why I was not undoing his stout tethering rope so that he could trot along merrily behind me. Not this morning, chum, I thought, as I grabbed my walking-stick from the water's edge and set off at a quiet but brisk pace up the familiar path. By the time I reached the brow of the hill overlooking the camp, I could begin to see my hand clearly in front of my face. This was always the sign that dawn was about to break, and I knew that within an hour or two the first rays of sunshine would be filtering through the dense jungle foliage on to my head.

I walked on past our tree-hide, forking left, and crossed over the narrow stream that fed the waterhole. The morning was crisp and still. Occasionally I would hear the startled screech of a squirrel or the alarm call of a racket-tailed drongo, alerting the forest creatures to my presence. I marvelled at how the sound travelled through the thick forest and how it would change as some other creature, recognising a danger signal, would pass it on down the line.

It was not surprising that a man on the move in the forest seldom saw a great abundance of wildlife. I longed for the day when I could peacefully sit in the tree-hide, without alerting the jungle to my whereabouts, and watch the deer drink quietly at the waterhole, oblivious to my presence.

It was getting light rapidly now, and I could make out a familiar patch of sandy earth up ahead upon which nothing had grown. As I got closer, a strangely familiar and pungent odour struck my senses and yet, try as I might, I simply couldn't recall what it was. I stopped, and twitching and flaring my nostrils, turned my head into the slight early-morning breeze diagonally to the right of me. The smell wafted through the air to me in waves. I recognised the scent, but what on earth was it?

And then it came to me. Tiger!

I stood frozen, riveted to the ground. Where on earth was he? His marking spray must be ahead, upwind somewhere, just off the trail. But was he still there? I flicked the switch on my camera and crouched down slowly, scanning the trees and the undergrowth for any movement. The tiger, I knew from my reading, had large soft pads of hardened flesh under each paw, enabling it to move almost silently through the undergrowth. He could be anywhere.

All the man-eating stories of Colonel Jim Corbett came flooding back into my mind. Get a grip, I told myself, man-eaters only attack for a reason, generally because they have been wounded and can't hunt, or through sheer old age and senility. Sometimes a tigress might roar and charge to protect her cubs, or a feeding tiger snarl to guard his food, but that was about it. What was it that he wrote? 'There can be no sound on earth more terrifying to man than that of the female tiger roaring in the forest at close quarters.'

There had never been any recorded incident of tiger attack here in Khao Sok, but then again, what happens if one doesn't live long enough to record it, I reasoned unreasonably. Nonsense, I told myself, pull yourself together, you're in the jungle now, you must expect to encounter the creatures that dwell here. If you can't cope with that, get out and go and live in the city and do your research from libraries like most sensible people!

Out of the corner of my eye, I saw a beautifully coloured bird looking quizzically at me from a high perch, its head askew. It was a banded kingfisher. Suddenly it burst into song – '*Chee-woo, chee-woo, chee-woo*' – the spell was broken. As the bird sang, the notes changed slightly and became a more staccato '*Chee, chee, chee, chee*'. The bird was laughing at me! And a revelation struck me so profoundly that I simply stood there and smiled, in spite of myself. There was no doubt that I had been deeply afraid, but then again I was completely harmless. The jungle had nothing to fear from me, and therefore I should not fear it. I carried no gun on my shoulder, I sought not to take life from this place, but to try and restore it. And from that moment on I began to walk boldly, with my head held confidently high, safe in the knowledge that nothing would possibly harm me unless I provoked it first.

As I got closer to the patch of sand, I could see the tracks. First a large deer, probably a samba, and then the unmistakable pug marks of the tiger. I followed them for some distance along the trail, and found some fresh faeces openly on view. Clearly the tiger was not as self-conscious about his ordure as the domestic cat, and probably left them deliberately as a form of warning token to other predators. I bent down and broke one open with a small twig. A biologist would have been able to discern exactly what the big cat had eaten, but I had no such specialist knowledge or equipment and could only guess at its contents. An hors d'oeuvre perhaps of jungle fowl, followed by haunch of venison and a purée of porcupine to finish it off! All much favoured by the tiger, but never in the same meal, I thought, and continued to follow the tracks until they veered off into the forest to my right.

Dwaila's jungle camp was less than a kilometre away, and as I advanced, I was acutely aware that I had much more to fear from the human animals in these parts than from the wildlife. I undid the safety strap from my M16 bayonet and let it hang slightly out to one side like a six-gun waiting for the draw. I had practised this for many hours, teaching Bun how to throw the knife with deadly precision into a small target ten paces away. He in turn had taught me how to fashion a lethal spear from bamboo that could pierce the heart of a wild pig from the same distance. I had no spear, but I had adapted the end of my stick so that I could attach the bayonet if need should arise. Like most insurance, I prayed that I'd never need to use it.

As I drew closer to the embankment overlooking the camp I could sense that it was deserted, but I also noticed a bitter, acrid charcoal smell in the air. As I clambered down I could see the scorched patches of ground where fire had destroyed the basic accommodations there.

The rattan poachers, bastards, I thought! Probably revenge for the stern ticking off that we had given them a few weeks before, but to set fire to everything? This wanton act of vandalism was clearly done with deliberate and uncaring menace, without any thought for the risk that the embers could touch off a major forest fire that might devastate thousands of acres of land and everything upon it. It was also a message. The maniac that was capable of doing this was also leaving behind a warning: 'Don't mess with me.'

I kicked around in the ashes for a while, remembering the very first night that I'd spent there, and I was both angry and sad at the same time. I was filled with hatred for the base and selfish mentality that had destroyed the serene beauty of this place. It had been defiled by man, and man had used the ultimate weapon of mass destruction, always the same old thing, fire.

And I was suddenly ashamed to be human. All at once I felt a greater affinity with the fauna around me than I did with my fellow man. I remembered the words of a Buddhist monk who once said, 'Greed will show quicker on a landscape than on a man's face. And so will kindness.' The precepts of Buddhism were clearly forgotten by the men who stalked these parts, and the bile rose in my throat at the duplicity of man. There was no hypocrisy in the animal kingdom, I thought; what you see is what you get. Animals do not scheme and lie, but man, despite his extraordinary skills and talents, continues to develop his ability for deceit, cheating and taking that which is not his at every opportunity, purely out of greed and self-interest. And the legacy and proof of that rapacity was every-where to be found, even in this most precious corner of the world. That reality made me shiver with a fear far more intense than any tiger could ever induce.

I went down to the stream for the last time to wash and bathe my face. Its waters would never be the same. I sat on the rock where I had last thought of my life and near death in Sweden, and looked mournfully about me. This sacred place which had first shown me the true spirit and life of the forest was now desecrated.

I scrambled back up the bank on to the path, and headed back toward the raft-houses with a heavy heart. The discovery of the fire had cast a desolate gloom upon the day that was difficult to shake off. The sun was not yet over the hills, and this should have been a time when the birds of the forest were at their most apparent, and yet I saw only a pair of coucals, a common enough sight, ducking through the trees before me.

Something was wrong. I thought for a moment that perhaps I was reading too much into the destruction of Dwaila's camp and that the charred remains had frightened away the wildlife; but it was more than that. Each morning, at about this time, the jungle would be alive with a cacophony of birdsong and insects all fighting to be heard, but now there was only silence; just like it was on that fateful morning when I had first awoken in this jungle, knowing that 'the big boy' was close by. Had he come back now? My heart missed a

107

beat and then quickened as I looked nervously around me. Leaves moved and branches swayed slowly in the low undergrowth. Behind every movement, every shadow, I was convinced the tiger lay, crouched close to the ground, waiting to pounce. Instinctively I reached for my knife; time and again I touched its handle until finally I held it tightly in my hand and began walking slowly back the way I had come.

Visibility can vary dramatically in tropical forests: dust can hang in the air, evaporating rain can precipitate a thick fog, and the morning mist can conceal even the largest tree. But now the air was clear and although my range of vision was at its optimum, I somehow didn't notice the obvious until I was upon it.

I had passed the broken tiger faeces, and had been looking at 'the big boy's' tracks, less discernible now as the ground began to dry. There was something distinctly different about the pattern. When I reached the area of sandy soil where my own footprints were plainly in evidence, it suddenly dawned on me what was wrong.

There, on the ground, clearly visible, were yet another set of prints superimposed over my own. These tracks were fresh and quite unmistakable. They were the paw marks of the tiger!

I bent down in amazement and there, plain to be seen, were three sets of tracks. First the tiger's, then my own, and then the tiger's again. He must have come round full circle and followed me up the trail, but how far behind, I wondered.

The crafty devil, I thought. He can only have been a few metres away from me when I noticed his scent earlier, and after I walked off, he had decided to have a closer look at me. And I hadn't known a thing.

So much for all those horror stories of the malevolence of the wild tiger. He was just being typically curious and wanted to check me out. I was hugely relieved that I obviously met with his approval. I had no great desire to hear the roar of the angry tiger at close quarters!

Chuckling to myself more out of relief than anything else, I strolled back to the river camp, much happier now. It was only ten-thirty by the time I arrived, and it felt as though I had been gone for a week.

For the next two days we hauled all the heavy equipment up to the tree-hide: the generator and its elaborate sound-proof housing, plus the lighting rigs that held the 500-watt halogen lamps. There were four separate rigs, and each could deliver a maximum of 3,000 watts of light if needed, more than enough to illuminate a large area of ground and allow the cameras to work efficiently. The six lamps on each rig could all be operated individually, and the sophisticated dimmer unit that I had bought in Singapore would permit me to gradually increase the light output without frightening the animal that I was trying to film.

This was all untried and untested theory of course. No one to my knowledge had attempted to film like this, and even if they had, there was no manual that I could find to aid me in my endeavours. Light gradation, I reasoned, was vital. To suddenly throw a switch and turn night into day in the middle of the forest would surely frighten every living thing for miles around. And yet it was just possible that the gradual introduction of light might seem like the full moon rising in the mind of a wild animal.

I had no way of knowing. The idea had to be tested *in situ* and if it didn't work, then I would simply have to try something else, because without light, there would be no vision, and that meant no film.

Whilst a seemingly endless procession of bearers, all kindly arranged by Dwaila, carried the kit up to our camp, Sophy, Thao and I busied ourselves stretching the cables from the tree-hide down to the camera positions and back beyond the waterhole to where we had located the generator.

I had asked one of the workers the previous week to dig three separate holes because I was anxious to test the water-table and had no wish for poor Hugo to drown at the first sight of rain! We inspected each hole in turn, and the one that I had most hoped would remain dry seemed to be fine. Another had filled with water very quickly, a great shame because from a sound attenuation perspective it was the best, as any excess engine noise would have been softened by a sheer rise of rock on both sides. I had seen this one before and discounted it immediately, but nevertheless for some reason stopped and pointed it out to Sophy as we walked back slowly toward the hide to inspect the last hole.

The diversion can only have taken a few seconds and as we stepped back on to the path we heard the most tumultuous commotion in the undergrowth to the left of us. Something was moving very fast and heading across the track in our general direction. We froze, and I reached for my knife. Suddenly a large, black, dragon-like creature, about six foot long, broke cover running at high speed, its head darting this way and that, hissing wildly, as if desperately looking for somewhere to hide. The giant water monitor, a lizard, has the awesome reputation of being a fearless predator, but this one was clearly very frightened.

From behind it something suddenly broke cover, and a dread shiver went down my spine. As it emerged we both saw the aggressor quite plainly, and gasped in terror. Although I had never seen one before, with its flattened head held so high, poised to strike, it looked every bit as deadly as I had imagined.

We had been warned many times that, if we came across a king cobra, we should freeze and stand absolutely rigid until the thing lost interest, and under no circumstances whatsoever try to run away.

The king cobra is, without doubt, the most dangerous of all the poisonous snakes in Thailand, both because of its highly lethal neurotoxic venom and the massive amounts it can deliver in one bite. The poison rapidly attacks the central nervous system and, without immediate treatment, death follows quickly from respiratory and cardiac failure. Although I always carried a powerful antivenin syringe, I had no wish to succumb to the fangs of this brute whose head was at least four feet off the ground. Cobras can raise up to a third of their total body length vertically in order to strike. This beast was big!

The monitor lizard reached the path, where it had three choices: to turn left and away from us on to the flat ground and run off past the tree-hide, to cross the path and continue through the dense undergrowth of ferns, brambles and creepers and try to reach the water, or to turn right and run straight toward us. I had my heavy wooden stick on to which I could attach the bayonet, but would I have time? The creature seemed to hesitate for an instant and then crossed straight over about fifteen feet ahead of us and fled down the bank in a last-minute bid to reach the water. The cobra followed, without ever losing sight of its quarry. If it noticed us, then it didn't care. God, it must have been angry!

We stood still for several long minutes after that, half expecting the huge snake to reappear at any moment, but it was gone.

At the time I would have fully understood if Sophy had said, 'OK, that's it. I've had enough.' But all she said was, 'Thank heaven that's over.' And we walked on in silence.

Bun thought later that the lizard had been disturbed trying to make off with the cobra's eggs or offspring, because the female will always defend her young brood with a vengeance. But whatever the case, once more I had witnessed at close hand the formidable creatures of the jungle, and they had done me no harm.

Thao thought the whole incident hilarious, and spent the afternoon strutting around like a cross between a giant lizard and Mick Jagger. This would have been extraordinary enough in itself but was made even more so by the fact that early on in the morning he had stepped on a nail which had penetrated right through his foot. Newt and I had applied copious amounts of disinfectant and bandaged the thing up as best we could because we were fearful of a nasty infection taking hold. And yet Thao seemed completely unconcerned by the injury, and a couple of days later it had healed up almost without trace.

By the end of that week, the lighting rigs were safely erected. It was the middle of May and we were starting to run out of time, not only because the monsoon season was just around the corner, but our visas would need renewing by the end of the month.

We had already experienced one day of torrential rain and, as sod's law invariably would have it, this was the day put aside to secure the guy-ropes to the lighting towers. The rigs, as we called them, were made of twenty-foot sections of inch-square boxed steel welded together with a latticed framework of flat steel cross-bars, eighteen inches wide. Each section looked rather like a long ladder with criss-cross bars instead of rungs. Three of these sections were bolted together to form an arch with four lamps at the top and one on each side. When this was assembled the whole unit had to be hauled upright using forked sticks to prop it up, whilst the ropes were tightened at strategic angles from the top of the tower rather like the rigging of an enormous tent.

It was whilst four of our helpers were precariously holding up the rig that the first drops of rain started to fall, and within minutes we were wallowing around in thick mud up to our ankles. Most sensible people would have thrown in the towel right there and then and run for cover, but the day was warm and the rain refreshing, at least to begin with, so with considerable cajoling, bullying and promises of an early finish to the day, we stayed. Our gallant troopers didn't complain, but stood there, faces turned against the downpour, holding the twenty-foot-high scaffolding tower against the heavens.

When the last rope was finally secured, I stood back, telling the men to release their poles one by one, and by some extraordinary miracle the thing didn't collapse. It remained standing, proud and

111

erect; apparently this alien structure deep in the jungle was there to stay.

It rained solidly for two more days, keeping us confined to the raft-houses. Our living quarters were very cramped. The hut was about ten feet long by six feet wide and five feet high at the centre. The pitched roof was made of dried coconut palm leaves cleverly woven together to make a thatch. Inside, not only did we have our mattress, clothes and personal belongings, but all of the camera equipment, batteries and film stock as well.

We spent the time mostly reading, checking over the equipment, and trying out the cameras under the shelter of the large roof in the dining area. The rain was depressing. Around us there were hundreds of acres of beautiful terrain, but the appalling weather kept us apart.

I had not expected to be able to do too much serious filming until after the rainy season, but I was determined that all the work around the site should be completed and everything fully tested and operational before Mother Nature could work her wonders during the wet period and remove all trace of our activity with new plant life and vegetation.

On the third day, the rain let up, and we marched back up to the tree-hide carrying all the filming gear ready for a test. I was anxious to see how well everything had fared after the inclement weather, and was content to see that, despite the lashings of wind and rain, the tree-hide was perfectly dry inside and obviously quite weather-proof.

Don had carefully labelled every cable individually, so that it was easy to connect all the wires correctly, and by lunch-time I was in position, aloft in the hide, fingers on the buttons poised for the big trial-run. It was one of the most anxious moments of my life. There was no real reason why things should not work, and yet I knew only too well the law of Mr Sod. Most worrying was that there was no Hollywood genius any more to put things right. It was all up to me, I thought with trepidation, and if something went wrong and a capacitor blew up or a fuse burnt out, we were in big trouble.

First the generator. Please, Hugo, I thought, do your stuff, and as I touched the black button I saw a light flickering on the console and then shine bright green. The needles on the voltage meter danced for a few seconds and then held steady on 230v. It was remarkable: I had power, and yet I couldn't hear a thing.

I called down to Newt and Bun, both of whom had very acute

hearing, asking them if they could detect any sound. They shook their heads solemnly. I then moved my attention to the lighting board and tested each light in turn pushing the delicate levers up and down and watched each lamp blink softly at me in the contrasting brightness of the daylight. With an enormous sense of satisfaction I watched the amazing effects of the controls at my fingertips, and thought it a great shame that Don could not be here to witness this extraordinary pioneering breakthrough. I made the bulbs dance for a while longer as though I was illuminating some unseen rock concert, and then faded each one gently and slowly shut them down.

It was time to try the camera. I took a deep breath and flexed my fingers like a pianist about to embark on a concerto and, just as Don and I had rehearsed back at the Mansion, I went carefully through the check-list. Orange and green lamps glimmered up at me from the console and, after a while, I had only one button left to press, beside which was written the word PLAY. I touched it gently.

I waited. Nothing seemed to be happening, and my heart sank. And then, slowly, the camera images flickered into life on the TV monitor high up above the ground in the remote jungle theatre.

I let out a huge cheer of delight. 'It's working, it's bloody well working!' I called down, hardly able to believe it myself, and beckoning for Sophy and Bun to come up first to see for themselves.

Thao thought it was hysterical watching Newt making faces at the camera, and I thought what a great team we all made and what an extraordinary achievement had just been accomplished by a curious combination of hard work, ingenuity, fate and good luck.

Now all we had to do was coax a tiger to come into the area and that, I thought to myself ruefully, is perhaps going to be the most difficult part of all.

That evening, Sophy and I spent our first full night in the hide. We had a mattress in one corner with a mosquito net and took with us some food and blankets. We listened to the sounds of the forest: the ubiquitous cicadas and tree-frogs, and squirrels screeching into the darkness of the jungle, alerting everything to our presence. And in the morning, a family of langur monkeys came very close to inspect us before swinging away into the trees, gritting their teeth in disapproval.

At around midnight, I completed another full test, and was overjoyed to see how well the lamps responded to the delicate controls on the console, introducing just the right amount of light, and illuminating a vast area when I increased the power to just below its maximum output potential. There had been no sign of our quarry. That would take many all-night vigils, and an enormous amount of patience, I was sure.

Although we had enough food and supplies to stay all day in the tree-hide, I had awoken with a severe pain in my left ear and we had foolishly left the first-aid kit back at the raft-houses. I knew that the discomfort was indicative of a deeper problem requiring some form of medical attention, but I was optimistic that Dwaila would be able to help out. With stiff and weary legs I climbed down from the tree-hide and plodded back to her camp, feeling the vibration of each step resounding inside my ear. Something was definitely wrong.

Once back at her river camp, Dwaila had a good poke around inside my ear with cotton buds, but couldn't locate the problem. The ache was getting much worse, and a difficult decision had to be made. Newt had taken the boat over to the fishing village and had to wait around for some tourists who were to visit the lake and Dwaila's camp. He was not expected to be back until early evening. Without transport therefore, we were stranded and at his mercy. The only alternative was to walk out, a hike of about seventeen kilometres at the hottest time of the day.

Dwaila had some 2% hydrogen peroxide solution which might clean the ear for a while, although instinctively I knew that I was in urgent need of professional help and so, after I swallowed three powerful pain-killing tablets, we walked.

Bun came along as guide, Thao for company, and with full water-bottles we set off. After a while, as the drugs took effect, the pain subsided and I marched along in a vacant haze, my blurred vision obscuring all but the nearest of objects. My stout walking-stick kept me upright and I fell into pace with the others, oblivious to my surroundings and intent on staying awake, although at times all I wanted to do was simply lie down and sleep. We stopped every so often to rest and at least once I dozed off for a few minutes, coming round to the gentle sound of Sophy's voice encouraging me to stand up and walk.

We stopped for lunch and I remember her taking off her boots at one stage and seeing her ankles covered in blood. It was a leech attack. She took a mixture of lime juice and tobacco and gently squeezed small drops on to those that still clung on, making them release their powerful suction and fall to the ground in a writhing, bloody mess. Leeches inject a mild anti-coagulant into the skin when they take hold, and the wound bleeds continuously for quite some time after they have departed. Sophy was a truly remarkable girl, I thought, quietly cleaning her wounds with antiseptic solution, accepting the discomfort as simply one of the not-so-pleasant aspects of jungle life. Her injuries were clearly visible but there was no obvious sign of my discomfort, and yet *she* was there for me, as supportive as ever.

Eventually, nearly six hours after we had set off, we arrived on the main Takua Pa to Surat Thani road, and Thao began frantically trying to wave down a passing car that would give us a lift into town. A minibus pulled up after a while and demanded *bhat* 500, an extortionate amount, but we were in no mood to argue, and with blessed relief we climbed aboard.

I had never been to Surat Thani before and was glad that the boys were with us to help navigate the unfamiliar streets. It was a bank holiday in Thailand, one of the many festivals that litter the fun-loving Thai calendar. That afternoon, every doctor's surgery that we visited was closed, all except one, which by some miraculous coincidence happened to be that of an ear, nose and throat specialist.

Dr Manette tut-tutted as he peered inside my ear with his otoscope. 'Good job you came today,' he said finally. 'Tomorrow it would be much worse, maybe too difficult to treat.'

From the circular examination mirror atop his balding oval head to the multi-coloured biro stains on his hospital white coat, Dr Pakorn Manette gave the impression of being the epitome of his chosen profession. His double chin and halitosis, however, betrayed a penchant for good food and a disinclination towards dental hygiene and strenuous physical exercise that was impossible to ignore.

He explained that I had contracted a form of otitis media, an infection of the middle ear. He told me about the dark warm cavities in the hypotympanic recess and the narrow tracts of the eustachian tube and how they were highly fertile breeding grounds for all sorts of nefarious bacteria which multiplied at a phenomenal rate in the damp and fetid atmosphere of the jungle. He prescribed antibiotics and steroid drops for the ear and gave me two injections: one, a shock dose of penicillin, the other to reduce the swelling.

During the lengthy examination, he had been making small talk, the way doctors do all over the world, and had expressed a keen interest in what we were trying to achieve in the jungle. He seemed genuinely fascinated, and after my treatment was over insisted on showing us something at the back of his surgery. He said that he needed some advice.

As we proceeded out into the rear courtyard, the stench suddenly hit us like a battering ram. I noticed the broken glass and razor wire atop the eight-foot wall before I recognised the growling noises emanating from a row of cages. There were six in all and each one housed a snarling, hissing, spitting, pitiful and terribly frightened clouded leopard. One was missing a front paw, another had a large section of its tail missing, and they had all been quite obviously trapped in the wild.

Manette explained in a calm, matter-of-fact sort of way that he had been trying to breed them, and wanted to know the reason why the females devoured their young within minutes of them being born.

Irrespective of the fact that this man had just treated me, I could not restrain myself from explaining in uncompromising detail not only my opinion of people who took such graceful creatures from their natural habitat but also my theory as to why the females had no wish for their own offspring to endure similar torture imprisoned in a box no bigger than a broom cupboard.

Although I felt a lot better, I should have known a lot better, and might just as well have held my breath. Manette simply looked at me dumbfounded, unable to fathom why I didn't share his perverse curiosity in the captive breeding of wild jungle predators. He simply couldn't comprehend why any creature, wild or otherwise, would not prefer a life of comfort and security in a cage to the hazards and hardships of an existence in the wild.

Despite his medical training, he was a hostage to the theory of humanising all living creatures and utterly oblivious to the stark reality that when man tries to rise above nature, he invariably falls beneath it.

Thailand is a country littered with temples, Buddha images, and other material reminders of its Buddhist heritage and faith, the precepts of which include a reverence for all life. Most visitors erroneously believe this includes respect for wildlife, but nothing could be further from the truth. For many Thai, an interest in wildlife is synonymous with cages. Their inflated sense of self-importance dictates somehow that giving a wild creature a caged home is an act of great value upon which the Lord Buddha will smile favourably. The Thai government for years has myopically supported this view, allowing each citizen the right to own two wild animals of almost any variety. The legacy of that political lunacy can be seen in the country's rapidly diminishing flora and fauna, and the luxurious lifestyles of the nation's hundreds of exploitative and unprincipled wildlife traders.

Dr Manette's leopards had been snatched from the wild, and two of them severely injured in the process. People like him – the wealthy, urbanised and supposedly well-educated Thai who should know better – were supporting a trade that was pushing some species to the brink of extinction.

His cats could never be tamed, and would never successfully readjust to a natural life even if they were fortunate enough ever to be released back into the wild. That much I had learned from my studies of similar experiments in the past. Once a big cat had lost its instinctive fear of mankind, it never regained it. A lion or tiger might well become a man-eater; a leopard would, likely as not, become a nuisance, and raid farms and domestic livestock whenever hunger and the opportunity arose.

Dr Manette's clouded leopards didn't just smell of urine and excrement, they smelled of fear, the sort that comes with the realisation that captivity is for ever. The mothers instinctively understood this and responded with maternal compassion for their offspring, killing them promptly at birth.

I left the place with a profound empathy for the absolute sacrifice of those wretched leopards. It was as if I now understood the abject misery in their hollow eyes, but I was equally plagued by the apprehension that Dr Manette and his kind never would.

CHAPTER ELEVEN

Phuket, June 1990

We needed a boat, and we needed one fast. My ear problem had been an unpleasant reminder of the frailty of the human body and just how much we sometimes depend, like it or not, on the comforts of the modern world, the cities, and the skills of the people that dwell within them.

Our remote location left us cut off from the rest of the world and that was wonderful. Nevertheless, in the event of an emergency, we would need rapid transport to enable us to reach civilisation, and we couldn't expect Dwaila to always be on hand to help us out. I had been fortunate in being able to walk out of the jungle before. Next time we might not be quite so lucky.

The island of Ko Samui seemed a convenient enough place to start looking, lying only a few miles off the coast of Surat Thani in the Gulf of Siam. The island turned out to be a playground for holidaymakers from all corners of the world, and a pleasant enough distraction from the labours of jungle-camp construction. My ear infection soon cleared up, and it was fun playing tourist with Sophy for a few days, indulging in good food and wine, and romping around on the beach. Curiously enough, there were few boats for sale, and those that were invariably proved to be too expensive or totally unacceptable, so we returned to that other island in the sun, Phuket.

Even Phuket turned out to be vaguely tolerable, mostly perhaps because we had our bolthole in the rainforest already secured, and could leave at any time. We stayed in the centre of town at the Pearl Hotel, and decided to make this our communications base. The staff were most friendly, and obligingly agreed to hold mail and faxes for us, and to give us a room at a generous discount whenever we needed in the future.

Eventually we found a suitable boat in the form of a twenty-one-foot fibreglass Boston whaler, complete with its own trailer and a somewhat temperamental 115 horse-power Yamaha outboard engine. We agreed a suitable price with its expatriate owner, a peculiar chap called Howie.

Howie was one of those extraordinary individuals that seemed to have been everywhere and done most things in life, however bizarre. He had been a postman in England, a ranch-hand in the Australian outback, a deck-hand on yachts all over the world, and a roustabout on an oil-rig in the Gulf of Thailand.

He also had a pet dog called Boris that he found one night adhered to an odd instrument of Thai rodent control, called a 'rat-buster', which is, in fact, a tray of highly cohesive glue. Some people use cats, others use traps, but only the Thai could dream up something as diabolical and dastardly as glue in order to trap rats. The sticky mass is of course somewhat indiscriminate, as Boris found out to his peril one evening, whilst doing his habitual round of the neighbourhood.

Howie heard his pitiful whimpering from the inside of a discarded section of sewage pipe and prised the poor creature out of the glutinous mess. And so grateful was the young pup that he adopted Howie to show his appreciation. The two of them had become more or less inseparable ever since.

Both Sophy and I thought at the time that such an endearing and charismatic individual couldn't be all that bad, and therefore that his boat had probably been well looked after; an unwise assumption, and one that we were later to regret.

I went to see my old friend, Theo the blacksmith, who volunteered to weld a tow-bar on to the back of his own pick-up truck and drive the boat up to the lake for us. And, in the third week of May, we all set off back to Khao Sok.

We didn't hear the axle grating against the wheel. If we had, we would have probably stopped before the wheel sheered off. Which it eventually did, pitching the boat and the trailer dangerously over to one side, fortunately without serious injury. For several anxious seconds it scraped along the road with Theo fighting the steering wheel to prevent the entire equipage jack-knifing into the path of the oncoming traffic. As we ground to a halt he hit the dashboard with his huge fist more out of relief than annoyance, and together we gingerly got out to inspect the damage.

120

The bearings on the wheel hub had obviously not been oiled or greased for months and the constant friction had caused such intense heat that the metal had more or less melted. An incredibly unlucky man would have had a piano-tuner as companion in such a disaster; luckily I had a blacksmith. And that really was the only consolation that I could muster as Theo loaded up the errant wheel-housing into the back of his pick-up, and set off in search of a repair workshop, leaving Sophy and me behind to guard the boat.

Three hours later he returned, beaming from ear to ear, signalling that his mission had been fruitful although he was several dollars lighter. Many hours delayed, we eventually resumed our journey just as it was getting dark.

The gates of the EGAT compound were locked by the time we arrived and we were forced to spend a most uncomfortable night sleeping fitfully in the back of the boat. At seven o'clock the guard nonchalantly waved us through, and an hour later the boat was safely deposited into the water and a genuinely relieved blacksmith was on his way back to Phuket.

For Sophy and me it was to be the beginning of a new voyage of discovery as the boat made every nook and cranny of the lake accessible to us. We found hidden caves with huge stalactites that were home to thousands of fruit bats during the day, and at sunset we'd watch them emerge, swarming off into the night sky to raid some unsuspecting plantation. In isolated coves we found tiny floating raft-houses nestled up against the rocks where nomadic fishermen kept their prize specimens in submerged holding pens made of bamboo. We learned to bargain for *blaboo*, a delicious freshwater fish, and taught the locals how to cook it, chip-shop-style in batter, possibly undoing or perhaps beginning many generations of cultural tradition in the process.

Bun took us on expeditions, pointing out narrow tributaries that led us deep inland. On one of these trips, in water only a few inches deep, we spotted the very rare *serow*, a type of mountain goat that was remorselessly poached for the perceived healing power of its short antlers. Invariably we would see white-handed gibbon and langur monkeys and they would always thrill us with their incredible agility and tree-top acrobatics. One evening as we watched a family troop romping around high up in the branches, a youngster decided to show off and swung down through the foliage to a point less than thirty feet above our heads. He stood on a chosen branch and did backflips until he did one too many, lost his grip and came crashing

121

to the ground. He was on his feet again in seconds, but buried his face miserably in his hands and slouched off, shoulders bent in shame, to hide behind a tree until his embarrassment wore off. He eventually emerged with renewed composure, and slowly, and much more carefully, clambered up again to rejoin the others.

Almost every day we would visit the tree-hide, and for three nights in a row Sophy and I slept high up in the trees hoping for the opportunity to spot 'the big boy' or some other wildlife. Barney the goat had obliged, and we now had an excellent rendition of his voice which I played into the night air at periodic intervals, but to no avail.

On the last night we came to the unhappy conclusion that the disturbance we had made in the surrounding locality when building the hide, and the obvious scent of our presence, would keep the animals at bay for some considerable time. It might possibly take weeks to finally evaporate and disappear altogether.

We therefore decided to leave the area totally alone for at least a month, and Dwaila agreed that she would find a new trail for her tourist visitors. In the meantime, we would return to Phuket before travelling on down to Singapore to collect new visas. It was a difficult decision. We had come so far and achieved so much, and yet we were being hampered by the spirit of our own enterprise. Time was the great healer we decided, and after the rains there would be little sign on the ground of any human activity whatsoever, and so the following day we said a sad farewell to Dwaila and the boys and set off back to Phuket and out to the airport.

Sophy had never been to Singapore. We stayed at the Metropole and made frequent trips out to the zoo to observe at close hand, not only the tigers, but their entire collection of rare animals and birds of the Asian region. I developed into something of a camera-shop junkie, always finding some obscure reason to slope off in search of a new filter, lens cloth or some other plausible excuse to talk cameras with Danny Chew. In the evenings we would read quietly or go out to a movie, or, on one indelible occasion, we drank champagne in the skytop restaurant of the Westin Stamford Hotel.

For some weeks a thought had been maturing inside my head. In the beginning, when it first struck me, I had banished it from my mind without hesitation as being both frivolous and nonsensical. But it kept popping back up at odd times and, try as I might, it simply wouldn't go away. The notion would visit me in my dreams, whilst I was out walking, swimming around in the lake, brushing my teeth, or when I was desperately trying to concentrate hard on just about anything. At these times I would be seized by this strange concept and disappear into a private flight of fancy from which I would invariably emerge one tiny step closer to an understanding and acceptance of my predicament. Now, in Singapore, the pieces were beginning to take shape, everything seemed to fit perfectly together, and it was time.

We sat at a window table of the Compass Rose lounge looking down on the spectacular lights of the city. The night was clear, without a cloud in the sky, and it was possible to see the Straits and the hundreds of boats, all brilliantly lit up, moored far out to sea. We drank a superb New Zealand sauvignon with the delicious seafood and a bottle of excellent Chateau Margaux with the steaks, and by the time we were ready to look at the pudding list, I was sufficiently pickled to broach the subject that had been tormenting me for weeks.

'Sophy, will you marry me?' I asked, falling to my knees. 'Take the weekend to think about it if you wish, but I would prefer an answer this evening.'

I took her hand and struggled back to my seat on shaky limbs. Her eyes welled up with tears. I didn't think I could surprise her any more, and for some reason I thought she might have seen this coming, but she just looked at me, ever so slightly shaking her head from side to side.

She's going to turn me down, I thought. Common sense is going to tell her that she couldn't possibly spend the rest of her life with someone as harebrained and unpredictable as myself. She's going to say no, I thought over and over again. And then she dabbed her eyes gently with her napkin, and, looking me squarely in the eyes, said, 'Yes, I'll marry you!' We kissed, and then I ordered the most outrageous bottle of champagne they had on ice!

To celebrate, we flew to Kota Kinabalu, in Sabah, the Malaysian north-east of the island of Borneo. We visited the orang-utan rehabilitation project in Sepilok, went white-water rafting, and saw the extraordinary proboscis monkey on the banks of the crocodile-infested waters of the Danum river. But that, as Kipling once remarked, is another story.

On June 22nd we returned to Tree-Tops. Dwaila and Lai were thrilled with our news, and invited some friends around for a celebration lunch. As their world was normally so full of transient visitors, we were pleased to discover that they now accepted us as

123

semi-permanent fixtures and wanted us to get to know the local crowd. It was at that luncheon that we met a man who was to make a deep impression on us both, and someone who turned out to be a real friend.

Aroon Srisowan was no more than fifty years old and yet he had the wise and mellow composure of a man very much older. He was tall for a Thai, with broad shoulders and a strong, well-seasoned face which radiated both warmth and compassion when he spoke. He had lived in Khao Sok most of his life, and had always loved the forest; he had spent his childhood and much of his youth learning about its ways and the lore of the jungle.

It was therefore quite natural that when it came to choosing a career, he opted for a life with the forestry commission, and went away to study at the university in Bangkok. It was whilst he was there that he met the legendary Dr Sueb Nakhasathien, a man who had devoted all his life to the preservation of wildlife throughout his country and most particularly at the Huay Kha Kaeng National Park close to the Burmese border in western Thailand. During the 1980s the park had come under intense poaching pressure and Dr Sueb's continued protestations to the Royal Forestry Department's wildlife conservation division fell on deaf ears. Sueb had worked hard to protect the park from encroachment and degradation, his efforts had received international acclaim throughout the scientific community, and yet he could not seem to influence his own government to crack down on the endemic corruption and avarice that was systematically undoing his life's work. One tragic evening, in a final act of self sacrifice to provoke the administration into action, he took his own life.

Aroon spoke in a lilting broken English, and I could see that he was deeply saddened by the degradation of his native land. It was plain to see that Sueb's work had a profound and inspiring effect on this man. He was sickened that the corrupt officials who permitted such wanton pillage were still in office and continued to profit from the rape of his beloved country's wildlife heritage.

One such man was currently in charge of Khao Sok National Park, and there was no hiding Aroon's bitter contempt for this evil and unprincipled individual. As I listened, and tiny pieces of the jigsaw fell into place, I began to realise that unless something was done very quickly, this beautiful park would soon be stripped of its most precious resources and become the next victim of an all-pervasive sickness that was engulfing the whole country.

124

Toward the end of the afternoon another man turned up, driving a battered minibus. He was in his mid forties, and had a kind and studious face that befitted his work at the local university as a language professor. Dwaila referred to him as Adjan, an honorific meaning 'learned teacher'. And although he didn't stay for long, he left me with a wonderful feeling of hope because he was campaigning hard with his students for a new awareness about the perilous decline of the nation's wildlife and the dangers of habitat destruction. Like Dr Sueb, his was a tiny voice in the wilderness, but a voice nonetheless.

We travelled back to the lake the next day, my head still buzzing with the candid discussions of that fateful luncheon. I had yet to meet the park superintendent since, whenever I had called by his office, he had been away in Bangkok. It was obvious that he despised his job and spent as little time in the park as possible, preferring the bright lights of the big city and the distractions of its nightlife to the business of preserving the integrity of the park's natural wilderness.

Most of his employees, it appeared, turned up for work in the mornings, clocked in and then went promptly home again or busied themselves with casual construction work or went poaching. Although it was difficult to prove, it was widely rumoured that he submitted full time-sheets for each one to park headquarters in Bangkok, paid the men half salaries and pocketed the rest.

It was further rumoured that he was in the process of re-defining the park's boundaries so that large areas could be sold off under the table to neighbouring landowners, and that a so-called 'security road' would be constructed along the new border. If that ever happened, then not only would the natural corridors for the park's wildlife be broken up but, more perniciously, the area would become completely accessible from all sides, enabling even more devastation and pillage and, of course, more back-handers for the men at the top.

The odd part about all this seemed to me that we were being allowed free access to the park and might ultimately discover its secrets. Either the superintendent was a complete fool, or he was so arrogantly confident of his own power and position that he cared little about who uncovered his wicked schemes. His network obviously encompassed the neighbouring villages and his staff presumably would report to him regularly about our activities. I made a mental note to be very careful about whom I spoke to in future.

We arrived at the raft-houses late in the evening. There was a full house. Dwaila's tourist business was apparently thriving, and her trips into the jungle were proving very popular. She was developing a solid reputation almost entirely by word of mouth.

Sophy and I were anxious to see how the pre-monsoon rains had affected the area around the tree-hide, and the following morning we got up very early to investigate. By the time we got to the final rise before the camp, we felt that something was wrong. The track was still well beaten and we had no need to use our machetes to cut through the undergrowth and creepers; which would otherwise have grown at phenomenal speed across the path after the first rains of the previous weeks. At the base of the hide there were more obvious signs of human activity, and I rushed to where I had hidden the bamboo ladder, dreading that the hide itself had been disturbed. Once up on the platform everything seemed to be in order, and yet there were signs that someone had been there. Furious at the realisation that Dwaila's tourists were still using this trail, I ran back to the raft-houses to confront her.

'Well, what did you expect, Mike?' she said dismissively. 'I have a business to run here. I can't make huge detours around your hide just to keep you happy.'

'It's not just a question of keeping me happy,' I replied angrily. 'We are trying to achieve something here, something that will ultimately benefit the park and its wildlife. You know how hard we have worked, and how vital it was to leave the area completely undisturbed. You agreed to that, for Christ's sake.'

'Yeah, well, there's no other way round to the communists' cave. Besides, I've been running these trips long before you showed up with your fancy ideas.'

'Now that's not fair, and you damn well know it,' I said bitterly. 'If I had known this would happen, I would have located the hide somewhere completely different. There's no way that anything can be accomplished there with herds of tourists traipsing by every day.'

'Well, you're just going to have to put up with it,' she said, trying to end the conversation.

'We'll see about that,' I said furiously. 'Don't you forget that it's our research permit that helps you stay here inside the park boundaries. You are supposed to be our back-up and support camp. Now I don't care if you do run tour groups, that's your business, but it surely can't be that difficult to find other spots to take them, miles away from where we are trying to work.'

126

She wouldn't see our point of view or, if she did, wouldn't accept it. We were devastated, and it was pointless staying there any longer to continue arguing. I tried once more to see if we could reach a compromise solution, but she was obstinate. Her mind was made up, and as far as she was concerned, we would have to adapt to her tour groups or leave. And faced with that sort of ultimatum, we threw our belongings in to the boat and left.

We stayed with Aroon for a couple of days, hoping that Dwaila would cool off and see reason, but we were to be disappointed. He suggested that we move to the national park raft-houses on the lake, and agreed to arrange permission with the park superintendent. I hated the idea; the thought of asking him for anything disgusted me. On the other hand, the opportunity to monitor the activities of his so-called rangers on a day-to-day basis had some merit, and after a long soul-searching debate with Sophy, we agreed to give it a try.

The next day we collected all our remaining possessions from Tree-Tops and travelled with Aroon back across the lake to what was to be our new home. The complex was much larger than I had imagined, about 150 metres long from end to end. The raft-houses were extremely well made, and constructed almost entirely out of timber with solid floorboards, windows and with insect-screens, pitched roofs of corrugated steel that didn't leak, and a proper bathroom!

When we arrived I noticed a procession of young men appear and bow respectfully, in the Thai fashion with hands pressed together as if in prayer, to our new friend Aroon. Bringing up the rear was a short podgy individual with narrow-set piggy eyes and a tussock of black curly hair that sat atop his blubbery face like an ill-fitting wig. His name was Weewat. He bowed, although not quite so deeply, and I clearly detected some considerable friction between the two men. Behind him was the pop-eyed youth with the moronic stare; he was Weewat's brother-in-law.

We were introduced to everybody, and as far as I could understand Aroon asked that we be made to feel welcome and explained briefly what we were doing on the lake. Weewat smiled in mawkish acquiescence, and sauntered off back, as we discovered later, to his hammock.

'Him, superintendent deputy,' said Aroon.

'I beg your pardon?' I exclaimed, aghast. '*That* is the park superintendent's second in command, and *those* were rangers?'

'Yes, better not speak about too much what you do,' he added,

127

his voice low, 'him no can speak English but other man can. Be careful. Boy called Boon you can trust, my nephew.'

'OK,' I said, 'thanks. Will you come and visit us?'

'Yes, maybe, when I get time.'

And with that he was off to talk with the rangers. A short time afterwards I heard the sound of a long-tail engine starting up and the boat appeared from the far end of the complex and tied up beside our whaler. Aroon smiled proudly at a young man with a mop of black hair and an engaging lop-sided grin, and introduced him as Boon. With a final wave, the two of them sped off across the lake into the evening. We stood there on the jetty and watched them depart, feeling alone and somewhat abandoned, and wondering desperately if we had made the right decision.

That night I cooked dinner, a ragout of chicken with boiled rice and green salad. We had chosen a hut at the back of the complex with three rooms, one of which I had converted into a kitchen. There was a walk-around platform two feet wide, and a large balcony at the front.

The cooking aroma emanating from our quarters must have been irresistible to our neighbours because before too long our porch had been taken over by a gaggle of women and their assorted children and menfolk who had come to see what the smell was all about. They sat on our chairs and on the floor, nattering to each other and bursting into fits of laughter every so often. Strangely enough, they refused our offers of food or refreshment. It seemed they were perfectly content to just sit and observe the *farangs* at work in the kitchen, and were fascinated by the way we cooked and the sound of our voices. After a while they got bored, packed up their knitting and sauntered off into the night. This was to be a regular evening event for them whenever we cooked, and must presumably have been an amusing distraction, although because of the language barrier we were never quite sure.

In the morning we got up early and went over to try and make our peace with Dwaila. She was not there and her camp was deserted except for cousin-of-Bun who had been left to guard it. He explained very carefully that Dwaila had been summoned to the park headquarters by none other than the superintendent himself, and was not expected back for two days.

In actual fact, we didn't see her again for two weeks, and by the time we did she seemed to have forgotten all about the row and was determined to make amends. As it turned out, it was probably for

128

the best that we had moved away from her raft-houses, for both she and I, and Sophy for that matter, were strong-willed, independent people, and living on top of each other as we did was a recipe for disaster.

From that time on, we seemed to understand and respect one another's individuality a great deal more, and she agreed to cut a new trail for her tourists far away from our tree-hide.

Although we spent many more nights hidden away in the trees waiting for the tiger, he never came. We often saw his tracks though. It was the same large male, 'the big boy' that had disturbed me from my sleep all those months before, but now he was proving to be very elusive indeed.

Trying to coax him into our filming area became a battle of wits, but it was almost as if he knew when we were around and deliberately stayed away. We would work the tree-hide in shifts, arriving early on in the day with plenty of provisions, then we would haul up the ladder and stay there for two days and two nights before returning to our new base for three days and the cycle would begin again.

We saw wild pig, barking deer, the strange binturong or bear-cat, and porcupine. Gibbons and the family of langur monkeys were regular visitors to the waterhole, but the great gentlemen of the forest, as Colonel Jim Corbett once called the tiger, kept well hidden.

One morning, as we were creeping down slowly to the hide, trying to disturb things as little as possible, we saw his tracks within twenty yards of the base of the ladder and well within filming range. It was sod's law, I suppose. Had we been there the night before, we would have seen him walk by, but it was not to be. 'The big boy' was just too crafty.

By the third week of July, the rains had set in and we reluctantly decided to pull out altogether until after the monsoon. We collected all the valuables from the tree-hide, dug up old Hugo and trundled everything back to our base. Thao presented us with some snake eggs that he had found as a parting gift, insisting that they weren't dangerous, adding that they would make good pets and remind us of the park. It would have been churlish to refuse and we kept them with us at the park raft-houses for a few days in a Tupperware container until they began to shrivel up. (We thought they had died, of course, but in fact snake eggs do that a few days before they hatch!)

The rain just wouldn't let up long enough for us to make the one-hour crossing to the EGAT pontoon. We had planned to take the boat with us back to Phuket, as it needed completely repainting and an engine overhaul, and would be much safer with friends there. Our jeep now had a tow-bar, but the journey back would take a whole day, and each morning as we looked out on to the lake, boiling with the continuous pounding of the rain, we quietly resolved to wait.

One afternoon, a familiar and frightening sensation began deep inside my ear. We found the drops that Dr Manette had prescribed before and the last of the pain-killers, and the discomfort lessened by the following evening. But it was a false dawn, because that night the pain returned with a vengeance and we decided that, come what may, we had to get out the following morning.

We awoke early, the skies had cleared although there were ominous looking clouds on the horizon, and so we made a dash for it. Crossing the lake in record time, I hooked the trailer up to the jeep, reversed down into the water and secured the boat without difficulty. By ten o'clock we were on the main road heading west toward Phuket. So far so good.

An hour later, the pain in my ear was back again, thundering inside my head. I knew that I needed help, but we were still three hours at least away from Phuket Town. Although I noticed the familiar Tupperware box on the back seat of the jeep as I grabbed the very last pain-killer, I thought nothing of it. We needed to keep going.

The first puncture on the trailer didn't really surprise me at all. It was almost as if I had expected it to happen, and was glad that it had, sooner rather than later. The second puncture, coming as it did on a steep hill overlooking a sheer drop on to the jagged cliffs below, however, was a complete and utter shock. This unexpected nightmare was made all the worse by the reality that we had not only used up our spare tyre but that we had, by necessity, ground to a halt on a particularly dangerous piece of road.

There was nothing to be done other than to unhitch the boat and go in search of a replacement tyre. As I was doing this, Sophy tried to warn the oncoming traffic of the hazard, waving in desperation for them to slow down. But the Thai weren't to be put off that easily, and one near-miss became a series of reckless death-defying manoeuvres as lorries, buses and cars swerved around our broken-down obstacle without losing speed. She insisted on staying with the boat as I raced off to get help from the highway patrol station that I knew to be a few kilometres further up the road.

I found the traffic cops busily watching afternoon television, the most senior officer demonstrating his superiority by sprawling his well-polished boots across his desk.

'Please come quickly,' I spluttered, out of breath, addressing the man in boots. 'We have broken down. The situation is very dangerous.'

There was no reaction. I should have known that, his being in charge didn't necessarily mean he spoke English. And so I made the same announcement much more slowly, to the entire room, addressing no-one in particular, searching inside each face for some sign of recognition. I was competing with some garbage karate comedy on the television into the bargain.

For some totally inexplicable reason the peace-loving Thai have a great liking for imported junk television from Japan. These programmes typically have an enormous cast of unbelievable characters, many of whom are dressed in the traditional Japanese costume of the Samurai warrior. These men, with heavily painted faces and long black hair severely tied into a bun at the back, prance around the screen in the most incongruous of settings, until for some unknown reason they all begin to knock the living daylights out of each other. With extraordinary physical agility the actors engage in triple somersaults, backflips, cartwheels and handsprings to the accompaniment of the sound of broken bones and smashed furniture, until finally the fight sequence ends, everybody dusts themselves off without a hair out of place and they have a jolly good laugh. I switched the TV off angrily.

'Please,' I repeated, 'my wife and I need your help. There could be an accident.'

'Accident?' chirped up the man in boots. 'Why you not say so before. Where is the accident?'

'Well, actually, there is no accident,' I began, 'but the situation is very dangerous. There could be an accident at any minute.'

'No accident?' said the boots, clearly surprised, and turned the TV back on. 'OK, you come back after there has been accident, then we come!' he bellowed with obvious finality.

I couldn't believe it. This man was an officer, clearly intelligent and in charge, and I was expected to go back and wait for the inevitable to occur and *then* seek their help? I turned the TV off again, risking his wrath but demanding his attention.

'Look,' I said, trying a different tack. 'My wife is back there in the middle of the road trying to *prevent*, to stop, an accident from happening. She is all alone. Someone could be killed. You must help us please!'

'You lady wife alone?' he asked.

'Yes.'

And with that he barked off some orders in rapid Thai to his underlings, turning to me finally and saying, 'OK, you show them, we help you.'

Four men then stood smartly to attention, marched off briskly outside and jumped into a waiting patrol car. With siren blaring, we sped off down the mountain to the rescue.

When we arrived Sophy was not alone. An American missionary and his wife had stopped and the three of them were holding the fort, frantically waving to other road-users to slow down. The police quickly took charge and within minutes the situation was under control, and I had learned a valuable lesson in the subtle art of police persuasion.

The pain was beginning to return as I drove off back in the direction of Khao Sok to buy a spare tyre. By the time I got back the light was fading fast, and the police insisted on changing the wheel and then gave us an escort back up the mountain.

The drive was a nightmare, as we had no lights on the trailer, and I had to rig up a beacon using the boat's battery. At times I felt as though my eardrum was about to explode. We eventually arrived at the Pearl Hotel in darkness, so neither of us noticed the infant reptiles crawling around in the back of the jeep. My head was on fire, and I prayed that the casualty unit at the Mission hospital would be open all night.

We dumped our bags at reception and took a taxi. I'd done enough driving to last me a lifetime.

Dr Thrasher, a kindly American with a slight stoop, took one look inside my ear, tut-tutted and admitted me on the spot. He shook his head gravely as he described the seriousness of the infection, adding, with a slight sigh, that I would need round-the-clock observation with intravenous antibiotics or I could be dead within the month.

CHAPTER TWELVE

Phuket, July 1990

The fetid atmosphere of the jungle is full of strange microbes, most of which are completely harmless to mankind. Nevertheless, all it takes is one microscopic spore of noxious bacteria to alight upon the right fertile medium, and a chain reaction will commence that can be both frighteningly prolific and potentially lethal.

Somewhere in the dark chambers between the middle ear and my eustachian tubes, an extremely hostile bacteria had taken up residence and was breeding at a phenomenal rate. Natural antibodies within my immune system had been thrown into a frenzy of activity, but their potential for effect had already been severely weakened by the drugs prescribed earlier by the hapless Dr Manette. This time more drastic measures were needed in order to evacuate the poison that was surging through my veins, wreaking havoc in its path, leaving me drenched in perspiration and helpless with a dangerously high fever.

And now, as I began to drift in and out of a make-believe world haunted by strange hallucinations and distant echoing sounds, Dr Thrasher's antibiotic penicillin dripped silently into my blood system through a narrow catheter taped to the inside of my arm. With one stroke of his pen he had served an eviction notice, and the powerful drug was thundering through my arteries searching out the epicentre of the infection before it spread further and attacked my brain.

For two whole days I remained virtually immobile and largely oblivious to my surroundings. Blurred visions came and went, soft voices whispered close to my head as my blood pressure was taken or a thermometer placed in my armpit. I ate nothing, as my head felt as though it weighed over a ton, and was impossible to raise from

133

the pillow. What nutrients my body needed were being fed in through the hole in my arm. And so I lay there, feeble and debilitated, incapable of any resistance, my future endowed to the one man whom I believed had the power and skill to cure me, the indomitable Dr Thrasher.

He had left the quiet backwaters of his native Minneapolis during the late 1960s already a highly qualified and experienced medical practitioner, having made sure his two children had graduated through his own alma mater with honours. President John F. Kennedy had recently consigned many thousands of America's finest to a so-called policing operation in Vietnam, and field doctors were needed on hand in case the conflict began to escalate.

Quite how quickly and dramatically the situation deteriorated surprised even the seasoned Dr Thrasher, but he was a veteran of two wars and was about to become one of the longest-serving physicians and one of the last to leave in the airlift from Saigon six years later. The army offered him a healthy pension but his old practice in St Paul had long been absorbed into a state-run facility that had no place for the ageing field surgeon. Thrasher was not the sort to retire and grow old gracefully. He had acquired a taste for the tropics and its people and chose to visit Thailand, where he had read that a head of white hair still afforded respect rather than derision.

Almost twenty years later he was still working twelve-hour days and loving every one of them. He took great pride and delight in his vocation and shared freely of his considerable knowledge with a long succession of eager young students keen to learn the old doctor's secrets. He was a man truly blessed with the gift of healing, and as the days wore on, his magic began to work deep inside my ear and eventually the pain subsided, the fever passed, and I slowly began to recover.

Sophy visited me several times a day, and on one occasion made me laugh so much that I thought my eardrum would burst. It appeared that on the way back from Khao Sok the snake eggs had started to hatch and that several of them were frantically crawling around inside the Tupperware box by the time she emptied the jeep on that first fateful night back at the Pearl Hotel.

The next day she had taken the box to show Phil Watkins, the island's resident snake-charmer, who had pronounced them harmless wolf snakes and agreed to contact a chum of his who would know exactly how to feed them and give them a good home. In the meantime Sophy had taken them back to the Pearl and transferred them to a much larger container with plenty of fresh earth and vegetation and placed it outside on the balcony of the bedroom. When she had gone to check on her infant charges the following morning, the container was empty.

Her room was on the third floor overlooking the swimming-pool which had been bestowed with a series of waterfalls carefully set in a landscaped tropical garden environment to give bathers the feeling that they were swimming in some isolated pool in the depths of the jungle. The adventurous young snakes had obviously wriggled out to the edge of the balcony, taken one short peek, thought 'This looks inviting', and jumped for freedom. Quite what the hotel guests were going to think when tiny green eyes peered out at them from behind the lush foliage we dared not imagine!

Tears ran down Sophy's face as she told me of the hilarious encounter with the pool attendant when she had ventured downstairs to try and find them. The garden was vast and the snakes were tiny, but nevertheless she padded around in a vain attempt at locating them until a young man came out to enquire what she was doing.

'Er . . . looking for an ear-ring,' she said hesitantly.

'I'll help you,' he replied courteously.

'No, it's really quite all right, I can manage.'

'It's no trouble. I'm sure it's expensive,' he had said.

She then had to act out this charade for ten minutes, peering around for some imaginary object before excusing herself, dashing upstairs, grabbing a golden ear-ring from her modest jewellery collection, and returning to the garden. Whereupon, with a conjurer's sleight of foot, she let the thing slip down the inside leg of her trousers, allowing the young man the honour of finding it. During the whole episode not a sign had been seen of the escapees, and from that point on they were left in peace by the poolside.

Dr Thrasher was greatly amused by the thought of harmless slithering reptiles chasing hysterical holidaymakers around the Pearl Hotel, and I'm sure the tale became greatly embellished as it did its rounds of the wards.

By the beginning of the second week I was allowed out of bed, my appetite had returned and I was feeling altogether much improved. The good doctor obligingly made arrangements for me to visit a specialist in Singapore before the long flight home to England and more prolonged treatment in London. He explained that there was only so much he could do with the limited resources at his disposal, and that in order to make a full recovery, I would need considerable rest and several weeks away from the constant humidity of the tropics.

It was late July, the rains were incessant, and there was little enough reason to remain even if I was fit and well. So a couple of days before the end of the month, Dr Thrasher discharged me out of his care, and Sophy and I began the long trek back home.

England was basking in record summer temperatures by the time we arrived, and we spent several days rushing around locally visiting family and friends, sharing all our news, and making frequent trips to Guy's Hospital where the specialist, Mr Gleeson, had taken a keen and personal interest in my case.

A sad telephone call to my mother in the wilds of the East Anglian countryside revealed that all was far from well at home. In one of the more grotesque ironies of life, I was gradually recovering from a near fatal tropical disease whilst my father, at the age of seventy-two, who had not left the shores of England for more than a decade, was slowly dying of another – an intransigent sickness that he contracted during World War Two as a prisoner of the Japanese in the jungle camps of Kanchanburi province in Thailand. For over forty-five years the virus, transmitted by the bite of a Thai mosquito, had lain dormant. However, as a cancer invaded his abdominal organs, the yellow fever awoke, releasing hideous bile pigments into his blood which jaundiced every inch of his ailing body. Within two weeks of my return he was dead.

My father and I had agreed to differ on many aspects of life, our two worlds were completely disparate and at times unreconcilable, and yet at the end I held his hand as the fragments of life left his frail body knowing that he had been a good man and profoundly saddened by his sudden death.

For the next few weeks my life was taken up by the unpleasant realities of family bereavement, although I must confess to never feeling that I had not done enough to comfort my griefstricken mother. She had gallantly nursed my father through one long illness after another, with the shadow of death never too far away. And yet for the last six or seven years, the cancer had abated and in the early summer of 1990 the life sentence had been lifted and he was given the all-clear. It was not difficult to understand the agonising torment she must have felt when a few short weeks later the vile disease re-emerged and there was simply nothing left in her power to prevent it taking the life of the man she had known and loved for more than four decades.

By late October I returned to Thailand, as the monsoon season was drawing to a close, and I needed to get back to the jungle. There was much to do, as the equipment would need completely re-checking and a thorough overhaul. We resolved that I should fly out alone and prepare everything, and that Sophy would follow on later.

I should have waited. Phuket was still in the grips of severe storms, and I discovered the origins of the word aquaplaning when the Thai Airways Boeing 737-300 on which I arrived nearly skidded off the runway into the Andaman Sea. The Pearl Hotel had not floated away, although the street outside was at least two feet deep in water. On the east coast, a typhoon whipping itself up far out in the Gulf of Siam was threatening the town of Surat Thani for the second year in succession. The phone lines were down around Takua Pa, and it was impossible to get through to Dwaila, so every day I drove over to the yard of a company called Sea Nomad and worked on the boat in the shelter of their enormous barn-like warehouse.

Sea Nomad specialised in manufacturing inflatable rubber dinghies and was founded and owned by an ebullient Swiss by the name of Luca Schuelli, with whom I became great friends.

One day Luca announced in his lilting English that he had mentioned my work to some journalist friends in Germany who would be visiting Thailand in late November to cover the King's Cup Regatta. As an additional piece, they were keen to visit the lake and possibly write a feature article about the eccentric Englishman living in the jungle trying to film tigers. I was naturally flattered, although I couldn't quite see the angle of importance, but nevertheless agreed to show the gentlemen of the press my little corner of the world. Luca thought it would be a good idea if I showed him the lake first so that he could brief his friends later with the benefit of first-hand knowledge, and so it was decided that when the rains had passed we would journey up to Khao Sok together.

It was two weeks into November and still the rain hadn't stopped. Sophy was due to arrive on the 25th and I wanted everything to be ready by then, so Luca and I risked it.

We left at seven-thirty in the morning in the midst of yet another monumental deluge. One hour later it stopped quite suddenly and, although we didn't know it at the time and joked amicably about our good fortune, the monsoon was over for another year. Getting through the swamp to Dwaila's tested the four-wheel-drive vehicle to the limits, and we were forced to unhitch the trailer and leave the boat on the edge of what used to be her driveway.

She said that we were the first vehicle to reach her in over a month and her food supplies had been drastically depleted as a result. We were therefore extra specially welcome, arriving as we did with cartons of beer, fresh meat and vegetables, and box-loads of provisions that we had collected from the supermarket earlier on.

During the previous three months, much had happened. There had been a major row with the park superintendent, and she had been forced to relocate her raft-houses or face eviction from the lake on the spot. Since that time no-one had been near our tree-hide and she was anxious that everything was safe and still intact. Activity more or less ground to a halt in the park during the rainy season, and the rangers were forced to do even less work than usual. Even the poachers were reluctant to work, as much of the wildlife sought higher ground away from the floods and became inaccessible and therefore harder to trap.

In the coming months, as the forest cover dried up, the animals would return to the lowlands and hopefully to our waterhole, which by now probably resembled a small reservoir.

We set off before sunrise the next day, and by nine o'clock the boat was safely in the water and Luca and I were heading across the lake. An hour and a half later we had tied up in the spot where Dwaila's floating raft-houses used to be and were hacking our way through the thick new growth up the hill to our tree-house. As we stood atop the last rise I could hardly see the hide such was the density of the new foliage. Dwaila had been as good as her word, as it was obvious nobody had come this way for several weeks. As we approached the tree-hide, I looked around carefully for other signs of life. We spotted Malayan sun bear and leopard tracks, and the usual small deer, wild boar and civet cat that were regular visitors to the area, but no tiger.

I was keen to find evidence of 'the big boy' and prove to both Luca and myself of his continued existence. Less than two kilometres away along the old familiar trail, we saw the unmistakable paw marks of my old friend not far away from the spot where I had last seen them.

Tigers are solitary, semi-nocturnal carnivores requiring little more than sufficient prey, water, shade and an adequate gene pool in order to survive. Adult tigers can vary in length from two to four metres and be as high as one metre at the shoulder and weigh over 300 kilograms. The males are always larger, and are distinctive in a number of ways but perhaps most strikingly because of a ruff of hair around the neck. They possess acute powers of hearing and vision, and their nostrils can be flared in a peculiar grimace-like way to detect the smell of other tigers that may have strayed into their territory. This they mark out in many curious ways. 'The big boy', like all dominant males, regularly patrolled his area, leaving obvious signs to other tigers marking the boundaries of his domain. Luca was fascinated when I pointed out to him various points along the path where the huge tiger had scraped the earth with his back paws and the tree where he regularly sharpened his formidable front claws. The faeces were another deliberate marker as was the faint smell of urine on a nearby rock. The tiger hadn't been by for a few days, but he was a creature of habit, he'd be back – something the poachers knew only too well.

We had a wonderful few days on the lake. Every morning the gibbons would wake us with their deep throaty whistles, and we would fall asleep at night to the sound of bull-frogs croaking on the floating rafts beneath us. Boon had brought two delightful kittens to live with him, and they were wonderful to watch as they played hide and seek and chased each other around the base. Even Weewat seemed vaguely agreeable: perhaps he was impressed by the imposing size of Luca, or maybe he had just resigned himself to the fact that I was back to stay.

Although hauling Hugo and all the other equipment back to the hide during the daytime was tedious and hard work, it was tremendous fun to see everything working again. For some reason I was satisfied that this time things would all fall into place, and I would be successful in capturing the elusive tiger on film. It was not to be.

On November 24th I drove back with Luca to Phuket. Sophy was due to arrive the next day, and three days after that, his journalist friends were flying in from Frankfurt. It was going to be a busy week.

They say that things happen in threes, especially bad things, and the worst always happens last. For Sophy and me, it all began in the dead of night two days after returning to the national park raft-houses.

139

I awoke from a deep sleep to the sound of urgent hammering on our wickerwork door. Weewat stood on the threshold in his sarong, a useless torch in his hand, jabbering frantically for me to come with a powerful flash-lamp. I grabbed a 40-watt lamp that I kept permanently hooked up to a 20-amp car battery, and followed him into the night. I had no idea where we were going. We crossed the rough bamboo floor of the main reception area and I could see a group of people huddled around the lean-to kitchen on the far side.

The light was playing hideous games with their shadows. Their misshapen forms danced eerily across the walls and upon the water as they pointed as if with one giant finger toward the floor of the cookhouse. I shivered in the cool air. Whatever they were all looking at, my instincts told me was malevolent and wrong.

Boon appeared from the shadows, his face contorted in anguish, and led me to the edge of the platform. He gestured feverishly ahead of him into the darkness, warning me to be careful. I scanned the floor with my lamp: there were pots and pans, unwashed plates, a large wooden chopping block, and then I saw it. Squirming heavily beside a discarded sack of rice was a massive reticulated python. Another bloody snake, I thought. So this is what all the fuss was about, I've been woken up to look at a venturesome reptile. I turned to go, but Boon took my arm urgently.

'Look, look!' he cried.

As I looked more carefully, I could see its great body flexing, muscles expanding and contracting as its whole being seemed to writhe around some unseen object. And then very slowly, first one eye, then his head and finally his mouth came into view. With great deliberation, the giant snake was swallowing the ginger kitten.

I shuddered, and yet I could not turn away. I was transfixed. The great pythons are quite capable of taking pigs, dogs and, on extremely rare occasions, even small children. A python eating a deer is a gruesome enough sight, but one devouring a domestic pet is abhorrent and sickening. And although I told myself over and over again that this was nature at work, I was filled with loathing and disgust for this abominable creature.

There were many infants on the national park raft-houses; Weewat's boy was only fifteen months old. I could see the dread fear in the men's eyes and hear their spoken obscenities as they too watched the repulsive beast gorge itself. From behind me a man appeared with a pump-action shotgun, but the wily old snake was already on the move and slithered quietly into the water and was gone before he could fire.

Sophy was devastated, as she loved cats and had taken in dozens of kittens from her home farm as a child. Only that afternoon she had played with both kittens on her lap, amazed by the strong bond between them. We sat on the back porch of our hut watching the reflection of the full moon in the water, our toes well back from the edge in case the great monster came back again. We thought of the number of times that we had swum and bathed here, and how easy it would have been for the huge snake to overpower us in the water.

We sat there for many hours, talking quietly, drinking Mekong whisky and soda, trying to make the alcohol drive the cruel memory away. And then finally we returned to our room and slept.

The story was all round the lake by the next morning, considerably embroidered no doubt. Most Thai people, in their typically fatalistic manner, simply brushed it off as one of those things and it was soon forgotten, but for us the ominous and foreboding undertone would not disappear.

Nevertheless we had to put it to the back of our minds. Luca would be arriving around noon with his guests, and we had to entertain them as best we could. We met them at the smelly fishing village. Luca quite mischievously thought that this would give them a good introduction to the lake and if they survived that, he reasoned, the rest would be a breeze.

Harald Mertes and Peter Mueller had experienced decay and degradation far worse than the villagers of the lake could serve up. They both seized upon the wonderful photo-opportunity and zapped away with their expensive Canons, dispensing smiles and good cheer to the children, and leaving a conspicuous bottle of Mekong behind for the adults.

Harald was in his late forties, short with wild curly brown hair and a dishevelled beard that covered most of his otherwise expressionless face. He had travelled around the world many times and had been a war correspondent for over ten years. He told me about the escalating situation in the Gulf with a great sense of relief that he no longer had to witness such horror.

Now he was a successful travel writer who could pick his destinations. He explained with genuine sincerity how much he had been looking forward to this trip. He and Luca had been sailing friends for many years and he had covered most of the world's leading yacht races.

Peter was much quieter and somewhat older than Harald, probably just into his sixties. It struck me that he was too sharp to be working for a yachting magazine, but then again the sport is huge business in Germany and its journalistic corps must be of the highest calibre.

Luca had brought along the pride of the Sea Nomad fleet, an eighteen-foot inflatable with an 85HP outboard that four of his workers were now assembling in the water. Trust him, I thought, not to miss the chance of some professional quality pictures in this fabulous setting. With one deft twist of the key the gleaming engine roared into life and, with his not inconsiderable supply of provisions neatly stowed away, we were ready to leave. Except that my engine wouldn't start.

For over two hours in the midday heat, his mechanic slaved away in the bowels of the ancient Yamaha engine. He stripped away the cylinder head exposing the pistons, rubbed them down with emery paper, cleaned all the vents and reassembled the machine using copious amounts of liquid gasket compound. Each plug lead was removed, cut back and replaced. The fuel system was thoroughly cleaned, with the carburettor receiving close and meticulous attention. We watched from the shade of four pieces of sacking untidily sewn together the ice in our Mekong whisky visibly melting before our eyes.

Finally the young mechanic replaced the hood of the engine, pumped fresh fuel from the tank into the unclogged system, and turned the ignition key. With a brief groan and a splutter the motor fired once, then twice, then thundered alive, belching out great billows of dense blue smoke that hung upon the surface of the water until a gentle breeze whisked them away.

With an audible sigh of relief from myself, and a thumping great pat on the back from Luca, we set off across the lake with a final wave to his dauntless team who were to hold the fort at the village. For the next couple of days we had a wonderfully relaxed time showing our guests around the lake, introducing them to some of the hideaway groups of fisher folk, exploring the small caves and watching the antics of the monkeys high above us on the limestone cliffs.

On their last day we got up early and went trekking up to our tree-hide. Neither of the journalists had ever seen anything quite like it, and were fascinated by the entire concept and the amount of equipment we had managed to haul out into the middle of nowhere and then magically make disappear into the natural surroundings. I had to confess that although most of our kit appeared well camouflaged to us, it didn't seem to fool our main quarry who had been playing hide and seek with us for several months.

Harald told me to have faith. His experience told him that these things weren't easy, but he recognised that we were on the right track. 'Give it time,' he said quietly.

We walked up the trail away from our hide, looking for signs of the tiger. Peter was a keen bird watcher and was thrilled to see brightly coloured barbets and a racket-tailed drongo. The blue-eared kingfisher would be at his usual haunt close to Dwaila's burnt-out camp, but I had no wish to show these people that side of the park.

We were looking for fresh signs of 'the big boy', and yet there were none. Almost without exception, on every occasion that I had walked these paths, there were signs of his presence. He was a creature of habit and guarded his territory jealously. He knew that he could chase me out at any time, and yet he majestically allowed me freedom of passage throughout his domain. I had never seen him, and yet I always knew he was there. Now it was almost as though he was too conspicuous by the absence of any sign. A shudder went down my spine. Something was wrong.

Peter and Harald were not disappointed, as they had both seen tigers in India and Nepal and knew just how elusive they could be. We saw great-crested hornbills on the walk back, and a massive blue metallic scorpion lay in wait for us on the sandy stretch where I had seen 'the big boy's' footprints covering my own all those months before. The scorpion was just sunbathing, and we stepped around it without incident. We returned to our base where Weewat's wife had prepared an enormous farewell meal from Luca's ample provisions. Sophy and I knew that she would have stashed away the best to feed her gluttonous husband later, but we didn't care; we were used to it by now, and accepted it as all part of the game.

By mid-afternoon, just as the worst of the heat of the sun was passing, our guests climbed aboard their inflatable and we said our goodbyes.

That evening Sophy and I were feeling a little lonely after the excitement of the previous days, and I was particularly troubled and uneasy about something, although I couldn't define exactly what it was. Luca had left us with five bottles of Sang Thip rum, a case of beer and three flagons of wine. More than enough to sink a battleship, and our melancholy, so we grabbed a few bottles, jumped into our boat and went to share them with Dwaila.

Drunk but not disorderly we clambered back into the boat at about ten-thirty. There was plenty of light from the moon by which to navigate, and we set off into the night, turning left into a narrow passage before it opened up into the vast open water of the lake.

It began with a distant rattling sound which then became a louder clank. Instinctively I knew that something was wrong with the engine and closed the throttle, but even as I did the clanking became a fierce metallic thumping and then the outboard died. I cursed loudly into the empty black air. The problem was serious, and my simple tool-kit was of no use. We had no reserve motor and no oars. We were dressed in shorts and T-shirts and had no food. As I looked up, dark clouds were gathering around the moon and the wind began to tug at my sleeves. Within minutes the first spots of rain began to sting our exposed faces.

We huddled down in the well of the boat praying that the squall would soon pass.

CHAPTER THIRTEEN

Khao Sok, December 1990

I sat cross-legged and sheepish at the front of the whaler, my bush hat pulled down well over my head, watching Boon's long-tail pull us laboriously across the lake. Out of the corner of my eye I could see Dwaila waving furiously from her boat in our direction. It was the second tow we'd had that morning and probably a great opportunity for her to amuse her tourists at our expense, I thought. She stood in the bows of her garishly painted wooden bath-tub as it chugged wearily toward us. I imagined the mocking and self-satisfied look on her face that came with owning perhaps not quite the ugliest and most sluggish boat in the universe, but at least one with a thoroughly reliable engine.

As her boat swung in a huge arc, bearing down on us all too quickly, I began to notice not mockery but an anguish on her face as she frantically signalled for Boon to cut his engine. Something was wrong . . .

The last night had been terrifying as the freak storm whipped itself into a frenzy on the lake. To begin with we drifted hopelessly at its mercy, the wind and rain lashing both sides of the boat. Tied up on the pier at the national park raft-houses the Boston whaler had looked sleek and impressive; in this massive expanse of water we felt tiny, helpless and insignificant. As the storm increased, the wind careered through the mountain gorge; emerging as a twisted, violent tornado that seemed to pick up the flimsy boat and throw it to one side like discarded driftwood.

The torrent of rain collected rapidly in the well of the boat. When the bilge pump died, I stuffed some paper in the nozzle of the plastic fuel funnel and baled out the water by hand. The whaler was reputed to be unsinkable, but I had no desire to test that. We struck submerged boulders several times and just as I thought that we were about to be battered against the rocks for the final, fatal blow, the boat was whisked out into the lake again as if on some violent unseen underwater current.

For three terror-stricken hours we were hurled around in the water, and for three hours I pleaded with Sophy to hang on, telling her that the storm would soon pass. A hundred times I told myself that I must be insane bringing her out to face situations like this. She just looked back and forced a smile.

By four o'clock in the morning the tempest had subsided and we were carried along aimlessly towards the shore. I was able to grab hold of some bamboo and pull us into shallow water less than two feet deep, and wedge the boat securely between some friendly rocks. We slept.

About two hours later I awoke from the depths of a frightening dream in which sea-serpents were trying to pull me into a massive whirlpool. Sophy sat on a rock stroking a baby tiger, calling mournfully, 'Goodbyeeee . . .'

I could hear the sound of an engine. Sophy was still asleep, so I let her rest and went to investigate. It was a young fisherman and his wife whom we had met before. I shouted and waved my arms, he turned his tiny boat around and we were saved.

Quite how he managed to tow us with his fragile craft I shall never know, as his engine looked no bigger than a sewing machine, and yet we eventually made it back to the raft-houses in one piece. He refused any offer of reward, smiling joyfully at us as they left.

By mid morning I had diagnosed the problem with the engine – shorn piston rings and probably end bearings as well. We would have to take it back to Phuket for repair. Boon helped me lift the engine off its mountings and into the well of the boat, and agreed to tow us back to the smelly village. We packed a few items of clothing and locked up the cameras and other valuables in the spare room. Aroon had already laid down the law, and I knew our belongings would be safe. We set off slowly at first until the long-tail adjusted to the weight of our boat behind it, then Boon opened up the throttle and with a tremendous roar we headed off across the lake . . .

Dwaila was kneeling, rope in hand, at the sharp end of her tub.

Boon had cut his motor and there was only the quiet rhythmic thud of her diesel engine and the gentle lapping of the waves against our boat as she approached. She shouted something to Newt the boat-boy, who deftly brought his craft alongside as Dwaila called to me.

'Take my arm,' and she jumped across into the whaler. Newt gently manoeuvred his boat away, and she sat on the side of our boat clutching the hand-rail tightly.

'Mike, I've got some bad news.'

'What is it, what's happened?' I asked urgently.

'A tiger has been killed up by my old camp. We think it's "the big boy".'

My right hand curled instinctively into a fist which I wrapped with my left and bit my knuckles hard. 'My God, no! Are you sure?' I cried angrily.

'Sure about the tiger, yes, sure that it's "the big boy", no. But it's his territory, you know how he patrols it, and so do the poachers. He must have gotten unlucky.'

'Unlucky!' I screamed. 'It's his bloody jungle, for Christ's sake, he shouldn't have to worry about bad luck. Do you know exactly what happened?'

'No, there are only rumours at the moment; you know what this place is like. All I've heard is that a large tiger was snared, and that the poachers couldn't get anywhere near him he was so mad. His foot was badly damaged in the trap, so they shot him and carried him out on the old lumber road close to the marker at Kilometre 92.'

'Where is he now? What are the police doing? Who killed him?' I demanded, enraged now.

'Look, I only heard this a short while ago at the fishing village. Go talk to Aroon, he'll know more.'

And with that she whistled over to Newt who brought back her boat and she prepared to leave. 'These are bad people, Mike, don't mess with them.'

'Mess with them!' I bellowed. 'If I find out who they are, I'll bloody crucify them.'

'Just be careful, and in case you're wondering, Panas is in Bangkok,' she said as her boat chugged away.

'Fucking typical,' I shouted at her back, and she was gone.

Boon looked at me quizzically, and was visibly shocked when I told him what I knew. He fixed me with a sad and anxious gaze. It was as if he could read my mind, and he said simply, 'I help you.'

147

With that he clambered back into his long-tail and we sped across to the fishing village at high speed. When we arrived I asked Sophy to help me act out a hopeless charade where the broken engine was the lead player. Boon and I went to get the jeep, and I told him my plan. He was to deride us unmercifully to the villagers, which shouldn't be difficult, I thought. He was then to find out everything he could about the poaching, and meet us three hours later at Kilometre 92.

I gave him 500 *bhat* that I told him to say he had won from us gambling, which should boost his street cred, I thought. We returned to unload the boat. Some villagers came to help us manhandle the outboard into the back of the jeep, and I gave them an absurdly large tip for their trouble. In ten minutes I knew that it would have been exchanged for a bottle of Mekong, all the better to loosen tongues.

With a heavy heart we left Boon behind, ostensibly to tie up and take care of the whaler, and drove off to find Aroon. Sophy had said very little since Dwaila had delivered the shattering news, but I knew the cogs were turning deep inside her sagacious mind.

'First the kitten, then the storm and now this,' she said quietly. 'What does it all mean?'

'It means we should pack our bags, get the hell out of here and go back home to civilisation,' I said without conviction. 'Except for some reason I don't think we're going to do that.'

'What *are* you thinking of doing?'

'I don't know yet exactly,' I replied, 'but I don't think we'll get much satisfaction from the park authorities. I'm hoping that Aroon will come up with something.'

He was sitting on his porch when we arrived, talking earnestly with a park ranger. I signalled that I wanted to talk and drove round and parked up at the back of his house. His wife ran a small sideline entertaining visitors to the park, and we sat in the shade of her café and drank ice-cold Coke until Aroon finally joined us.

'Hello,' he smiled in his normal warm and welcoming manner. 'What a surprise, why are you not on the lake?'

'The boat has broken down again,' I said. 'We have to take the engine back to Phuket Town to get it mended.'

Aroon laughed, not out of scorn but to insulate himself against the inevitable confrontation; he knew exactly why we were there. I disliked this small talk and hedging, but it was so typically Thai to dance around an unpleasant topic until the very last possible moment.

Finally he looked deep into my eyes and said, 'You have heard?'

'Yes, I have heard.'

'It is a terrible thing, if it is true,' he said with finality.

'What do you mean, "if it is true"?' I asked, clearly amazed.

'The teachings of the Lord Buddha tell me that if I have not seen it with my own eyes, then it is only a rumour,' he said somewhat piously.

'I have a generator up at my camp that can turn night into day,' I said.

'Yes, I know.'

'But you have never seen it?'

'You have told me that it is there.'

'And do you believe me?' I asked.

'Yes.'

'You believe me because I have no reason to lie. Just as I believe the person that told me about the tiger, and I know that deep in your heart, you believe the person that told you.'

'Yes,' said Aroon very quietly.

'Please tell me what you have been told,' I asked gently.

'Yesterday afternoon, before the storm,' he began, 'a policeman saw six men carrying a dead tiger out from the track at Kilometre 92. They put it into a pick-up truck and drove away.'

'A policeman?' I said incredulously. 'Why didn't he stop them, why didn't he do something?'

'He was too frightened.'

'Well, what about the rest of the police, have they done anything?'

'He has not made a report,' said Aroon gravely.

'I can't believe this,' I said. 'OK, so the policeman was too frightened to get involved, that's bad enough. But not to have reported an incident that happened almost twenty-four hours ago, that's incompetence to the point of collusion. The tiger and all the evidence will have disappeared by now.'

'Yes,' said Aroon solemnly. 'Maybe they don't care.'

'Well, I care. Will you help me?'

'There is nothing more I can do,' he said.

'Well, I'm going to find out the truth,' I said indignantly, 'and when I find out there is going to be one hell of a stink, I can assure you.'

'Mike,' he said very seriously, 'don't get involved, these are bad people, there could be danger.'

'If someone doesn't do something, then these bad people will keep killing and killing until there is nothing left,' I said. 'They just have to be stopped!'

Aroon rubbed his forehead thoughtfully with the heels of his hands, pushing his fingers back through his wavy hair. He shook his head slowly. I could see that he was paralysed, powerless to act. Someone had already got to him, and he had been warned off. Now he was feeling impotent and ashamed. There was nothing more that I could say. He would have to wrestle with his own conscience.

Sophy was furious when I said that I was going back to Kilometre 92 to meet Boon. I tried to calm her, telling her that I would be careful, insisting that she stay behind and wait. My mind was made up, and I drove off in a fury.

Boon sat on the edge of the lane, out of sight of the traffic. I turned into the track telling him to get in whilst slamming the engine into four-wheel-drive to climb the precariously steep slope up away from the road and out of view. At the top I stopped and looked down. We were well hidden and there was no-one in sight. I turned to Boon.

'What have you found out?' I demanded.

'The tiger, a very big male, was killed not far from here, maybe five kilometres only. They carried him down this trail to a white pick-up truck, then to a man in the town of Amphoe Phanom. You know where it is?'

'Yes, I know,' I said. 'Did you find out anything else?'

'They sold it for 7,000 *bhat*.'

Less than 200 pounds sterling for the life of 'the big boy'. I wanted to throw up. 'Anything more?'

'Yes, the man who killed it, his name is Jouey. He lives not far from here. He has killed tigers before. He has a white Mazda pick-up.'

'Do you think you can show me where the tiger was killed?' I asked.

'Why you want to go there?' asked Boon, clearly puzzled.

'I don't know,' I said. 'I just want to be close one last time, to see where he died. Can you find it?'

'It should be easy, many tracks,' he said.

We walked in silence on up the track. The rain had washed away almost all of the footprints but we were looking for the point where they had left the path. In the dense undergrowth that would be easy to spot. It was hard going but not difficult, and I was possessed with a new energy that drove me forward, an energy that drained instantly from my body the moment we found the spot.

We had followed a clear path that the six men must have cut for themselves until it opened up into a small clearing. I had never been there before and yet I knew instantly that this was where the great beast had taken his last breath. Despite the rain, the smell of the tiger hung in the air all around me, the smell of fear and rage as he must have struggled and torn against the wire snare, desperately trying to break free. I could feel the very soul of the tiger was still there, in the trees, in the ground; its presence was all about me.

Boon found the stout sapling that the poacher had used to spring his trap and I could see where the wire had chafed against its bark. Underneath there was an area that seemed to have been hollowed out of the undergrowth, broken branches, crushed leaves and scrapes of earth gorged out from the ground. Here the poor creature must have frantically thrashed about in blind panic, unable to understand what had happened to his trapped leg. There was blood everywhere. And there was the smell of death.

Boon stood silently looking at the pitiful scene of devastation before him. With a great sigh he told me the last of his information. 'The big boy' had suffered for over two days as the poachers waited for him to lose his strength so that they could take him alive. On the third day, when he had almost completely severed his own leg in the snare, they shot him through the head for fear that he might finally break loose and attack them.

We walked back to the jeep in silence. It was getting dark and I desperately needed a drink. Sophy hadn't moved from her chair.

'Where's Aroon?' I asked.

'He's gone into Takua Pa, to the restaurant that sells jungle food.'

So he is sniffing around, I thought; good for him.

'Come on, darling,' I said, 'let's get out of here. I've seen quite enough of Khao Sok for one day.'

'Do you want me to drive? You look as though you need a drink.'

'I do need a drink,' I replied, 'but I also need to digest the last few hours with a clear head. I'll save the drink until we get to the Pearl.'

And so we left Khao Sok and drove off into the early evening dusk. My mind was whirling, turning things over and over, and by the time we arrived at the Pearl I had worked myself into a complete rage, so utterly sickened was I by the sheer waste of the tiger's life. I was possessed by a dread loathing of the man Jouey that killed him. I knew that if I had stayed up at Khao Sok, I might have been perfectly capable of dragging him into the forest, nailing him to a tree and leaving him there.

Such notions I had to work out of my system very rapidly, as this was Thailand, where the value of the life of a tiger was beneath contempt. Taking the life of a poacher, on the other hand, would have put me in prison for life.

Sophy suffered with me throughout all this, although in her own way. She had always been much more spiritually inclined than I could ever be. For her, all this had happened for a reason. She knew that the death of the tiger would affect many people in many different ways. For most it would be an item of hot gossip. For others it would be a profitable encounter as they benefited financially from the trade of the tiger's life. For still more it would represent the end of a feared predator. For a few it would be a martyr for all endangered wildlife. And for one person in particular, it would be the end of a filming expedition and the start of a whole new way of life. All this she knew deep inside, because she believed in destiny and was therefore powerless to prevent it.

She was also gracious enough to get drunk with me that night, and we both woke with exceedingly sore heads the following morning. We dropped off the stricken engine with Luca's mechanic, who shook his head with hopeless indignation. I told him to patch it up the best he could, because we would not be needing it for too much longer, and left him to it and drove away to find his boss somewhere down near the Phuket Yacht Club.

It was the regatta's final day and the big man was nowhere to be found so we sat in the shade of the Coconut Café and drank ice-cold beer and ate shark steaks in garlic. By lunch-time our hangovers had been pleasantly surpassed by a wonderful new feeling of mild insobriety.

We didn't care. I remembered an old Rechabite's admonition: 'First the man taketh a drink. Then the drink taketh a drink. Then the drink taketh the man.' Well, the hell with that, I thought, let the wretched drink take me and be damned!

We met Harald Mertes coming down the lane arm in arm with a most distinguished-looking gentleman. I called out to him and they staggered over to join us. They'd obviously been drinking lunch as well.

'This is Señor Ermano Traversso,' he said with great eloquence.

'Delighted,' I said, stumbling to my feet to shake his hand. 'Do please join us.'

They sat down and we ordered some beers. Ermano was in his mid-forties, deeply tanned with a strong, angular face and immaculately groomed black hair. He was master of an equally elegant vessel that lay at anchor out in the bay. His yacht was called the *Storm Vogel*, and it had starred alongside Nicole Kidman and Sam Neill in the film *Dead Calm*. It was now, however, the undignified repository of a particularly inebriated Swiss friend of ours.

After our drinks we all decided to go over to the boat and attempt to pitch the slumbering colossus into the briny. A task of Herculean proportions which we miserably failed to accomplish.

Harald and I sat talking all afternoon. He was deeply sympathetic, and his words were profoundly wise. Any thoughts of enacting my revenge on the hapless Jouey were systematically dismantled and thrown unceremoniously overboard. You must box clever, he told me. Box with your head, not with your heart. And of course he was right. The slaughter of the tiger was indicative of a much greater and pervasive problem, he said. If you want to do something, then make sure that he didn't die in vain. He then outlined a strategy which he said would have optimum impact. But I had to be sure and follow each point in turn, even if they felt trivial or inconsequential at the time. It made perfect sense and I began to feel better. In that brief encounter, Harald Mertes unwittingly tempered a resolve deep inside me that I'm sure he didn't realise at the time. But he gave me a new strength of purpose and I remain deeply indebted to him to this day.

Later that evening, at the regatta's gala presentation of prizes, I met with one or two journalists from the Thai press who were covering the yachting. They were drunk, and I foolishly mentioned the tiger incident.

'Who cares?' asked one. 'Thai people don't want to read about stuff like that. It happens all the time.'

'My editor would laugh at me if I wanted to publish a story like that. People don't give a damn about animals,' said another.

I left them to drown, I hoped, in their own vomit. Such arrogance was atypical of Thai journalists, I was sure. These men were only there to cover an event that owed its success solely to foreign involvement. To dismiss the concerns of foreigners, therefore, with such conceit and insensitivity was pompous and high-handed.

Harald's plan involved the sympathy of the Thai media, but if these people were its ambassadors, I was sunk.

The next day I sent a stern fax up to the Royal Forestry Department's National Parks division in Bangkok, addressed to the Khao Sok superintendent, Mr Panas Ratnarathorn.

Dear Sir,

It has come to our attention that an adult male tiger was snared and, after more than two days of suffering, shot by poachers in Khao Sok National Park close to Kilometre 92. The dead tiger was then sold to a man in Amphoe Phanom for *bhat* 7,000.

Please do not allow this terrible act to pass without investigation. I am even prepared to offer my own money as a reward if it will help you to successfully find and punish the men responsible. I trust this matter will receive your urgent attention.

Yours faithfully, Michael Day.

The following day, having received no form of acknowledgement, I sent a similar but more detailed fax to the editors of *The Bangkok Post* and *The Nation*, both highly respected English-language newspapers in Thailand.

When I returned to Khao Sok, Aroon had no new information, or if he had, he was reluctant to share it with me. He had received a discourteous phone-call from the park superintendent who had travelled down overnight and was expected any minute. Part of that call presumably forbade him to talk further with me on the subject, and we spoke no more about it.

Someone once told me that Panas 'had the most evil eyes of any man I've ever met'. That statement was particularly accurate that morning as he stared at me across his desk. It was impossible for him to hide his loathing and contempt. As for me, I sat confidently in my chair, enjoying his unease. He had, of course, received my fax, but had chosen to ignore it. Until, that is, he was summoned to the office of the Director General of The Royal Forestry Department, the formidable Khun Phairote Suwannakorn.

Phairote had received two embarrassing and intrusive phone-calls in quick succession, both from highly inquisitive journalists demanding to know what was being done about the alleged killing of a tiger in Khao Sok National Park. He had nothing to tell them

154

because he had not been informed of the incident, and demanded an explanation from Panas who in his turn was typically evasive. I can only speculate as to what happened next, but it was obvious that Panas had been dispatched with haste to come up with some answers.

'I have looked into the alleged incident, and have found no evidence whatsoever to support your accusations,' he began.

'I see.'

'I also understand that you have been making some enquiries of your own. The matter is none of your business, and these interfering questions must stop,' he said with finality.

'Do you intend to pursue the matter yourself?' I enquired.

'I have already made my position quite clear. As far as I am concerned, the matter is closed.' He made to get up, but I wasn't finished with him yet.

'Well, in that case I regret to have to inform you that I *will* be pursuing this matter. As far as I am concerned, a tiger was very definitely killed. I have seen the place where the incident took place.'

Panas was clearly taken aback. He began to visibly shake with barely controlled anger. 'What have you seen?' he demanded.

'I have seen an area covered in blood where a large animal has recently put up a violent struggle before being brutally killed,' I said steadily.

'And where was this?'

'Close to Kilometre 92, as I made clear in my fax.'

'This animal that you say was killed there, how do you know it was a tiger?'

'It doesn't matter much what type of animal it was,' I said deliberately. 'The spot was well inside the park boundaries where no killing of any kind should occur.'

'I'll be the judge of that,' he growled at me. 'From now on you are not to go near Kilometre 92. That area is strictly off limits!'

'And if I do?' I enquired gently.

'Then I'll have your permit revoked and you will be thrown out of the park,' he said dismissively.

'If that is the way you feel, then this meeting is concluded,' I said, getting up and marching out of his office.

Sophy was outside and I told her what had happened, adding that we had better round up some help quickly and go and retrieve our things from the tree-hide.

155

Dwaila was at Tree-Tops when we stopped by to recruit some volunteer workers.

'Well, you sure as hell stirred things up around here,' she said with a grin.

'News travels fast,' I said, 'and so must I. Can I borrow some muscle for an hour or two?'

'Sure,' she said, barking orders at her team. And in a couple of minutes the jeep was full of smiling young faces and we were off back to the lake.

By the time the engine was hooked up and ready, it was beginning to get dark. Dwaila knew what my 'hour or two' meant and as long as her crew were back by the following evening, she wouldn't worry too much. We stocked up on provisions and cooked everyone a huge meal that night and at the crack of dawn set off across the lake towards our camp, saddened by the apprehension that we might be making the journey for the last time.

By noon, Hugo the generator was safely stowed in the well of the boat and a procession of keen young helpers were carrying all the valuable equipment down from the hide. The lighting rigs were left in place along with the cables and we hid the ladder so that no-one could climb up to the platform. With a last look we said a silent goodbye to our tree-house and returned to our base at the national park raft-houses. We locked everything away in the store-room, and took the boat back to the EGAT pontoon, hooked it up to the trailer and by mid-afternoon we were on our way back to Tree-Tops.

Dwaila, Sophy and I sat solemnly around her circular dining-table that night eating excellent food and mulling over the events of the past few days. Harald had warned me that the battle could not be fought and won on a local level. This was a small community, and people had to somehow exist side by side whatever their personal grievances. It was the Thai way to avoid confrontation at all costs, and they would always choose the path of least resistance. The root cause of the poaching problem and all the other illegalities surrounding the park lay not here, but at the top, in Bangkok. It was there that I would have to expose injustice. The people here were just the pawns in an enormous game of chess and would be as easily sacrificed by the key players up north if it came to the crunch.

'The big boy' did not end his life's journey here in the south of Thailand, of that much I was sure. By now his mighty carcass had been spirited away to the capital to the north, and it was there that I would have to look in order to find his killers.

PART THREE

THE CAMPAIGN

*'It hath been falsely believed that all tigers
be females, and that they engender in
copulation with the wind.'*

Edward Topsell,
History of Four Footed Beasts, 1607

CHAPTER FOURTEEN

England, December 1990

Cold winds and icy rain greeted our return to England. Christmas and New Year came and went with the usual round of parties and family get-togethers, long wintry walks in the woods and afternoon naps in front of blazing log-fires with dogs and cats snuggled disobediently on the sofa.

Frequently, conversation would come round to our adventures in Thailand, although we tried our best to avoid it. Somehow we wanted to distance ourselves for as long as we could from the inevitable reality that, when the seasonal festivities were over, we would have to make some very serious long-term decisions. Instead we would turn discussions round to wedding plans.

We settled on the date, June 15th, although the count-down had really already begun shortly after our official engagement announcement appeared in the *Daily Telegraph*. There were a thousand-and-one things to arrange, and I kept myself well clear of all of them. For me, seeing beyond the end of January was in itself a difficult enough task; half a year ahead, an impossibility. Besides, I could see that Sophy and her mother were enjoying the preparations far too much to want me involved, and I quietly resolved to keep it that way for as long as possible.

Christmas had brought a mighty harvest of books, mostly about tigers, conservation and the environment, and I read enthusiastically, absorbing anything and everything I could get my hands on. Meanwhile, my future wife and mother-in-law planned happily for hours at a time around the farmhouse kitchen-table. Sophy's father, on the other hand, seemed to take everything in his stride. When I had telephoned in the middle of the night from Kota Kinabalu in Malaysia to ask for her hand six months earlier, he had consented without question, even though he knew that I was far from ready to settle down and provide a stable family home for his daughter. And now, as it appeared that our lives were about to take a turn toward the increasingly unstable, he uttered not a word of objection. In his youth he had followed his own wanderlust, finally settling for an expatriate's life in Kenya. He knew only too well the powerful call that defies all logic and reason and makes one abandon security and dive headlong into the unknown. He knew that to attempt to stand in the way and block its path was both vain and futile. He understood that I would have to live out my own calling, and that until I worked things from my system once and for all, his daughter might never know true happiness. For that forbearance and understanding, I owe him a great debt of gratitude.

Sophy and I needed to find some neutral territory from which to think and work effectively. Both Norfolk and the London house provided too many distractions, so we decided to pile everything into the car and head for the south coast. On January 3rd we arrived at the seaside town of Rye in Sussex and checked into the Wayfarer bed and breakfast, one of those quaint and quintessentially British establishments with deep sagging beds, electric blankets and a rubber shower-hose on the bath taps.

From a small second-hand shop next door to the Co-op in the High Street we bought an old but serviceable Olivetti typewriter. And, armed with spare ribbon, writing paper and plenty of Tipp-Ex, we locked ourselves away in our spacious bedroom and began the arduous task of alerting the unsuspecting world to the plight of the tiger in the jungles of faraway Thailand.

Whilst Sophy scoured the local library for the names and addresses of those with whom we wished to make contact, I began to draft out a letter that we both hoped would bring the cavalry rushing over the hills to the tiger's defence.

Dear Sir,

For the past year, my fiancée and I have been living in southern Thailand, studying the tigers of the Khao Sok National Park. Khao Sok lies approximately 100 kilometres west of the coastal town of Surat Thani and was declared a national park by royal decree in 1986, when vast land masses were flooded as part of EGAT's (Electricity Generating Authority of Thailand) Rajjaphrabda Dam project. Needless

160

to say, untold damage was done to the natural wildlife infrastructure as more than 150 kilometres of rainforest became submerged within a remarkably short period of time. However, the resulting man-made lake has, by way of its many feeder branches and tributaries reaching deep into the jungle, made previously very remote areas now accessible by boat.

It is at the head of one of these tributaries, and approximately two kilometres inland, that we have built a fully habitable tree-hide some six metres above ground, overlooking a waterhole. This platform now gives us the unique opportunity to study and film the tiger, at close range, in his natural jungle habitat. It further gives us the chance to observe and document the many species of both flora and fauna that make up this hitherto little known area of the world . . .

. . . Wildlife have returned to the area since the disruption of the construction period and, on our last visit, we came face to face with a wild pig absentmindedly ambling along past the foot of the ladder. Within a 1,000-metre radius of the hide, and on either game path or in the jungle itself, we have observed, sometimes directly through sitings or indirectly by evidence of fresh tracks, the following: tiger, leopard, clouded leopard, fishing cat, leopard cat, wild elephant, tapir, gaur, samba, barking and mouse deer, binturong, porcupine, wild pig, sun bear, civet cat, langur and macaque monkeys, gibbon, monitor lizard, several species of snake including reticulated python and king cobra, plus innumerable varieties of birds and small insects including a magnificent assortment of butterflies.

This is, then, the truly definitive natural jungle habitat of the tiger, and yet, why is it that so little is known of the Indo-Chinese tiger when so much has been written and documented about his perhaps more readily accessible Indian cousin?

When statistics showed that the Indian tiger was rapidly facing extinction (and these figures alone were a credit to the work of the men responsible), clearly something drastic had to be done. Full tribute must be paid to the late Indira Gandhi who responded quickly to the call from Mr Guy Mountfort and helped to set up the tiger reserves as outlined in the WWF's 'Project Tiger' proposals. It was undoubtedly

161

this swift co-operation between her government officials and the international expertise of the WWF (not to mention considerable bulldozing of red tape) that precipitated much that has led to the revival of the Indian tiger today. Some neighbouring countries were quick to follow India's example, and yet Thailand has been demonstrably slow in showing any positive and sustainable initiative. How can this be?

Thailand owes much of its present comparative economic strength to tourism, although the price paid through deforestation and the subsequent decline of a once magnificent wildlife heritage has been extremely high.

When people ask me what I do and I reply that I am studying tigers, they frequently misunderstand the word and assume that I mean Thai girls! Incredible as it may seem, the majority of visitors to the country, and indeed Thai people themselves, have no idea that tigers still (or ever did) exist there in the wild.

Sadly, only about 500 tigers are now left in Thailand. Moreover, this figure is only really a guesstimate on the part of the Thai authorities, and I suspect the true figure to be considerably less. In Khao Sok, perhaps in the total park area of 650 square kilometres, probably fewer than six survive.

The acute problem facing the future of the tiger today in the 'tourist-infested' southern regions is not the blatant disregard of the logging ban and the continuing illegal deforestation, although this is all too serious, but the almost epidemic rate at which poaching has been allowed to escalate by the inept and largely disinterested and especially ill-equipped officials of the forestry commission and local police.

Recently, just over a month ago, an adult male tiger became entangled in a poacher's snare. For over forty-eight hours the poor wretched animal tried desperately to break free. The snare had been set deliberately to entrap a live tiger, commissioned by a local dealer. This live specimen would then be sold to produce archaic remedies for the cure of backache and impotence. The poachers, fearing that the tiger would tear itself free in a last-ditch attempt at escape, cowardly shot the beast in cold blood and subsequently carried the dead animal out through the thick undergrowth (this must have taken at least eight men!) to a nearby road. It was later delivered and sold to the dealer for £145. Despite my having supplied the authorities with the name of the poacher and protestations to the national press, no criminal proceedings have been brought.

You will, no doubt, have heard of the work of the late Dr Sueb Nakhasathien at the Huay Kha Kaeng wildlife sanctuary in Uthai Thani Province in Thailand. Dr Sueb dedicated his life's work to the conservation and protection of some of Thailand's rarest species of deer, alas to no avail. And it was only after he sacrificed his own life in a last desperate attempt to halt the catastrophic damage caused by the poachers of the area that the authorities finally woke up and sent in a military detachment to restore law and order.

Some of the ex-poachers have now surrendered their rifles (mostly home-made weapons), and help to assist the rangers with their work, whilst in the affluent South where hordes of Japanese, Taiwanese, Korean and Singaporean visitors arrive daily, expecting to gorge themselves on the bounty of the rainforest, the problem is all too frightening and acute. As the restaurants perpetuate their demand for wild game – bear, pig, deer, monkey, snake and no end of other animals and birds – the poachers continue, undisturbed and unpunished, to supply them.

For the hunter, the rewards are tantalising and high, and with little or no chance of discovery, who can blame them? It is unlikely that they realise the full impact of their actions, as hunting and poaching have been a key feature of village life for generations. And, with the net proceeds from the sale of one wild pig exceeding that which can be earned in two months' hard toil in the fields, the easy-money option is hard to refuse.

For the tiger, the almost daily depletion of his natural food supply spells disaster, and ultimate extinction is the price Thailand might have to pay for her contented tourists.

The magnificent coral reefs of Koh Pi Pi were once the pride of Thailand and justifiably amongst the most spectacular in the world. Until about six years ago. Now the coral is dead, devoid of almost all sea life, the terrible legacy of the poacher's dynamite. This has been the price, catastrophically high, paid by the undersea world as the once prolific Phuket lobster was pursued to oblivion.

Surely, this mistake cannot happen again, this time in the

rainforest? Surely there is some way to educate the people of Thailand and inform them of the irreversible consequences of their short-term greed? Tourism at any price?

I am convinced that if the Thai people were made aware of the dangers and the potential environmental calamity that such short-sighted avarice can only precipitate, perhaps by way of a simple documentary film shown on their favourite media, the TV, that a fire could be lit under the feet of those who, through their own ignorance and self-interest, could change the face of their country for ever.

I am fully prepared to offer every means at my disposal to help bring this about and to halt this sad, short-sighted and fatal attack on the wildlife of Thailand. Unfortunately what I lack desperately is contacts and *clout*. Therefore I turn to you in the hope that you will be able to come up with some form of direction and advice.

Apart from the aforementioned tree-hide, we have a twenty-foot Boston whaler with a 115HP Yamaha outboard; a 4500-watt Honda petrol generator; a fully modified and remote-controlled Panasonic MSI Super VHS video camera steered through electrical impulses transmitted over 100 metres of cable and monitored by way of a six-inch television monitor; video and stills cameras, lenses, tripods etc.; halogen lighting, spotlights, heavy-duty batteries, walkie-talkies, camouflage, several hundred metres of cable of one sort or another and a host of other vital and not so vital equipment. We naturally have the full permission from the Khao Sok authorities to cover the entire area and there is excellent floating accommodation on the lake.

In short, we have the basics, local knowledge and expertise. We are on friendly terms with the rangers, for there are those that care although, like us, they often feel powerless to act.

If saving the wildlife of Khao Sok and throughout Thailand is indeed a matter of consequence, then you will treat this letter not only as an appeal for help, but a statement of the ultimate, inevitable and impending environmental catastrophe that faces the country today.

Would you please take the time to consider this matter urgently. We are more than prepared to be guided and to assist those with the experience and wherewithal to help save this situation before it goes beyond all redemption.

We would be most happy to meet at your convenience should you so decide, and to bring along any slides or material that may assist in your endeavours.

In the meantime, we remain,

Yours faithfully,
Michael Day and Sophy Pilkington

PS Please feel free to call me day or night on the above number at any time, should you wish to discuss things further.

I read over the draft. I wondered if anyone would notice the paraphrasing of Winston Churchill's famous wartime letter to Roosevelt in the closing paragraphs. I wondered if anyone would care. The letter itself was far too long and hardly a masterpiece of literary achievement, but I didn't have the luxury of a word processor and the document was by that time already well-daubed with Tipp-Ex. I hoped it would be judged on its content rather than its form. It would have to do.

We made over thirty copies of the letter, leaving the address area blank. I then customised each one with the typewriter to the extensive list that Sophy had produced. She had split the names into essentially three groups: conservation and environmental organisations; writers, journalists and celebrities known for their interest in the environment; and finally, film-makers, television producers and broadcast media generally.

By Twelfth Night we had posted our appeals to World Wide Fund for Nature, Greenpeace, Anglia Survival, BBC Natural History Unit, Professor David Bellamy, Sir David Attenborough, Uncle Tom Cobleigh and all, and we returned to London to field the deluge of concern we naïvely envisaged our impassioned cry for help would precipitate. We were to be bitterly disappointed. Those few replies that we did receive were discouraging. Mostly, our letter was completely ignored.

One correspondent did stand out from the rest, John Nichol, author of a magnificent publication entitled *The Mighty Rainforest*. Were it not for him, we might well have abandoned our conservation endeavours there and then. John had also written a book called *The Animal Smugglers*, and was fully aware of the illegal wildlife trade in South-east Asia.

We finally met up with him in London's Covent Garden and over coffee one afternoon he gave us some very valuable advice on whom we should contact further. One of the suggestions he made was for us to get in touch with an organisation called the EIA, the Environmental Investigation Agency. He was also the first to tell us that, if we were going to take this matter seriously, we would ultimately have to do it all ourselves. He had seen and worked with the top-heavy bureaucracies of the leading conservation groups at first hand.

'Forget them,' he said, 'they won't be able to help you make a difference.'

The second man to make a similar statement was Ian MacPhail, a co-founder of The World Wildlife Fund, as it was originally known, more than thirty years earlier. His formidable experience with that organisation and the giant International Fund for Animal Welfare (IFAW) had left him shaken and disillusioned with much of the conservation movement. I think he found in me some of the fire and spirit that had shaped his thinking all those years before.

'Go back and find out more,' he had said on one of our long telephone conversations. 'Discover the real truth and when you get it, beware of those that will try to twist it to suit their own ends.'

Wise words indeed, and counsel that I was to heed later when the wolves came knocking at our door.

Whilst back in London, we spent the long winter days writing more letters, waiting for the phone to ring, looking out for the postman, or collating the many hundreds of slides and photographs that we had taken in both Thailand and Singapore into some orderly collection. We submitted a selection to the picture libraries of Anglia Survival and Oxford Scientific Films, and were graciously accepted as bona-fide wildlife photographers by them both. Although these companies had formidable reputations in natural history film-making, they were sadly unable to commit the sort of manpower and funds necessary to fully document our tiger story.

The effects of the recession and Margaret Thatcher's extraordinary commercial television licensing reforms combined to freeze us out. Five years earlier we might have stood a good chance of finding a suitable partner. Nowadays, independent broadcasters had to find the horrendous franchise fees to pay to the government. Quality commissions were axed in favour of cheap American and Australian soap-operas as a result. The TV companies weren't unsympathetic, they were simply unable to help. We were getting nowhere.

One afternoon we had a visit from a representative of the EIA. It was to be a memorable wake-up call. The Environmental Investigation Agency had been conceived in the eighties by veteran Greenpeace campaigner, Alan Thornton. He realised that change could only result from effective lobbying, which in its turn relied heavily upon solid and irrefutable intelligence information.

'Politicians won't listen to anything else,' said our visitor, 'however much you might want them to. Unless your facts stack up, governments will completely ignore you.'

'But they are supposed to care, to do something,' I said.

'They are supposed to care about and do a lot of things,' he said, 'but saving the planet won't win them votes, so essentially they don't give a damn.'

'You mean it's all lip-service?'

'You got it, and politics,' he said with disgust. 'Take the fur industry labelling orders for example,' he began. 'A couple of years ago, spring 1988 I think, the trade minister Alan Clark was working on a new bill that would compel the British fur industry to label all garments made from animals caught in those barbaric leg-hold traps. He was good, he believed in it. Anyway, the anti-fur campaigners at LYNX fought a brilliant campaign, and the furriers were going ape-shit. As things were hotting up, the Canadian Government jumped in behind their trappers. It was rumoured at the time that Britain was trying to sell three nuclear submarines to the Canadians and their Prime Minister, Brian Mulroney, eventually wrote and complained to Maggie Thatcher. You can imagine the sort of drivel, no direct mention of cancelling the order of course, but the message was clear. Anyway she fell for it, buckled under the pressure and personally axed the bill as a consequence. It never got off the ground.'

'You're joking,' I said incredulously. 'You mean to say that she went up against one of her senior ministers to keep the bloody armaments industry and fur-trade happy?'

'Yes, and the joke was that the Canadians never did buy the subs. Totally bluffed her out. So don't kid yourself that she's going to be any more sympathetic about tigers. Especially with the Chinese gobbling them up. This government doesn't have the balls to upset Beijing. Don't forget Hong Kong and all that.'

I began to feel decidedly dejected, as one does when the enormity of any obstacle is graphically unveiled for the first time. 'But you guys had a tremendous victory with the ivory ban two years ago,' I said.

'Yeah, but that was only through detailed and meticulously researched investigation, backed up with hard film evidence.'

'But didn't you have a great deal of support from other large groups, WWF for example?' I asked him.

'Hardly,' he said, with thinly disguised contempt. 'They were against us every step of the way. Right up until the middle of the CITES conference in Switzerland, and then they only reversed their position because they knew they were losing.'

'What's CITES?' I asked, with unashamed ignorance.

'The Convention on International Trade in Endangered Species,' he said. 'It's the only global legislation in the world that's supposed to protect endangered wildlife. But don't worry, most people have never heard of it, and even fewer respect it. Nevertheless, it's all we have to work with.'

'Can the EIA get involved with the tiger problem?' I asked.

'Not directly. We are a small organisation and we have to keep focused. At the moment we're fully committed on elephants, rhinos, marine mammals and the bird trade. We don't have the staff to take on anything else.'

'If you were me, where would you start?'

'You've got to look at the trade. Find out who's behind it, who the key players are. Video them in action. Get hold of documents, any scrap of information upon which you can build your case. You've made a good start already. Buy a good camcorder, hide it in a bag, and keep it with you all the time. You never know when you might need it.'

He then went on to describe in detail how to effectively conceal a video camera in a shoulder-bag so that it could operate quietly and without suspicion. Although I didn't realise it at the time, I was getting my first lesson in covert surveillance technique, and from a master of the trade.

Finally he wished me luck and went, leaving me alone with my thoughts. It was the beginning of March. It had become increasingly apparent that, if we were going to help save the tiger, Sophy and I would have to go it alone.

On Saturday March 15th, three months before our planned wedding day, we returned to Thailand determined to get to the bottom of the tiger slaughter, and equally determined to document every step of the way. The main problem was to find the right place to start. It

168

was Sunday afternoon by the time we checked into the Pearl Hotel in Phuket, and I grabbed a copy of the English-language Sunday newspapers as the bell-boy helped take our bags up to the room.

On the front page of one of the papers was a large photograph of a man pictured amongst a gruesome assortment of wildlife trophies including a full-length tiger-skin. His name was Boonlerd Angsirijinda, and the caption told me that he was head of law enforcement at the Wildlife Conservation Division of the Royal Forestry Department in Bangkok. He had a strong, kind face with eyes that conveyed a strange combination of serenity, compassion and depth of character. He had the look of someone that could be trusted, and I resolved there and then to travel to Bangkok and meet him.

Who knows why we chose to return to Thailand on that particular day, or why I picked up just that particular newspaper. Or perhaps why the feature article on Thailand's endangered wildlife and the one man who was crusading to fight the poachers and smugglers appeared on that particular day at all? Nevertheless, these seemingly unrelated facts combined to reinforce my commitment to tiger conservation, because from the very first moment I set eyes on Boonlerd, I knew that I had found the man to help me.

I eventually found his cramped office at the back of the RFD's sprawling compound on Paholyothin Road in Bangkok's Bangkhen suburb. I expected to find him working alone, and was surprised to see that he shared his office with five other people. He was stationed somewhat incongruously in one corner behind three cackling women, one of whom was idly painting her nails when I arrived.

Boonlerd greeted me warmly from behind an ancient and over-laden metal desk that seemed to visibly sag with the mighty weight of thick files and enormous heaps of paperwork upon it. I had hurriedly arranged the meeting over the phone the day before and he had juggled his busy schedule around when I explained who I was and what I wished to discuss with him.

We drove to a small restaurant on the outskirts of town and went upstairs to a quiet room which slowly began to fill with early lunch-goers in need of good food and a discreet place to discuss business.

We talked for over three hours about his work and how he had single-handedly created his own position. It appeared that there was no long tradition of what one might call law enforcement within the RFD, basically because so many senior people were apparently on the take, none of whom had any wish to be discovered.

Despite a logging ban, vast areas of forest were still being felled, some of it well within national park boundaries. I told him that I had video film evidence of deforestation at Khao Sok, but he seemed not in the least bit surprised. Illegal hunting, it appeared, was a by-product of illicit logging; where you had one, invariably you'd find the other. And everybody was at it – government officials, the military, the police – it seemed everyone was out to make a fast buck. Boonlerd's chosen vocation seemed more and more impossible the more we talked.

He told me about the famous weekend market at Chatuchak, and how it was possible to find almost any species of wildlife from Kenyan lion cubs to Amazonian parrots quite openly on sale. Curiously, the market had a similar reputation to that of Harrods in that it could, given time, procure anything from anywhere in the world. And shamefully, Thailand's laws did nothing to prevent it. For over seven years, he told me, he had worked on a legislative proposal to change things, so that foreign species would receive at least the same documentary protection given to those indigenous to Thailand. For seven years he had worked until a change in government had knocked the entire concept back into the dark ages, and he was back to square one.

Boonlerd was a gentle man, he had little political power, he told me, and he had little money, but he had energy, and that was his only major asset in the fight against the illegal traffickers of Thailand's endangered wildlife. His life had been threatened many times, his wife and family intimidated by gangsters, and poisonous snakes had been put in his house. He had been shot at by poachers, and yet somehow had always found the will to carry on.

In those few hours, Boonlerd Angsirijinda made one of the most powerful impacts upon me that any man has ever done in my entire life. I was determined to do anything in my power to help him. He gave me his home telephone number and suggested that in future we meet well away from the RFD headquarters. It was impossible for me not to admire the intensity of the man's drive, particularly in the face of the animosity he must have felt from his working colleagues. From that time on he became my ally and my friend, and I became his.

John Nichol knew Thailand extremely well and had given me a number of pointers and people to contact that might shed light on the dark mysteries of the illegal wildlife trade. I had decided that somehow I must infiltrate the underground dealer network and gain their trust and find out their ways. I couldn't possibly do this from some flop-house in the back-packers' district of Banglamphu, and although the Shangri-La was a luxury hotel, I managed to negotiate a 50 per cent discount through a very good friend in Phuket.

For the next few days, Sophy and I followed up on John Nichol's leads. We had the names of Bangkok's more notorious wildlife traders: Mr Preecha of Pim Chai Birds, Mr Suchin of The Suchino Corporation, Mr Kampang of Bangkok Wildlife and the enigmatic Chanchai Onamphi. He also told us to visit the so-called zoo on the seventh floor of the Pata department store in the centre of town. In addition, we planned to visit the market at Chatuchak, and to follow up on an idea I had about Bangkok's Chinatown. Apart from that we would generally comb the streets looking for whatever clues we could find.

But only after we had called in to see a very old friend of his, who had her finger firmly on the pulse of the big city. Katherine Buri was petite, shrewd and businesslike. Most mornings she would attend the Bangkok stock market buying and selling equities, futures and bonds in vast quantities. By the afternoon session she would return home to tend to her otters for whom she had constructed a bizarre waterway network in her rambling three-acre garden. Hotels, office blocks and apartment buildings overlooked her oasis in the centre of the capital and, despite the traffic noise and pollution, not to mention the vast sums of money that developers had offered for her property, she had steadfastly refused to sell.

Over tea, Katie told us how she had once hidden the famous primatologist Shirley McGreal from gangsters dealing in smuggled orang-utans. Dr McGreal had obtained damaging evidence of their nefarious activities and that one or two quite senior politicians were also implicated. For three weeks she had remained out of sight until she was eventually spirited out of the country and back to America.

Later that afternoon we went to the Pata shopping complex. Nothing, but nothing could have prepared us for the depravity that we witnessed on the seventh floor. In one tiny cage a demented gorilla, frothing wildly at the mouth, gripped the bars and swung his old head back and forth in crazed psychosis. In another, we found a 'white' tiger that was almost black from the filth, pollution and excrement that obviously hadn't been cleaned from its pen in months. Everywhere we looked it was the same. By far the worst example was a polar bear languishing in that heat, without water to either drink or bathe in. When I first saw him I thought he was dead;

171

his apparently lifeless body was spreadeagled in the dirt of his totally inadequate enclosure, and grotesque wounds and callouses disfigured a once proud head. A bullet would have been merciful.

The Pata zoo was owned by the Onamphi family. At least now I knew what type of monsters I was up against.

We left in stunned silence, the stench and horror clinging to our skin like filthy cobwebs. If a place like this was openly on view, what hideous truths were there to be found lurking beneath the surface? Somehow I would have to find the courage to discover them.

The following day we got up early to join a typical tourist tour of Bangkok's floating market. We were collected from the pier at our hotel by a noisy long-tail boat and whisked away at high speed into the *klongs* (maze of tiny rivers) on the other side of the Chao Phraya river. In the narrow streams, dozens of sampans lay side by side, each piled high with brightly coloured fruits, vegetables and dried goods, and all rocking precariously in the swell of the larger boats that raced at high speed through the narrow waters. It soon became apparent that we were not permitted to stop and buy, but merely to look. The tour organisers evidently had their own ideas as to what foreign tourists liked in the way of entertainment.

Eventually we pulled alongside a small jetty with a garishly painted sign that announced to the world in appalling English the presence of men wrestling crocodiles, snake-handlers defying certain death charming highly venomous cobras, and the opportunity to be photographed beside a dangerous and bloodthirsty wild tiger. I held Sophy's hand a little tighter as we clambered ashore.

We first had to run the gauntlet of hawkers plying stuffed cobras, crocodile-skin handbags and elephant-hide boots and shoes before we were introduced to the show. Tourists of all nationalities were made to endure ninety minutes of stupefying bravado as young men put their heads inside the gaping jaws of uninterested reptiles whilst others whacked lethargic cobras over the head in an attempt at eliciting some form of aggressive response.

I watched the faces of the spectators. Many were shocked, some were in awe, mostly they were just bored. Sophy and I wandered off. Eventually, behind a small screen, we found the tiger. Katie had warned us, but the sight of the poor creature was too much to endure. His teeth had been filed down to blunt stumps, his claws extracted from each paw, and what was left could hardly keep its drugged head off the ground, despite repeated prodding from a youth with a sharp stick.

'Photo, mister?' he asked out of the corner of his mouth.

'Not even if my life depended on it,' I said, shaking my head sadly. And we walked back to the boat and sat in the empty bow until the rest of the herd were shepherded back to join us.

'You not like the show?' asked our guide, as if there was something peculiar about us.

'It was bloody awful,' I said with finality. Wisely, he didn't pursue the discussion.

When we got back to the hotel, there was a message waiting at reception.

'Mike. Please telephone my office urgently. Boonlerd.'

It took some time to get through. 'I got your message. What is it?'

'This morning we raided a wildlife dealer. We confiscated three baby tiger cubs. Can you come?'

'Yes, yes,' I said, 'I'm on my way.'

CHAPTER FIFTEEN

Bangkok, March 1991

Boonlerd looked up from behind his desk as I knocked gently on the glass door. His office was strangely deserted and then I remembered the time; it was four-thirty. The journey across town had taken over two and a half hours. Traffic jams in Bangkok were horrendous.

'We were very fortunate today,' he began. 'We were able to make an arrest and confiscate three young tigers. They are very small. We do not know how old. I would like you to see them.'

'I am no expert,' I said, 'but of course, anything that I can do to help.'

'Yesterday,' he went on, 'I received some information that these tigers were to be smuggled on to a ship; they were being kept in a warehouse near the harbour. This morning I took some men and alerted the police. By the time we arrived, the smugglers were already beginning their escape. We were only just in time . . .'

'You mean they were tipped off?'

'Yes, they knew we were coming. It happens all the time.'

'Tell me about the ship,' I said.

'It is a large container ship from Kaohsiung in Taiwan. It is due to return there tomorrow.'

'Taiwan,' I thought, how very interesting. Something that John Nichol had mentioned to me about the animal-smuggling racket was now beginning to make sense. 'How did they intend to get the tigers on to the ship?'

'It's really quite easy. There are many prostitutes that go aboard every night. They often carry all sorts of things for the smugglers.'

'And then what happens, to the cubs, I mean?'

'Normally the ship's cook is involved, because the animals must be fed. That is always the first place to look. But it is difficult to get

175

a warrant to inspect the ships. The Port Customs Authorities are not always that cooperative with my department.'

I could see his problem. There were obviously no end of fat bribes on offer to silence anyone that did hear plaintive squeals coming from the ship's galley. The sheer volume of paperwork and red tape involved would probably be enough to put most officers off the idea. I could also imagine the hookers wiggling their way up the gang-plank late at night, clutching fake Louis Vuitton vanity cases, their terrified contraband hidden deep inside.

Boonlerd had put the three tiger cubs in a straw-filled portable dog kennel. I had never seen cubs this small before; their eyes were only just beginning to open so they couldn't be more than a couple of weeks old; the dried umbilical cord still clung to their swollen bellies. They should never have been taken from their mothers so early. They needed urgent care and attention, otherwise they would be dead in a few hours.

'Have they been fed?' I asked Boonlerd.

'The smugglers had tried to give them chopped beef, but they didn't eat.'

'The fools,' I thought, that was like giving a T-bone steak to an infant child.

'They will need a compound milk formula, with the correct balance of vitamins and minerals,' I said. 'And the swollen bellies look bad. Have they, er, been to the toilet?'

'No, I don't think so,' he said.

'That's very important,' I replied. 'Normally the mother stimulates bowel movement with her tongue. Perhaps we can try with a towel or something later on. In the meantime I had better go to find the correct food. I'll be back as soon as I can.'

I knew that there was a veterinary college about half a mile away on the same road as the RFD, and a kindly old professor hastily scribbled the name of the compound for me in large Thai letters and told me of a specialist pharmacy down town that regularly stocked it. By the time I returned to Boonlerd's office it was getting dark.

That evening, Sophy and I bottle-fed the hungry tiger cubs in our laps. They were quite beautiful. It was an incredible feeling watching them guzzling the warm liquid with huge paws pressed tightly against our hands. Somehow I knew that we were giving them life. Now, at least, there might be a slim chance that they would survive. The gentle rubbing of the towel worked and later, much relieved, the three tiger cubs slept quietly.

It would have been all too easy to have become very attached to the young cubs, and to stay in Bangkok to take care of them. But I realised that they were just the innocent victims of something altogether much larger. Boonlerd had been lucky: this was the second time in less than three years that tigers had been intercepted on their way to Taiwan. I knew that sooner or later I would have to take my investigation there.

On Sunday, Sophy and I met up with Katie Buri at Chatuchak weekend market, and the wildlife section turned out to be everything that we had previously heard about it – and some. It was a crossroads, not only for Thailand's wildlife but, as Boonlerd had explained, species from around the world. We saw domestic species like white-handed gibbons, slow lorises and dusky leaf monkeys mixed with marmosets and golden tamarins from South America. In a small cardboard box I was shown four baby leopard cats.

Everywhere there were exotic birds from all corners of the globe, and in one cramped cage we even found a bizarre example of local exotica: day-old chicks dyed every colour of the rainbow! On the dirt floor in a cramped pen I found four young wallabies, God knows how they got there. There were tight-meshed cages containing snakes and other reptiles, and on the fringe of the market we found vast wads of cash changing hands as fighting cocks tore each other to pieces in a makeshift arena.

Katie explained about the wild animals and birds transported from all over Thailand to arrive here for the weekend. Every week, in the early hours of Friday morning, trains would arrive at the central Hualamphong railway station laden with boxes of poached wildlife from the north and north-east of the country. Poachers and traders in the south took advantage of newspaper and magazine distribution trucks that would otherwise return empty to the capital. The trains coming from Malaysia via Surat Thani were also frequently used, and goods were collected from Thonburi station, south-west of the city centre. The system didn't seem terribly sophisticated to me and would probably be very easy to infiltrate. The biggest problem would be in finding a dedicated corps of individuals able to resist the bribery and corruption endemic to the business. From what I could see, there weren't that many like Boonlerd around.

The export trade had no defined market centre and was therefore more difficult to intercept as exotic species were carefully hidden in remote warehouses before being smuggled aboard departing ships or aircraft. Boonlerd had been extremely lucky with his recent haul. I wondered just how much went undetected, and shuddered at the thought.

I now realised that there were two distinct sides to the tiger problem. On the one hand was the poaching and domestic trading within Thailand. On the other was the demand and illegal smuggling abroad to countries like Taiwan. Within Thailand there was little enough that I could do. I had already witnessed the arrogant disregard of the authorities in Khao Sok, and had seen at first hand the monumental task that poor Boonlerd had taken upon his shoulders. Although there would undoubtedly be areas where the two sides met and crossed over, essentially it was Thailand's sovereign right to do whatever she wished with her own wildlife. Any further overt involvement on my part would be deeply resented by all but a few of the officials in charge, and could land me in very hot water.

The alliance between Boonlerd and myself could not be jeopardised by foolhardy meddling on my part. In future I would channel all my findings within Thailand through him, and trust in his judgement.

Katie had already pointed out what should and what should not be on sale in the way of birdlife at the market. After she left us, Sophy and I went back and together we masqueraded as innocent tourists. I snapped away with a wide-angle lens on my camera as she pointed out one endangered species after another. Through the viewfinder I focused not on my lovely bride-to-be but the dealers and their illicit wares, and they haplessly ignored us as I joked and fooled around. The next day I had the film developed, and the most incriminating photographs enlarged. Over a quiet dinner with Boonlerd at a riverside restaurant that evening, I handed over the evidence and with it took my first step into the clandestine underworld of environmental espionage.

That brief encounter was to be the first of many as we traded information and contacts. Boonlerd had decided to trust me as instinctively as I had put my faith in him. He knew that I had considerably more to lose. This was his country, he knew its language, its ways and its people. He had the right to protest and make political statements. I was technically a guest, on a restricted tourist visa, and could be locked up or deported at the drop of a hat. However, I was a free agent and could come and go as I pleased. I was accountable to no-one, I could fade quietly into the background and that was a strength that I gradually learned to perfect.

It wasn't difficult blending into the ocean of humanity that flows around Bangkok. The city is a bustling metropolis and a favourite destination for millions of tourists every year. The locals have grown accustomed to the strange idiosyncrasies of the *farang* and have mastered the art of separating him from the contents of his wallet. For a novice spy, this was the perfect training ground. Each day I would try a new gambit on an unsuspecting merchant in a different part of town; it was an exciting game of cat and mouse as we both tried to outwit one another.

In England, my phoney accents and cheap disguises would have been transparent and easily exposed. In Thailand, the cosmopolitan atmosphere of the country worked to my advantage and I exploited the Thai's inherent love of foreign exchange to the limits. I was able to practise and develop a number of different characters and very slowly I perfected the art of duplicity until it became no longer a game.

Very early one morning, at a small stationer's offering a same-day service on the Surawongse Road, I arranged for a number of business cards to be printed. Later that afternoon I collected six discreet boxes, each containing a new identity and linked by phone and fax to an accommodation address in London. For some extraordinary reason, in the Far East, an elaborate business card immediately provides the bearer with credibility and authenticates his position in life. I simply invented a few for myself and depending on who, when or what the circumstances required, I would become a banker, a collector of antiques and exotica, a journalist, research scientist or whatever suited the moment. Walter Mitty would have enjoyed Thailand.

In the sprawling Chinatown district I was now able to march confidently into all sorts of shops and enquire discreetly about tiger and leopard skins, explaining that I was a collector or trading on to others in Europe and the United States. I developed a technique that invariably got me taken into some quiet back room or darkened cellar where furs, ivory or, in one case, dried bear paws were produced for me personally. I mastered the technique of extricating myself from negotiations without raising suspicion, and was invariably welcomed back by the traders on subsequent occasions when I needed more evidence to pass on to Boonlerd. I realised that I was slowly perfecting an act, a skill that I would need to rely upon with one hundred per cent confidence when I took my investigations further afield.

After a week or so, I felt that I knew enough about the Thai end of the sordid business to represent myself in Taiwan either as a dealer from Bangkok or, at the very least, one who regularly traded there. An old American economist's homily said: 'When you can no longer impress with statistics, baffle them with bullshit.' It was equally true in the spying game, and I learned how to lie like the best of them.

Boonlerd had also been busy. The courier for the tiger cubs had been thoroughly interrogated and talked extensively about the various zoos and crocodile farms that were secretly breeding tigers for export to Taiwan. Boonlerd had had his suspicions about these places for a long time, but this was conclusive evidence, and he could now proceed and prosecute. I also obtained corroborative evidence in a file containing the details of the Taiwanese container ship and the name of another vessel intercepted in Hong Kong a couple of years earlier.

Boonlerd was sure that he had only managed to scrape the surface of a large and highly profitable tiger-farming operation. On a restaurant napkin one evening we made a rough calculation of what it would cost to feed and care for a tigress for the fifteen weeks of her gestation. He added to that the cost of a stud male, hush-money and other incidentals, and it quickly became apparent that the racket was worth several tens of thousands of dollars. It was obvious that a commercial value had now been put on illegally bred tiger cubs. It was equally obvious that this same value applied to wild tigers, and therefore created an even bigger incentive for the poachers who needed only to go out into the forest and steal them.

Sophy and I decided to return to Phuket to pick up the trail there. We also needed to check up on things in Khao Sok and collect some equipment from the lake.

Whilst in London, there had been some vague film company interest in our work, most notably with ABC Keyne through Oxford Scientific Films. It was evident, however, that we could no longer expect to continue to work in the jungle ourselves and therefore some of our photographic and film kit had become dispensable. It was pointless keeping such valuable cameras when they could be sold and the money used for other essential items. We simply had to come to terms with the reality that our natural history film-making days were numbered. From then on, we would have to use small-format video concealed from view, and hope that some day we might persuade the men with the million-dollar camera rigs to take us seriously.

Back at the Pearl Hotel, there were a collection of messages and faxes for us, one of which jumped out of the pile. It was from a company called Ward & Associates in the United States.

Dear Michael and Sophy,

We are a Washington, DC, based television production company working on an environmental program on threatened and endangered species. We have been talking to the Environmental Investigation Agency's Peter Knights, who showed us your letter to Alan Root. We are very interested in pursuing the tiger story and would like to speak with you as soon as possible, etc, etc.

Best regards,
Kathleen Pearce
Producer

The fax was dated March 23rd, almost a week earlier, and three days after the tiger-cub seizure. I scribbled a quick note asking her to call us back urgently. At about midnight the phone woke me from a light sleep. It was Washington.

'Hello Michael, this is Kathleen Pearce. I hope I didn't wake you up. What time is it there, anyway?'

'It's around midnight. Thanks for calling back,' I said, still feeling half asleep, desperately trying to focus my fuzzled brain.

She explained exactly who she was and what she was up to. Intriguingly she was working with someone called Sam LaBudde from San Francisco, the man behind the dolphin/tuna issue. The very same man that I had talked to Don Watson about over a year before!

'He wants to talk to you,' she said. 'Can I give him your number?'

'You bet,' I said. 'I've been a fan of his for years.'

'OK, let's keep in touch,' she said, and was gone.

Well, I'll be damned, I thought. What a small world. Sam LaBudde had successfully campaigned against formidable commercial and political opposition to bring about dramatic changes in the United States. In October of 1987 his film of dozens of dolphins

181

trapped and drowning in the long-purse seine nets of a Panamanian-registered tuna boat was aired on television news across the United States. This triggered an American boycott of tuna in 1988 and forced the major canneries to change their ways and no longer buy tuna caught in the dolphin-killing nets.

If I could persuade him to help me expose the tiger issue even on one-tenth of that scale . . . I was still thinking about the incredible possibilities when the phone rang again.

'Hi, Michael? This is Sam LaBudde. Kate gave me your number. How are you doing?'

He spoke with intensity and passion about the Ward & Associates' project and was keen to hear exactly what Sophy and I had come up with so far. I explained that it was too early to say for sure, but all things indicated a huge smuggling operation of tigers from Thailand to Taiwan, both wild and captive bred. He was friendly and encouraging, and full of excellent advice, most important of which was to forget the immediate lure of working directly with a television production. This sounded irrational, until he explained that long ago he had tried the same route, namely to interest the media before the event. It didn't work because nobody really took him seriously until *after* he succeeded in obtaining his blockbuster evidence. Then he created what he called a 'feeding frenzy' and had to fight them off!

It all made perfect sense, except Kate had hinted that there might be some advance money to help with the next stage of my enquiries.

'She's incredibly well intentioned, Michael,' he replied, 'but take it from me, these things take time to work out. It could be weeks if not months before it gets off the ground, lawyers have to get involved, program controllers, commissioning editors, you name it. Are you stuck for funds?'

'Well, sort of, since you mention it, yes. The work so far has made a huge dent in my savings and I'm supposed to be getting married in a couple of months!'

'I might be able to help you out. Let me have a list of the things that you need, and I'll have a word with some people I know over here and see what we can come up with.'

I sat on the edge of the bed staring at the phone in my hand. In less than an hour I had received two of the most encouraging phone-calls I could possibly imagine. Somebody, somewhere, was smiling on me again.

The next morning I was still re-living the phone-calls and boring

A three-month-old Siberian tiger cub. Many will be trapped or killed by poachers supplying the Chinese medicine racket (*Michael Day*)

Dwaila's river camp in Khao Sok National Park, Thailand – my home for many months (*Sophy Day*)

Approaching my hide deep inside the Khao Sok National Park (*Sophy Day*)

Sophy holds a panda cub, Wolong, China, 1992 (*Michael Day*)

Now almost fully grown, one of the three tigers rescued by Boonlerd Angsirijinda relaxes on Tiger Mountain in Thailand (*Michael Day*)

Rebecca Chen (*Nick Gray*)

Tiger skins are still traded openly only a stone's throw from the Thai border in the Burmese village of Tachilek (*Sophy Day*)

A rare shot of a Siberian tiger on a wild boar kill (*Michael Day*)

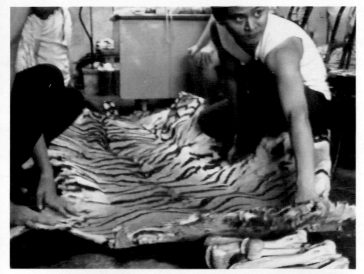

Hard evidence: Mr Wang displays both tiger skin and complete skeleton for my hidden camera (*Michael Day*)

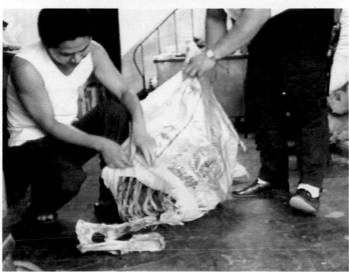

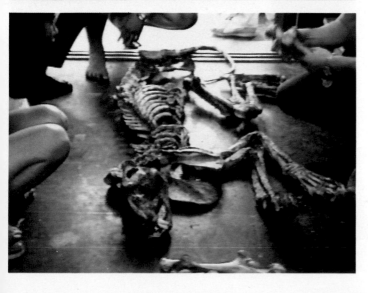

In my office at home, near Newmarket, with a range of tiger bone products (*Cambridge Evening News*)

A tiger poacher flays the bones of a young tigress (*Ron Orders*)

As the sun slowly sets over Tiger Mountain in Thailand, this rescued male slowly blends perfectly into his natural surroundings (*Michael Day*)

More evidence. Foetal embryonic tigers preserved in formaldehyde at a
Chinese tiger farm (*Michael Day*)

A magnificent Siberian male, in full winter coat, is perfectly equipped to
survive the harsh climate of the Russian Far East (*Michael Day*)

Little more than skin and bones, this old male awaits an undignified end at the Heilongjiang tiger farm in China (*Michael Day*)

An Operation Amba ranger holds the skin of a once proud Siberian tiger, Ussurisk, Russia (*Steve Galster*)

Only 180 Siberian tigers remain in the wild. Poaching could wipe them out altogether by the end of the decade (*Michael Day*)

Sophy with every detail as we drove back up the old familiar road to Khao Sok. She was as thrilled as I was, but only needed to be told once. For me, I needed to hear it over and over again, it was almost too incredible to be true.

'You realise what this means,' I said. 'All I have to do is get some evidence on film and they will do the rest. Sam's got the experience, the connections and the clout, and Kate is an award-winning producer. What a team!'

'Yes, but which tree are you going to climb every morning with your video camera on your back waiting for the bad guys to incriminate themselves?'

'I'll climb whatever tree I have to, metaphoric or otherwise,' I replied, somewhat dismayed by her pessimism. 'You know what's going on as well as I do. Don't you think we're both smart enough to catch them with their pants down?'

'Yes, I think *you* are, that's what frightens me,' she said sombrely. 'I know you, Mike, you won't stop until something awful happens.'

'Something awful *has* happened, and whether we like it or not, we are already involved. You knew that when you agreed to come back here.'

'But I never realised that so many terrible people were involved; it's just like the Mafia.'

'That's exactly what it is, darling. It's the bloody Mafia, which is probably why nobody wants to take them on. But they are systematically wiping species off the face of the earth. God knows how many elephants have died across the plains of Africa so that some bastard can make a fortune from the poached ivory. It's happening with the rhino as well. Somebody told me the horn sells for over 10,000 American dollars a kilogram on the streets of Hong Kong. It's hardly surprising with that much money to be made that there are so many people willing to get their hands dirty. Morals evaporate very quickly when there's too much cash around and it's happening right under our bloody noses with the tigers. And from what I've seen, nobody seems to give a damn.'

We drove on in silence for a while. She was frightened, I knew that. It was one thing bringing her here a year ago to face the creepy crawlies and the primitive conditions of jungle life, but this was altogether different. I had declared war on the illegal traders, and foolishly expected her to fight alongside me. It was too much to ask, she had done enough already, and I had no right to expect her to get in any deeper. The hardest part to accept was that she was far more frightened for me than she was for herself. And I had no sure-fire way to comfort her.

'Sophy,' I said, 'I don't know any other way to try and explain this thing to you except to say that you are far more spiritually aware than I am. You know that all this is happening for a reason. All those strange coincidences last year and now all this, meeting up with Boonlerd, the cubs, Sam. There is a pattern, and somewhere inside is a guardian angel keeping an eye on both of us. You have to believe that.'

She just looked across at me, and wiped a tear from her cheek.

'I'll be careful,' I said softly, and leaned across and kissed her.

We stopped in to see Dwaila on the way, but she wasn't at home. Probably up on the lake, I thought. I debated about whether to call in on Aroon, but decided that we could do that later. It was noon already, we had to get to the smelly fishing village and find a boat to rent, visit the tree-hide and raft-houses all before sun-down. It was better to keep on the move.

Rag-head, as we called him, the village head-man, stuck five stubby fingers under my nose as I bargained with him for the hire of his boat. I put up four and he laughed through gold-capped teeth, and we were on our way. His boat was very fast; the engine had been adapted from a Toyota pick-up. There was more than enough horse-power to push us across the lake at thirty knots.

We went to the national park raft-houses first, as I wanted to try and find Boon. Weewat appeared somewhat sheepishly on the mooring as we arrived, and there was a curiously smug look of self-satisfaction on his blubbery face. I thought for an instant that something might have happened with our kit, especially when I spotted the youth with the staring eyes disappear hastily out of sight as I stepped ashore on to the rickety bamboo boardwalk. However, as I unlocked our store-room I could sense that it hadn't been disturbed since our departure. There was a dank, dusty feel to the air and cobwebs everywhere. I quickly found the Pelican case containing the video camera and accessories, and a few other valuables that we had left behind, and re-locked the door. Boon appeared at my shoulder, smiling happily. It was good to see him again. I had a present for him in my shoulder-bag which I thought wise to give to him later. He agreed without question to accompany us to the tree-hide, and it was like old times again as we set off around the headland across the massive expanse of water.

There was no sign of Dwaila's boat at her camp, so we pressed on, up the narrow tributary to the spot where we had first camped and spent all those happy weeks almost a year before. It felt good to be back. Rag-head parked the long-tail deftly in the shade, and Boon, Sophy and myself set off up the hill to inspect the camp. It would be the first time back since we hurriedly shifted the generator before Christmas. There had been little rain since then and the ground was very dry.

If 'the big-boy' was still alive, I would know exactly where to find his tracks, I thought sadly, but today was not the day to be morbid. It was a brief reunion with our old friend Boon who was having a great deal of fun with the Instamatic camera that I'd given him.

As we approached the final brow before the camp, I knew something was wrong, and I bounded up the last few metres. Standing alone at the top, I gazed down in horror at the havoc by the familiar waterhole. There was a blackened and charred void where the tree-hide used to be. The fire had destroyed all but a few strands of plastic tarpaulin which flapped helplessly in the breeze. The branches of the trees were scorched and twisted, and the lighting rigs lay in a smashed and tangled heap on the ground.

I dropped to my knees and bellowed loudly into the hidden canopy above: 'Baaaaaastards.'

Sophy rushed to my side. 'Oh my God,' she cried. And I stood up and hugged her close. 'I knew something like this would happen,' she whispered after a while. 'I just knew it.'

We walked down the slope holding each other tightly, and kicked about in the ruins of our once idyllic tree-house. There was no doubt who had done this, and the sinister message this wanton destruction conveyed. It was a warning, Thai style.

There was no point in going back to Tree-Tops or to Aroon's now. We needed to find someone removed from all this, someone we could trust. And that man was in Surat Thani. 'Acharn', the professor, had said very little but listened a great deal when we had first met at Dwaila's luncheon party all those months ago. His quiet and reserved manner intrigued me and I was sure that it only served to hide a powerful intellect that understood all too well my impassioned ramblings. He was tall for a Thai, with a muscular, well-toned body, and I imagined him as a keen squash player with more than a passing interest in the martial arts. It was his parting words after that briefest of encounters that perhaps encouraged and

185

impressed me the most: 'Don't think for one minute that you are alone in all this, Michael. There are many who feel the way you do. When you are ready, come and see me, and I will do all I can to help you.' It was time, and somehow I knew that he would remember and be there for me. He was that kind of man.

There was nothing salvageable from the fire. I imagined that whoever had done this had already picked over the wreckage of our belongings like vultures.

It was time to leave Khao Sok. I would return to collect our things later, when I felt less like committing first-degree murder. And so Sophy and I turned our backs on a thousand shattered dreams and trudged wearily up the hill to the waiting boat, and the jeep that would eventually take us far away from that evil place.

CHAPTER SIXTEEN

Hong Kong, May 1991

Sam had been as good as his word, I thought, as I gazed out of the aircraft window down on to the South China Sea. Some 2,500 dollars had already been deposited into my bank account by this mystery man on the other side of the world, and another 5,000 was on its way.

I had sent him a laundry list of what I thought we would need from the Wang Thai Hotel in Surat Thani on the night we discovered the burnt-out tree-house. I added a caustic line or two about that as well. Whatever it was I said, it didn't take him long to respond, because less than a week later my bank in London confirmed that the money had arrived. And now I was finally on my way to Taiwan.

It had been a busy few days. That night we met up with the professor, and he introduced us to some local vigilantes who had been making some enquiries of their own following the death of 'the big boy' and were anxious to impart their findings. They were an odd bunch. The leader, a man called Montri, sported an old deerstalker and spoke fondly of his days walking the North Yorkshire moors as an engineering student attending Leeds University. There was an extraordinarily pretty girl called Lek who, from what I could gather, was an illegal immigrant from the Mon tribespeople across the border in Southern Burma. Two teaching colleagues of his from the Surat Thani University were here too, plus three students who listened intently to the hushed proceedings.

'We have found the dealer, the man that bought "the big boy",' said Montri. 'He is a Chinese merchant with a warehouse near the

187

station. We have been watching his premises for some time. We have seen a white Mazda pick-up with the registration number 9467, it belongs to Mr Jouey, coming and going a lot recently.'

'Good work,' I said, and meant it. 'Can you take me there.'

'Yes, we can go later. We also want to show you a restaurant selling wild boar and deer poached from Khao Sok. Also, Dr Manette, the ear, nose and throat specialist, has moved his collection of animals to a new house. He has many more clouded leopards now. We think Jouey supplies them to him through the Chinese trader, although we are not sure.'

'You have been busy. What do you want me to do?' I said, already guessing their answer.

'Acharn tells us that you have a good friend in Bangkok, someone that can be trusted. Please, give this information to him,' replied Montri, with great urgency.

Later that evening we drove north, about forty kilometres outside of Surat Thani, to a remote restaurant on the edge of the forest. The owner had been killed a few weeks earlier in a gang-land shoot-out, and his wife was running his business and, from what I could see, into the ground. The place was almost empty, but a large black-board on one wall had much of the food on offer scrawled in white chalk: bear, monkey, wild pig, barking deer.

We ordered some beer, and whilst the woman disappeared into the back I grabbed my camera and fired off three quick flash photographs of the menu. The place looked like it would go bankrupt of its own accord quite soon, but I knew the poachers would quickly find another to supply. We returned to town and headed out toward the train station.

Just as Montri had said, the anonymous-looking shop-front was only a stone's throw from the railway line. A perfect dropping-off point for all sorts of wildlife on their way to the weekend markets of Bangkok and beyond. We parked close to a line of taxis, and I slipped quietly out of the sliding door of the minibus. The street was quiet as I approached the large wooden gates of Mr Goh Lim's warehouse. I peered over them, straining my eyes and ears for any sign of life. There were large bundles of rattan, almost identical in form to the ones Bun, Newt and I had found a Dwaila's old camp over a year before. Some things never change, I thought. I decided to climb over and get some pictures, and hitched myself higher on to the top ledge of the gates.

From out of nowhere a massive Dobermann bounded frantically

across the yard, snarling and barking ferociously, eyes fixed menacingly on my head. In three great leaps it was upon me and jumped,
its huge mouth snapping wildly into the air. I felt its foul breath on
my face as I frantically forced myself backward from the gates and
fell on to the pavement. From there I could see its feet and vicious
teeth in the gap under the gate, scraping and biting desperately, its
crazed head growling madly, baying for my blood. I crawled away
backwards and stood up. Acharn had started the engine and the
minibus lurched forward, the side-door slid open, and three pairs of
hands grabbed my shirt and pulled me unceremoniously inside and
we sped away into the night.

We drove back to the Wang Thai Hotel. I was shaking with fear
all the way. Any man that keeps a dog like that on the loose
definitely has something to hide, I thought. He would have to be
caught red-handed, and that was the responsibility of the authorities
in Bangkok. I could only point the way.

As we pulled up outside, Acharn said something in rapid Thai to
Montri, touching me gently on the shoulder at the same time. He
obviously wanted a quiet word as Montri told Sophy rather loudly
that he could do with a stiff night-cap.

'Don't worry, darling, I'll be with you in a minute,' I said, turning
back to Acharn.

'Let's walk for a moment,' he said quietly. And we both got out of
the van and wandered away toward the river gardens.

'Mike . . .' he began, 'you've done so much here, we are all very
grateful.'

'Don't be silly,' I said, feeling embarrassed and a mite apprehensive at the same time. 'In a way, I've only just begun; the real fight
lies ahead.'

'Yes, that's what I mean. We think you've done enough. Let us
handle it from now on,' he said gravely.

'You can't be serious, there's so much left to do. Why show me all
these places tonight if you want me to quit?'

'We only decided a few days ago, and this evening . . . Well,
things happened so fast. It's my fault. I should never have taken you
to the warehouse.'

'There's something more, isn't there? It's not just Goh Lim.
You're keeping something back from me.'

He looked away and down at his shoes, his fingers and hands
fidgeting. He rubbed the back of his neck nervously, and then
looked at me with sad watery eyes.

'There could be danger,' he said softly.

'Acharn, my friend, I know there could be danger. You have warned me before. It's part of the work, don't worry. I'll be careful.'

'The danger is more serious now.'

'What do you mean?'

'Your life, somebody want to kill you.'

'What?'

'Somebody maybe try to kill you,' he said sternly, putting his hand firmly on my shoulder and shaking me hard. 'You understand?'

'No, I don't bloody well understand. What do you mean, what is all this about, Acharn. Tell me!'

'I have heard a rumour that someone will pay money to kill you.'

'You mean that there is a price on my head? Jesus Christ, a fucking contract out on me?' I shouted, barely able to control my anger and fear.

'Yes.'

'Do you know how much?'

'10,000 *bhat*.'

'10,000 *bhat*, 400 lousy dollars. Christ!' I said, shaking my head in disbelief. 'What do you suggest I do?'

'Go away from here. Don't come back for some time. Let us fight our own battles.'

I looked at him carefully now. I could see that he was very worried for me. He knew the whole thing had somehow got out of control. Death threats on Thai people were not uncommon; on a *farang* it was serious. First the tree-house, now this.

'Sophy?' I asked, my stomach in a constricted knot.

'No, only you.'

'Well, fuck them,' I bellowed. 'Fuck the lot of them. They are not going to scare me off like this. You find out if this is serious or not. You said it was a rumour, that could be all it is,' I said, clutching at a thin thread.

'Mike, these people are dangerous. Don't go back into the park.'

I could sense that he was backing off. Perhaps it was, after all, just a malicious rumour. I *had* stirred up quite a bit of trouble already, and the superintendent was furious with me. The hell with the lot of them, I thought. If they go to this extreme, they must have something to hide. The only thing to do was bluff them out, and keep Sophy well out of it all. If anything ever happened to her . . .

'OK,' I said, 'we were going back to the lake tomorrow to collect the rest of our things from Weewat. I'll wait awhile with that and get

Sophy back to Phuket. But I'm not giving up on this, I can assure you. I am going to see this bloody thing through, no matter what it takes. Have you got that?'

'Yes, but be careful.'

'Not a word to her about this, please. Otherwise there *will* be trouble,' I said and laughed.

'OK, not a word.'

And we walked back to the hotel in silence.

Montri agreed to come with us back to the Amphoe Phanom police station near Khao Sok the next day, so that we could file an official report on the destruction of our hide. It was a futile gesture, I knew, but we had to get something on record. We had discussed it all earlier. At the time, neither Sophy nor I were prepared to take things lying down, we felt it was time to hit back. If the wrecking of our hide was supposed to be a warning and frighten us away, it had absolutely the opposite effect on us both. I detected an entirely new spirit in Sophy: her resolve, like mine, had been hardened by the incident. She was now as determined as I was not to allow such cowardly intimidation to get the better of us. That was then, now things were different. I could never risk some crazed madman taking a shot at her.

When I met up with her in the bar, she could see that I was troubled, but knew me well enough not to pursue it.

Early next morning we were on the road. The police station was easy to find, sympathy and concerted action a little harder. After two hours with a less than uninterested police lieutenant, we could all see quite plainly that the local authorities were going to be of absolutely no help whatsoever. Finally, we left the Khao Sok area thanking Montri for his kind help and translation, and headed back to Phuket. I felt as though I was running away and I hate that feeling. I would have to bury Acharn's warning away in the back of my mind and forget about it, although that was much easier said than done. If what he said was true, I was now the target for a 'hit'. Something that I'd only read about and seen in films; but me? Surely not.

There were some faxes waiting back at the Pearl, mostly from Kate and Sam. Ward & Associates were now in discussion with both Fox Television and National Geographic's Explorer series, and really pushing hard. Things were beginning to look fairly promising.

I thought, not for the first time, what a great shame it was that none of the British networks had shown any solid interest in our work. Anglia Survival had an unwritten policy of rarely including presenters in their productions, and the BBC went over the top in

191

the other extreme and featured the same old faces in every imaginable setting, however incongruous they might appear. The concept of the investigative reporter in wildlife documentaries seemed to be anathema to the programme controllers back home in the UK. A great pity, because Great Britain had a well-earned and solid international reputation in world and current affairs chronicles like *Panorama, Horizon, Assignment* and *First Tuesday*.

There was a message to call Boonlerd at home, and I wondered if he had heard about our tree-house.

'Michael, when are you coming back to Bangkok?'

'Not for a day or two,' I replied. 'Is there something wrong?'

'Yes, perhaps. We raided another dealer this morning, but were too late. He had three more tiger cubs but he got away.'

'Tipped off?' I asked foolishly.

'Maybe you know the answer already,' was all he could say.

'I'm sorry,' I said. 'Sophy and I have had a bad few days. I think I'd better bring my plans forward and get over to Taiwan quickly. I'll call you when I get to Bangkok.'

Sophy was giving me one of her sad, dewy-eyed looks. I could tell what she was thinking. I had no training for this type of work. I wasn't a soldier or a detective, let alone a spy. We were both making up the rules as we went along, and clutching at straws wherever we could find them. The fact of the matter was that there was no international body we could turn to. Interpol was not interested in wildlife smuggling, and all our letter-writing back in England had produced little in the way of cavalry. Endangered wildlife, it became all too clear, was being left to the mercy of the poachers and smugglers and the ingenuity and courage of people like Sam and the EIA to stop them.

Like it or not, we were being drawn into the arena to champion the cause of the tiger, for no other reason than that there was nobody else prepared to do it. Sure, there were the massive international groups like IUCN and the WWF but, as we were rapidly discovering, it was their complacency that had allowed the situation to get out of hand in the first place. If they did get involved, it was always to take the path of least resistance which normally involved endless report-writing, futile workshops and, almost inevitably, a new fund-raising proposal. The tiger's survival was being threatened simply by basic schoolboy economics and the inequalities of supply and demand. There were not enough tigers to go round and yet demand was increasing. That forced up the price, tempting more people to make a fast buck. It was quite obvious where that path would lead, even the odious notion of captive breeding to meet some of the demand was fundamentally flawed. And yet time and time again we read articles by eminent scientists advocating one crack-pot idea after another. Nobody, it seemed, had the guts to take the bull by the horns and drag the whole sickening issue out into the glare of the public spotlight, except us. And we hardly knew where to begin.

It was years since I'd been to Hong Kong, and the final approach over the roof-tops of Kowloon was still as spectacular as ever. How these enormous aircraft navigated their way across the high-rise apartment blocks was an absolute miracle of engineering, and the Cathay Pacific Boeing 747-300 touched down perfectly.

I'd often thought that Hong Kong Central's skyline must have been conceived and designed during a monumental night on the bottle by the Colony's otherwise staid city planners. Each spectacular building, towering majestically into the clouds, seemed to compete with the next for originality of concept and form. And yet they all blended wonderfully together and formed one of the most breathtaking architectural landscapes in the world.

From my room on the forty-ninth floor of the Island Shangri-La I gazed in awe out across the harbour to the horizon and mainland China beyond. Great buzzards swooped and dived, caught in invisible thermal air currents that lifted them high into the air and out of sight.

Somewhere here in Hong Kong I hoped to pick up the trail of the three tiger cubs that had slipped through Boonlerd's net a few days before. We were both quite certain that they would pass this way, almost certainly en route to Taiwan. But as I looked out over the densely populated expanse of concrete below me, I wasn't sure quite where to begin.

David Melville, the bureau chief for the local WWF, shook my hand warmly and gestured for me to take a seat in his cramped office.

'I bring you greetings from Boonlerd,' I began.

'How is the old bugger?' he enquired with a wry grin. The tone was set and we both relaxed.

David was forty-something; it was hard to tell as most of his face was covered in a dense, curly brown beard. He was what they used

193

to call an old China hand. He knew the territory, the people and their ways. He knew what they got up to and therefore what they got away with. He understood Hong Kong's strengths and her shortcomings. All this was blatantly apparent after only a few brief minutes of conversation. My problem was getting him to share some of his closely guarded secrets with me. I didn't succeed.

WWF has a very close alliance with an organisation called TRAFFIC (Trade Records Analysis of Flora and Fauna In Commerce), a semi-autonomous network based in Cambridge and inextricably linked with the IUCN in Switzerland. TRAFFIC is mandated with the task of monitoring trade in wildlife, both legal and otherwise, and periodically reporting within the so-called WWF/IUCN 'family'. Much of this data never sees the light of day and what does is so severely edited and watered down it scarcely raises the eyebrows of those that read it, least of all the hard news hungry magazine and newspaper editors, but that's probably the intention. It is an excellent organisation full of very talented people who, for some reason best known to themselves, fail to share their findings openly and honestly with the outside world. Internal tampering with sensitive information is endemic to the system, and the wildlife of the world continues to suffer as a result.

Most senior WWF/IUCN personnel sign a confidentiality clause in their employment contract, and David Melville was no exception. What little snippets of information he did impart failed to provide the breakthrough I was so desperately looking for. As I stepped out into the blinding afternoon sunshine I thought, and not for the first time, what a curiously dark and secretive cloud envelops much of the wildlife conservation movement.

Of course, as far as *they* were concerned, I was just full of piss and vinegar and naïve ideology. But for me the equation was as simple as it was unfair. On the one side were the poachers, the dealers, the smugglers and the corrupt officials, and on the other were the innocent unsuspecting animals without a voice and therefore unable to fight a square battle. I was merely trying to redress that imbalance by exposing the people responsible. However, from what I'd witnessed so far, there was a distinct lack of support for my no-nonsense approach. I resolved to try and be a little more diplomatic in future, although I suspected that even that wouldn't be enough to break through the thick blanket of complacency that shrouded the established conservation movement.

I rode the MTR, the local underground train, across town and

194

under the Bay to Kowloon, the densely populated home to the majority of Hong Kong's six million ethnic Chinese inhabitants. Once there I wandered around from Tsim Tsa Tsui near the harbour to Mong Kok in the north. At almost every Chinese pharmacist I saw products made from tiger body parts, dried tiger penises, pieces of rhinoceros horn, bear gall-bladder and, in the tourist shops, elephant ivory as far as the eye could see.

David had explained that, despite the international ivory ban, which his organisation had shamelessly opposed right up to the last minute at the 1989 meeting of CITES in the Swiss mountain resort of Lucerne, Hong Kong dealers were still allowed to trade in the product under what was arcanely referred to as 'the grandfather clause'. This stupendous loophole provided the perfect cover for a massive laundering operation of un-cut ivory from the Southern African states for those wishing to exploit it.

A very similar situation prevailed with tiger products. Whilst I already had evidence of a thriving export market in live cubs from Thailand, I also knew that bizarre and archaic medicines made from tiger body parts were also readily available in Bangkok's China-town. Technically at least, the export of these products was against the rules of CITES. David had explained that that simply wasn't the case in Hong Kong. Once a dead tiger had been converted into something else – fortifying wine, virility pills, potions against devil possession etc. – it could enter Hong Kong with impunity. To all intents and purposes, tigers could even be smuggled out of Thailand and into Taiwan, fattened up and slaughtered, their body parts then manufactured into quack medicines, and then quite legally imported into the Colony. The evidence of that devastating loophole was all around me, and until the law was changed, the dreadful commerce would continue.

Over the next few days I hastily arranged meetings with various people in Hong Kong known for their concern for endangered wildlife. A picture began to emerge that seemed to square with my worst fears. The local government authority empowered with wildlife and CITES matters, the Ministry of Agriculture and Fisheries, appeared to have little domestic political will or outside British government support to pursue the 'in-transit' trade with too much vigour.

I had in my possession confidential documents detailing an exchange of information between the Thai and the Hong Kong authorities over the confiscation of tiger and bear cubs two years earlier. Her Majesty's Government, it appeared, couldn't even come up with the miserly amount of cash necessary to build a suitable holding area for confiscated wildlife, and yet they were about to leave $25 billion in the kitty for the Chinese when Hong Kong reverted to China in 1997! For years, the unfortunate victims of the trade had been sent to the Sha-Tin kennels, known locally as 'Belsen', and from there frequently died or mysteriously disappeared. No photographic journalist had been allowed inside the place for years.

Such was the fate of the confiscated young tigers and bears which languished at 'Belsen' for months on end. As the fax and telex messages bounced backwards and forwards across the South China Sea from Thailand to Hong Kong, with no side wishing to take responsibility for the poor creatures, one dark night they were spirited over the border to China, supposedly on a 'permanent loan' basis and never heard of again. It was hardly surprising from then on that customs officers and inspectors from 'Ag. & Fish' were reluctant to intervene whenever they heard plaintive whimpering from the depths of a transient cargo-ship after that fiasco.

I learned of local triad involvement in smuggling from the Chinese mainland when Hong Kong businessmen wished to impress clients with the grandiose display of barbecued tiger cub at private banquets. These same gangs were also involved in smuggling heroin concealed in baskets of highly venomous snakes destined for a similar undignified end. In May of 1991 it appeared that the illegal wildlife trade was alive and flourishing in the Colony, and few people were prepared to rock the boat. At that time, those that suspected the tiger was in critical danger of extinction either weren't being heard or, for their own perverse reasons, they were keeping very quiet. When I found out the truth, I thought to myself, I was going to shout it from the hill-tops and the hell with those who might try and stop me.

My camera repairman in Phuket, a wonderful chap called Virot with an unfortunate squint, had given me the name of his contact in Hong Kong along with 1,000 dollars in cash in exchange for the Panasonic MS1 which he readily bought from me. I had left one or two messages for Mr Wong Kwok Hung and one afternoon he called me back.

'Hello, Mr Day,' came a timid voice over the phone, 'this is Mr Wong here.'

'Well, good afternoon, thanks for calling back, please call me Michael.'

'Eh, Mr Michael, what can I do for you?' he enquired politely.

'I'm looking for a rather special type of camera. Virot in Thailand said you might be able to help. Something called a lipstick camera.'

'Ah yes, I think I can help you. Can you come to my office?'

Immediately I laid eyes on him Wong Kwok Hung reminded me of that wonderful Cambodian journalist in the film, *The Killing Fields*. He was physically, I suppose, about the same build, typically short, thirtyish, thin but with an agile wiry frame. He was dressed in well-worn, almost shabby, trousers, a short-sleeved white shirt and a plain blue tie slightly askew. He shuffled, rather than walked, his cheap leather shoes badly scuffed and in need of a polish. Attached to his belt was the paging device so ubiquitous in the Far East, and in an old canvas shoulder bag he kept his battered mobile phone, bound up with tape from years of excessive use.

After our first meeting we were friends, it was as easy as that. I told him exactly what I needed and I told him why. Perhaps that's what made him trust and like me. My instincts normally were to be evasive and cagey, giving little away about my real motives and mission, but Wong has never betrayed that trust. It was he who eventually found the vital photographic equipment that enabled me to become a spy.

The next day, Wong arrived at my room with a plain carrier bag containing a small package. He laid the contents out on the bed. The name 'lipstick' aptly described the tiny camera which must have been no more than three inches long and less than half an inch in diameter. This miniature video device was originally designed to be used in factory assembly lines to monitor the work of robots or other pieces of sensitive machinery from the comfort of a television monitor some distance away. However, undercover operators quickly realised that it could be adapted, modified and subsequently concealed for use in covert film work. The SAS and security agencies in the United Kingdom used them, as well as the CIA in the United States and the former KGB in Russia; in fact anyone who needed a perfect television image used them to silently and secretly record on video whatever found itself within range of the camera's almost invisible lens. Provided, of course, that they could get hold of one and had the requisite amount of cash.

It is a little-known fact, but the second largest American Embassy in the world is in Thailand. The largest is Cairo. That way, the two most volatile areas of the world are adequately covered by what is quaintly described as the CIA footprint. Each day, some five hundred or so US citizens of one security clearance category or another cross through its elaborate surveillance system in Witthayu Road opposite the famous Lumphini Park and boxing stadium in central Bangkok. Dotted around the capital there are other less conspicuous buildings that serve as perfectly adequate blinds for dozens of highly trained and specialist individuals on assignment in the area to monitor the activities of the entire Asiatic Far East for their masters back in Langley, Virginia. Boonlerd's secretive world brought him in contact with one or two of these people, and through him, I had come to know of the existence of such essential tools of the trade as the lip stick camera.

As I looked at the amazing device being put through its paces with great excitement by my new friend Wong, I wondered what on earth I was letting myself get into. Thus far, things had been relatively easy, a gentle bit of snooping around, nothing too strenuous or potentially damaging. But now I was looking at a blatant piece of spying equipment. Although I tried, I couldn't imagine talking my way out of a situation if I was caught using the thing. And yet its power and potential were magnetic.

I was fascinated by the camera, although I hadn't yet received the money to pay for it and was loathing the prospect of disappointing my new friend.

'Not to worry,' he said. 'Take it, you can pay me tomorrow.'

'No, I couldn't possibly. Besides, how do you know you can trust me? I could check out of the hotel tonight and you'd never see me again.'

'Would you do that?' he asked with a sad lilt to his voice.

'No, of course not.'

'Yes, I know that. Keep it. Phone me when you have got the money.'

And he was gone. I had only known the man less than forty-eight hours and yet he left me with a piece of valuable camera equipment worth over $4,000.

Two days later I had settled the debt, packed my incriminating hardware as unobtrusively as possible in my shoulder-bag and headed out to Kai Tak Airport on my way to Taiwan. I was worried about travelling alone. Although I had already prepared an elaborate story for the customs officials in Taipei and had arranged an overnight printing of a business card identifying me as an 'electronics engineer' for 'Precision Assembly Surveillance Ltd' with offices in London, New York and Hong Kong, I nevertheless would feel much happier going through the system with someone.

And then I spotted her. Across the departure lounge a stunningly attractive Chinese girl was looking forlornly at the China Airlines check-in desk above which a sign flashed 'CA 765 Taipei. GATE CLOSED'. She had obviously just missed her flight, because she then ran over to the Cathay Pacific desk waving her ticket frantically. I watched as the check-in clerk shook her head.

The two airlines run hourly departures to Taipei and normally the tickets are perfectly interchangeable. This particular evening, however, things were well over-booked with long waiting lists for all remaining flights.

'You miss your flight?' I asked in the friendliest manner I could muster.

'Yes, and now I don't know how I shall get home. Everything is booked solid,' she said in slightly accented English.

'May I see your ticket?' I said, trying not to sound too official, and wondering whether I'd be able to read, let alone understand, it.

She handed me the travel document. Mercifully it was printed in English; it was a standby, space-available-only ticket issued to airline employees and those in the know.

'Are you a stewardess?' I asked.

'No, I work for a courier and freight company, Air Express International.'

'Maybe I can help. Will you watch my bag for me, I won't be a minute?'

And, still clutching her ticket I strode off purposely toward the Cathay Pacific ticket office. 'Please, you just have to help me,' I began. 'My girlfriend and I have simply got to get back to Taipei this evening. She has only just started a new job in the airline business and her boss will be furious if she is not at work bright and early tomorrow.'

'Let me see the ticket, sir,' she said helpfully. 'Ah yes, this is a restricted-use ticket. May I see yours, please?' I handed over my documents. 'I see you are travelling business class and we have just one seat available in that section. If you would like your friend to up-grade, that will be another, let me see, HK$575.'

'Done!' I said, handing over six 100 dollar bills. And with that she re-issued the ticket for the seat next to mine on the flight leaving less than an hour later.

I walked back to the girl, smiling happily.

'Here,' I said, 'all arranged. Your flight leaves in one hour. By the way, my name's Michael, Michael Day.'

'I'm Rebecca, Rebecca Chen,' she said. Although I already knew that.

CHAPTER SEVENTEEN

Taiwan, May 1991

De-planing, as the Americans so quaintly put it, was an anxious ordeal as I fell into step with the thronging mass trudging wearily up the gangway. I carried Rebecca's cabin bag into the arrivals hall where dozens of passengers were already queuing up at the immigration desk. I had to stand in line in front of the sign marked 'Tourists and Foreigners', whilst she skipped neatly over on to the fast track reserved for citizens of Taiwan. We had agreed to meet at the luggage carousel if we lost contact. She gave me an embarrassed wave and a shrug that said, be patient.

The young bespectacled android looked at my visa, looked at me, tapped my passport number into his computer, adjusted his spectacles a fraction as he gazed at the screen, looked back at me, rubber-stamped an empty page with bright blue ink and handed back my documents without so much as a smile or a word. Welcome to Taiwan, I thought; now for the customs check.

I looked across at my ragged and rather tatty suit-bag as it tumbled out from the luggage conveyor-belt on to the carousel with a disconsolate thud. An old lady shoved me aside as she made a lunge for her gleaming blue and black Samsonite suitcase which had fallen with a crash before it. As I regained my balance, I watched my own bag disappear out of reach into the distance as the aged woman heaved her bulky possessions on to a waiting trolley. Rebecca had three matching bags, which I recognised from Hong Kong. As I glanced around, three seemed about the average for the Taiwanese. Perhaps much luggage meant much face, I didn't know. My spy-camera had passed through the security checks in Hong Kong without comment and as I loaded up a baggage wagon as unobtrusively as possible with Rebecca's bits and pieces, I prayed that Taiwanese Customs would also give them the most perfunctory of looks.

'This way,' said Rebecca, tugging at the handle-bar. 'Follow me.'

'Anything you say,' I replied, and zigzagged the squeaking cart through the crowds in her wake.

'*Ni ha*!' She said to a smiling young customs officer, resplendent in an immaculately pressed navy uniform, and launched into a torrent of Mandarin that I couldn't even begin to comprehend.

Finally he looked at me and said. 'Enjoy your stay in Taiwan, Mr Day,' and we were through, waving goodbye and thanking this courteous lieutenant as the electric doors to the arrival lounge engulfed us with a satisfying swoosh.

'Who was that?' I asked in surprise.

'That's my friend Anthony from school,' she said. 'He normally works with the marine customs, this is all part of the training programme.'

Anthony and Rebecca! No Wongs or Mai-Lees here as yet, I thought.

'Does everyone have a western name?' I asked.

'Mostly the young people, yes. My Taiwanese name is much too difficult to pronounce,' she replied with a grin.

We said goodbye as her parents came across to greet her, and agreed to keep in touch over the next few days. She had been interesting company on the flight; she was bright, and talked much about her work and friends. It seemed impossible to equate this vibrant, fun-loving young person with a people that ate tigers. It didn't make any sense. From what I'd seen of the Taiwanese so far, although they were somewhat abrupt to our way of thinking, they seemed to be a decent enough bunch. Hardly the type that would sit down around a banqueting table and gnaw away on a tiger bone. However, first impressions can be deceptive at times. I'd just have to find out.

In the expansive hall, a noxious and suffocating odour hit my nostrils like a cloud of stale fug. It came in waves, a stifling stench that caught in the back of my throat like burning pepper and then it was gone. Over the weeks to come, I was to notice that smell time and again, and yet try as I might I could never identify its source. Some say it is the scent of China and that could be true, for I have never noticed it anywhere else in the world.

Chiang Kai-shek airport was in dire need of a facelift, I thought, as I scanned around for a suitable hotel tout. I veered off toward the information desk as a dishevelled looking individual with a serious case of dandruff presented himself at my side.

'Are you looking for a hotel, sir?'

'No, I was rather hoping to spend the night here in this delightful lounge,' I said, testing his mettle.

'My name is Mike Tey,' he persisted.

'No, I'm supposed to say that,' I said automatically, and at the same time unable to believe my ears.

'I'm sorry?' he said, looking quizzically up at me.

'Actually my name is Mike Day,' I said. 'How did you know that anyway?'

'I don't understand,' he said, offering me his business card. 'My name is Mike Tey, and I work for the Cosmos Hotel, a very good hotel in down-town Taipei. Very good, very cheap, I give you very special discount.'

Here we go, I thought, just the man for the job. I was looking for a tout. I wanted to find somewhere unobtrusive, a place where I would just blend into the background with all the other transient visitors, a place to hide. As I looked at his name-card, the extraordinary coincidence was just too much to resist.

'OK, Mr Tey, how much is your hotel?'

'Normally, 1,800 New Taiwan dollars, but I give you a thirty per cent discount.'

Some 1,200 or thereabouts, I thought, 50 American, a snip if it's clean and comfortable. If it wasn't, there would be plenty more to choose from tomorrow. I was too tired to haggle. 'Done,' I said. 'Do you have a car?'

I waited a few minutes whilst he scouted around for more prey until, finally, just the two of us clambered aboard his severely beaten and battered mini-van and careered into town.

Mike Tey couldn't drive. At least not by any rules that I'd ever known. Gears crashed, lights flashed and tyres screeched as he manhandled the vehicle on and off the motorway hard shoulder. The Taiwanese drive on the right, although it's unwise to rely on that, especially if people like Mike Tey are coming in the opposite direction. Quite how we arrived in one piece outside the foyer of the Cosmos Hotel on Chunghsiao West Road, opposite the Hilton, without killing anyone en route I shall never know. But we did and I lived to tell the tale. Later, I was to discover that Mike was quite a considerate driver by Taiwanese standards. Another object lesson is not always taking things in this enigmatic land as they might first appear.

It was here, on the island of Taiwan, and in the murky under-world that sustained it with smuggled goods from the Chinese mainland, that I would have to look to find the truth behind the illegal tiger trade. And as I unpacked my spy camera on to the candlewick bedspread of my incommodious lodgings on the fif-teenth floor of the Cosmos Hotel, I thought with fearful trepidation of what might happen if I wasn't very, very careful indeed.

For two days and nights I walked the streets; watching, listening, photographing and filming the sights and sounds of the city. The lipstick camera stayed well hidden in my room and I used a Nikon and an innocuous Canon Hi8 video to record the prodigious quantities of endangered wildlife on offer throughout the town. For two whole days I bounced faxes across the Pacific Ocean and the continental United States to Sam in San Francisco and Kate in Washington. My message was always the same:

This is it. This is the end of the line. I've found the Necropolis and I can't believe my eyes.

On the third day I telephoned Rebecca. I wanted her to see things through my eyes. I needed some rationale, a native's perspective.

We met in the lobby of the hotel and walked out into the stifling afternoon air. Taipei, it appeared, was a city under siege. It was hostage to the relentless onslaught of construction. An elevated express public transport system was being built and the roads below it were in a constant state of chaos. The ground shook with the continuous pounding of pile-drivers, and huge mechanical diggers prodding the ground like giant yellow storks searching for food. Dusty clouds rose from the sweltering asphalt leaving filthy black stains in the white lint face-masks of the traffic-cops that bravely tried to keep order in the dangerously polluted air. Aluminium-panelled buses, windows darkened with dark blue translucent film, thundered by, belching thick smoke into the mouths of a thousand pedestrians that clogged the narrow pavements and overhead walkways.

'How can you live in this?' I asked her incredulously.

She just shrugged as if it were all part of the everyday trials of life in the capital, and we walked on, away from the immediate mayhem, past the sprawling central railway station and west towards the Tanshui river and the old part of town around Ti-hwa Street.

This bustling part of the city was a vestige of the rampant smuggling days of the fifties when Chiang Kai-shek's one and a half

204

million expatriate Chinese craved the dried seafood, mushrooms and fruits of the mainland. Here, as in many similar centres up and down the island, tons of illicit foodstuffs would arrive in bulk to be repackaged and then redistributed throughout Taiwan with complete impunity. The authorities never intervened; for them it was a question of '*mei yi si*', or, can't be bothered. They liked to eat well too! The narrow covered pavements were alive with people and produce spewing out from the open shop-fronts. The smell of sun-dried shrimps, squid and a plethora of brightly coloured seeds and chillies filled the air.

It would have been easy to miss the more sinister contraband, hidden as it was in this dazzling bazaar. Nevertheless, in open view for the world and my camera to see were the grisly remains of countless dead tigers, rhinos, bears and a host of other exotic species from the rest of Asia and beyond. In that single afternoon we counted over a dozen shops brazenly selling tiger bone, notably the femur or thighbone. We saw tiger skulls, stuffed baby cubs, skins and teeth, but the most sickening sight of all was the dried genitalia, believed by those who ingest it to be good for sex. A shudder went up my spine as I thought of the once proud tigers that had been callously slaughtered because of such utter nonsense.

Perhaps that's why 'the big-boy' really died, so that some pathetic old has-been could make a fool of himself in the boudoir of a ten-dollar whore.

Rebecca confessed that she'd not been in this neighbourhood since she was a child and found the wares on offer as distasteful as I did. Nevertheless she was defensive of her countrymen and wouldn't accept that they were responsible for the slaughter. She argued that the tigers were already dead and the merchants only traded in their by-products. She further reasoned that, for the vast majority of Chinese, all species of flora and fauna existed solely for the benefit of mankind. That every animal, insect and bird had some utilitarian value whether it be food, medicine, clothing or ornament.

It was time to prepare the spy camera. Over the last forty-eight hours I'd given a lot of thought as to how I could conceal it effectively. Wong had suggested that I take a good look around me, choose something unobtrusive and hide it in the least conspicuous place, somewhere no-one would ever dream of looking. I didn't quite take all of his advice, and bought myself a straw hat, a large blue bandanna, a set of miniaturised tools including a soldering iron, and locked myself away high above the streets of Taipei, and went to work.

Around Ti-hwa Street were a number of fabric shops and haberdasheries and I had carefully selected some ornate brass buttons, feathers and other bits and pieces of suitable costume jewellery. Once back in my room I matched the various items to the front of the hat until I was satisfied that I could create the J.R. Ewing look and then painstakingly began the arduous task of boring out the imitation gold plaque behind which I hoped to successfully hide the camera.

The delicate operation took over six hours, as the hole had to be perfectly symmetrical and fit the camera lens to within a minute fraction of an inch. Time and time again I blew away the golden dust and shavings from the tiny aperture and compared the two vital component parts up against the light. Each time I returned to my work with the delicate metal file that I had bought especially for the purpose. Finally I was satisfied and with trembling hands set about burning a tiny hole through the straw hat with the soldering iron. The smell reminded me of the stubble fires after the harvest at home on the farm of my childhood, all those thousands of years and miles away.

The lipstick camera had a miniature bracket which I loosely attached to the inside of the top of the hat, upside-down and just behind the little brown hole and I peered through. The alignment was spot on. With great care I firmly attached the four miniature black screws and the spy camera was finally in place. With a small dab of contact adhesive I pressed its outer rim hard up against the inside of the blackened orifice and held firmly until I was confident that the glue had set fast. Satisfied, I ran the camera's delicate transmission cable around the inside of the hat and sewed it tight with a needle and thread.

All that remained now was the hard part: the Dallas-look to the front.

Wong's sister-in-law, Cecilia Lau, was an extraordinarily talented make-up artist. One evening, as I was sitting patiently beside Wong as he ripped a perfectly good Sony handycam to bits trying to get at the vital recording mechanism, she arrived in a flurry, straight off the set of some ghastly kung-fu epic. We got to talking over some drinks and it quickly became apparent that Cecilia shared Wong's fascination for what I was hoping to achieve. Mostly for fun, but also as an object lesson in deception, she decided to administer a few tricks of her trade in order to disguise my appearance. We sat in front of an oval mirror and from her large make-up box she produced powders and liners, pastes and creams and a hideous fake moustache. By the time she was finished I had aged twenty years and my face looked sallow and worn. From a rack in the hall she found a battered old trilby and plonked it on top of my head; from her top pocket she produced a pair of wire-rimmed spectacles which she perched on the end of my nose. The transformation was remarkable. I was virtually unrecognisable to myself and an idea slowly began to take shape behind the extraordinary disguise.

And now, as I looked at the crest of feathers that I had laid out behind the brass plaque on the front of the hat, that image suddenly took on an entirely new spirit. I could become the aged Texan billionaire. From my wash-bag in the bathroom I found the various essentials that Cecilia had given me, and I touched each one in turn. I smiled at my reflection in the mirror as I slowly realised how I could make my impossible mission work.

The solitude of the hat project gave me a lot of time to consider the full implications of what I was getting myself into and how, if at all, I could involve Rebecca. She was in her late twenties, gainfully employed in the airline freight business earning a reasonable salary, still living at home with her parents and waiting for Mr Right. She had a happy circle of friends and a loving family, many of whom kept firm ties with the mainland. I was aware of just how easily my own personal mission in Taiwan might be misinterpreted. I was there, after all, to spy. To expect any Taiwanese citizen to collaborate with my endeavours would be asking them to betray their country. It was easy to draw parallels with England, and it would have taken a very brave English girl indeed to collude with a Chinese undercover agent looking into fox-hunting or hare-coursing in the wilds of Suffolk.

Rebecca had no previous experience of detective work, and why should she cooperate with me? She grew up learning that man was the supreme predator and exercised his free will over the animal kingdom, taking what he needed for himself or for trade. The concept that wildlife existed for its own sake was anathema to her forefathers, and to the vast majority of the Chinese people. Somehow I had to balance this with the reality of what was going on outside of Taiwan as a direct result of the continuing demand on places like Ti-hwa Street. Somehow I had to get her to understand that if that trade persisted, tigers would be wiped off the face of the planet forever, and her people would have to live with the blame and the consequences. Taiwan's lax wildlife laws had permitted a flourishing black market to blossom, and grow almost to the point that it was out of control.

She told me of a recent incident reported in the newspapers of a family dumping a juvenile orang-utan on the steps of a department store because it had started to wreck their home. This prompted some public debate, and it transpired that there were perhaps a thousand of these great apes on the island, every one of which had been illegally imported from Borneo and Malaysia. Baby orangutans had become instantly fashionable following the broadcast of an American soap opera where the lead family kept one as a pet. Smugglers cashed in on the fad, and the authorities did nothing to prevent them. Infant apes, however cute and cuddly they may be, grow up with an urge to move around and the living-room of a cramped apartment is not the ideal place for that to happen. Abandoning the creature on the street was one family's solution and that, inevitably, led to an epidemic of maladjusted primates being foisted on to the country's embryonic animal welfare groups. And one hell of a headache it had turned out to be, by all accounts.

In Rebecca, there was without doubt the makings of a shrewd and committed foot-soldier. I decided to test her out and see how she got on. I need not have worried. She was a natural, and she took to the task like a duck to water.

We sat in the coffee-shop on the ground floor of the Cosmos, a foolscap writing pad in front of me littered with expansive diagrams, doodles and calculations that I generally used when trying to make myself understood in foreign lands. I sketched a large wire basket and a cauldron to explain how Koreans preferred to boil their bear cubs alive before disembowelling them and chopping off their paws. And, as if in a bizarre game of one-upmanship, Rebecca produced a magazine article containing a series of photographs taken in Taiwan a few years earlier of a tiger strung upside-down in a cage, its head pulled through a large gap in the bars by a gawping youth with a stout rope. In the most gruesome shot, its throat had been slashed wide open and the young tiger was bleeding slowly to death into a plastic bucket. I shuddered as I held the folded piece of paper and shook my head in disbelief.

'Where did you get this?' I asked, still shocked by the graphic illustration and horror of the execution.

'My friend gave it to me. We were talking about tigers in the office yesterday, and she asked me whether I knew that this still went on. I had no idea. You were right all along, Mike. I'm sorry if I didn't believe you.'

We talked for a while, and it was plain to see that her mind was in turmoil. I had deliberately opened her eyes to something that was, for most people, better left unseen. All around us there are atrocities of one sort or another if only we care to investigate. Ninety-nine per cent of the population cleverly insulate themselves and never notice a thing. But that doesn't mean these things don't exist. They are real enough and as long as they remain undiscovered they will, by definition, never be exposed. It never ceased to astonish me, the levels to which some individuals would stoop in order to make a buck; child prostitution and barbarity to animals being the most vile to my way of thinking.

I eventually asked Rebecca if she would agree to do a little snooping around for me.

'What do you want to find?' she asked, clearly interested by the prospect.

'Well, we've already found considerable evidence of dead tigers. I want to now see if we can find some live ones, preferably for sale.'

'That won't be easy. Where do I start?'

'Try pet shops to begin with,' I began. 'Mostly they will sell the usual – cats, dogs and guinea pigs – but invariably they know someone that might have something more, how can I say, exotic.'

'And then what?'

'Well, then you're going to have to trust me,' I said. 'Upstairs in my room, I have a miniature camera. It can secretly take video film without people realising what's going on. I need to get solid documentary proof of tigers being bought and sold.'

'A secret camera. Sounds like you're some kind of spy.'

'No, not really. It's just that these people would never allow themselves to be filmed openly.'

'Where do you hide your camera?' she asked, more curious than ever.

'Actually I've got two,' I said. 'One is inside a shoulder-bag and the lens peeps out of a tiny hole in the front. It's almost impossible to detect. The other is inside a hat.'

'A hat!' she gasped. 'I don't believe it!'

'Trust me,' I said, 'it's true, and when I use that one I have to disguise my face so that I look very old, then people don't notice the hat.'

209

'You really are a spy,' she said.

'Maybe,' I said, 'if that's what you want to believe. I just think of myself as a sort of detective, trying to find out the truth.'

'OK,' she said, 'I will help you, but please don't tell anyone else about me. I don't want to get into trouble.'

'You won't get into trouble,' I said, 'and thanks, thanks very, very much.'

That night we decided to test the hat camera out in the famous 'Snake Alley', a grotesque part of town that came alive in the evenings and owed its name to the hundreds of cobras and other reptiles that died there each night, writhing in agony as their pumping hearts were cut out with a razor blade.

I'd been there before, and a huckster had sworn at me as I levelled my Hi8 video at him to record the grisly act. 'No picture!' he had bellowed, and the crowd of leering Taiwanese had pushed and jostled me to the back, forcing me to put away my camera. I'll be back, you bastard, I thought, and next time you won't have a clue.

I had bought a pale cream-coloured safari suit and an ebony cane. Over my shoulder I carried the tan leather bag-camera. And on my head I had my revolutionary innovation poised for the crucial test. The device had worked brilliantly in the controlled atmosphere of my hotel room; the images it recorded were well focused, sharp and steady. Wherever I turned my head and looked, the camera automatically followed. All that remained was to test it on the unsuspecting world.

It was a most peculiar feeling, dressed up in disguise. I felt self-conscious and mildly paranoid although as I looked around there was absolutely no evidence that anyone was giving me anything more than a passing glance. I certainly looked odd, perhaps mildly eccentric with my strange clothes. Rebecca was getting more double-takes than I, dressed as she was in bright red hot-pants and low-cut blouse.

She had fiercely objected at first: 'I can't wear clothes like that. What if my friends see me?'

'Do your friends go to Snake Alley?' I asked, hoping for the right answer.

'No, of course not. At least I don't think so.'

'Well, if you do bump into someone you know, you'll both be as surprised as each other. Besides, you can always tell them you're rehearsing for a part in a movie. I'll back you up, don't you worry.'

She had finally succumbed and agreed to play the part of the bimbo, although I was completely unprepared for just how far she'd take the role. She was spectacular, the absolute perfect distraction.

We wandered around Snake Alley arm in arm. Around my waist I had secured the wide surgical elastic abdomen belt that I had espccially bought for the purpose in Hong Kong. It held the batteries and video recording deck that Wong had adapted for me tightly into the well of my back. Tiny electrical leads ran down the inside of my leg and into my trouser pocket. I could feel the switches easily with the tip of my index finger and flicked them on and off as I stared at one grotesque sight after another.

I watched a man with a throat microphone drawing in the crowds as he lauded the benefits of drinking fresh blood from a turtle that he had just decapitated before my very eyes. In a darkened booth, a huckster was demonstrating the claimed aphrodisiac qualities of tiger-bone wine by performing what he termed to be blood-enhanced intercourse with a prostitute. I almost trod on a bag of live birds that some merchant was trying to foster on the Saturday night crowds. After an hour or two I lost count of the number of snakes that I saw snipped open with a rusty blade to reveal their quivering hearts pumping blood into a cocktail of neat whisky.

'Good for sex, can fuck all night,' was the message in Chinese. Personally, I would have rather gone without. It was not surprising that none of the traders wished for this nauseating turpitude to be recorded on film. But it was too late, I thought, I've already done it.

Earlier I had spotted an orang-utan locked up in a cage barely larger than itself. I had switched on the bag-camera and shot several minutes of film which I was sure fully illustrated the poor creature's torment. He had watched me quizzically through the bars, staring hard with his doleful blue-grey eyes. I could see what he was thinking: just get me out of here, he seemed to say. When I passed by again he was chained to a trapeze, swinging maniacally back and forth. When he caught sight of me he stopped abruptly and sat on the rung with his index finger resting on his lower lip as if deep in thought and watched as I came closer. Suddenly he lunged madly at me, his great hairy arm reaching out to grab my hat. I ducked out of his way much faster than a sixty-year-old man was supposed to do, and stepped back out of range. People were looking at me, and I turned to Rebecca and laughed.

'Did you see that, my dear?' I said. 'The damn stupid monkey tried to steal my hat!'

'Yes,' she said quietly, 'that was a close shave. I think we'd better go.'

CHAPTER EIGHTEEN

Taiwan, May 1991

The following afternoon, Rebecca called me at the hotel. She had been busy and her voice was full of excitement.

'Mike, I think I've found someone selling tigers,' she said.

'You can't be serious,' I said. 'So quickly? Well done! Tell me more.'

'Well, I don't know for sure, but my friend thinks that this man sells all sorts of wild animals. He had a baby orang-utan for sale yesterday, we know that.'

'When can we go and look?' I asked, desperate to follow up on this extraordinary lead.

'Maybe tomorrow in the afternoon. I'll try and get some time off work. We can pretend that we're looking for a birthday present for me. Would that be OK?'

I could hardly contain my excitement. I wanted to go right there and then, but it was Sunday and the shop was almost definitely closed.

'Yes, good idea, that would be fantastic,' I said. 'I can't wait. I'll expect your call tomorrow morning then. Good work, Rebecca, well done!'

Things were beginning to happen very rapidly. I'd been in the country less than a week, and had already documented twenty-six Chinese medicine shops. Eleven of them had tiger bone openly on sale in the front window. Five had complete legs, chopped off at the knee-joint, and three more had skulls. In eight shops we spotted rhinoceros horn, all clear violations of Taiwan's domestic wildlife act which had come into effect almost two years earlier.

Article 33 of that law categorically stated:

'For illegal import, export, trade, exchange or display with

213

intent to sell conservation wildlife: a prison sentence of up to two years maximum and/or a fine of up to NT$60,000 [£1,500] maximum. For illegal import, export, processing, trade, exchange or display with intent to sell carcasses, bones, horns, antlers, teeth, hides, furs, organs or their products of an endangered or rare and valuable species: a prison sentence of up to one year maximum and/or a fine of up to NT$30,000 [£750] maximum. Repeat offenders or professional violators should be subject to a prison sentence of up to three years maximum and/or a fine of up to NT$90,000 [£2,250] maximum.'

There had never been tigers in Taiwan, or rhinos for that matter, nor had the species been artificially introduced. Anything there now had to have been imported. Why wasn't this law being enforced, I wondered? For the answer to that I had to wait for the deputy chairman of the Council of Agriculture, Mr Ling Shiang-nung, to denounce me as an 'interfering westerner' and an 'environmental terrorist', but that came later. For the time being I was on a fact-finding mission. And facts, it appeared, weren't proving that difficult to find.

When I returned to my room the night before I had hastily stripped to the waist and removed the constricting elastic belt holding the Sony video recorder. I hooked the machine up to a tiny, six-inch, battery-operated TV monitor and watched in amazement as the flickering images unfolded before me. I was curious to notice just how many people the hidden camera had recorded walking straight toward me, glancing ever so briefly at my eyes and then look away. None of them looked directly into the camera's lens. It was obviously invisible to them.

I'd done it. The camera worked, and I let out a huge cheer that must have woken half my neighbours on the fifteenth floor! I noticed that the position of the lens, high as it was on top of my head, gave a perfect panorama above everyone else. More interesting was the discovery that all I had to do was to peer closer at any particular object and it appeared that the camera was zooming in as the image grew on the tiny screen. The turtle decapitation was terrifyingly graphic. And towards the end of the film I was more than satisfied to note that Mr 'No Picture' had been irrevocably committed to video, his unsuspecting face full-frame in the picture, his bloody hands ripping open the belly and tearing out the living flesh and blood of yet another sacrificial cobra.

214

I watched the tape over and over again, analysing every detail, for this was, after all, only a trial run. And yet I'd captured some startling and quite terrifying images. The hat-camera's potential was clearly tremendous as long as I learned to use it wisely and not to get too confident. Practising in my room was easy. On the street at night had not proven too difficult. But how would I fare in broad daylight, when there were no convenient shadows to hide the wires running down the back of my neck, no artificial light to help conceal my painted face? The make-up was very good – the best the film industry had to work with – but it was still make-up.

In Hong Kong I'd bought a few extra props, a fake gold Rolex, a flamboyant sapphire fraternity ring and an imitation diamond lapel badge in the shape of a treble clef, all to complement the extravagantly wealthy American image. I'd seen some ageing rock-star wearing a similar badge in *Time* magazine and I now tried it on. It looked ridiculous, but that was the point. It looked overblown, but it caught the eye, moved it down and away from my face. But would the ostentatious sparkle trigger increased interest in the rest of me, or would I be written off as a western eccentric? The more I agonised about it, the more I thought that I'd gone completely over the top. Why couldn't I just make do with the bag-camera like so many undercover investigators? Why did I always have to go one step further than everyone else?

I was growing increasingly nervous. Rebecca had telephoned two hours earlier and confirmed that she was free for the afternoon. We would meet at two-thirty. The mission was on!

Who knows where those early, needling symptoms of dread come from? My stomach constricted into a tight knot first, making it impossible to eat. It was still only one o'clock. Perhaps it was just acute tension that triggered some sort of chain reaction, but no matter how it began, my heart seemed to kick prematurely into overdrive. I paced around the room, unable to relax. Damn this waiting!

Years ago, I would taunt danger with a bold and arrogant disregard for my own safety. In Sweden, as an expatriate bachelor, I didn't care. Now, thoughts of Sophy, asleep many miles away in another world, flooded my mind. I would do nothing foolish, I told myself. Nothing to hurt her, nothing to betray the love and trust she had in me. In a month's time we would be married, and I would have put Taiwan behind me.

Focus, I told myself, and absolute concentration were the key, coupled with a keen sense for the first signs of the unpredictable. I had to be able to spot the trip wires, avoid the traps. The people that I was about to meet would be playing by their own rules. It was their sleazy world that I now had to infiltrate and in which I had to establish my credentials. They would probe deep, attempting to penetrate my defences with trick questions. If I let my guard down for a split second, I would be at their mercy. Except I doubted if there was much mercy in the sordid underworld of the tiger smuggler.

I re-read a fax from Kate. There was no great encouraging news from Washington as things were in the hands of lawyers and legal executives where they could stagnate for all eternity. Sam had just won the prestigious Goldman Award, a kind of Nobel Prize for the environment, and was touring the United States shaking hands and giving lectures. They were relying on me to make a breakthrough. The tigers were out there, not far away, of that much I was absolutely convinced.

The phone rattled by the bedside. It was Rebecca, downstairs and waiting. I took one last look at myself in the bedroom mirror and slipped quietly out of the room. The lift was thankfully empty and I met no-one in the hallway. Downstairs in the lobby, I ducked out of the door to find Rebecca waiting in the car that she had rented. The driver touched his cap briefly as he held open the door for me, and I slid painfully into the back seat.

'Hello,' said Rebecca smiling. 'You look different.'

'You too,' I replied, 'very elegant. Did you buy that dress here in Taipei?'

'No, Singapore.'

We kept up the small talk for a while. I could see that she was nervous, but the idle chatter helped to relieve our tension. She had told me briefly over the phone that the man we were going to see had a reputation for being able to supply any kind of animal or bird. He owned a 'poodle parlour' which apparently provided the perfect front for his operation.

The car sped smoothly through the streets of the capital heading east toward the Municipal Stadium. At Fuhsing Road we turned left and then almost immediately right until we eventually pulled to a halt beside a row of narrow streets that led to the Dinghao Market.

'This is it,' said Rebecca.

'OK,' I said, forcing a smile. 'Let's go and find you a birthday present.'

We found the place at once. Outside on the ground, as if by way of advertisement, was a battered cage containing an emaciated white-handed gibbon and a Burmese cat. I put the leather bag-camera on the ground for a good steady shot, quietly flicked the switch in my inside trouser pocket, and the tiny device in my hat sprang to life.

The shop door yielded with a light shove and tinkled unnecessarily to announce our presence. Inside were dozens of wire pens holding many different breeds of small dog, all of whom began yapping madly as soon as we entered the shop. The room smelled of stale urine. At the back was a dark curtain and an empty clipping table. Apart from the dogs, the place seemed deserted.

From behind the cloth I heard a deep guttural noise, a low extended growl like an angry tom-cat. Except no ordinary cat could make such a hoarse rasping sound. Whatever was hidden behind the drapes had frightened the dogs into silence. I moved closer to the dark fabric one step at a time.

'Is anyone there?' I called, in my rough Texan drawl.

'Be careful,' said Rebecca. 'It sounds angry and dangerous to me.'

As I went to take hold of the curtain, the door opened behind us and a bustling, heavy-set woman with dark orange hair squeezed her way through. She wore an apron with large combs and scissors sticking out of the pockets. Either a hairdresser or a poodle-clipper, I thought, opting for the latter.

She told Rebecca that she worked for the proprietor, and then promptly disappeared behind the rear curtain.

'The woman is not the owner,' said Rebecca. 'She is going to phone him and he will come. In the meantime, she wants to show us something else.'

And as if on cue she re-emerged carrying an infant orang-utan that could only have been a few months old. I shuddered to think what had happened to its mother; normally poachers shoot them out of the trees, and if the baby survives the fall it is then sold abroad. It was impossible not to feel compassion for the tiny ape, orphaned as it must have been in such a bloody way. It clung to Rebecca's neck, nestling its soft hairy head on her shoulder. It should have been clinging to its mother somewhere in the wilds of Borneo, I thought. This sickening wildlife trade had claimed yet another victim.

The woman wanted NT$150,000 for the tiny creature, about £4,000. We declined, insisting that we were looking for a large exotic cat. She looked disappointed and then, with a shrug, beckoned

217

us to follow her and drew back the heavy black drapes. There was no window in the back room and the place was lit by a flickering strip-light which made all movement seem disjointed, like an old silent movie. In a small cubby-hole in one corner were two stainless-steel cages about three feet square and four feet deep. In one was a clouded leopard, pacing round and round in the cramped interior. In the other, barely visible in the darkened hideaway, its eyes sparkling in the fragmented light, was a black panther which snarled viciously as we approached. The leopard growled again as I crouched down to rest the shoulder-bag on the floor. I prayed that there was enough light for the camera; the device was completely automatic and would adjust itself, I hoped.

I could just make out the fabulous rosette markings of the black panther. These are really melanistic leopards that owe their black pigmentation to a recessive gene factor dominating when two carriers mate. It's not that uncommon to find just one black cub in a litter of commonly marked leopards, although for centuries men believed they were a completely separate species.

These two large cats, like the orang-utan, had been taken from the wild, of that much I was sure. It was impossible not to notice the torment in their eyes, the wild spirit that had not been dampened by their severe confinement. They wanted to break free and run back to the jungles from whence they came. Instead they had been trapped and would spend the rest of their miserable days behind bars, guilty of no other offence than their own beauty and the desire of man to brag of his power and to possess them.

Rebecca looked horrified by the sight of the two caged animals, and I could tell what she was thinking. Even she had not expected that such barbaric and selfish trade went on in her own city, but she was trying to rise above such emotion and keep our play-acting on track. We walked back into the main shop.

I shook my head. 'I don't think that they are really suitable, darling, however beautiful they might appear. They look quite wild to me. I don't think that you could actually cuddle one. You'd be badly scratched, I'm sure.'

She took my cue and launched into a lengthy explanation to the fat woman with much subtle gesticulation and cradling of arms. The point was eventually made. We insisted that we actually wanted a cute and cuddly animal, something that Rebecca could stroke and make a huge fuss of. The woman understood, but nevertheless tried one last attempt to sell the snarling pair of leopards for less than

218

£3,000, including the cages and delivery.

'Thanks, but no thanks,' I said, and Rebecca dutifully translated.

'There is a man who has tigers,' Rebecca then told me. 'Not far from here, on the outskirts of town. When the owner comes he will take us there.'

She looked flushed and excited. My adrenaline was flowing overtime as well. If we could keep this up, I thought, maybe I could record the vital evidence that was needed. Suddenly I remembered the hat-camera and flicked the machine off. We had been in the shop about ten minutes and the battery life was only twice that long. I needed to save power in the event that I didn't get another opportunity to change them.

The phone rang and the woman disappeared into the back to answer it. The conversation was very brief, and she re-emerged smiling cheerfully, and spoke rapidly to Rebecca.

'She wants a commission if you buy me a tiger cub. I said OK,' whispered Rebecca.

'Is that all?' I asked.

'No, the owner is outside waiting in his car. He will take us.'

'Make sure we can follow in our car,' I said. 'Tell him not to drive too fast.'

We stepped out into the afternoon sunshine and walked briskly back to our waiting chauffeur. Rebecca went over to a sleek Mazda sports car and spoke briefly to the driver. I watched in horror as she prepared to get in the passenger door.

'Don't worry,' she shouted with a wave and climbed in.

Good grief, I thought, what the hell is she playing at?

'Get a move on,' I barked at the driver, telling him not to lose sight of the car in front.

Whatever was she thinking of, getting into a car with a complete stranger, and one that dealt in smuggled tigers! Rebecca was a remarkably resourceful girl and knew what she was doing, I reasoned. I had no choice but to trust her instincts.

We drove rapidly out of town heading south-east into the suburbs, through tunnels and darting on and off short stretches of motorway. Eventually we began to climb up through a mixed neighbourhood of small factories and detached houses until the road became very steep and narrow. We wound our way carefully round blind corners until we ran out of road and the lead car ground to a halt on a disused piece of rough land. We parked beside him and got out.

'Mike, this is Mr Leung,' began Rebecca, with a look that said he was a real creep.

'Pleasure,' I said, shaking his clammy hand.

I took her arm possessively and we strolled together away from the cars.

'Why did you just go off with him like that?' I demanded.

'He said something to me.'

'What?'

'It wasn't what he said, but the way that he said it. I'll tell you later. Don't worry. I know what I'm doing.'

But I was worried. One week ago she was an office secretary, now she was getting into flashy sports cars with men involved in tiger-smuggling. This wasn't a game, these people knew they were breaking the law.

We walked back down the hill. On the left was what looked like a scrap-yard with a particularly aggressive Alsatian dog on the loose. As I got closer I could make out the contours of a number of ramshackle cages and behind them several twenty-foot containers. The area looked like a tip with discarded cans and plastic containers everywhere and large pale-blue polythene bags flapping around in the wind. And then, as if from nowhere, an old familiar smell hit my nostrils and I was somehow transported back to the jungles of Khao Sok. It was the smell of a tiger!

Rebecca was chatting away merrily to Mr Leung as I flicked the switch in my pocket and walked nonchalantly up to the chain-link fence. In the yard I could make out at least a dozen rusty iron enclosures of one sort or another and, as I focused my eyes through the coarse wire mesh, I could make out the distinctive lines of first one tiger, then another. A cold shiver ran up my spine. There were five tigers in all that I could see, and more dark cages at the back.

This was it! I was looking at an illegal tiger farm. And yet it was right here in full view of a suburban neighbourhood. There were kids on the street riding bicycles, there were many more houses further up the hill that looked down on this area. The stench was quite overpowering, and the animals were too big to hide. How the hell did this man get away with it? Had he bought his neighbour's silence, had the laissez-faire economy gone crazy or were they simply scared of him? I prayed that my cameras were recording every detail.

Opposite the compound, on the other side of the street, was a steep stone staircase up which Mr Leung was now leading Rebecca.

220

I tore myself away from the horrors of this contemptible prison and followed them. We emerged at the top on to a wide balcony that looked back down across the road on to the tigers. It was a much better view. The bag-camera wouldn't fail to pick it all up, I thought. The verandah was about twenty feet long by twelve feet wide. In the centre was a chipped lacquered coffee-table and a tatty three-piece suite. At one end was what looked to be another stainless-steel cage, similar to the one I'd seen in the shop earlier. It was covered in a pale green velvet cloth with an elaborate gold-tasselled fringe. For some reason my eyes were drawn to it, and I couldn't take my eyes off it even as I heard a voice coming from inside the elevated house.

I'd already made up my mind about what type of man would keep tigers in such purgatory, and Eddie Chen did nothing to disappoint. He was a slob. His pallid, greasy complexion looked as though he bathed in Johnson's baby oil, or lard. A shirt might have helped disguise his disgusting bloated appearance; instead we had to endure the sight of his blubbery torso bulging through the contours of a string vest. His massive belly quivered as he parked his otherwise unremarkable frame in an armchair having pumped my hand enthusiastically.

'My friend Leung say me you want tiger,' he began in pidgin English.

'Perhaps . . .' I said, nodding to Rebecca, 'you would be more comfortable speaking Chinese.'

'OK,' he said, watching my gaze return to the velvet cloth. 'Look, look,' he said repeatedly gesturing toward the cage.

I was worried about turning my back on them. The cable from the hat-camera was thin but not invisible. I got up awkwardly, shooting an apprehensive glance at Rebecca. She understood immediately, and distracted them with a flourish of her Yves St Laurent cigarette case. As Leung leaned across with his outstretched lighter I took my chance, stood up, and stepped neatly over to the corner edge of the balcony and turned to face the group.

'He says to take off the cloth,' said Rebecca as Chen spat out some words through the smoke and nicotine-stained teeth.

They were all watching me, so I'd better get on with it, I thought, and pulled the cloth slowly down to the floor. I wasn't prepared for what I'd see next. It was a truly unusual and extraordinary sight. Inside the cage was a cardboard box with a hole roughly cut out making it look like a flimsy dog kennel. Half in and half out of the entrance to the box and fast asleep was a young Yorkshire terrier and beside it, lying on its back with its enormous paws in the air, was a baby tiger.

'He's beautiful!' said Rebecca. 'Can I take him home with me? Please!'

Steady on, I thought. Let's not rush into situations that might prove difficult to get out of. 'Well, let's see, honey. This is a big decision to make. He ain't always going to be so cute and cuddly. Ain't that right, Mr Chen?' I asked.

Eddie Chen grunted.

'Perhaps Mr Chen would like to show us his mommy and daddy,' I said, pointing at the sleeping cub. 'I guess he was born here, or maybe he wasn't. Perhaps you'd care to ask him, hon',' I drooled.

'I get him two weeks ago,' interrupted Chen, 'from my friend in Kaohsiung.'

'Is that a fact? And did your friend breed him?'

'No.'

'Do you know where he came from?'

'I think Hong Kong. Why you ask?'

'Oh, it's just because we're worried about disease, papers, documents, that sort of stuff,' I said, trying not to sound alarmist.

'Not to worry,' announced Eddie Chen with a huge smile. 'I can fix licence, no problem!'

'Excellent,' I said turning to Rebecca, planning our next move. 'Perhaps if you ask Mr Chen real nicely, he might show us them growed-up tigers down there.'

He seemed to think that was a good idea because suddenly everyone was standing up and trooping down the concrete steps. I held back, ushering them in front of me. Somehow I would have to do something about those damn cables, I thought.

As we got downstairs, I turned to Eddie Chen and asked quietly, 'How much?'

He stopped momentarily and hissed at me as if to a fellow conspirator, 'Not expensive, only NT$150,000.'

About £4,000, I thought. Christ almighty, the price had more than trebled since Bangkok, because I was now sure that this tiger cub was one of the ones that had slipped through Boonlerd's net.

We walked over to his compound which he kept secured with an enormous chain and padlock. The guard dog bounded over, slobbering madly.

'Not to worry,' said Chen, pointing to the dog which promptly deposited a huge wad of saliva on my trouser leg. It could have been worse, I thought, as we approached the cages, that dog was a killer. I was saving power now with the hidden camera, and flicked the switch in my pocket on and off as we were shown around the cages.

There were seven tigers altogether, two at the back which I hadn't spotted earlier. In an adjacent cage I saw an aged chimpanzee, an enormous orang-utan, and a sorry-looking American mountain lion. A total of ten rare animals from around the globe were cooped up in this abysmal hole, and the authorities just looked the other way.

'Why do you have so many tigers?' I asked Chen.

'I try to breed. Is very good business.'

'Isn't it illegal?' I asked, feigning concern for the man's livelihood.

'Yes, ah no, not really, but not to worry. We can come to an arrangement. No problem.'

I was sure he meant it. There was nothing subtle or surreptitious about this man's operation. It was totally out in the open. Anyone could come and inspect it if they had a mind or a will to. It was plainly obvious that nobody had, the authorities didn't care, or if they did, Eddie Chen was paying them to leave him alone.

The tigers were in a pitiful state. They were being fed, but not enough, and certainly not the correct balance of red meat, vitamins and minerals. Their coats were dry and lacklustre, weals showed through the hindquarters where they had continuously rubbed against the confining bars of the cage. Their eyes were dull, and one young male had an almost psychotic look as he lolloped around the cramped interior of his pen. I guessed he was in-bred, his parents probably siblings.

'They must cost a lot to feed,' I said to Chen, leading him on.

'Oh, too much money,' he said excitedly.

'It must be difficult to make a profit,' I ventured. Mentioning the money incentive could be the kiss of death for this conversation, I thought, but worth a try.

'In the winter-time, easy to sell,' he said flatly, dodging my question.

'Why in winter?'

'Oh, ha, ha. You don't know?' He pulled me to one side, away from Rebecca, out of earshot. 'Chinese man like to eat tiger in winter-time. Meat very good. Good for fucking.'

I wanted to strangle him on the spot; instead I said, 'You sell them to restaurants?'

223

'Yes. Here in Taiwan there are many. Very good business.'

'How much for a big one?'

'Oh, too much questions,' he said.

'I was only wondering if we buy the baby tiger and then one day it gets too dangerous, how much it would be worth.'

'Not to worry,' he said. 'I buy from you. You make profit, not to worry.'

It was time to go. I'd seen and heard enough, and by now I was sure the camera batteries had died. Leung was still avidly chatting up Rebecca as I stepped over to interrupt them. I took her by the arm and steered her away, making sure that I didn't get in front of him.

'Come now, honey, we just have to get going. You know that diamond bracelet ain't going to stay in the shop window forever. Maybe we should go have one last look at it,' I drawled.

'And thank you, Mr Chen,' I continued. 'You've been real hospitable. Now me and my young lady here have to do some serious thinking.'

I took him to one side. 'What's your last price?'

'NT$120,000,' he said.

'And you'd guarantee to buy him back if things didn't work out?'

'Not to worry,' he said.

We left him locking up the chain-link fence. Mr Leung opted to stay behind. Rebecca thought they were going to sit and drink whisky. What the hell, just so long as they didn't get suspicious about us. The chauffeur was snoozing behind the wheel as we approached the car. I tapped on the side window and he snapped into life as only professional drivers can.

The car rolled down the steep hill and I took one last look at the tigers and their miserable compound. Chen and Leung waved as we drifted past. I didn't look back.

'Well,' I said to Rebecca, 'what did you make of all that?'

'He's a nice man,' she said.

'What?' I said incredulously. 'That bastard keeps beautiful animals in squalor like that, and you say he's a nice man!'

'You English,' she said, 'you must understand that he doesn't see it that way. He is just making business, that's all he knows.'

'And you agree with what he is doing?'

'Of course I don't agree, but these are my people, all they care about is making money. As long as he can, he will do such business. It is the same, I think, in England?'

She was right of course. It was the same everywhere in the world.

224

People would always risk breaking the law for high profits. If the law was never enforced, who could blame them? Chen had no qualms about what he was doing. Animals for the Chinese are strictly utilitarian. In his mind there could never be any question of immorality. If there was a demand, he would supply it. That was his speciality. I could never compete with such deeply entrenched values; there simply wasn't enough time. Wild tigers were rapidly becoming the victims of the inequalities of supply and demand. It was going to take much more than this video evidence to change things. I would have to dig much deeper. Much deeper indeed.

CHAPTER NINETEEN

England, 1991

June 15th 1991 will forever go down in the history books as being one of the coldest, wettest and most miserable days of the summer months, certainly in the living memory of all the 120 guests seated under the enormous marquee on the lawn of Sophy's parental home in Norfolk.

Nevertheless, for the bride and groom it was a dream-like day, for many reasons, not least of which that it passed so incredibly quickly. We'd been warned, of course, to savour every moment, but the minutes raced by in seconds and the hours disappeared in minutes. No sooner had we dutifully plighted our troth, one unto the other, than we were whisked away in a fairy-tale carriage under a sea of umbrellas to the reception. To the champagne, the endless congratulations, the cake and the eulogies.

'Sophy and Michael have been trying . . .' began my new father-in-law. His timely pause was, I'm sure, quite unintentional; nevertheless the room erupted as salacious minds, well primed with good wine, innocently but wrongly predicted what was about to follow. He went on through the banter, not in the traditional manner by lauding the virtues of his beautiful daughter upon the gathered assembly, but to salute our work in conservation. It was quite unexpected and his words will be forever etched on my heart. Since that day he has never once questioned our motives and has remained an unfailing source of wise counsel and sound judgement. If we have achieved anything over the years to help save the tigers, it is in no small part due to that man's untiring countenance and moral support.

We honeymooned in Kenya and the Seychelles then, on returning to England, set about the business of finding a suitable home. Both

227

Sophy and I were born and raised in rural East Anglia and had no intention of ever returning to actually live there ourselves. In fact, we could have chosen just about anywhere in the world to live, from Hawaii to Hong Kong.

So we chose East Anglia. Or rather it chose us. We'd met a particularly rumbustious race-horse trainer and his bride whilst on holiday, the sort of man that told my kind of irreverent and filthy stories and enjoyed a glass or two of whisky. We decided to look them up when we got back. One thing led to another and before we knew what had happened, we'd rented a house in the village of Ousden just outside Newmarket in Suffolk. The owner was a jockey that lived in Hong Kong and the mysterious circle was somehow completed.

From the comparative anonymity of that quiet village we planned our future work in conservation. We had a couple of extra phone-lines connected to the house, but to the outside world we were just a couple of newlyweds enjoying the novelty of married life. Few people ever suspected that it was from this unexceptional dwelling that a strategy was being meticulously mapped out that we hoped would catapult the plight of the tiger out into the unsuspecting world. We worked long into the night, sometimes all night, putting together a tight network upon which we were to rely in the coming months. I had learned enough to know that my methods were seen by many as crude and unorthodox. I had already received a damning letter from a published New York biologist, castigating my interference with tiger politics in Thailand. Little did he or anyone else know just how much Sophy and I had already risked in getting this far. He and his kind had their own agenda. Neither Sophy nor myself wished to have any part in that process. I was the reluctant conservationist caught up in something that I didn't pretend to really understand.

All I knew was that the tiger was heading rapidly down the slippery slope toward extinction and all the elaborate rhetoric that I'd heard up to then wasn't doing a damn thing to prevent it. If the tiger was to be saved, it was going to be through unorthodox and militant action. The odds were already too heavily stacked against a pragmatic or diplomatic approach. There simply wasn't time.

Whilst on honeymoon, Sophy and I had decided to invest a further two years of our lives in trying to save the tiger. No more. We were not professional conservationists, we had no other vested

228

career interest in environmental work. We simply decided that we could not stand idly by and watch the world blindly kiss goodbye to a species that had captured the imagination of not only ourselves but millions of men, women and children around the world since time immemorial.

And so in December of 1991, I went back to Taiwan, determined to seek out the truth.

The short train journey down from the busy west-coast town of Tainan had been uneventful. Rebecca and I attracted little more than a passing glance and a hissed 'tut tut' from an old biddy, wondering what a pretty young Taiwanese was doing with such a loathsome foreign devil. There was no shortage of westerners in Taiwan these days, as Taiwanese joint ventures were blossoming everywhere, their business partners coming from all corners of the globe. Blending in to this community was therefore easy. I could be anyone I wanted to be. A printed business card was the only passport, and I had several of those.

The bustling railway station at Kaohsiung paid no attention to the arrival of 'Michael Dane PhD, Gems, Antiques, Exotica' that day as I navigated my way through the thronging masses to the men's room. There was no hook in the filthy cubicle, but my Parker pen fitted neatly into a deviant's peephole making a convenient peg for my jacket. I put my leather shoulder-bag and the rest of my things on to the floor and stripped to the waist. Cathay Pacific Airways' Marco Polo Class graciously provides its passengers with a handy and very compact wash-bag which I had recently adapted to contain a few extras. From the bag I took a small mirror and tore away the protective paper from a double-sided sticker that I had attached earlier and pushed the mirror against the wall.

The fine grey lines that I had pencilled around my cheek and nose earlier that morning made my reflection seem much older. I added more of the powder to the soft skin under my eyes, and now looked as though I hadn't slept for a week! Cathay's complimentary toothbrush proved to be the perfect tool for applying a light silvery-pink paste to the hair of my temples. Next I smoothed the rest of my hair severely away from my forehead with some super-hold gel, and streaked in some more paste. The wash-bag also contained a fake moustache, glue and a pair of gold-rimmed glasses that I popped into the inside pocket of my jacket. I called these glasses my 'image intensifiers' – it was my 'image' they were intensifying!

False moustaches are the most uncomfortable things to wear for someone who has been clean-shaven all his life, and they are also extremely tricky to attach, especially if the upper lip is moist with sweat, a mistake that I'd made earlier. Today I'd used liberal amounts of aftershave, and although I must have smelt overpowering, at least my face felt dry and smooth. With great care I applied the special glue to the back of the moustache, blew out my upper lip slightly, as I'd been taught to do, and stuck it on. It felt alien and terrible. I sat down miserably on the cracked plastic seat and waited patiently for the glue to dry. After a few minutes I gingerly twitched my nostrils and the muscles around my cheek and nose. I peered at my reflection in the mirror. The glue was dry but malleable. Perfect.

Next I took the straw hat from a large and elegant carrier bag and put it carefully on my head, allowing the thin black cable to hang loosely down my back. Wrapped in a tight bundle at the bottom of the carrier bag was the wide elastic body-belt, bought from a surgical supplier in Hong Kong, into which I had sewn the video tape recorder, the crucial analogue decoder and a battery pack. More cables, tiny and unobtrusive, were attached to the belt, switches that would later trigger this vital equipment into life. Reaching behind me I carefully took the delicate cable and attached it to the decoder and stretched the belt around my middle, keeping it very taut and the recorder pressed tightly into the well of my back. Loosening my trousers at the front I gently slipped the switching cable through a hole and into the left pocket. Satisfied, I pulled the baggy shirt back on, buttoning it to the neck and making absolutely sure that there was enough slack cable for the delicate switches. I zipped up, and fastened my trousers. I felt absurd, standing here in this cramped and stinking lavatory. From the highly polished and toe-capped cowboy boots, to the wide-brimmed straw hat, with its feather cluster, I felt like some third-rate J.R. Ewing impersonator, but I managed a smile as I put on the spectacles. Some intensified image!

My leather shoulder-bag was lighter now, and inside I attached a freshly recharged battery to the other concealed camera, then neatly folded the carrier bag and placed it on top. The bag-camera was essential in case the tiny lipstick camera in my hat failed to operate. Finally, I double-checked to make sure that all the switches and batteries were well connected, took down the mirror, packed it away and prepared to leave. As I put on my jacket, I stretched to allow some freedom of movement for the cables, took a deep breath and steeled myself for the first glance of other people outside in the lobby of the men's room.

I briskly opened the door and stepped out. The room was empty. Suppressing a smile, I approached the sink area and the much larger mirrors. If I could fool myself, I could fool anyone. The moustache was good, the hat needed straightening slightly, but only I knew its secret. The rest was fine; I looked ridiculous, but sufficiently convincing, so I felt fine. Confident now, I strode out, head held high, scanning the concourse for Rebecca. I looked at my fake Rolex watch; the transformation had taken only ten minutes.

She had been busy as well. Whereas I had aged thirty years, she seemed ten years younger with her hair in bunches, her white ankle socks (virgin socks, I remember we called them at school), and striped shorts. Her make-up was sensual and provocative; it said, 'Beneath this child-like exterior lies a money-grabbing, promiscuous bitch, but don't touch, I'm spoken for and I bite!' She looked perfect. She was a very clever and resourceful girl, and I told her so.

It was time to find our contact. I was not sure who to look for, but felt confident that I would recognise him somehow. In any case, he surely could not fail to notice me! I was growing tense and impatient. In situations like these, I do not like to be kept waiting. When we could bear it no longer, Rebecca decided to telephone. She returned looking happier.

'It's all right,' she said, 'he's sending a car.'

Within minutes, a white Mercedes with blackened windows pulled up at the station taxi-rank, and a stocky Chinese squeezed out from behind the wheel. He was sweating profusely. I shook a cold hand which motioned me to sit in the back with Rebecca. He said little by way of a greeting; his partner in the front seat stared vacantly ahead and did not even glance at us as we climbed in.

The car pulled abruptly away from the station and headed north into the back-streets of Kaohsiung. By now it was early afternoon and Saturday morning workers on their way home were now mingling with shoppers as the town began to wind down for the weekend. I glanced over at Rebecca who smiled as she engaged the driver in cheerful small talk. I wrinkled my face slightly to indicate the discomfort of the camera equipment pressing into my back; the recorder kept digging into my spine every time the driver over-did it on the brakes. I did my best to appear relaxed, gazing aimlessly

231

outside and occasionally pointing at short-skirted ladies, much to Rebecca's amusement. It was vital not to appear as uneasy as I felt.

After what seemed like an hour, but was probably only about fifteen minutes, the Mercedes pulled to a halt in a narrow street. The pavement was covered by typical Taiwanese awnings of cheap timber and dull canvas to keep the sun and rain out of a row of tatty, open-fronted shops and offices.

Two young children stopped chasing each other around a lamp-post as the silent passenger in the front seat squeezed out of the car into the daylight. There was nothing remarkable about this street. Yet here, waiting for me inside one of these undistinguished façades, I hoped to meet the man whose bloody trail I had followed across three countries.

When I had returned to Taipei, the Taiwanese capital, I had discovered this man's identity quite by chance.

A few days before, and 100 kilometres to the north, I had been sitting in an ancient apothecary's shop grilling an aged Chinese herbalist for information about the underground trade and getting nowhere. My translator, a teacher called Lilly who owned an ice-cream parlour next door, shrugged as if to say, 'Why should he tell you!'

Suddenly there was a terrifying scream and instinctively I jumped up to place its cause and direction.

'It's my shop,' cried Lilly, and she was gone.

At the back of her shop a few seconds later, we found her young female assistant screaming in agony as her hand was slowly being crushed inside an ice-cream blender. Somehow the girl had managed to turn off the machine but her small hand was trapped. Quickly I went to work, barking orders to anyone that could understand them.

'Bring me ice, soap, towels. Quickly!' Within minutes I had stripped away the head of the machine and released some of the pressure on her hand. Lilly appeared with some washing-up liquid which I poured down over the little girl's wrist.

'This is going to hurt,' I told her. Lilly translated and the girl squealed in anticipation. I gently prised her hand out from inside the errant machine and felt for signs of lost fingers or broken bones. She had been very lucky.

I crushed the ice and made a pack around her hand and wrist, and told her not to worry, that within a couple of hours the swelling would begin to go down and a few spectacular bruises and a dull ache would be the only reminder of the unfortunate incident.

'What would we have done without you,' said Lilly finally.

Feeling somewhat embarrassed by all the attention and the looks of the small crowd that had gathered outside in the street, I returned to the old herbalist's shop to collect my things. Lilly followed and excitedly told the old man exactly what had happened. He beckoned me to sit, I was invited to take tea, and from that moment on I was accepted as a 'friend'.

Later, as I sipped the rancid brew, he began to tell me what he knew of the illegal tiger-bone trade in Taiwan. I'd explained earlier to Lilly that I was a university lecturer, researching a paper on traditional Chinese medicine. This seemed harmless to her, and she freely translated as the old man told her the name of an illegal importer in Kaohsiung. That evening I telephoned Rebecca in Taipei, and she in turn fed the name to one of her vast network of friends and contacts and the following morning verified his name and address.

And now, after all this time, I was about to meet him. His name was Mr Chan.

Rebecca got out of the car first, giving me the opportunity to swing my legs over and follow through the same rear offside door, thus keeping the bulge in my back out of sight. I straightened up and stretched slightly, adjusting my hat at the same time. I gestured to the others to lead the way.

Rebecca and I had discussed this meeting long into the night. What would this man be like? How should we approach him? We had drilled repeatedly for this moment, practised our act time and again. Finally I was satisfied, and slept confidently knowing that, come what may, she would quickly assume the right role for almost every eventuality. Our safety was in her hands, she was speaking for both of us, and now, at long last, the curtain was about to go up.

As we stepped across the pavement I was conscious of the two small boys staring at me. I smiled and waved, and in the broadest Texan accent I could muster said, 'Hi there, how ya doin'?' They giggled shamelessly.

Once inside the shop Rebecca presented herself, and introduced me as her 'special friend'. Chan nodded, staring at her without expression. He had the look of a mariner with deeply tanned and wrinkled skin. He squinted at me through broken spectacles, patched up with Sellotape in one corner and slightly uneven across the bridge of his nose. He extended a rough and calloused hand for me to shake. I sensed that here was a man who was cautious to the

233

core. His sea-faring peasant appearance clearly belied a shrewd intellect and a quick mind. I knew that we would need to be on our guard. He was about to test me out to satisfy himself that I was safe. Rebecca had spoken with him twice now on the phone, and they continued to exchange polite greetings, but were soon down to business as he fired off a series of questions: 'Who is he?' 'What does he want?' 'Can he afford to buy?' 'Can he be trusted?'

The answers had been carefully rehearsed. Although I could not understand Rebecca's language, I felt I knew exactly what she was saying because I had drafted most of the script.

I was American, she told Chan: a big-game hunter from Texas who had collected many trophies on his travels throughout Africa, Asia and South America. In Taiwan, I was acting on behalf of an associate who wished to establish a regular supply of tiger skins for the United States market. I also wanted a supplier of tiger-bone wine. There was always a huge demand for any new sort of aphrodisiac.

She wrinkled her nose in disgust. 'Frankly, from his performance last night, he could do with a bottle himself!' she said in guttural Chinese, at exactly the right moment.

The implacable Chan permitted himself a sneer. I could see him thinking what a ludicrous figure I cut with my absurd outfit, and he obviously despised my inability to conduct business negotiations myself. Those skills of Rebecca's were paying off again. Chan was starting to relax. She forced home the advantage with an offer we hoped he would not be able to refuse.

'If you work with me, I can show you how we can really cheat the old bugger out of his millions,' she said. 'All I want is a little money so that I can get rid of him and start my own business. He's not exactly my type!'

The deal was this: he would demand an excessive price which she would explain was the best and bottom offer; having secured my agreement, they would later split the excess proceeds between them. Chan nodded gravely and promised her a cash commission. Then he smiled at me. For a gangster with so much blood on his hands, it was a charming smile, but typical of the grasping Chinese who will deal with anyone if they can smell a fat profit.

Chan leaned backwards on his swivel chair, reaching high above his head to a row of cellophane bags. Seizing one, he threw it across the desk in my general direction. Another test, I thought, as I caught it without losing his stare. The contents of the bag looked

234

like a sun-dried sponge except it was hard and brittle. I met Chan's gaze. His smile had become almost a sneer, and while his manner may have been courteous, his watery eyes mocked me.

'He wants to know if you can tell what this is,' said Rebecca. She looked as mystified as me. Clearly this was no sponge. I shrugged my shoulders. 'He says it comes from China. He buys many thousands each month. Very good to eat.'

I still had no idea and said so. Chan spoke again, watching me closely, barely able to contain his glee. Rebecca's interpreting faltered. 'Placenta,' she said, 'human placenta. Collected from the labour wards of Chinese hospitals and dried with great skill. Highly nutritious.'

'So what?' I said loftily. 'I am not interested in this *product*.'

I looked at Rebecca as she translated. I wanted her to be firm. This man was teasing me, and I didn't like it. There are some areas of business where it pays to indulge the whims of one's counterpart. With gangsters I preferred to get straight to the point, and as I watched for some sign of understanding from her, I slid the placenta on to Chan's desk with my left hand and settled back in my chair to see what would happen next. All at once my eyes seemed to register something different in Chan's demeanour, and there was a sense of triumph almost as if he had telepathically picked up my thoughts. He looked smug and then I saw why, because cupped in his hand, as an assassin would carry a knife, was a large bone.

With the panache of a magician producing a magic wand, he flicked the bone into full view, waving it slowly from side to side. Oh yes, he knew what we were thinking, and he was playing the game to perfection. So far, my hands had stayed in my lap, my camera switched off. I was saving the short life of the batteries but now, in retrospect, I wish I had recorded that extraordinary scene. He reached across the desk and, with a slight wag of the bone, beckoned me to take it.

As soon as I touched it, I knew it was tiger. It was a femur, the most highly prized of all bones, with a small hole to the side of the hip joint, what some people call 'the eye of the needle'. This and other characteristics distinguished it from the femurs of deer and cows, which are sometimes passed off as tiger in the Far East by small-time crooks with no access to the real thing. The tiger's femur had been moulded by evolution to allow this most powerful animal to spring at its prey with supreme suppleness and awesome force. A slight curve in the shaft produced a peculiar twist quite unlike that of any other animal. There was no question about it.

I fixed Chan with a knowing look. '*Hu Gu!*' I said, the Chinese name for tiger bone.

He grinned, at ease now. 'Yes,' he said. 'Come, we drink tea, after, there is one man you shall meet.'

The bastard spoke English! I nodded and conceded round one to this masterful player. Rebecca was laughing. There was nothing else to do but laugh. I had done it, I'd passed his test.

The small talk that followed was mostly about trading. Chan, his round shoulders hunched over the tiny china cup from which he slurped his tea, was certainly no financial academic. But his inherent Chinese business acumen coupled with a good nose for a deal and a lifetime of profiteering from all manner of contraband had generated for him riches of which he was as protective and proud as the wiliest trader in stocks and shares. He wanted to know how I had made my own fortune. I told him that it was partly old family money, but that I had traded to considerable advantage in 'Rolex' watches that originated in Hong Kong and Taiwan. As Rebecca translated, he tapped his own genuine solid gold watch and chortled. The idea of profiting from breaches of international copyright seemed to appeal to him and he toasted me with a fresh cup of tea.

I was beginning to allow him to think we were becoming friends, when the driver reappeared from the back of the store, accompanied by the sinister silent passenger from our trip in the Mercedes. The thought of another car journey into the unknown quickened my senses. I shot a reassuring glance at Rebecca, and she blew me a kiss and winked. We all laughed one last time as I shook hands with Chan and walked around to the blind side of the car and climbed in, taking excruciating care not to displace my hat and expose the feeder cable stuck down the back of my neck. However fruitful our interview with Chan might have seemed, it had yielded no evidence of any extensive illegal trading, as he had been extremely cautious. As we drove away I pictured him telephoning the man we were about to meet to forewarn him of our arrival. So far I had not recorded a single foot of film. We needed to have sight of something significantly more incriminating than a solitary bone. Otherwise, it would just be our word against theirs.

As the Mercedes sped off again, I saw the blood rush to Rebecca's face. The adrenaline was flowing now. If Chan had the slightest suspicion that we might be deceiving him, we were in grave danger. For the second time that day, I had an intense feeling of helplessness

236

in the back of that car. I wished, in more ways than one, that I could be in the driver's seat.

We must have driven for at least twenty minutes, weaving through one back-street after another until I was completely disorientated. Finally we came to a halt outside a small warehouse. Its front was partly obscured by a row of sacks, some of which were spilling their contents on to the pavement. Rebecca shot me an expectant glance, a look which said 'This is it!' I reached down to the bag between my feet and felt inside around the contours of the camera. The batteries would last about forty minutes; it was a gamble, but one I had to take. I triggered a tiny switch. Painfully slowly I slipped out of the back seat of the car and into the street behind Rebecca.

We stepped past a number of small boys who were busily weighing out packets of exotic seeds, mushrooms and fruit. I stopped. It looked like contraband, probably smuggled in from China. A few more steps and we were inside. The interior of the shop was quite bare except for rows of shelves lining the walls, crammed with all manner of strange produce, and a battered and solitary desk tucked away in one corner. Beside it was a door leading into the back. The floor was typically grey marble, an aid to keeping the place cool in the height of summer. From behind the desk a man emerged, his shoulders and arms protruding from a shabby white singlet and glistening as if covered with oil. His short cropped hair made him look strangely menacing and yet his smile was lopsided and boyish by comparison. His name was Wang. He was obviously master over all the bustling activity in and around the shop, and explained that he was in the middle of making up orders for market.

'I don't have much time,' he said abruptly, and he obviously wasn't about to waste it on polite conversation.

Casually I scanned the shelves that stretched from floor to ceiling all around us. Could it be? Yes, there it was on open view. Rebecca was busily talking to the man as I slipped my left hand into the pocket of my trousers and quietly pressed three switches. The hidden eye in my hat sprang to life.

'He wants to know how much you can buy,' said Rebecca.

'That very much depends on the price.'

For a few minutes, we parried each other's questions, see-sawing back and forth. He was much more direct than Mr Chan.

'Why do you want tiger bone, only Chinese people use this item in

237

medicine?' 'Who do you buy from now, why have you come to me?' 'Do you have the cash with you?' 'Where do you want me to deliver?'

I had made it clear to Rebecca that this man must understand that even if he didn't like the way westerners do business, the essential thing was to establish ourselves as bona-fide traders with sufficient cash to spend. However, under no circumstances would there be any immediate deal. She would always have to leave the door open so that she could return quietly and fine-tune the mechanism designed to cheat me. It was essential to always devise a way to back out of even the most advanced of business negotiations. The greed element invariably worked!

It was not long before he began to show the first sign of impatience. He turned abruptly away from me, grabbed a bag from one of his shelves and thrust it down in front of me. The bag contained eight bones. I saw immediately that it was a complete set of leg bones from a single tiger.

Except I wanted to make him feel uncomfortable for a little longer.

'What about skins?' I demanded. Rebecca translated and he grinned to reveal a set of rotten and discoloured teeth, interspersed with a few gold-plated dentures. He spoke rapidly to one of the many youths bustling around us with packages that were being whisked away on mopeds. The youth sprinted away down the street and out of sight. He reappeared mysteriously from the back of the store, walking slowly towards us under the weight of a large bundle. On Wang's orders, he slashed the twine that bound it with a Stanley knife. Four animal skins unfurled with a flop on the floor.

I put my shoulder-bag down in the shadow of a sack of strange seeds close to the door, pointing it deliberately at the spectacle unfolding on the cold marble. Then, moving purposefully forward, trying not to spoil the line of vision and tilting my head downwards slightly, I gave the hat-camera the best possible chance of a full close-up.

The skins were very dry and had been poorly preserved. I knelt down for a closer look. Three tigers and a leopard had died to provide this hideous merchandise. I turned the skins over to search for bullet holes. They had been badly patched. With a little tug at one of the tiger skins, a tuft of fur came away in my fingers. This would not have happened if they had been professionally cured. What was on offer was not only obscene, but the quality was extremely poor.

I decided to go on the offensive, hoping to goad Wang into bringing out anything else that he might have hidden away.

'This is no damn good for the American market,' I said. 'I can buy better than this. Where did this crap come from?'

Rebecca shot me a glance. 'Translate word for word,' I said.

'Thailand,' said Mr Wang. I silently prayed that my cameras were working and the microphone was picking up every word in the chaotic atmosphere of the warehouse. At long last, this was the conclusive proof that I needed.

I realised that my feigned irritation with the decrepit state of the skins had paid off. I was now in a strong position. I picked up the bag of bones.

'How am I supposed to know if these are real?' I demanded. 'How do you expect me to believe they aren't fake? I expected to see quality and you show me this shit!'

I nodded urgently to Rebecca when she hesitated to translate the outburst. 'Word for word,' I repeated firmly.

Wang recoiled, then indignantly snapped his grubby fingers and bellowed an order to one of his boys. The youth scurried off and returned almost immediately, dragging two sacks made from a thick fibre of woven nylon. My pulse quickened again. The cameras had already been on for ten minutes. Please God, let the batteries last!

What followed was both macabre and abhorrent. Wang picked up the first sack at the bottom and flipped it upside-down, so that the contents came clattering out with a dull thud on to the tiles. Barely able to believe what I was seeing, I stood momentarily frozen to the spot, my mind racing. The tiniest flaw in my recording equipment would be enough to destroy the finest opportunity I would ever have of proving the existence of this despicable trade.

First came a rib cage, then a skull, both intact. Then the twisted vertebrae of a long tail. The second bag was emptied with as little ceremony. Wang bent down to examine the next lot of bones. The partially dried fat and sinews dangling from them showed that the animal from which they had come had been killed within the last few months. I was looking at the gruesome remains of a tiger.

Wang, Rebecca and two of the boys knelt down to examine the bones and attempted to piece them together. I stepped back quietly and, hiding in the confusion and excitement of this grotesque jigsaw puzzle, picked up the camera-bag on the pretext of getting a pen, and moved it to get a better angle.

They all seemed intent on reassembling the skeleton to show that every last piece was present, and as I approached, Wang brandished a leg in one hand and a bone from his display stock in the other. He was knocking them together, repeating over and over again, 'See, same, same. Tiger, tiger!'

I nodded. 'Yes, it looks like a tiger,' I said. 'Where does it come from?'

'Thailand,' said Wang.

Assembling the skeleton was causing difficulties. They were having problems with the legs. Confident now, I took my life and my opportunity in my hands and, ignoring the risk that my wires would be exposed, bent down and grasped the tiger's rib cage and dragged it closer to the entrance of the shop where the light was better for filming. The other bones were pushed towards me. I picked up the skull. It felt greasy and yet strangely placid, the soul of this magnificent creature long departed. I turned the once proud head in my hand and there, in the back of the cranium, was a large hole. It could only have been made by a primitive gun, fired at close range. Typical of the crude home-made muskets used by the poachers of Thailand.

More angry now than afraid, I replaced the skull on the cold tiles of the floor with the respect of an elder statesman laying a wreath at the tomb of the unknown warrior. One piece after another was handed to me and laid out in its proper place: the neck vertebrae, still held together by desiccated strands of cartilage, then the elegant curvature of the spine; the legs assumed a curious foetal position that seemed strangely appropriate to this hideous spectacle; and finally the tail, arched as if in a final gesture of defiance at its undignified place of rest.

The bare head, empty chest, twisted limbs, and the small patches of orange and black fur around the feet would leave no witness in any doubt that this had once been truly a magnificent tiger. I retrieved my bag and walked it round the skeleton to make sure that we had the best shots from every angle of this squalid scene. Wang walked with me, talking with animation, admiring the handiwork.

Once again and for the record, I asked him to state the origin of this great beast.

'Oh yes, Thailand,' he said. 'I can get many. How many you want?'

CHAPTER TWENTY

Bangkok, December 1991

Boonlerd Angsirijinda stared at the television screen unable to believe his eyes. He sat bolt upright in his chair, his back rigid, hands pressed tightly together in his lap. Sometimes he would nervously touch his brow with the index finger of his right hand. Otherwise he kept absolutely still, as if in shock.

We were in my room on the eleventh floor at the Bangkok Shangri-La. Over two weeks of squalid hotels working undercover in Taiwan had been more than enough to prepare me for the comforts of my old riverside haunt. I needed to feel human again. The last place I stayed at in the west-coast town of Taichung had been a real dump, what they call a 'happy hotel', frequented mostly by businessmen paying for the use of a room in cash and by the hour. It was convenient for me because it was next door to a restaurant called *Bu Jung Bao*. The name meant 'precious healthy soup bowl'. The speciality of the house was tiger-penis soup.

'Where did you get this?' he asked softly.

'In Taiwan, a few days ago.'

'But how?'

'You remember what you told me about the use of hidden cameras?'

'Yes, but this is incredible. I've never seen anything like it before. How?'

'Modern technology,' I said, 'and a whole lot of good luck.'

We watched as the camera panned around the entrance of the restaurant, the picture jumping around a lot, swimming in and out of focus. This was a first-generation VHS copy of the original eight-millimetre tape. I'd had no time on my short stop-over in Hong Kong to edit out the shaky parts.

241

Rebecca's bright red jacket and gold-chained Gucci handbag came into view several times and then blurred out of frame. There was a shot of my rhinestone-studded cowboy boots and then a number of swirling faces moving away up what could only have been stairs. The camera jerked away again and a beautiful woman's face came plainly into view. She was explaining something carefully in Taiwanese, counting on her fingers as she talked, oblivious of the hidden microphone picking up her every word. Her left hand pointed to something out of frame and slowly the camera tracked right and came to rest on what appeared to be a glass cabinet. The lens slowly adjusted itself to the new picture and the edges sharpened and held steady. There, quite distinctly on display, laid out on neat squares of brightly coloured cloth, were the dried genitals of four male tigers.

Boonlerd looked at me in horror. 'From Thailand?' he asked.

'Yes, at least that's what the owner told us.'

Rebecca and I were following up a lead from a good source in Taipei. There had been an obscure article in a provincial newspaper reporting that a group of twelve Taiwanese businessmen had recently run up a huge restaurant bill in the town of Taichung to the tune of NT$500,000. Over £1,000 a head! Such extravagant feasts were not entirely unheard of, but what made this one particularly special was the type of food on offer. An emperor's banquet, according to the report, including a course of virility-enhancing tiger-penis soup.

It was one more piece of the jigsaw that seemed to fit in with the smugglers in Kaohsiung. I was more than ready to leave Taiwan after that episode. Almost every visual detail of events and the entire conversation on that fateful Saturday afternoon had been recorded. Mr Wang had clearly stated that his source for tigers, dead or alive, was Thailand. This squared with the inference from Chen the breeder, when he said his cub had come from Hong Kong which probably meant *via* the Colony at about the same time that three cubs slipped through Boonlerd's net in Bangkok. And yet I had to check out this new lead.

A pattern was definitely emerging. One of my contacts in Taipei had recently undertaken a thorough survey of wildlife trade across the Taiwan Straits from the Chinese mainland. Business, it appeared, was booming. In one memorable quote from the subsequent report the interviewer asked a senior Taiwanese customs

242

officer to estimate the percentage of the many hundreds of local fishing vessels that might be engaged in illegal trade. Apparently he replied, 'All of them!'

In London, the Environmental Investigation Agency had begun to look into alleged cases of rhino-horn smuggling from the southern African states and quickly concluded that they weren't so alleged after all. Taiwan was rapidly gaining a reputation in some circles as the environmental cesspool of the world. The evidence was overwhelming: open-water drift-net violations and dolphin slaughter in the Penghu Islands (Pescadores); ivory and rhino-horn smuggling from Africa; orang-utans from Borneo and Malaysia; exotic birds from South America and Indonesia; and now tigers from Thailand. The insatiable appetite of the Taiwanese for endangered wildlife, it appeared, was responsible for untold amounts of bloodshed across the globe. And a massive black-market operation worth millions of dollars had been allowed to blossom which the authorities in Taipei were doing nothing whatsoever to prevent.

Even this latest newspaper report stating publicly that Taiwanese nationals were eating tiger-penis soup had failed to arouse their concern. Such arrogant disregard for the critically endangered wildlife of the world was not only shameful but also negligent, almost to the point of collusion. If I, a six-foot, fair-haired, brown-eyed Caucasian could infiltrate the local underworld *and* secretly film their nefarious activities, then that surely was further damning testimony of the prevailing inefficiency and incompetence of the domestic forces who had thus far miserably failed to make one single arrest or confiscation.

And so, even though I had the Kaohsiung tapes safely under my belt and locked away, Rebecca and I planned one final sortie into the Taiwanese underworld.

I hired a four-wheel-drive vehicle, a Toyota Super Zace, in Taipei and had the rental company strip out the back seat so that I could sleep inside if necessary. Mostly I needed to stake out the restaurant and film the various comings and goings. It was mid-December. Eddie Chen had said that Taiwanese like to eat tiger meat in winter-time, so there was a slim chance that I could film a delivery. I drove down the west-coast road making wide detours into the towns of Kuanyin and Hsinchu. On the narrow section between Houlung and Yuanli, near the village of Paishatun, I saw fresh tracks on the beach, where a landing craft had come ashore and unloaded its illicit cargo on to a waiting heavy-duty off-road vehicle. The sand was churned up everywhere. I thought of the comment by the customs officer about all the fishing craft being involved in smuggling from the mainland. Here was the proof.

I'd seen the type of beach landing craft before. They were one of the most ubiquitous sights up and down the coastline. They were more of a raft than a boat, and of very simple construction: basically just a number of long sections of ten-inch reinforced plastic piping, welded together, sealed at the ends and bent up at an angle of about thirty degrees at the bow. They were virtually unsinkable and robust; propelled by a sturdy outboard engine, they sat high in the water with a draught of only a few inches. They were cheap and disposable, and they did the job. It was on high-speed vessels like these that the tigers were being brought ashore under the cover of darkness.

Of course I realised that the police and customs had a difficult task patrolling these waters. But not one single arrest?

I continued down toward my destination, passing pale, feature-less, high-rise buildings, some clean with a well-scrubbed appear-ance, others adorned with Chinese scribble and tattered advertising banners flapping in the wind. There were row upon row of low-level manufacturing plants with pitched asbestos roofs beside neatly regimented lines of detached houses. The dwellings and the facto-ries seemed somehow inextricably linked, and probably were. At about 83 per cent, Taiwan has one of the world's highest rates of home ownership in the world. I began to think more about this perplexing land, to try and reach some sort of understanding of its complex and frequently disparate ways.

Taiwan was not some third-world backwater country desperately struggling to repay crippling IMF loans. It was the world's four-teenth largest trading nation with estimated foreign exchange and gold deposits second only to those of Switzerland. On the face of it, Taiwan was an extremely healthy democratic and highly industrial-ised nation, exporting billions of dollars-worth of manufactured goods like computers and electronics, sportswear and plastics to Europe and the United States each year. They had remained largely unaffected by the recession that dogged the rest of the world in the late eighties and early nineties, so what was wrong with the place?

The answer could only lie in consumption. The Taiwanese did not like to save their money; they sought the instant gratification of spend, spend, spend! Much of the Taiwanese obsession with materi-alism had to do with gaining 'face', not material wealth. Having

244

'big face' was synonymous with prestige, and prestige is very important to the Chinese. I'd even heard of people owning luxury cars when they couldn't drive and some buying pianos without ever intending to play, simply because the higher the price tag, the bigger the 'face'.

Such conspicuous consumption indicated to me an underlying insecurity which could only stem from a sense of inferiority probably rooted in the Taiwanese people's humble origins. In one generation they had made the gigantic leap from a poor, war-torn, agricultural economy to a thriving and hugely successful industrialised nation. And they were now grabbing every opportunity to show off their new-found prosperity. This in itself was perhaps harmless enough, except that it didn't stop there, because prestige status-symbols were becoming commonplace and increasingly available to more and more people.

So the unscrupulous 'avant-garde' had to look elsewhere and invariably found 'big-face' items on the black market. Perversely, the underground trade offered even greater face, since it was a measure of the buyers' *guanxi* or connections to be able to circumvent the law and acquire such things. And thus a massive multibillion dollar black economy had developed over the years to supply the whims and fantasies of an ever-growing volume of Taiwanese seeking exclusive products outside and regardless of the law.

The tiger had long been a symbol of great strength and power to the Taiwanese and their Chinese forefathers. Myths and legends abound, and the tiger features in books, poems, paintings and songs. Perhaps no other creature on earth has captured the imagination of the Chinese quite so much as the tiger, and bedtime stories of its stealth, prowess, bravery and cunning were told to millions of children across the land each night. Yet for some, this very nobility made it the object of desire, and its rarity only increased that wanton avarice.

Tucked away in a book that I had once read about tigers was an obscure reference to a tiger eradication policy that prevailed across south-eastern China throughout much of the latter half of the 1960s and well into the 1970s. I had decided to dig deeper into this and discovered that Chairman Mao Tse-tung had in fact declared the indigenous tiger species vermin in 1966 and ordered its virtual extermination. The move was tied into the wide-scale agriculturalisation of vast tracts of pristine tiger habitat during the Great Proletarian Cultural Revolution of the time. Bounties were offered

245

to hunters for every tiger they killed and the authorities didn't much care how they went about it. The ensuing slaughter produced a flood of cheap tiger meat and other body parts on to the market upon which a number of scheming individuals resolved to capitalise. They knew of the ancient writings in the traditional Chinese pharmacopoeia and of the references to the apparent mystical healing powers of various parts of the tiger. Such 'delicacies' had hitherto been totally out of reach of all but a handful of Chinese emperors, mandarins and warlords. These unscrupulous merchants exploited the fundamental communist philosophy that everyone is equal and prayed upon the credulous nature of their people. Many Chinese believe in *jinbu* – that is to say, you are what you eat – and thousands lined up to test the theories foisted upon them by the enterprising Chinese medicine manufacturers. Tiger-bone tablets to banish rheumatism and arthritis, tiger-eye potions to improve vision, powdered tiger genitalia as the ultimate aphrodisiac. Other remedies were even more arcane, and the tiger's nose was sold to hang above the marital bed as a talisman to induce the conception of male children.

Tiger products rapidly found favour amongst the highly superstitious Chinese people, and prices rose dramatically as demand began to outstrip supply. By the mid to late eighties their stockpiles and indeed their own tiger population had all but disappeared and the merchants were forced to look further afield for supplies. The tiger reserves in India were amongst the first to be targeted, although nobody in authority dared to admit that this was the case until 1992. The current poaching epidemic affecting all remaining tiger populations throughout Asia was certainly not the result of centuries of popular cultural tradition but the product of post-revolution capitalistic enterprise – Chinese style!

And therefore it became clear to me that it was in the Taiwanese neo-consumerism that I would find the answer to the tiger's demise. To believe that the species' prevailing plight in the wild was the product of hundreds of years of traditional consumption was utterly absurd to my way of thinking. If that was indeed the case, as many non-adversarial conservationists believed, the tiger would surely have gone extinct centuries before.

What staggered me even more was that none of the big-name wildlife groups seemed to have given the subject any serious degree of thought. They simply accepted the Chinese agitprop that eating tigers was deeply entrenched in their hallowed medicinal pharmacopoeia, and therefore off-limits. They appeared totally paralysed, responding timidly and with stupefying predictability by commissioning more scientific surveys and reports. These inevitably took months if not years to prepare, cost a great deal of money and ultimately reaffirmed only one major point, that the tiger was rapidly going down the tubes. And the slaughter continued.

The answer was right under everyone's nose. It was the old story of the emperor's new clothes, and yet there was no quiet voice of dissent in the crowd. It was clear to me that the new Asian prosperity was responsible for the decline of the tiger. The Taiwanese could now buy all the Mercedes motor cars, the Rolex watches or the Louis Vuitton handbags they desired. Western television had taught them to covet these things, and now they wanted more.

Exotic species had become fashion items; the orang-utan craze was testament to that. The motto was now 'endangered is best', and unless a way could be found to tackle that new wave of underground consumerism, we could all kiss goodbye to the tiger. There was no other way. There was not enough time for elaborate scientific experiments like the ill-fated de-horning of the rhino. The amount of cash stacked up in opposition was too enormous.

It was time to go to war and I would need a campaigning machine in order to do that. It would take money, guts, tenacity and no end of creative energy to save the tiger, and a dynamic organisation behind it. And as I drove into the outskirts of Taichung, a name came into my head. I would call it The Tiger Trust.

I found the restaurant without difficulty. Rebecca had tracked it down in a trice and told me that I would find it located close to an opulent new karaoke bar built like a pyramid. Taichung was a rich town; it could afford grandiose indulgences like that.

She also knew of *Bu Jung Bao* through another unrelated source. American Express were running a financial incentive offer to their cardholders who ate at specially chosen prestige restaurants throughout Taiwan: coupons to the value of several hundred dollars off the cost of their meal. If this eatery really did serve tiger-penis soup, she told me, then Amex were more or less subsidising the tab!

She met me at the 'happy hotel' and we ran through our act together. We planned to eat at the restaurant so I wouldn't be able to use the hat-camera. I would take the leather shoulder-bag and rig the Hi8 video-camcorder so that I could change the batteries and tape

247

quickly in the men's washroom. It would be the old sugar-daddy and honey-child routine, with me poking my nose and camera around as much as possible whilst Rebecca provided the necessary distractions.

At seven o'clock we left the sleazy hotel. Taiwanese like to eat early. The restaurant building itself was long and sleek and expensively clad in glass. We were met at the downstairs entrance by an attractive young lady, named Claelia, who checked our reservation against a computerised list.

'You're seated upstairs, on table 11, by the window. Ben will show you the way,' she said in disjointed English and in obvious deference to my singularly un-Chinese appearance.

In the lobby beside the reception desk I had noticed an ornate bow-fronted mahogany cabinet. It was an exquisite piece with beautifully carved gothic motifs and magnificent cabriole legs, most probably Chippendale, I thought; this place could obviously afford it. Through the curved glass of the doors I could see a number of shelves. On each were laid out the delicacies of the house. I could see wild ginseng from North Korea, dried sea cucumbers from the Sea of Japan, abalone from Tasmania, shark's fin from the Great Barrier Reef and beautifully woven birds nests from Phang Na Bay. And in the centre of the display were delicately folded squares of coloured satin upon which, Claelia willingly explained, reposed the male genitals of tigers from India, Siberia, China and Thailand.

'What is this?' I enquired with nonchalant disinterest.

'That is a tiger penis.'

'Oh really?'

'All the ones with a spike on the end are tiger penises. We import them from Northern China and Thailand,' she continued. 'Sometimes from India as well, but the Siberian tiger is the best.'

'Fascinating. And then what do you do with them?'

'We make soup with them.'

'How revolting.'

There was no stopping her, she was like a museum guide, impossible to turn off. 'Because the tiger penis is dried, we have to soak it in water for a week. It takes that time to soften it. Then we add twelve different kinds of herbs which are good for men. It takes twelve to sixteen hours to make this soup.'

'Good for men, you say?'

'Yes, it is a popular dish among men in Taiwan. We serve it in winter. When they eat the soup with all the medicine in it they get horny.'

'How absolutely extraordinary. And how much does this all cost?'

'Each bowl of soup, served for eight people, costs £250. For a table of fourteen or fifteen people we need two tiger penises to make the soup rich enough, so that would cost £500.'

'Is that all?' I said. 'Well, you've been a great help, hasn't she, sweetheart?'

'Yes, you've no idea how helpful,' said Rebecca with a smile, and we allowed Ben, the maître d'hôtel, to show us to our table.

'And that's really just about it,' I said to Boonlerd. 'We went upstairs and I dashed off to the loo and checked the tape. The Canon Hi8 plays back through the viewfinder and the images were fine, as you can see.'

'Has anyone else seen this?' he enquired nervously.

'Only Rebecca and my man in Hong Kong.'

'You know that Thailand has been under a lot of pressure recently to clean up its act?'

'Yes, I know.'

'These pictures demonstrate something far worse than what is happening here,' he said.

'I wouldn't go so far as to say that. You know that there are Korean restaurants here boiling bear cubs alive.'

'Yes, but we have no proof.'

'Well, that doesn't mean it's not going on. You must find the proof. Then perhaps the international pressure will be relaxed.'

'Yes, you are right. Personally I do not mind the pressure. It helps me to do my job. People now want results and what you've done here is to demonstrate that the evidence can be found.'

'But you don't have the technology . . .' I said sadly.

'No, and even if we did I doubt that there is anyone here that could use it successfully, unless of course . . .'

'Oh, no,' I said, 'not me. I've had quite enough of this cloak and dagger work for a while, thank you very much, and besides it's Christmas, and I have to get back to Hong Kong to meet up with Sophy.'

'She is a very special lady.'

'Yes, I know, thank you. And thank you for keeping her company while I have been away. She worries about me and you have been a great source of comfort and support. I'm very grateful.'

He stood up and began pacing around by the window as if he was agonising within himself, trying to decide what to say or how to put it.

'Michael,' he began, 'I have an American friend to whom I would like to show these tapes.'

'What sort of American friend?'

'He knows about your work already. He told me about the special spy-cameras.'

'I see,' I said, thinking that this gambit had CIA written all over it!

'He might be able to do something politically. You remember what I told you about the Korean Embassy official who wanted two hundred bears just before the 1988 Olympics?'

I remembered only too well. The Koreans had made an unofficial request to purchase Malayan sun bears from Thailand, apparently to fortify their athletes during the international games. Boonlerd had diplomatically told them to sling their hook. I said, 'Yes, that can't have been an easy request to dodge.'

'Well, my friend supported me on that and had a quiet word with them. They said at the time that it didn't matter because they could easily get the bears elsewhere. But I know I offended them.'

'Tough shit,' I said, getting annoyed, and thinking how hard it must be at times to be a government servant.

'He might be willing to intervene again,' said Boonlerd.

'What you're really asking me to do is to help divert pressure away from Thailand on to some other country, isn't that it?' I asked angrily, instantly regretting what I had said.

I could see that I had deeply offended him. 'I'm sorry, Boonlerd, but I just can't see how people consuming tigers in Taiwan is going to help you in your work. As far as the Taiwanese are concerned, they are not responsible for the poaching. Not guilty. Their traders are only buying up debris.'

'You know that's nonsense. They are creating the demand. It is their money that is corrupting the Thai people. Your video proves that.'

I had never seen him quite so upset. It was so unlike the Thai. 'Do you really think it would help?' I asked.

'Yes, I think it might,' he replied carefully.

'Take them,' I said. 'I have copies. Please use them wisely.'

'You have my word. Thank you,' he said solemnly. 'And now, please, allow me to invite you for a pre-Christmas dinner.'

'On one condition.'

'What's that?'

'You don't ask me to try tiger-penis soup,' I said, and we both laughed.

CHAPTER TWENTY-ONE

Hong Kong, December 1991

Another Christmas came and went. Sophy and I stayed with our jockey-landlord in Hong Kong. We sat down to an enormous roast turkey at exactly one o'clock in the afternoon having just toasted absent friends with the first bottle from a case of well-chilled Moët et Chandon champagne. At midnight we were still at the table with twelve green bottles lying on the floor. I don't remember much happening after that.

We had planned to visit mainland China in the New Year, ostensibly to photograph the giant pandas at the WWF-sponsored Wolong breeding centre in the western province of Sichuan. I also wanted to see for myself the extent of the tiger trade in the old 'Middle Kingdom'.

My good friend Wong Kwok Hung agreed to accompany me on a recce and permit-securing mission, and we flew out together in the early hours of New Year's Day, 1992. The alternative and perhaps more civilised Dragonair flight was hopelessly overbooked as usual, so wc had no choice but to fly the communist-owned airline instead. The CAAC flight from Hong Kong to the provincial capital of Chengdu was uneventful. The plane was filthy, the food inedible and the sick-bags hadn't been emptied since God knows when. It was the first day of 'Visit China 1992 Year' and therefore, one could only assume, probably better than usual. The Chinese obviously liked to create the right sort of impression for their distinguished visitors, I thought dryly at the time. Sitting beside me was a representative of the International Olympic Committee having a quiet look behind the scenes at China's bid for the year 2000 Olympic Games. He wasn't terribly impressed either.

We spent four days in the freezing cold, mostly sitting across from

Chinese officials in woolly hats and overcoats shivering at their desks, and bemoaning the total absence of any adequate heating system. I produced letters of introduction, passport and visas, cartons of cigarettes and bottles of whisky. They nodded approvingly and shuffled voluminous amounts of unnecessary paperwork around aimlessly from one building to another.

On one occasion, when we could endure the endless waiting around no longer, we went for a walk, which took us in the general direction of the food market. Once there we were surrounded by pedlars offering all sorts of weird merchandise. On a whim I asked Wong if he could discreetly let it be known that we might be interested in tiger products. Within minutes there was a tug at my sleeve and we were led through a throng of people paddling in a sea of bicycles and away from the market. We were led up a damp unlit staircase of a grimy tenement building and into a rancid chamber that appeared to serve as a dwelling place for seven equally fusty inhabitants. By the light of an oil-lamp we watched as our urchin guide groped under an ancient and sagging bedstead producing at length a newspaper package tied up with brown twine. He carefully unwrapped the parcel in the flickering glow of the lantern. Finally, with tea-stained teeth, he smiled up at us as he removed the last crumpled piece of newsprint. Wong and I stared down in horror at the neatly severed paws of a bear-cub.

We trudged in silence back to our hotel, scarcely able to contain our rage. Mercifully the bar was open and we got completely plastered. Alcohol might not solve the problems of the world, but it definitely puts them into another perspective. The following morning we wearily traipsed back to the State government offices and by early evening had finally acquired the requisite number of rubber stamps and signatures to allow our return in three weeks.

With three cheers to the gods of patience, fortitude and equanimity, we flew back to Hong Kong, also on CAAC. A journey that was only marginally better than the first simply because we were travelling in a civilised direction.

'Sophy, you don't really want to go to China,' I said, pleading.

'Yes I do. You promised me a holiday.'

'A holiday! This will be bloody purgatory. Let's go somewhere else.'

'What's wrong with China?' she asked incredulously.

'I'm not quite sure how else I can put it, darling. It's cold, it's damp, it's miserable. The food is awful, everything is filthy, nothing works. The place stinks.'

'Sounds interesting to me . . .'

And so we went to China. We were met at the airport by odd little men with rosy cheeks and oversize uniforms who couldn't stand still and were forever hopping from one foot to the other and rubbing their hands to banish the cold. I hated it. Why me, I thought?

And then I started to enjoy it. I had to. There was simply no other choice.

They say it's not where you are, but who you're with. I was with the person I loved most in all the world, and accompanied by a Chinese guide and interpreter who turned out to be an absolute scream. Sophy christened him Joe; his real name was completely unpronounceable. In the next two weeks we saw things that few westerners could ever imagine, let alone get the opportunity to view. I still carry the photograph of Sophy cuddling a baby panda in my address book to this day.

We found evidence of wide-scale consumption of tiger bone and body parts, but at the time China made no pretence to the outside world that she was doing anything to control the situation. We obtained video footage of a giant panda trap well within the exclusive Wolong reserve which substantiated claims in the TRAFFIC report that the animals were being offered for sale on the other side of the country just across the sea from Taiwan. The trap was an exact model of the type used by the American research biologist, Dr George Schaller, when he radio-collared and studied the species back in the seventies. I still have the hair samples taken from inside the trap. They were later positively identified as *Ailuropoda melanoleuca*, the giant panda.

This alarming discovery squared with rumours I'd been hearing earlier that there was at least one panda penned up somewhere back in Taiwan, and that somebody had already acquired photographs to prove it. Such a disclosure would have had the effect of a political H-bomb on Sino-Taiwanese relations. And therefore not surprisingly, nobody was doing a damn thing to pursue the matter. Regrettably I only had one pair of hands and the rumours eventually died. Probably not long after the poor creature itself.

On the way back from Wolong, Joe took us to a bear farm. I knew he was a card-carrying member of the Party and reported back regularly to the authorities about what we were up to. Equally, however, he couldn't be expected to watch over us twenty-four hours a day. On the nineteen or so when he wasn't looking, we harvested our information. He'd been quite open about the farm, what it did and why. He knew people that worked there. We feigned uninterest to begin with, then disbelief, saying it wasn't possible to stick a catheter into a live bear and milk its bile fluids.

Although we knew perfectly well that it was, except that nobody had ever filmed it before.

There were over four hundred Asiatic bears at the farm, each in their own individual hell. The cages stood on concrete plinths, four feet off the ground. It was easier that way they said: food went in through the bars and excrement out the underside on to the concrete floor below. Inside the three by three by four feet solitary units, pairs of dark rheumy eyes would gaze dolefully at the beasts opposite. The wretched and feeble creatures had lost the ability to stand. The cramped interior and their own obesity prevented any appreciable body movement. The farm's production line didn't require it. The bears needed to be kept docile and acquiescent so that their bile could be milked twice a day and then crystallised into a highly lucrative foreign-exchange earner.

We visited the farm-shop, a veritable Pandora's box of arcane remedies from a plethora of endangered species. There were the ubiquitous one-gram files of bear-bile crystals, said to be the great panacea in Chinese medicine; oil made from the scent glands of the rare musk deer; laryngitis pills containing rhinoceros horn; and a dozen different preparations containing tiger-body parts in one form or another.

There was only a handful of people in the store, and Sophy neatly steered Joe off to talk with the shop assistant whilst I panned around the shelves with my camcorder. The battery was low, the camera had been very busy that morning, but I got the images that I wanted including a shot of the manager as he appeared behind the counter.

'You have a lot of interesting merchandise here.' I asked Joe to translate.

'Yes, we have many different products because we have many different customers that come to my farm.'

'Not many *gweilos*, I shouldn't imagine?' I enquired, leading him on.

'Oh no!' he laughed. 'You are the first for a long, long time.'

'Where do your best customers come from?'

'Taiwan!'

'Anywhere else?'

'Also from Korea and Japan. They buy a lot. Especially the bear bile.'

I knew that the province of Sichuan had been a great stronghold of the KMT and the Chiang Kai-shek regime before the 1949 revolution. It was not surprising that so many Taiwanese wished to visit the 'old country'. What was more of a surprise was their willingness to import the old ways. Kentucky Fried Chicken and tiger-bone wine made strange bedfellows to my way of thinking.

In the afternoon we were taken to the Chengdu Zoo. The overall squalor of the place was no great shock. We had already been in China for two weeks and had become accustomed to animal deprivation. Sophy and I left when the batteries died in my camera. We'd seen enough, and it was time to get back to Hong Kong.

We returned on February 4th and our jockey friend, Tony Ives, met us at the airport. Money was getting tight, and he'd generously invited us to stay at his spacious apartment on the island. He felt it was the least he could do to help. We had been renting his house in England for the past six months and had not been anywhere near it for the last five.

Of course Sophy and I hadn't planned it that way. We were being sucked into the world of environmental espionage, at least I was. There was no predicting what would happen from one week to the next. I had to follow up the leads as and where I found them, and to be prepared to jump on a plane at a moment's notice.

It was no life for newlyweds; we spent weeks apart, days without any form of contact whatsoever. I was becoming obsessed by the notion that somehow, if I looked long and hard enough, I would find the key that unlocked the mystery as to just why the world was doing nothing to prevent the tiger from vanishing into oblivion. And Sophy, bless her heart, was always there for me, always supportive and never complaining. She knew in her heart that all this was happening for a reason, and that perhaps, one day, I might just get lucky.

A week later I was back in Taiwan. Rebecca had heard a rumour that a live tiger was to be sacrificed in honour of the first moon of the Chinese New Year, somewhere near the town of Paiho in Tainan county. If this was true it would be a recurrence of a similar incident several years earlier. I'd already seen the gory photographs. No-one, to my knowledge, had ever succeeded in filming the horrific practice.

I also had something else up my sleeve. For some time now I had watched the growing debate surrounding the demise of the black rhinoceros in southern Africa, and the possible reasons behind it. It appeared to me that there were many similarities with what was also happening to the tiger, except that nobody was talking about the big cat at the time. Debate was centred around the rhino. I reasoned that if I could establish a common ground between the plight of the two species, then I would have a fast track on to the negotiating table with the tiger. I'd therefore kept my ear very closely to the ground on matters concerning the mighty herbivore, and trading information with one or two organisations that were concentrating on the subject.

The World Wide Fund for Nature's trade monitoring arm, TRAFFIC, had convened a special workshop in Taipei that week to discuss the rhino, and I had accepted an invitation to go along. I knew that Taiwan's Council of Agriculture vice chairman, Ling Shiang-nung, would be there, and I hoped to buttonhole him on the question of tigers as well.

Kristin Nowel, TRAFFIC's local bureau chief, presented her well-documented report entitled 'The Horns of a Dilemma' to a packed room. I sat beside an eminent authority on the subject, Dr Andrew Laurie from Cambridge University. We introduced ourselves and sat back to listen to an eloquent if not somewhat obsequious presentation followed by a stream of Taiwanese speakers, all huffing and puffing about the just and proper position of rhinoceros horn in traditional Chinese medicine. It was all a bit one-sided. Andrew got up and tried to say his piece in defence of the poor creature, showing slides of his studies across Africa, although nobody had the decency to dim the lights. His microphone spluttered on and off intermittently, and eventually he returned to his seat without anyone being quite sure of what they had seen or quite what had been said. Had I been a conspiracy theorist, I might well have suspected sabotage.

He shrugged and said 'Blast', as he sat down beside me. From that point on things progressively went downhill. At the afternoon coffee-break, I stood dumbfounded and listened to Ling castigate Dr Laurie and his position on rhino conservation, and when Andrew retreated, clearly unnerved and offended, I jumped into the breach.

'Good afternoon, Dr Ling, my name is Michael Day.' He had no PhD, but he did have a massive ego.

258

'Eh, howsay . . . good afternoon,' he replied, fumbling for a business card.

'I'd like to ask you about the tiger farms in Taiwan and what your government is doing to prevent the illegal import of tiger bone from abroad,' I began quickly, not sure which of my cards to give him.

'There are no eh, eh, howsay . . . tiger farms on Taiwan,' he stammered.

'With respect, sir, I beg to differ. I have evidence of massive tiger-smuggling, illegal tiger-breeding and restaurants selling tiger-penis soup all here in Taiwan.' His neck began to swell and turn red and his bottom lip started to quiver. 'There are no restaurants selling, eh, eh, eh, howsay . . . tiger-penis soup!'

'But I have video proof,' I said.

'Why you, eh, howsay . . . interfere in, eh, howsay . . . Taiwan affairs?'

'Because it is a matter of international concern. Uncontrolled demand in this country is responsible for the slaughter of tigers abroad.'

'This is not, eh, eh, eh, howsay . . . your concern!' he ranted at me.

'I have made it my concern. I would like to request a meeting with you to discuss my findings,' I said as clearly and respectfully as I could muster.

'I refuse! I have no time, for, eh, eh, howsay . . . terrorists!' and he stormed off.

'Terrorist?' I shouted at his departing back, but he was gone. And Kristin Nowel immediately came over with a look that said, don't you dare ruin my workshop.

'What the hell was that all about?' she demanded.

I just shook my head in disbelief. 'Nothing,' I said, 'absolutely nothing.'

The meeting reconvened, and the discussion centred around TRAFFIC's proposals and recommendations. I was only an observer and was therefore not allowed to speak. So for the next two hours I scribbled messages to my neighbour Andrew who appeared as outraged as I at what we were hearing.

I knew enough by then to realise that although TRAFFIC was ostensibly only a trade monitoring and statistical analysis organisa-tion, they were having a bloody good try at prescribing policy to the Taiwanese. Dr Laurie couldn't help but agree. I was flabbergasted at the grovelling and power politics going on before me. A critically endangered species was at stake here, and I began to think if this is what goes on behind the scenes no wonder the wildlife of the world is in such dire straits.

I needed to talk to Kristin, to try and understand what the hell was going on. As the meeting broke up, she just glared at me and I could only surmise that Ling had spoken to her about me.

'Kristin, I need to talk with you,' I called across the room.

'Not now, Mike,' she said with a look that meant, as far as she was concerned, that I'd said quite enough already.

Andrew and I shared a taxi back to my hotel. He was staying at the YMCA and had an early flight out in the morning, and declined the offer of a drink. I was left alone to my troubled thoughts. I desperately needed advice and decided that the only place I was likely to get it was from my old friends at the Environmental Investigation Agency. Peter Knights was now stationed at their Washington office and I sat down at the cramped bedside desk and hastily wrote him my report.

Taipei, February 12th, 1992

Observers were clearly baffled here today on this, the second day of a TRAFFIC-initiated workshop, to discuss proposals to control the use and trade in rhino horn (and rhino powder) in the Taiwan area.

Confusion began late yesterday afternoon when the local TRAFFIC office senior representative clearly stated that her organisation, and therefore the WWF, would support an open-ended time limit for the disposal of current stocks of rhino horn on the island, estimated to be as much as nine tonnes.

A recent survey, conducted by TRAFFIC, showed annual consumption to be in the region of 300–400 kilograms, which would therefore allow Taiwan up to twenty-five years to empty their stores!

In June 1989 Taiwan enacted their long-awaited wildlife conservation law. The new law allowed traders and traditional medicine shops until November 1989 to register their stocks. The penalty thereafter for possession with intent to sell (Article 33) carries a prison sentence of up to two years and/or a fine up to US$2,400 (tough measures indeed). However, since that time, not one single prosecution has been brought before the courts despite the TRAFFIC survey's findings that only four of

260

the 2,453 pharmacists interviewed had bothered to register their rhino-horn stocks!

The four-day workshop, intending to 'cooperate with the world's conservation of wild rhinoceros species', quickly degenerated into a face-saving exercise on the part of the Taiwanese authorities who paraded endless speakers, all charged with the task of promoting the efficacy of rhino horn in traditional Chinese medicine, to the assembled gathering and thus manoeuvring the conference deftly on to the subject of licensing (again) existing stocks and the people allowed to dispense them.

There are currently in excess of 8,000 unlicensed pharmacists practising in Taiwan, mainly because the owners are unqualified but also because as an unlicensed business the majority of trade is conducted in cash and is therefore untaxed. Some sources estimate that up to 40 per cent of Taiwan's economy operates outside of the law and therefore doesn't show up in official statistics. Clearly any effort on the part of the Taiwanese authorities to enact new legislation would be met with the same disregard and contempt by the trade as in previous cases.

So where does all this leave the poor rhino? Dr Andrew Laurie clearly stated that rhino poaching in the southern African countries is once more on the increase. Conclusive evidence has been obtained to prove that the end market is still Taiwan. Since the enactment of the 1989 law, several tonnes have been smuggled into the country and it is only the gross incompetence of the Taiwanese authorities in enforcing the law that has given rise to these new compromise discussions intended to appease citizens trading in and stockpiling their illegal merchandise currently valued at well over US$60,000,000!

In conclusion, now is not the time to begin to discuss traditional, cultural or historic uses of rhino horn. Times change. Traditions change with them. Cannibalism, slavery, foot-binding etc., latterly even drift-net fishing methods, have succumbed to world opinion. To now license and therefore legalise approximately ten tonnes of rhino horn opens the door to continued trade abuse by perpetuating virtually ad infinitum the demand. And if the market subsequently begins to accept powdered rhino horn, to quote Dr George Schaller, 'The blueprint for extinction will have been established'.

Taiwan not only holds these large stocks of rhino horn, but

elephant ivory, tiger bone, bear gall-bladder, musk-deer glands etc. Any sanctioning of relaxed proposals by TRAFFIC and therefore ultimately the WWF on the Taiwanese, allowing them an open-ended time period to dispose of stock, sets a precedent that will send shock-waves around the conservationists of the world and will sign the death warrant of countless rhinos, tigers, bears etc. in the immediate future.

I looked long and hard at the hastily written document. It was totally accurate as far as I was concerned, although somewhat unconventional. The hell with that, I thought. If the rhino-horn stocks were registered and legalised then the underworld would use them to launder fresh material, and the killing across the plains of Africa would continue unabated. TRAFFIC was promoting the path of appeasement and least resistance, a thoroughly self-serving and defeatist approach, to my way of thinking. I was sure that a Taiwanese speaker at the meeting had suggested a limited period of two years to consume existing stocks, and that Kristin had rejected the idea as unworkable. I had needed to ask her about that and she hadn't given me the chance and so I left all reference to it out of the report.

It was late as I padded barefoot down to the reception desk and gave the clerk the fax number to the EIA's Washington office. I stood tapping my fingers on the counter as the three pages were swept smoothly through the machine and were handed back to me with the transmission report.

There had been very little news from Kate Pearce regarding the American TV documentary, and I began to accept that the project had either failed to excite the commissioning moguls, or that lawyers were sitting on the concept to the point of suffocation. Either way it was dead or dying. Sam was somewhere in France badgering the European government on marine mammal conservation issues, and Sophy was holding the fort at our temporarily rented house in Phuket. I was in the field and had a lead to run down, and so for the next few days I stationed myself at the Redhill Hotel in Tainan and searched.

I found more orang-utans, clouded leopards, scarlet macaws and abundant domestic species being secretly traded and butchered, recording it all on hidden cameras. But no tiger slaughter. I found another farm just outside the town of Hsinhua and that led me to the village of Tsochen and then on a wild-goose chase across the county to a place called Chiali. Some new American friends from Tainan who invariably came along with me to translate began to think I was completely nuts. They couldn't understand the point of risking one's neck to save a wild animal, and had no desire to jeopardise their tenuous residence visas on my dangerous crusade. In the end I drove around alone.

Finally I returned to Taipei. My last stop had been at the east-coast town of Hualien. I had been taken deep into the Taroko National Park, through the magnificent marble gorge on yet another wild-goose chase looking for a poacher that supposedly stored frozen monkey heads in his deep freeze. My guide bolted when he heard the first sign of the man and his hunting dogs coming down the hillside. For a while I thought that I'd been set up. A man could easily disappear in that terrain and never be seen again. I hid well away from the poacher's house and slowly beat my own retreat back along the narrow and perilous mountain path to the four-wheel-drive and left, vowing never to take such an idiotic risk ever again.

Once back in the capital I called up an old friend, Keith Highley, who was the local representative of an environmental organisation called Earthtrust. He'd done great work on marine mammals around Taiwan, recording some of the bloodiest scenes of dolphin slaughter imaginable. More recently, he had taken up the plight of the rhino, and had established a definite illegal trade link with South Africa. He was a quiet, non-combative sort of man, and if I was the bad cop in the old scenario, he was the good guy. His Hawaii-based organisation kept him invariably strapped for funds, and I enjoyed buying him a beer. He graciously invited me over to his house that evening, and on the way I stopped to pick up a dozen cans of Tiger beer.

The Taipei streets are never quiet, even at the best of times. One in five of its 2.5 million inhabitants owns a car and the city has more than one million motor cycles, so making a positive identification of any one particular driver in such traffic was almost impossible. Nevertheless, as I pulled away from where I'd bought the beer, I was convinced that someone deliberately pulled out and followed me. The black Honda scooter stayed on my tail past the central railway station and out on to the Hsinsheng road north toward the Sun Yat-sen freeway. We crossed the Keelung river east of the domestic airport and I began to meander my way up the hills into the suburb of Neihu. And then I lost sight of him. He'd been clearly visible in my rear-view mirror all the way up to that point and only one of three things could have happened: 1) either it was a complete coincidence and he continued on his journey; 2) I lost him; 3) he guessed exactly where I was going and fell back deliberately.

Five minutes later I knocked on Keith's door and proudly handed him the beer as he came to greet me. I looked down the steep stone steps to the car and said. 'Will it be all right there? I've got some important papers, a camera, clothes, that sort of thing inside.'

'No problem,' said Keith. 'This is a decent neighbourhood. I've never heard of any break-ins. I'm sure it will be OK.'

I had no intention of staying the night, but one beer led to another. I was tired and still a bit shaken by the Taroko Gorge incident. Keith and his Taiwanese wife Suzie were fun and interesting company, and around midnight I gratefully accepted their kind offer of a bed.

At seven o'clock the next morning, Keith came into my room and shook me awake. 'Mike, wake up,' he said. 'You'd better get dressed and get down here.'

'Go away,' I moaned, 'my brain hurts.'

'Mike, wake up, for Christ's sake. Your truck's been trashed.'

'Oh shit!' I said dragging my head off the pillow. 'Why am I not surprised to hear that?'

CHAPTER TWENTY-TWO

Kyoto, Japan, March 1992

In every war there can be any number of battle grounds. Traditionally, the skies, the sea and strategic land positions must be secured
before any one side can claim victory. In the fight to save the tiger, a
thousand troops were already deployed across Asia, often engaging
the enemy poachers in bloody and sometimes fatal exchange of fire.
These courageous game-wardens were poorly paid, ill-equipped and
strategically outnumbered, and yet they fought on, praying each day
to their spirit-deities that the relentless onslaught of the poachers
would soon abate. Their prayers remained unanswered as more and
more cattle-herders, foresters and impoverished village dwellers
took up arms against them. This growing army of people had heard
of the mighty fortune to be earned by selling the bones of a tiger to
the foreign buyers that traded through the corrupt merchants in the
bazaars of Delhi, Jakarta and Bangkok. But the brave rangers never
gave up hope.

In Taiwan, the enemy was having a very easy time of it. There was
no opposition, and therefore no conflict. In Taiwan, the illegal
traders were having a field-day because, so far as the authorities in
the capital Taipei were concerned, there were no tiger farms, no
smuggling of tigers from abroad, and no restaurants selling tiger-
penis soup. Such things, quite simply, didn't happen in Taiwan.

Except that I knew they did. I had proof. Irrefutable, in-your-face
type proof, all carefully catalogued and recorded on eight-
millimetre video tape.

The Japanese say that 'business is war'. That suited me just fine,
because in March 1992 they were hosting the eighth global Conference of the Parties to CITES, the Convention on International
Trade in Endangered Species in the southern town of Kyoto. And

when I left Keith Highley in Taipei that fateful morning, without ever having the time to discover who broke into my car, I had only seventy-two hours to get there. A camera and some clothes had been stolen, along with some important notes and the video tape from the Taroko Gorge. I no longer believed in coincidence, and my instincts told me that it was time to leave Taiwan, before something really serious happened.

So far as I was concerned, the business of trading endangered wildlife was war. The thousands of courageous rangers around the world had every right to expect that their heroism in defence of the wild be acknowledged and upheld. They were, after all, not only defending the animals, but the law.

Someone once wrote that: 'When you set up a czarship, rest assured that however wonderful and brilliant the original people are, those that come after will be swine; that's the way it works.' He was probably thinking about CITES at the time.

Any fanciful notions that I might have had about the mighty forces of conservationism uniting against a common foe at the conference were quickly dispelled when I discovered an eight-foot sound-proofed partition separating the WWF/IUCN/TRAFFIC alliance away from the rest of the world's several hundred non-governmental organisations in the otherwise communal meeting area. As if the sheer magnitude of the poaching crisis was not enough to contend with, there was even an enormous divide among the so-called good guys as well!

Ah, ha! I thought, *so that's the way it works.*

Judging by what I had personally witnessed with TRAFFIC's performance in Taipei, and what I'd heard about the WWF's pro-ivory trade stance at the previous CITES conference in 1989, nobody seemed to trust them any more. In the obviously acrimonious and possibly anachronistic world of the acronym, things were beginning to get quite murky. This was no ordinary war; it was impossible to separate one side from the other!

CITES had been conceived and set up in the early seventies, a time of widescale, pro-reformist intransigence, and massive public demonstration to back it up. Out of the ranks of the anti-war protesters and the peace movement came a number of strident activists who saw much that was wrong with the industrialised world and how it was mistreating the planet. Greenpeace, WWF and

Friends of the Earth were all formed as a result. Not surprisingly, within the ranks of the Establishment there was a growing debate that an international body needed to be formed to regulate and control the free-for-all plundering of the earth's flora and fauna.

Conceptual discussions first took place at the IUCN family gathering back in 1960. The seed idea was then carefully nurtured and delicately transplanted into the womb of the United Nations and its human environment program. There were many extremely able and committed architects of that original concept, men and women of strength and vision. Sadly none of them had the political clout to keep the pernicious pettifoggers out of the drafting process. The first embryonic CITES draft which appeared in 1964 was spawned from a formal IUCN General Assembly resolution passed the year before. At the 1969 Assembly, a list of proposed species was drawn up, redrafted and circulated in 1971. The following year, at the United Nations Conference on the Human Environment held in Stockholm, Recommendation 99.3 was passed in response to which eighty-eight countries discussed a draft convention at a conference held a year later.

It took CITES *thirteen* long years to gestate, and even before the ink had begun to dry on the ratification papers signed in Washington by the twenty-one founding nations on March 3rd, 1973, fissures began to emerge that nobody in authority seemed to have the presence of mind to either notice or redress. By the time the eighth convention was held in Japan, these cracks were big enough to drive a herd of elephants through and, paradoxically, that was exactly what a coalition of South African nations was hoping to achieve.

All the original and honourable intentions of CITES appeared to have been watered down or dissolved completely. It was no longer a conservation tool but a trade agreement to be flouted, circumvented and ignored whenever possible. The largest document for review in the entire two weeks' proceedings was something called the 'infractions report'. Over one hundred pages of flagrant violations of the Treaty which can only have represented the smallest tip of the iceberg.

And whilst the glad-handing politicians and low-level bureaucrats in attendance tut-tutted in affected disdain, the illegal traders were laughing all the way to the bank.

CITES was premised on science, and yet half of the delegates present probably wouldn't have known the chemical formula for water, let alone the difference between a bear and a panda. Almost without exception, none of the 112 countries represented had the authority to make crucial voting decisions without checking the political implications in advance with their foreign ministries back home. They were there supposedly to safeguard the future survival of the planet's endangered wildlife, and yet they were collectively terrified to the point of paralysis of upsetting diplomatic relations with their international trading partners in the process.

It was easy to see how such kow-towing to the mighty endangered wildlife consumers of the world could be manipulated, exploited and used to knock the stuffing out of any vaguely ground-breaking initiative on sensitive issues such as the consumption of oriental delicacies like 'tiger-penis soup'!

During the first few days, many conflicting images were going through my mind. I shrugged off the angry show-down with the TRAFFIC hierarchy as a mere confirmation of my original fears. There were so many slick operators, wolves in sheep's clothing, it was difficult to know whom to trust. The rudiments of the treaty – do we trade or do we conserve? – seemed to be being systematically ripped to shreds. The so-called 'precautionary principle' – always giving the benefit of the doubt to the species – was being severely and systematically undermined by the pro-trade lobby, rumoured to have been heavily funded by the Japanese themselves.

Even the CITES logo, with stupefying insensitivity, had been redesigned in the form of an elephant. If the crucial vote re-opened the ivory trade, then the organisation's own motif would forever be linked with the entire blood-thirsty business, so graphically depicted in a dozen full-colour pamphlets available at the conference.

The buzz-phrase of the convention was 'sustainable utilisation'. That is to say, using wildlife without using it up. An utterly naïve and fanciful concept, to my way of thinking, especially in the absence of adequate law-enforcement to back it up; not to mention a fundamental respect for the CITES treaty itself. A respect that was clearly not held by the 60 per cent or so of member-nations who had thus far failed to pay their dues to the Secretariat.

The bitter irony seemed to me that the only people in possession of the most up-to-date, straight-from-the-street information – the NGOs – had to pay entrance fees up-front in cash and yet had very little say in procedures. The NGO community, it seemed to me, was treated with contemptuous disregard and derision by the vast majority of the undistinguished delegates at the meeting. Apparently it had always been that way. It was about time things started to change, I thought wearily.

One look around the conference hall on the first few days formed an indelible impression. The Indonesian delegation, for example, was made up of a number of highly disreputable wildlife traders. The austere Swiss Secretariat personnel sat aloof from the proceedings, their former Secretary General banished in disgrace for allegedly conniving with the ivory merchants.

If only people realised what *really* went on, I thought. Except they were never likely to. Although momentous resolutions concerning the extinction or otherwise of the world's wildlife heritage were being hatched up, and then invariably hashed up by the sophists in attendance, the major-league press was conspicuous by its absence. This conference was *dull*, as far as any self-respecting editor was concerned and they were probably right. The CITES Swiss Secretariat knew that, of course, and had every intention of keeping things that way.

The trouble was that this was all I had to work with. CITES was *the* only accredited form of international wildlife trade regulation. There was nothing else. This was the law. This was where proposals were discussed, decisions were made, contacts established and allegiances pledged. This *was* the debate and whether I liked it or not, I would have to adapt my approach or fall miserably by the wayside in the process.

And so I bought a new suit, cut my hair, polished my shoes and watched, waited and listened. I also did a lot of hand-shaking, card distribution and talking. Man, did I talk!

The business cards had been the result of rail-roading poor Sophy into going along with The Tiger Trust idea and I had subsequently ordered a stack of them whilst I was in Hong Kong. My usual printing-man smiled ruefully as I handed him the design layout. Little did he know that it was the first genuine order that I'd ever given him!

On the second day in Kyoto I spied an extremely distinguished-looking gentleman in bright red tartan trousers, tweed jacket, a long flowing white mane, monocle and ebony walking-stick. I had no idea who he was, but he looked wonderfully eccentric and as interesting an individual as I'd seen in a long time. I went up to him as he was rummaging around in his pigeon hole and caught sight of his name scribbled on a hand-written envelope.

'Well, well, Ian MacPhail,' I began. 'We meet at last. My name is Michael Day.'

'Dear boy,' he said, 'I wondered if I would bump into you.

Delighted to meet you. Do come and have a drink.'

And we moved away toward the bar, which sold remarkably good beer and the finest imported Scotch whisky. It was to be a veritable oasis over the next fortnight and an area where, I surmised, much of the real decision-making took place. Ian and I talked for a while until he suddenly looked at his watch, downed his drink, stood up rather painfully and said, 'Must be off now, I'm afraid. One of these awful working-group meetings to attend. I expect I'll see you at the NGO post-mortem later on,' and he limped away.

So that was the legendary Ian MacPhail, I thought, founding father of the World Wildlife Fund, great patriarch of the conservation movement. What a thoroughly fascinating character.

I had come to Japan with two main objectives. To endeavour to get the critical plight of the tiger somehow on to the agenda, and also to torpedo out of the water an horrific motion submitted by the People's Republic of China.

The first objective wasn't going to be easy. There wasn't a single tiger-specialist that had bothered to show up, none of the big-name scientists or writers on the subject. By comparison, the African elephant had a veritable legion. There was Ian and Orja Douglas-Hamilton, Dr Richard Leakey, Daphne Sheldrick, the naturalist and film-maker Simon Trevor, Dr Bill Jordan, Will Travers, Ian Redmond and a host of NGOs that had concentrated solely on the issue for years.

But no tiger people. A quite obvious indication as far as I was concerned that nobody really understood the depth of the crisis. If they did, then they should have been there. Just because there was only one proposal on the agenda was no excuse. CITES was about fringe meetings, forging contacts, forcing things into the limelight. And as far as I could see, that one tiger proposal was so potentially catastrophic for the species as to warrant a battalion of specialists to fight it. In the event, there was only one tiger specialist at the eighth CITES conference in Kyoto, Japan. Me!

At about 12.35 p.m. on Friday March 6th, the Chinese government's spokesman, Liu Yuan, was given the floor by the presiding chairman, Dr Martin Holgate, Secretary General of the IUCN.

'Thank you, Mr Chairman,' he began. 'The People's Republic of China would like to submit . . .'

For the previous forty-eight hours, the subject of this proposal hadn't left my mind. I'd read it over and over again, together with all the supporting documentation, until I was finally able to string a coherent written sentence together in defiance of this outrageous proposal.

The Chinese were endeavouring to legalise tiger-farming! They had been doing it domestically for over five years. Now they wanted a slice of the lucrative export market.

I knew it was a scam. It had to be. The proposal talked about captive-breeding and ultimate reintroduction to the wild. It was absolute nonsense. Reintroduction was supposedly the point of the giant panda-breeding programme in Wolong, except I'd been there and witnessed things with my own eyes. The Chinese were *taking* pandas from the wild. So far, in over ten years' work, they had miserably failed to reintroduce one single animal. They hadn't even tried. The Chinese panda programme, ably aided and abetted by the WWF, was simply a glorified captive-breeding experiment to produce pandas for the Chinese government to rent out to zoos overseas where they could earn staggering amounts of foreign exchange. Why on earth would a people with the finely hued business acumen of the Chinese release something into the wilderness potentially worth millions of dollars in export revenue? Particularly when they had no protective or adequate defence mechanism against the poachers!

There had only been one occasion when a giant panda had returned to the wild from the Wolong centre. It was in 1991, and the creature had quietly let itself out of its unlocked cage and wandered off into the springtime sunset. They bought padlocks after that, although after the summer, when the weather started to turn cold, the prodigal panda couldn't let himself back in again. A keeper found him outside the compound one morning looking very miserable and a tad hungry. He never ran away again after that!

Systematically I prepared my defence against this latest dollar-earning ruse. Piece by piece I assembled my arguments as objectively and cohesively as possible. Within CITES, there was little place for subjective unsubstantiated sentiment, and that meant facts. Emotion was a handy tool, but to be used sparingly, and only to hammer home an advantage built upon hard information.

However in this particular instance, there were so few details, and the Chinese knew that. Few westerners had ever seen the tiger farm and they liked to keep it that way. One that had was Dr Esmond

Bradley Martin, an adviser to WWF and UNEP, who had been there in April of 1990. In his subsequent report he noted:

> . . . The Chinese claim that they must obtain some financial return from the parts of dead tigers in order for the breeding project to survive economically. The manager of the centre believes that he can obtain a considerable sum of money by selling Siberian tiger bones as it is the most valuable type of tiger. Sumatran tiger bones sell in South-east Asia for about half the price of Siberian 'ones. An adult male tiger could produce, according to the manager, fifteen kilos of bones acceptable to the medicine trade and an adult female eight or nine kilos.

I already knew from the tiger-penis soup restaurant in Taichung that Siberian males were top-drawer as far as the Chinese were concerned, and judging by my chat with the bear-farm manager in Chengdu only a month earlier, there were no end of cash-rich consumers across the water in Taiwan, Korea and here in Japan anxious to gobble up tiger-based products.

Dr Bradley Martin was fortunately in attendance, and he agreed to raise the question of the genetic origin of the tigers at the farm. In his opinion, there was some doubt as to whether they were all pure Siberian. Introduction of hybrids into the wild clearly violated the scientific code as far as he was concerned, and he resolved to pursue that line of debate. His approach squared neatly with mine because in the supporting literature to the Chinese proposal I noticed the words: '. . . nurse cubs artificially and let the tiger go to another oestrus period early, and practise the technique which allows tigers to produce two litters within one year.'

As any student of the big cat will know, the tigress keeps her litter with her for two years in order to teach all the necessary hunting and survival skills necessary for life in the wild. Since the Chinese were separating them shortly after birth, there was no way they would ever be reintroduced.

One day, I resolved, I shall go back to China myself and find out the truth. In the meantime there were any number of other points that I listed carefully in a two-page report. I hastily made up forty or so copies at the NGO communal facilities room, returned to the conference hall and began to distribute them to the delegates.

'May I have one of those?' said a familiar voice behind me.

'Boonlerd! How wonderful to see you. I didn't know you'd be here.'

'Well, it was sort of touch and go until the last minute, but as you can see, here I am,' he said happily.

It was so good to see him. 'Are you here for the duration?' I asked, hoping he was.

'Yes. I want to support the Danish proposal to protect the American black bear. It's the only look-alike species left unguarded, and the smugglers know this.'

I knew what he meant. Although the Asian bears were supposedly protected from excessive trade by CITES, traders could always claim their stock came from the United States. It was virtually impossible to distinguish the species.

'I got inside a bear farm in China last month,' I told him. 'I have the video with me. Perhaps we should have one of our quiet meetings.'

'Good idea. Besides, there is someone here I'd like you to meet,' he said.

'Oh yes, sounds intriguing. Who is that then?'

'My American friend from Bangkok,' he said quietly.

'I'll look forward to that,' I said. 'I've been wanting to thank him personally for the secret camera idea.' He took me gently by the arm and walked slowly away from the bar.

'I have also something to show you,' he said. 'My department has made an extraordinary breakthrough. We raided a restaurant in Bangkok a few weeks ago, selling bear meat and paws. It was one of the worst experiences of my life. There were heads and body parts everywhere.'

We continued to talk for a while until I finally asked him about the Chinese tiger-farm proposal.

'Personally I'm dead set against it. The whole idea disgusts me. But I suspect my government might look upon it in a different way. These things are very political, you know.'

I was beginning to realise only too well. Endangered species had somehow become relegated to the status of mere pawns on a vast political and diplomatic chessboard, and China held many of the key pieces. They intended to win the tiger-farm issue; anything else would involve an intolerable loss of face. They had done their homework and lobbied hard for support.

And as the Chinese spokesman, Liu Yuan, finished his presentation, I

273

was totally unprepared for where that first endorsement would come from.

The Australian delegate raised his flag. I couldn't believe my eyes!

'Mr Chairman. The Australian government would like to applaud the proposal as presented by the distinguished delegate from China . . .'

The bastards, I thought, *so that's the way it works!*

The Australians earn reasonable amounts of foreign exchange farming and exporting crocodile skins and products, some of which go to China. The Chinese had obviously had a quiet word with them; something probably along the lines of 'What is sauce for the goose is sauce for the gander'.

Either that or they were too blind to see what the Chinese were really up to. Or they didn't care. Whichever it was, it had the desired effect because it signalled the position of a significant voting block, and a number of other nations piled in with their support.

CITES relies heavily on the reports and findings of three subordinate committees: the Standing Committee which meets every six months *in secret* and prohibits the attendance of the press or NGO observers; and the two specialist bodies which review matters regarding plants and animals. The Animals Committee, as one of them is known, is chaired by the Australians, and in supporting the Chinese tiger-farm proposal they were therefore giving a huge and quite obvious signal to the rest of the assembly that tiger-farming was fair dinkum as far as they were concerned.

In Thailand, legalised crocodile farming had caused the almost total extermination of its previously healthy domestic wild species. In South America, rare caiman skins were being passed off as anything but the real thing; few argued, let alone cared. And now the Siberian tiger was being threatened with the same fate by the sanctioning of a clearly transparent Chinese scheme by the Australians, and everyone else that had decided to play follow the leader. It was outrageous. The proposal was being steam-rollered through the committee and there wasn't a damn thing I could do to stop it. I looked at my watch; it was nearly one o'clock. Thank God.

Conservation is war, I thought again, as the committee chairman called time out for lunch. Had it gone to the vote at that stage, I felt sure the Chinese would have won hands down.

For the next ninety minutes I brow-beat and bullied, cajoled and pleaded with anyone that would listen to intervene and undo what seemed increasingly like an impossible 'done deal'. The more powerful tiger-range countries of India, Thailand and Malaysia were all sympathetic to my arguments, but even collectively they were not nearly as powerful as China.

China holds a significant place on the United Nations Security Council, but nevertheless remains on friendly terms with the hard-line extremist government in North Korea. Nobody really knows its true wealth or military capacity, but it's safe to say that by any standards it's awesome. Furthermore at the drop of a green cap from the old immortals in Beijing, friendly neighbours are invaded, protesting students crushed to death in the streets, nuclear test-bans shunned, and weapons of mass destruction shifted around the world. That is not to mention the relatively minor infractions of imprisoning dissidents without trial, manufacturing cheap export items with forced labour, mass-pirating of intellectual copyrights, etc.

China is the most populous nation on earth, and without doubt *the* number one emerging market, and it gleefully rattles the keys to Hong Kong in the face of anyone that might be daft enough to dispute it. Only the very brave go head to head against odds like that. The bitter irony was of course that Beijing is well aware of all that power, and can afford to be humble every once in a while, although she deeply resents the spineless and abject grovelling of so many politicians in the western world.

Whatever it was that happened during that lunch-time, I shall probably never really find out. Suffice to say that if China wanted to proceed and farm tigers there wasn't anyone present in Kyoto at the time that could have stopped them. As it was, I witnessed an extraordinary act of humility.

When the meeting reconvened in the afternoon, Liu Yuan politely withdrew his country's proposal and probably saved the Siberian tiger from immediate extinction in the process.

I looked up to the heavens in amazement. Somebody thumped me on the shoulder and said, well done. And yet I was stunned. Had I made the Chinese climb down? No, absolutely impossible. They made the decision themselves. I stood up on shaky legs, picked up my papers and left the committee chamber. I needed a drink.

There was more back-slapping and hand-pumping at the bar, but I couldn't take it all in. The only hand I really wanted to shake was that of the head of the Chinese delegation and he was nowhere to be seen.

Boonlerd came over, all smiles. With him was a tall, lean

individual with carefully groomed grey hair. He had a sharp, angular face with piercing steel-blue eyes that seemed to gaze into the depths of my soul from behind gold-rimmed spectacles. The man was mid-fifties, I guessed, and stood erect with a ramrod-straight back. He was extremely fit for his age and he shook my hand in a vice-like grip. The CIA really do pick their men well, I thought, retrieving my hand.

'Mike,' said Boonlerd, 'I'd like to introduce an American friend of mine . . .'

Over the weekend recess I tackled my second CITES objective, and began looking into ways of getting Taiwan under the microscope and clarifying its role in the decline of the African black rhino. Once the spotlight was on, I reasoned, it would be perfectly possible to introduce the plight of the tiger into the equation.

With the help of the EIA's Dr Ros Reeve, I set about drafting a resolution condemning Taiwan's failure to stem rhino-horn imports, and cast my net into the sea of CITES documentation in the hope of finding a convenient Trojan horse for the operation.

American NGOs take CITES very seriously and there were at least half a dozen excellent and highly qualified environmental lawyers at the conference. By way of comparison the United Kingdom delegation, for example, had none. I enlisted the help and support of three of the best, and even though they had impossible schedules and deadlines to meet, through the combined efforts of John Fitzgerald, Chris Wold and Professor David S. Favre, we eventually found the ideal vehicle and went to work.

By Thursday of the following week, we were ready to submit our amendment to an existing Dutch proposal that was up for review. Dr Bill Clark on behalf of the Israeli delegation graciously agreed to introduce it to the floor and with it almost committed political suicide in the process.

In the panic to get the draft amendment tabled in time, and like an absolute bungling fool, I had totally overlooked one of the basic principles of political manoeuvring: namely, 'if you are intending to hijack a sovereign nation's proposal in international fora, it is only polite to ask permission beforehand.'

Quite naturally, the Dutch representative, on hearing the proposed amendment, shot it down in flames. I don't think he wanted to, but my political blundering left him no other possible choice. All that hard work was in tatters, and there were only twenty-four hours to go before the meeting broke up for its two and a half year recess!

That night was, strangely enough, party night, the last opportunity for everyone to gather together before the great human dispersal out of Kyoto the following day. Nevertheless I remained sober, searching high and low for the one and only chance to get some remnant of our ill-fated proposal into the record books. The only person that could do that was the Committee Chairman himself in his summing-up address to the plenary meeting the next morning. I eventually found Dr Martin Holgate at a small reception on the seventh floor of the conference hotel, and asked to speak with him.

The Takaragaike Prince Hotel is roughly circular in shape, with each floor built around a central atrium that towers up through the middle like an enormous gilded chimney. Round and round I walked with Dr Holgate, first apologising for my lack of experience and the ham-fisted bungling, and then explaining the major importance of the issue and the huge implications it could have on all endangered species. Finally, I appealed to him for some words of support in his final address the next day. Something from his position as chairman that might ultimately be entered into the minute books. Vital words upon which we might build a more coordinated action plan in the future . . .

He said very little and listened very patiently. After seven circuits of the corridor he politely wished me goodnight and returned to his room. I had done my penance and said my piece. There was nothing left to do but get plastered.

In the hushed assembly hall of Committee Room One the following morning, all eyes were on the podium as the chairman began his summing-up address. Dr Holgate studiously worked his way through the long agenda report of the previous two weeks' proceedings until he finally came to the question of rhinoceros conservation.

'CITES seems to have failed in its duty . . .' he began, and I breathed an almighty sigh of relief.

We had done it!

Sophy met me at Phuket airport forty-eight hours later. It was March 15th, and I hadn't seen her in over a month. The outside temperature was in the nineties and yet I was cold. I was physically and mentally wasted. I'd lost more than a stone in weight, and was

277

in no shape to fight off the tropical bacteria that immediately invaded my system. Within hours of my arrival I collapsed with exhaustion.

After three weeks of continual antibiotics, I'd had enough. It was time to go home.

CHAPTER TWENTY-THREE

England, Spring 1992

Whatever pathological germ it was that took hold of my body in the spring of 1992, it had no intention of letting go without a hard fight. I took weeks to recover fully. Although unwell and under strength, in some respects I didn't mind. Sophy pampered me back to health, and it felt good to be with her all the time again. I was tired of crusading. I wanted my life back. I wanted to do all the things that most people take for granted – get a good job, raise a family, save up for holidays, go to the pub on Fridays. Routine does have a certain positive appeal at times.

After Japan, the phones were silent. It was as if everyone had gone back to their own lives. Lucky them, I thought. There was no news from Kate in Washington, and it seemed that the American TV documentary idea had shrivelled up and finally died. The EIA didn't call and neither did Sam. Ian MacPhail telephoned every once in a while but that was about it. The walking wounded from the battlefields of Kyoto had all disappeared into the sunset.

The fledgling Tiger Trust needed serious funds if we were to continue our work. I tried to make some money trading equities on the London Stock Exchange in order to bolster our private conservation war-chest, and got severely mauled in the process. The gods of good fortune appeared to have left me. Without significant funding, our save-the-tiger campaign was going nowhere.

The video material that I already had was good enough to excite many of the conservationists at CITES, but it certainly wasn't yet good enough for general consumption, and without public awareness there would be no major fund-raising opportunities. It was a vicious circle. England was still in the grips of recession. British Finance Minister, Chancellor Norman Lamont's famous green shoots of recovery had withered on the stem and money was tight everywhere. The Charity Commissioners in Liverpool seemed to be taking forever to officially recognise and register full charitable status for The Tiger Trust and, until they did, we were financially paralysed. There was nothing to do but wait. We dipped into Sophy's savings and somehow muddled by.

Towards the beginning of June I received a phone-call from a production executive at Yorkshire Television. He was researching a three-part series commissioned by Channel Four called 'Defenders of the Wild'. He had heard about my investigations and was keen to feature the work of Boonlerd and the plight of the Thai tigers in one of the programmes. Were we interested?

I told him that we would have to think about it and call him back.

Martin Belderson politely thanked me for my time and was about to hang up when I said, 'For Christ's sake. I'm only joking! Of course we're interested. When can we meet?'

The following week he drove down, accompanied by the series director, Nick Gray, and we sat outside our rented home in the summer afternoon sunshine, and thrashed out the basics of a deal.

The programme concept was to concentrate on the work of conservationists indigenous to the country featured in the documentary. They felt, quite rightly, that too many existing wildlife programmes relied upon the posturing of western commentators highlighting the problems of the developing world. Yorkshire TV was looking for the homespun variety, and if those people's endeavours were being helped from abroad, all well and good.

As far as I was concerned, it was the perfect formula. Boonlerd thoroughly deserved public recognition for his extraordinary work, and both Sophy and I were more than happy to help in any way at all.

And then tragedy struck, like a savage bolt out of the blue.

I had grown used to the sound of Martin's voice on the phone. He called regularly to discuss the film project, and for background information on tigers, the illegal trade, that sort of thing. One afternoon when he called, there was a faltering, deeply distressed tone to his voice. 'Mike,' he began, 'I have something awful to tell you. Boonlerd is dead.'

I put the telephone down quietly and wept.

Up to that point in my life, I'd never really understood the emotional pain caused by cruel and unexpected bereavement. I'd seen examples of grown men in some parts of the world openly wailing in anguish at the sudden death of a loved one, never truly understanding their inner torment, perhaps believing that such unashamed displays of grief were simply a cultural thing. But the untimely loss of my dear friend Boonlerd Angsirijinda tore at my heart in a way that I could never have believed possible, and it was several days before I could bring myself to call back and find out the circumstances of his tragic death.

It had happened in Washington DC. He was visiting the United States on behalf of his department in Bangkok. Nobody was exactly sure of the details. He had suffered a massive stroke in his hotel room one morning, and was taken to hospital. There had been some initial confusion as to his condition and a delay in calling an ambulance, as I understood. Foul play was not suspected. He had died of a massive brain haemorrhage at the age of forty-nine, probably brought on by stress and overwork. His body was being flown back to Thailand for a traditional Buddhist funeral. He was survived by a wife and one daughter.

Time, they say, is the great healer and with the passing of the weeks, Sophy and I began to come to terms with our grief and accept that he was gone. I shall never forget his passionate speech in defence of the bears in Kyoto. His tearful words had shattered the hearts and minds of the pro-trade delegates at the conference, and succeeded in overturning a crucial vote. I had hugged him warmly in the assembly room after that. It was the final day of talks and he wanted me to change my flight and fly back to Bangkok with him to keep him company. He didn't want to travel alone. It was not possible. I had things to attend to in Hong Kong. I never saw him again.

In early August, Martin and Nick drove down again from Leeds to see us. They wanted to know if anything could be salvaged from their plans. Would it be possible to build a programme around my own investigations in Thailand and Taiwan? Was there anyone else that could fill the tragic gap? We talked for several hours. I thought that it might just be possible if I could only persuade Aroon at the Khao Sok National Park to cooperate. He had been on the front line for over twenty years. And then there was the question of Taiwan: who would be 'the defender' in that country? As we talked, an idea came to me. It would mean that I would have to swallow an awful lot of pride and take a back seat. Nevertheless the story would be finally told and that was the main thing.

Finally I stood up and said, 'Gentlemen, there is only one decent thing we can do. We must somehow make this documentary as a tribute to Boonlerd. His work and inspiration must go on.' And with that, we toasted the success of the project that was already beginning to take shape inside my head.

From then on things happened very quickly. Up to that point I'd been loosely cooperating with the EIA on a Taiwan campaign. They had valuable information on the rhino-horn trade, I had my evidence on tigers. Between us, I reasoned, we should be able to cause quite a storm. The problem was that now I had to stay completely focused on the film documentary. I therefore resolved to put all my information and film into a great big cardboard box, and sent it down to them by special courier. They were clever and experienced strategists. They would know how best to use it.

Sophy and I gave all our time to the preparations for the Yorkshire TV production. Nick Gray had by now accepted just how important it was to highlight Taiwan's role in creating the demand for tiger products, although at the time I'm sure he wasn't terribly confident that we would be able to pull it off. He had good reason to feel cautious. Taiwan was not an easy nut to crack.

Nevertheless, several days were allocated in the film schedule to fully explore all the avenues that I had already uncovered, and on September 6th, 1992, Nick and I flew out to Bangkok to meet with Royal Forestry Department officials and reconnoitre the area around the Khao Sok National Park. Martin Belderson left two days later to check out Taipei.

It felt good to be part of a team. Together I was sure we could piece together the intricate web of deceit and corruption that lay behind the tiger's demise. We met with the top brass at the RFD and I explained carefully about the film concept, taking great pains to fully establish that the main thrust of the documentary would be aimed at the consumption of tigers in Taiwan. I needed them to understand that we were not intending to make a film that would be unjustly critical of their country. The tigers of Thailand were being slaughtered to feed a demand that was out of control in the consuming nations, and courageous people like the late Boonlerd and Aroon had devoted their lives to protecting wild animals from the sheer enormity of that trade. They were the good guys. The crooks were in Taiwan.

The senior directors of the RFD, the National Parks and Wildlife Conservation division met at length and deliberated until finally they gave their blessing. They would give the project their fullest support and cooperation. Nick and I breathed an almighty sigh of relief and took them at their word.

A big mistake as it happened, because somebody somewhere didn't want the truth to be told.

In order to work, the documentary would need good close-ups of tigers, and I suggested that we go and see how the three cubs that Boonlerd had rescued eighteen months earlier were getting along. We found them in an abysmally small enclosure out at the RFD's Khao Pradap Chang captive-breeding centre near Rajburi, two hours south of the capital.

The tigers were being fed, but their overall living conditions were atrocious. The Thai were trying, I suppose, but they didn't have a clue. They couldn't really be blamed, as they relied to a great deal on the so-called experts of the IUCN's Captive Breeding Specialist Group, often jokingly, but nevertheless appropriately, referred to as the Wildlife Farmers' Club.

The proponents of commercial captive breeding as a valuable conservation tool were barking up the wrong tree, as far as I was concerned. The cuddly captive-breeding concept was an affront to nature, although it was being touted as the final solution. The general public loved to see baby tigers, of course they did, but they weren't being told the truth. Any livestock farmer with five minutes' tuition could breed tigers; in fact it's quite hard to *stop* tigers from breeding. The species is in its evolutionary prime, that's not the problem. The problem was to get due recognition of the situation *in the wild*, and the ease with which it could be solved if only everyone would pool their wealth of talent and resources. Except the captive-breeding specialists would never agree. Because if they did, they would quite simply work themselves out of a job in the process!

I looked down at the three tigers, now almost fully grown, and remembered the time when Sophy and I had held each one on our knee and fed them with a warm bottle of milk formula. In the wild, they would carve out a territory for themselves, the males staking out anything from twenty to over a hundred square kilometres. These three had to make do with less than a hundred square metres between them. It was a disgrace.

It was probably out of my hands by now, I thought, falling headlong into the defeatist's trap. There was little to be done short of building them a new home and so we prepared to leave. Before we left, Nick and I somewhat reluctantly accepted an invitation to look over the breeding project by the regional supervisor, a bright young man called Pornchai. He had studied big cat welfare in the UK and the Channel Islands the previous summer, and had phoned me to ask if we could help with the purchase of some refrigeration equipment for the tigers' food. We sent the money, the cold-storage units were bought, and we thought no more about it. Now he wanted to give me the guided tour. He was a pleasant enough sort of chap, and it would have been churlish to refuse.

For the next hour or so we were shown the centre's entire collection of rare and endangered wildlife all trapped, confiscated, captive-bred or handed in by the people of Thailand. The complex was huge, well over a hundred acres, but the cages were tiny. The Thai simply didn't comprehend the concept of space. As far as they were concerned, they wanted to be able to *see* the animals. Most wild animals like to hide from gawping humans, but they need space to be able to do that. Most people don't think that's fair; they want the instant gratification of spotting the creature quickly, however miserable the surroundings.

As we were nearing the end of our guided tour, out on the perimeter of the area, I looked up at a large rock-covered hill and said, 'If we could only build a fence around that, it would make a better home for the tigers.'

'It is possible, I am sure,' said Pornchai.

'You mean it?' I said, 'because I do, I'm not messing about.'

'Sure,' he said, 'we have the land and the labour to build it, but no money to buy materials.'

Enough to build comfortable living quarters for staff and visiting officials from Bangkok, I thought, but never enough for the poor animals. 'Maybe I can help out,' I said.

Nick Gray took off his spectacles and began to polish them. He looked strange without his glasses. His expression seemed even more peculiar. I think he must have thought that I had gone barking mad. He was probably right.

Nevertheless the original concept of 'Tiger Mountain' was conceived on the spot. We paced around the base of the hill, scratched about in the dirt, came up with some numbers, and I said that I would get back to him with a plan.

Two weeks later I was sitting in the office of Mike Lockyer, director of John Aspinall's Howletts Zoo in south Kent, picking his brains for the engineering formula behind the safe construction of enormous tiger enclosures. One week after that, I had sent the

284

drawings along with some cash to Pornchai, and building commenced.

Tiger Mountain, as it became known, was paid for privately, and cost Sophy and me our entire earnings from the Yorkshire TV production, but it was worth it. By the time the film crew arrived in late November, it was complete, and we were ready to set about making the documentary that would finally expose the horrors of the illegal tiger-bone trade. And Boonlerd's tiger cubs would star in the production. It was indeed a fitting tribute.

I had flown out with Sophy in advance to attend the first Asian regional meeting of CITES in Chiang Mai. There I was able to meet up with colleagues from Kyoto and make new contacts amongst the world conservation community. Once again there were no recognised tiger-people apart from The Tiger Trust in attendance, simply because, as far as they were aware, there was no tiger item on the agenda. However the meeting was much more relaxed than in Japan, and it was easy to raise the issue and draw similarities with the much-publicised plight of the rhinoceros. There were few formal resolutions agreed upon at the conference, but we did force through a document that voiced concern about the continuing illegal consumption of the species in traditional medicines. It was hardly a ground-breaking initiative, and the Chinese delegate ruthlessly attacked the whole concept. The result was the usual wishy-washy compromise, but nevertheless it was a positive step in the right direction, and something upon which greater things could be built in the future.

After the conference, Sophy and I journeyed north into The Golden Triangle, the notorious opium heartland where the borders of Laos, Burma and Thailand meet at one point, to follow up rumours we had heard of tiger skins and body parts being smuggled over the border from Burma. We didn't have to look too far or for very long. The area was a veritable jamboree of wildlife. Everything was available for a price. Uncut ivory, rhino horn, bear gall, leopard and tiger skins and bone as far as the eye could see. And the authorities, as usual, weren't lifting a finger to stop it. The bridge across the narrow stream that separated the Thai border town of Mae Sai from Tachilek in Burma was awash with pedestrians, bicycles, trucks and motor bikes all toing and froing, and stacked high with all manner of contraband. There was absolutely no customs or immigration control in evidence whatsoever. Until we showed up.

285

When white-skinned, dollar-carrying foreigners arrived at the border, they had to pay US$10 in cash to get across. That's the way things work in Thailand. Everyone else circulated with complete impunity. We coughed up and crossed the busy bridge to the other side, took reels of film and video tape, and finally trudged wearily back to our hotel thinking that there was no end to the illegal wildlife trade and wondering whether the world would ever come to its senses.

That night, we heard news of Bill Clinton's election to the White House. The Reagan years were over, and the Democrats were back in power. Positive news perhaps. President Clinton's running mate and new Vice President, Al Gore, had strong views on the state of the planet. Now it would be very interesting to see if there was going to be any real action. The Clinton/Gore team appeared on the face of it to actually care about conservation and might possibly stand up to the free-trade-at-all-costs lobby that had dogged Capitol Hill for so long. Back in the United Kingdom, there was perhaps now a faint glimmer of hope that the ruling Conservative government might just support tough US action on the environment. Just a glimmer. We would have to wait and see.

We flew back to Phuket and began to make arrangements for the arrival of the Yorkshire TV film crew. In Khao Sok we fully briefed Dwaila and Aroon, and then went on to Surat Thani to talk with Acharn and the underground cell of environmental activists. They were busy trying to thwart another hideous dam-building project that threatened many tens of thousands of acres of pristine wildlife habitat. Nevertheless they were able to report that the two leading poachers, Jouey and a man called Prasit, were regularly helping themselves to whatever they could trap in Khao Sok. Mr Goh Lim was still actively breaking the law shipping contraband up to the capital and beyond, despite their protestations to the local authorities. The wildlife restaurants still served all manner of poached meat from the sanctuaries around the area. In fact, things were about usual for the region at that time of year.

Acharn took me aside and warned me again of the danger to my life in Khao Sok. I was most concerned about Sophy.

'Don't worry about Sophy,' he said sombrely. 'It's you they're after.'

'I must have upset them rather badly,' I said, trying to make light of the whole thing.

286

'Don't underestimate these people, Mike,' he said. 'Prasit is a convicted murderer. It is no idle threat. He has killed before.'

An icy shiver ran down my spine and I swallowed hard. I remembered the time I had tried to organise insurance for my camera equipment when we were working on the lake. Lloyd's of London had refused. Their maps for the region were pinned with the red flags of communist insurgence, so as far as they were concerned, Khao Sok was still a war zone.

Dwaila had told me of the day she had met the stranger in a village noodle shop. He was an old man who lived on the edge of community life. No-one knew much about him, although he knew intricate and personal details about her childhood and family in the United States. He introduced these snippets of information delicately and without obvious menace into the conversation. But Dwaila understood. Deeply troubled, she finally excused herself and went to the bathroom; when she returned he had gone.

'Don't you worry, my friend. I'll be careful,' I said.

The next day I returned to Bangkok to meet up with Nick Gray and checked into the Maruay Garden Hotel opposite the RFD's offices in the Bangken suburb. For two days we met with officials, shuffled papers and permits around, collecting signatures and rubber stamps en route. There were no exact details on the film schedule, and I intended to keep it that way until the last possible moment.

By night I schemed and plotted quietly away in my room. The Environmental Investigation Agency in London had just launched their massive UK campaign aimed at boycotting Taiwanese-made imports under the damning slogan of 'Made in Die-Wan'.

When the EIA hit, they hit hard, and the target was already feeling the pain. My co-conspirator from Kyoto, Dr Ros Reeve, had already flown out to Taipei hot on the heels of Jörgen Thomsen from the TRAFFIC office in Cambridge who had accepted an urgent invitation from the Taiwanese Government to down tools and attempt a conciliation. The Council of Agriculture had made some damning comments about their report, and it was rumoured that the TRAFFIC executive was none too pleased with them at the time. For twenty-four hours Ros and Jörgen had played cat and mouse in the Taiwanese capital. I thought it might be interesting to try and stir things up.

Ros was an extremely able campaigner, and whilst I was sure she could easily handle the interference from the TRAFFIC directorate,

I thought it might not be a bad idea for her to have some high-calibre moral support. It was now time to strike, and so I phoned Sam LaBudde in San Francisco and pleaded with him to get on a flight to Taipei and help her out. I risked jeopardising our entire filming plans in the process; it was brinkmanship almost to the point of madness.

Equally, however, I knew that we might never get another opportunity quite like it. Sam had the issue at his fingertips and was a master at working the media. I certainly didn't have the experience, and my hands were tied because of the film contract. With a lot of skill and juggling, I thought, it might just be possible to pull off a minor coup; with luck, even a blitzkrieg. Sam had never been known to shy away from a good fight and mercifully agreed on condition that I met him at the airport with some sustenance. I suggested a six-pack of cold beer. The deal was done.

Meanwhile I continued to work on the film schedule. After the death of Boonlerd, there hadn't been much in the way of wildlife law enforcement in Bangkok. His department had been thrown into confusion, and nobody really knew where to begin. Boonlerd had carved out his job himself, persuading his department of the necessity of tough action against the illegal wildlife trade. Now he was gone, things were rapidly reverting to apathy and chaos.

Until we showed up. Yorkshire Television wanted to film the Law Enforcement Division in action and I knew exactly where to find it. The problem was that the word 'action' seemed to be getting lost somewhere in the translation. As far as the authorities were concerned, action meant traipsing around after boring clerks and bureaucrats checking documents and tagging the hideous collection of stuffed animals by some of the wealthier members of Thai society.

We, on the other hand, had a completely different interpretation. Action meant crack-down. It meant raids on known dealers. It meant enforcing the law and rooting out the villains. It meant giving the Thai authorities a chance of proving to the world that they were living up to their publicly stated international obligations and doing something to protect endangered wildlife. Action meant action, with a capital A.

The man that was eventually given Boonlerd's desk, and who became the one upon whom we relied to deliver all the 'action', was called Sorasit Kanitasut. I had first met him at the Chiang Mai CITES conference. His English was excellent and his knowledge of computers and general office hardware was superb. He was a nice guy, I liked him. But he was no Clint Eastwood. He was an administrator, not a law-man, and had been thrown in completely out of his depth.

Nevertheless he was the one we had to work with and, like it or not, I had to trust him. Up to that point we had been working with a sanitised script, no name, no detailed locations, just abstract references to vague areas and the amount of time needed to cover each one. Eventually I had to fill in the blanks for Sorasit, and although he was out of the country at the time, I especially flew over to Hong Kong in order to brief him personally. David Melville kindly allowed me to use the conference room at WWF headquarters, and over coffee on the afternoon of November 25th, I quietly spelled out the facts.

I told him about the secret warehouse owned by the man that ran the hideous zoo at the Pata department store in central Bangkok; the shop in Silom Road selling tiger and leopard skins smuggled in from Burma; the pharmacy in Chinatown with the stocks of tiger bone in the back storeroom; the Korean restaurant selling bear-paw soup; Goh Lim's address in Surat Thani; the names and abodes of the poachers, Jouey and Prasit; the girlie-bars in Patong with the baby gibbons chained to the counter; and plenty more besides. He listened intently, clearly surprised at my catalogue of information, and saying very little.

That evening I flew on to join the crew in Taipei with assurances from Sorasit that we would receive maximum cooperation from his division. He returned to Bangkok to prepare his team for our arrival.

What happened after that is unclear. All I do know is that ten days later, when we arrived at the first item on the list, the souvenir shop selling tiger and leopard skins, they had already been tipped off. We were expected and there was nothing incriminating to be found. It was the same everywhere else. The restaurant allowed us a full inspection of their cold-storage facilities knowing full well that we would find nothing. Goh Lim had put a sign up that his business was 'temporarily closed'. Aroon had been threatened not to cooperate with us. Prasit's house was as clean as a whistle, although he did state on camera that he would kill whoever had denounced him as a poacher. In Patong, the nine gibbons that I had personally counted two weeks before had mysteriously vanished; even the ubiquitous wandering man with the python had heard we were coming and looked totally miserable with just the Polaroid camera dangling around his neck. It was a fiasco and a complete contrast to the previous week in Taiwan where we hit sixes with every stroke.

Upon arrival in Taipei I had gone to ground at my old haunt at the Cosmos Hotel and stayed holed up there for forty-eight hours. The film crew were at another hotel and I thought it unwise to openly publicise my direct involvement with them. I was also juggling with another ball: the boycott Taiwan campaign.

I picked Sam up at the airport in the most outrageous beaten-up old limousine I could find, and we swigged beer all the way back into town. Late into the night we worked on a statement to the press and a fact-sheet hand-out to whoever might be interested in the background to our allegations.

What happened next can only be retold in the approximate words of an extraordinary Taiwanese environmentalist called Jay Fang. He said, 'What you guys did was rather like making a fist and putting it into the government's face. They should have bluffed you out. Instead they walked right into it.'

Within forty-eight hours, Sam and Ros were headline news. Their pictures were on the front pages of every newspaper from Taipei to Kaohsiung, and *the* story on every major radio and television news channel. The Taiwanese Council of Agriculture didn't quite know what had hit them.

Meanwhile I moved quietly out of the Cosmos and into the Grand Hotel with the Yorkshire television crew and went to work. The first obstacle was to satisfy Nick Gray with the bona-fides of the indigenous Taiwanese main character, the local 'defender'. He and Martin had talked with a few 'possibles' but were far from happy. I knew that, because as far as I was concerned, there really was only one candidate. And that person was in a league of her own.

She had changed so much since that fateful meeting at Kai Tak airport in Hong Kong all those months ago. When we had first met, she was a mildly ambitious young secretary, quietly on the lookout for promotion, a husband, and a stable career. Since that time she had undergone a remarkable metamorphosis, from office girl to courageous environmental campaigner. She had examined her own ideas, challenged the philosophies of her friends and family, and lobbied hard within the apathetic Taiwanese government to do the same. She had become a new voice in the wilderness, crying out to be heard against the cruel injustice of illegal wildlife trade. Over the past year she had sought out like-minded people within her own community in Taipei, forged new contacts and made new friends.

Her life had been turned upside-down as she helped wage war on the animal smugglers, her task made all the more difficult by generations of prejudice against female Chinese endeavour. Nevertheless she fought on, and slowly, ever so slowly, succeeded in turning the tables on her country's wanton consumption of the world's critically endangered wildlife.

One evening I tapped on Nick's bedroom door and told him that there was somebody that I would very much like him to meet. He followed me down the corridor to my room and we found her sitting quietly by the window looking out over the magnificent panorama high above the city.

'Nick, I'd like to introduce Rebecca Chen,' I said as she looked up.

'Delighted, delighted,' he said. 'Mike has told me so much about you, but, I'm amazed. I don't know what to say. Are you sure you want to do this?'

'Yes,' she said, 'yes, I am.'

'Mike, you old rogue,' he said to me, 'how on earth did you pull this off? I had no idea. Does she really know what she's letting herself in for?'

'Oh, yes, she realises only too well, Nick. You are looking at a very brave young lady. A very brave young lady indeed,' I said.

And with that, we set about planning to revisit all the nasty people and localities that we had uncovered over the previous eighteen months. For the next week I stayed well hidden in the background and pulled strings. Nick directed, Martin produced and Rebecca gave the most stunning performance of her life. We wangled our way back inside the tiger farm pretending that we were scouting a pop-video for Michael Jackson. The footage was incredible; the cameraman, Mike Shrimpton, was an absolute genius. In Taichung, we penetrated the defences of the *Bu Jung Bao* restaurant where sound recordist Chris Barker brilliantly picked up the vital evidence that the place was still importing tiger penises from Thailand. In Kaohsiung we returned to Mr Wang's warehouse, but he was away in China on business at the time. Probably buying more tiger bone.

We succeeded in getting everything we could possibly dream of on film. There was only one tricky moment when we were filming in Tainan, not far from the Redhill Hotel. We were looking at tiger skulls, bones and penises, the usual thing, when an old man appeared from behind a grimy partitioning curtain in the shop and asked, 'You're not with the EIA, are you?'

Nick looked at me, I looked at Rebecca, we all looked at each other and laughed out loud: 'The EIA, good heavens no.'

'OK, that's all right then,' said the old man, and shuffled off again.

The last item on our agenda was to film the three tigers inside the huge Tiger Mountain enclosure at Rajburi. We had already recorded the actual release two weeks earlier, shortly after our return from Taiwan. Pornchai and his team had done a wonderful job; the compound was absolutely magnificent. The tigers had seemed fretful at first, not quite understanding what exactly was happening to them. Suddenly, one of the males gave a huge jump for joy and bounded off into the thick undergrowth and for several hours played hide-and-seek with the other two.

We had left them to settle down after that and moved on to the south to film in Khao Sok. Now it was time to return and see just how they were readjusting to a life in natural habitat, although not quite in the wild.

The transformation was incredible. Their eyes sparkled, their muscles rippled through shining coats. They looked lean and healthy and brimming with vigour and vitality. They quite obviously approved of their new home.

As we left Tiger Mountain at the end of our film trip, an old Buddhist monk arrived and pitched a small sun-bleached brown tent close to the perimeter. I went over to talk with him. He sat serenely in the lotus position, his English measured and slow. I asked him what he was doing.

'I have come to be close to the nature,' he said quietly. 'Here it is peaceful and I can meditate. I know of no other place where the spirit of the tiger is so strong. This is a beautiful place.'

CHAPTER TWENTY-FOUR

England, 1993

Someone once claimed that 'life begins at forty'. If that was indeed the case, then I'd been having an extraordinary dream for the last thirty-nine years. At times it seemed that way, just a dream. I'd lost count of the number of grubby hotels I'd stayed in, or cheap flights from one country to another. I'd met heroes and villains, and some that were so slick they could have been either. Truth sometimes fused with fiction as I tried to separate good from evil, and in the early months of 1993, my instincts for right and wrong were tested to the limit.

Conservation is war, and in the battle that was blazing in Taiwan, many hitherto uninvolved and unconcerned individuals were jumping on the bandwagon and putting their collective boot in. The word was out that The Tiger Trust and Yorkshire Television had succeeded in obtaining damning evidence that was broadcastable, authenticated and genuine. The tiger gravy-train was about to pull out of the station and everyone, it appeared, wanted a piece of the action. The enemy was on the run.

The established conservation and environmental movements had totally underestimated the seriousness of the tiger's plight. Now journalists were wanting to know why, and often played down the issue as alarmist for no other reason than they had no knowledge of the facts. Nevertheless, tiger-related articles began to appear, and a dozen different names and organisations grabbed the credit for bringing the crisis to a head. Some were already familiar to me, although for distinctly different reasons than their interest in tiger conservation. Welcome to the world, I thought.

'We are getting noticed at last,' I said to Sophy one morning, as I opened a hopelessly inaccurate letter from a member of the conservation intelligentsia. 'I wonder how they will feel when they find out that we are going after China!'

The trouble was that there were so few people I felt I could confide in. China was the ultimate goal, the last frontier, the keystone of the Asian wildlife trade. If I could find a chink in their armour and utilise it effectively, it would provide an axis for the entire illegal trade war. And yet nobody could ever really know what I was planning. I became excessively secretive; even Sophy was excluded from many of my plans. She would worry, I told myself, and worry never achieved anything.

Undercover investigative work bred mistrust. I began to look at people in a completely different way, and inadvertently I would pigeon-hole them into a number of categories: those that my information would incriminate; those that would be guilty by association; those that would be embarrassed through failure of duty; those that would be shamed by their incompetence; those that sought to profit from my findings; those that sought to claim my material as their own; those that sought to discredit me because of their own ineptitude. For every ten new people, eight would fall into one or many of these categories, one would be hard to define, and the last would give unequivocal support. I hated it and clung on to the last vestige of my naïve belief that the world really did care about endangered species. The film would prove that, I was sure.

The first weeks of 1993 were taken up with post-production work on the Yorkshire Television documentary that was now to be called 'The Tigers of Thailand'. Sophy and I made repeated trips up to Leeds to help where we could, and to see the programme slowly take shape. It was my first real encounter with life behind the scenes in a major broadcasting studio, a fascinating time, and valuable experience.

Sam LaBudde was riding on the crest of a new wave following the commotion in Taiwan, and since the production of the Channel Four documentary was co-sponsored by the American Discovery Channel, he set about looking to find ways to help market the programme in the United States.

Sam and I had differing views on a number of things, some of which bordered on mild antipathy. One thing we did agree upon, however, was the way in which to present the tiger crisis to the American people. Americans are still slightly suspicious of foreigners, regardless of what many people claim to the contrary. That suspicion is only fractionally eroded once allegiance to the star-spangled banner has been duly sworn. For those of us that visit their shores on a strictly temporary basis, the friendly locals remain guarded and apprehensive behind the warm handshakes and beaming smiles. And when bad news has to be told, they take it more seriously and respond in a more cohesive, unified manner when they hear it first from a fellow American. At least, that was the theory.

On February 24th, I flew out to Washington DC to attend a press conference and to prepare for the CITES Standing Committee meeting to be held there at the beginning of March. The American NGOs had been very busy. In an historic alliance, they had joined forces with the local WWF, still known in the United States as The World Wildlife Fund, and petitioned the American government to impose trade sanctions on Taiwan and China under the terms of an obscure piece of federal legislation called the Pelly Amendment. The charge was one of gross negligence in stemming the supply and demand of tiger and rhinoceros parts and products across their borders. If found guilty, those countries could face punitive trade restrictions potentially worth millions of export dollars a month.

Once again, it felt good to be part of a team again, albeit from a strategic position at the back of the press conference, watching my hidden camera footage unveiled to the American media for the first time. Sam was still the darling of the environmental community in the United States, and he put over our case with passion, eloquence and a carefully measured amount of righteous indignation. Cameras flashed, tape-recorders quietly whirred, pencils scratched vigorously on notebook, and television crews panned and zoomed in for the vital close-ups. That night, millions of Americans saw the tiger skeleton on the cold marble floor of the warehouse in Taiwan for the first time. The following day, newspapers were carrying the story.

It had taken me three long years, but the big cat was now well and truly out of the bag.

It was winter in Washington and I stayed at a modest hotel just off Dupont Circle. Most days I would trudge through the snow to meet fellow campaigners at the offices of one of the many American NGOs in the neighbourhood. We would sit drinking endless cups of coffee and discuss strategy for the up-and-coming CITES standing committee meeting to be held at the American Fish and Wildlife headquarters in Arlington, Virginia.

The UN-sponsored Convention on International Trade in Endangered Species relies on the inter-sessionary secret meetings of its Standing Committee which assembles every six months at various locations around the globe. For simplicity of operations, the CITES world is split into six regions: America and Canada, Central and South America, Europe, Asia, Africa and finally Australasia. Countries within each group decide largely amongst themselves which nation is to represent them at these meetings. Because of the extraordinary politics endemic to the system, something only a bureaucrat could explain, Europe was represented by Sweden, a country which had yet to join the EEC. The tiny and largely impoverished state of Senegal carried the all-powerful African vote, and Thailand, the nation most recently hammered by conservationists and CITES itself for flagrant abuses and breach of the Convention, carried the entire Asian mandate.

The big guns that made all the noise and actually pulled the strings like China, Japan, South Africa and, to a lesser degree, Zimbabwe, Canada and Switzerland, were always represented and made sure matters proceeded precisely in the way that they intended. Israel always fought valiantly to redress the balance, invariably in vain. I couldn't help but notice a disproportionate amount of anti-Semitism in CITES matters.

At the twenty-ninth CITES Standing Committee meeting, the Senegalese delegate got completely 'lost' in Washington on the first day of talks, and therefore the entire African continent was conveniently represented by the alternate and pro-trade delegate from Namibia. The American delegation, who were already quietly nodding favourably at the Pelly Amendment petition, had to behave with excruciating impartiality for fear of upsetting the diplomatic status quo. And the Thai delegation spent most of their time out partying and consequently absented themselves from perhaps the most radical reform in recent CITES's history.

And this meeting was to discuss the critical plight of the world's endangered species?

If this nonsense persisted much longer, I thought, we can all kiss goodbye to the tiger, the rhino, the bears and the elephants. CITES had been totally corrupted by politics. Hardly surprising, therefore, that they had to hide behind locked doors; out of sight and sound, and away from the scrutiny of the world's press! Small wonder then that the endangered wildlife trade had been allowed to blossom into the second largest illegal racket after narcotics!

God knows what nasty little deals were being cooked up. I had to rely for my information on 'friendly' delegates who were otherwise forbidden to discuss proceedings with outsiders. Without the help of those courageous people, who risked political alienation in the process, it is safe to say that the tigers of the world would be largely extinct by the year 2000.

For the previous two years, I had been cultivating an association with the IUCN's Cat Specialist Group based in Switzerland. This expert body of men and women is made up of over 150 leading scientists and wildlife managers from more than forty countries who serve as consultants on the conservation and management of the world's thirty-six species of wild cat. Their chairman was a former Reuters chief correspondent and passionate tiger specialist by the name of Peter Jackson.

Peter and I had spoken a dozen times on the phone and exchanged several hundred feet of fax paper. He seemed to delight in my buccaneering exploits and no-nonsense approach, and a sort of friendship began to develop even though we had never met. He was no great fan of large formal political gatherings, and after a lifetime of involvement had learned to avoid such meetings wherever possible. His time was more than occupied attending smaller specialised get-togethers around the feline world. If there was nothing significantly cat-like on the agenda, he would give things a miss. From my limited experience of CITES, who could blame him.

Nevertheless, Peter Jackson played a crucial role in getting the plight of the tiger on to the agenda and into the public domain, albeit from his Swiss mountain residence several thousand miles and six time-zones away.

Meanwhile, back in Arlington, Virginia, I had left repeated messages at the hotel of Mr Pong Leng-ee, head of the Thai delegation, to contact me. I wanted to discuss the progress of the film documentary and the possibility of The Tiger Trust injecting significant amounts of funding into his under-equipped and over-whelmed national park rangers. There was also one other item that needed to be talked through, the critical plight of the tiger and the possibility of an emergency resolution being submitted to CITES. None of my messages were ever acknowledged despite the fact that I had freely donated almost US$15,000 to the Tiger Mountain project three months earlier. An extraordinarily arrogant and pernicious error of judgement, I thought, especially from the one man that represented Asia and therefore the world's tigers at that

297

meeting. Until, that is, I found out that he favoured the idea of tiger-farming, and then the reason behind his taciturnity became obvious.

CITES believes that specific regions should generally decide themselves on how best to manage their indigenous wildlife. A laudable theory, but like all theories, that's where it ends. Were it not for the expressed wishes of some of the poorer African countries opposing legalised trade in ivory backed up by western nations and NGOs, South Africa and Zimbabwe would have wiped the floor with their proposals at the Kyoto conference a year earlier. Similarly now, the poorer Asian countries were being browbeaten by China and Japan, only this time the species at stake was the tiger. Mr Pong Leng-ee was doing a deplorable job, being neither sympathetic nor impartial. He also displayed a lamentable lack of initiative. The fate of the tiger was up for grabs and once again the NGOs stole the march.

The tiger desperately needed a forthright voice, and so Sam and I decided to forge ahead with a formal request to address the Standing Committee and submit our findings. Such NGO impertinence was unheard of, it was said. How dare they? Who on earth do they think they are? We had prepared for this reaction, and we were not alone. The EIA had already made a similar request, as had a coalition of NGOs researching arguments against a complete revision of the original CITES listing criteria. It was to be an historic day.

The Chairman of the Standing Committee, Mr Murray Hoskin from New Zealand, granted our request and at 5.30 p.m. on the first day of talks, we were given the floor. I glanced around the debating chamber. The room was packed except for a handful of empty seats at the conference table itself. There wasn't a Thai face in sight!

After the presentation, the IUCN representative at the meeting, Dr Simon Stuart, stood up and acknowledged our investigative work and admitted the possible extent of the issue with the memorable words: '. . . This tiger problem has rather crept up on us from nowhere!'

A rather fitting response, given the tiger's legendary stealth, I thought at the time.

Sam and I worked late into the night drafting and re-drafting an emergency proposal. The following morning we submitted it for consideration. For two days it was knocked back at us for being overly polemic and confrontational. Tone it down, they said, these things take time; moderate the language. The tiger doesn't have time, we said, it doesn't have ten years for you to deliberate, it needs help *now*. And so backwards and forwards it went. It was quite obvious that the document was beginning to suffer the traditional fate of all CITES draft resolutions: it was being watered down beyond all recognition.

Finally, on the night of the third day I said to Sam, 'Listen, mate, I've had enough. The way this is going, there will be no resolution. The majority of delegates don't want anything on tigers, they don't want anything even remotely controversial on *anything*. They want an easy time of it. They don't have the balls to go head to head on any issue. All the bastards want to do is wallow with their inflated egos like bloated hippos in a quagmire of self-righteous compromise. That way they can slouch back to their masters and safely report that the Chinese or the Japanese weren't offended.'

'You got that right, pal,' murmured Sam, half asleep.

'Well, tough shit,' I said, 'life just isn't that simple. Japan might be buying up half the western world and China might be consuming the rest of it, but I'm not about to allow them to suck the tiger down the tubes in the process.'

'So what's new?'

'I'll tell you what's new,' I said. 'I'm going to fax this draft over to Peter Jackson right now and try and ask him to endorse it.'

'Do you know what time it is over there?'

'I don't give a flying fuck what time it is,' I said. 'If you and I can work half the night, I can certainly disturb Peter at midnight or whatever time it is in Europe.'

'Worth a try,' he said.

And so I risked the wrath of a sleepy Cat Specialist Group Chairman and woke him up in order for him to receive my fax.

'Michael, do you know what time it is?' came a sleepy voice over the phone.

'I'm sorry, Peter, this is important. Would you please switch your phone on to fax mode and let me know as a matter of urgency your views on the document?'

'Very well,' he grumbled, 'I'll see what I can do.'

The following morning there was a return fax lying unobtrusively on the deep-pile carpet, that had been silently put under my door during the night. It was a copy of our emergency resolution and at the bottom, six words had been added: 'Seems fine to me. Peter Jackson.'

Thank God for the fax machine, I thought. If the world's leading authority on tigers agreed with our proposals, and given the inextricable links between the IUCN and CITES, then there was no way that the delegates could ignore it now. At long last we were in with a fighting chance!

There was little more that I could do other than make sure the endorsed fax was given to the most effective individual in the CITES decision-making process. I resolved to deliver it myself, and from then on it was entirely out of my hands.

On the last day of talks, under agenda item 'Other Matters', the draft proposal was presented to the meeting for formal discussion. The final document, which acknowledged '. . . that the most recent population estimates for all remaining populations of *Panthera tigris* give rise to the most serious concern, due to indiscriminate and uncontrolled poaching and smuggling of tigers and tiger parts and derivatives to sustain markets for traditional medicines', and calling on all parties 'to take such measures as are required to halt the current illegal trade in tiger parts', was adopted later that day by consensus.

The political process had begun. I'd achieved precisely what I had set out to achieve, with the added bonus that this historic decision now added even further weight to the Amcrican NGO campaign to certify the consuming nations under the terms of the Pelly Amendment. The writing was now firmly on the wall for Taiwan.

It was time for me to return home and finalise my plans for a look behind the scenes at what was going on in China.

Once back in England, the phones started to buzz. The Tiger Trust had scored its first major international victory, and we saw no reason to hide that fact from the media. Both Sophy and I were dismayed at first when we discovered that other groups, much larger and hotter off the mark with their press releases than ourselves, were claiming all the credit for the Washington declaration. With the notable exception of the EIA, which has a Washington office, we were the *only* British-based NGO at the conference! And then I remembered, once again, that conservation is war, and when the good guys are not fighting the enemy without, they compete amongst themselves within. It was a valuable lesson and if the fledgling Tiger Trust was going to battle for funds with the other much larger conservation groups around the world, we would just have to sharpen up our act.

It was still early March and yet the publicity machinery at

Yorkshire TV had already kicked into action. 'The Tigers of Thailand' was scheduled to be broadcast on May 2nd, 1993. The BBC World Service and Radio Four wanted interviews. Journalists called wanting statements. Writers preparing articles for the TV listings magazincs wanted photographs, and letters of congratulations arrived from the most unlikely of places. Any notions I harboured about a trip abroad were put on ice as Sophy and I fielded this wave of attention as best we could.

Whether I liked it or not, The Tiger Trust was losing its relative anonymity. Up to that point, we had been quietly beavering away behind the scenes, away from the immediate glare of publicity. I now felt that although there was still so much left to do, we would nevertheless have to sacrifice some of our privacy. We had earned our recognition the hard way, and by the same token we would have to earn the funds for future work and investigations. For that we would need the help and support of the Great British people. There was only one thing for it: we would have to meet the press and the public head on.

Sophy and I prepared a brief synopsis of our work and together with Katie Metcalf and Guy Davis from Channel Four, we set about drumming up some advance media coverage for the forthcoming TV documentary. Will Travers at The Born Free Foundation was an endless source of advice and encouragement, and as the runaway express train of our lives careered through the month of April, both the *Sunday Times* and the *Mail on Sunday* newspapers wanted to write about the tiger issue, both on the day of broadcast. Somehow we managed to keep the two competing journalists apart and focused on their own particular angles. Had they found out about each other beforehand, the stories would most probably have been axed. As it turned out, both articles were excellent and complemented the seriousness of the crisis superbly well. The media plays a vital role in shaping the views of the public on so many different topics; Martin Hennessy and Sean Ryan did the cause of tiger conservation a monumental service on that particular Sunday, the very day that the tiger possibly took one tiny step back from the brink of extinction.

The media critics were extremely kind about the documentary, and 'The Tigers of Thailand' was hailed 'pick of the day' in many of the big-name newspapers throughout Great Britain. Channel Four had generously allowed a caption following the broadcast giving a contact address for The Tiger Trust for further information on tiger conservation.

We were deluged with mail. I'd always thought that there must be many thousands of British people that cared passionately about tigers, but we were totally unprepared for the outpour of response that followed the Sunday newspaper articles and the evening television transmission. And were it not for the generous help of friends around the Newmarket area, we would never have coped with the piles of letters that arrived on our doorstep each morning for weeks afterwards.

The Tiger Trust was launched straight into the deep end. It took considerable time before we could properly float, but we were totally drenched from day one!

Back in Washington things were hotting up. The new Secretary of the Interior, Bruce Babbitt, had taken a personal interest in the Pelly Amendment initiative, and under his watchful eye the proceedings were gaining momentum. Sam LaBudde was lobbying hard and whipping up a media storm by taking out huge advertisements in the national press encouraging people to pledge their support for tough action by the government against Taiwan in defence of the tigers.

Towards the end of May, Secretary Babbitt began preparing a stern letter to both the Chinese and Taiwanese governments informing them of his intention to pursue with the certification process under the terms of the Pelly Amendment. He saw no reason to delay any longer; the tigers and rhinos were running out of time, and the consuming nations were dragging their feet daring him to confront them. It was by now twelve weeks after the CITES emergency resolution, and just over three weeks since the first broadcast of our tiger documentary.

There is no doubt that a draft of that letter was somehow leaked to the mandarins in Beijing because two days before the official letter was signed, something quite remarkable happened. On May 29th, 1993, the Chinese government pre-empted the American attack and made yet another extraordinary and completely unexpected announcement.

They totally banned the domestic use and possession of tiger-bone products! With the stroke of a pen, the Chinese State Council cancelled the pharmaceutical criteria of tiger bone, and its further use or manufacture in traditional Chinese medicines. Fourteen months after their unprecedented climb-down on tiger-farming in

Kyoto, the old immortals in Beijing conceded that continued uncontrolled demand for the species in medicine and other quack remedies would eventually wipe out the tiger. And they wanted no part in it.

That historic announcement also served to pull the rug unceremoniously right out from under the feet of the mealy-mouthed protagonists of 'sustainable utilisation' who had been consistently defending the Chinese right to pursue what *they* perceived to be centuries of cultural tradition whilst simultaneously selling the tiger down the river in the process. Beijing knew only too well that over 99 per cent of its population neither needed nor used tiger bone, and were never likely to. The rest constituted not only a minority but a significant threat to a species whose historical significance in Chinese history and art was firmly established. The Tiger Trust had made a significant contribution to that realisation process, and we duly celebrated in the time-honoured and traditional manner.

When the hangover subsided, we started to digest the full scale and importance of this monumental breakthrough. There were many aspects to consider. We had always set out to expose and therefore undermine the illegal demand for tiger products. On the face of it, we were winning. The largest consumer had just prohibited domestic consumption, and Taiwan was still reeling from the effects of our public exposure of their dirty linen. If we could keep up this pressure, we would soon be able to switch attention away from the demand side of the equation to the supply. And help beef up anti-poaching efforts wherever needed. It was a heady time indeed.

Peter Jackson and I spoke regularly on the phone after the Washington meeting. Part of the resolution required him to contact representatives of the fourteen countries that still had wild tigers, and request up-to-date statistical information. He knew the enormous difficulties of this task. He knew what government officials would never dare to admit. The truth. And the truth was that nobody really had any idea just how many tigers were left in the wild. Statistics were traditionally formulated from anecdotal accounts, guesstimates and extrapolations based on primitive counting techniques. One thing that most people did agree upon, however, was that the tiger was in very serious trouble. Perversely, though, accurate and reliable statistics would inevitably demonstrate most countries' inability to tackle the illegal trade. So the real truth remained buried.

In response to Peter Jackson's questionnaire, the venerable authorities failed to agree. In India, the Project Tiger experts reckoned that between 2,500 and 4,500 of the great Bengal tiger remained. Almost a staggering 100 per cent margin of error! In Thailand, the discrepancy was even greater, with conflicting reports of between 106 and 500 tigers remaining. The Beijing government didn't even bother to respond, and in an unholy show of solidarity with the Chinese consumers of tiger bone, the Indonesians snubbed the IUCN request as well.

His subsequent report was evidently the best that the high-technology scientific world of 1993 could offer in defence of one of the most majestic animals on earth. It wasn't Peter's fault, of course – he could only compile the information to hand – but it was a damning indictment on political compassion and expenditure on critically endangered wildlife.

The rounded totals concluded that between 4,400 and 7,700 tigers remained in the wild.

Towards the end of June of that year and about three weeks after the Chinese government's prohibition announcement, we heard a piece of very alarming news. The owners of a Siberian tiger farm in China had cut off funding in protest, and were intending to allow the seventy-odd tigers to starve to death.

The tiger farm, in the north-eastern province of Heilongjiang, was the subject of the Chinese proposal to CITES in Japan, the proposal that claimed to be captive-breeding Siberian tigers as a conservation tool for eventual release into the wild. The very same proposal that received such a hearty and very public pat-on-the-back by the Australian government.

It now appeared as though I had been right from the very beginning. The farm was just a scam to supply tiger bone to the medicine trade after all. Their market had been abruptly cut off, and so now they saw no reason to continue the business and care for the tigers. As far as the Native Animal By-Product Import-Export Company Limited, which owned the enterprise, was concerned, the tigers could rot in hell.

So much for the ethic of captive-breeding as a conservation tool, I thought. Bloody hypocrites. It was time for me to blow the dust off my spy-cameras and get back to work.

CHAPTER TWENTY-FIVE

Harbin, People's Republic of China, July 1993

It was late evening by the time I arrived at the remote airport of the provincial capital of north-east China. It had been a long day. I had left Hong Kong at eight o'clock, travelling first to Beijing. The connecting flight should have left shortly after lunch. Instead I waited around in a filthy transit lounge for nine hours as I watched the short flight to Harbin being rescheduled time and time again. I was beginning to think that I would have to find somewhere to sleep when the flight was finally called. With relief, I joined the sea of weary and overladen travellers, and flew off to the city of tiger farms.

I had sent a fax to the Native Animal By-Product Import-Export Company two weeks earlier, requesting permission to visit. They had readily agreed. I was convinced that the tiger farm they owned, 'The Breeding Centre of Felid of Hengdaohezi (Heilongjiang) China', was a front although the Chinese representatives at CITES had succeeded in convincing a lot of people that their intention was simply to breed genetically pure Siberian tigers for eventual release into the wild.

What puzzled me now, of course, was that *if* the Chinese government were being so sincere, why had they sanctioned the turning-off of the food tap? What was to become of their honourable captive-breeding experiment now, I wondered? China had banned the use of tiger-body parts in medicine because the inevitable consequences of continued consumption had been made all too obvious. The State Council also realised that even restricted or controlled use was completely unworkable. They knew only too well that any finely honed business acumen would soon find a way to abuse the system, especially where such attractive profits were to be

305

made. By the same token, I thought, they should have been equally conscious of the devastating effects that legalised farming would have on wild tiger populations. Somewhere, however, that message was being lost in the translation.

I rode the shuttle bus into the town centre and found my hotel without difficulty. I collected my key from the unsmiling concierge in the corridor, and trudged down the creaking hallway anxious to scrub the traveller's grime from my skin. The hotel was a medium-class sort of place with large rooms and rusty bath water. After five minutes, the gushing liquid turned pale yellow and I knew then that I would have to cut my losses before it ran cold altogether. Knowing when to compromise was an integral part of survival in north-eastern China. I wrote a brief fax to Rebecca in Taipei and retired to bed.

Professor Shi Shaoye of the local Forestry University met me the following day. He was a 'special adviser' on captive-breeding, and explained over breakfast a little about the tiger farm. It was originally set up in 1985, and financed and managed by two Chinese government agencies reporting to the Ministry of Forestry and the Ministry of Foreign Trade. By 1989, he told me, a staggering US$880,000 had been spent on the project. The centre's initial breeding stock was made up of eight tigers collected from various zoos in China during 1986. He insisted that the main aim was to breed pedigree Siberian tigers for eventual release into the wild. He only smiled when I asked him what the secondary aim might be.

The professor was a mild-mannered individual with silvery white hair swept tightly back over a deep and furrowed forehead. The rest of his pale white face was equally craggy, and years of bending over a microscope had produced deep and baggy pouches under his eyes. He told me that he was a specialist in DNA, bio-genetics and cloning. Useful skills, I thought, and quite invaluable in the field of reproductive engineering, especially if commercial interests really were behind the tiger farm.

It was Saturday morning, and he was looking forward to a weekend together with his family. We agreed to meet again on Monday and drive out to the centre. He left at about ten-thirty and I returned to my room to make one or two phone-calls. I had been given the name of a suitable translator by a journalist friend. He was at home when I called and agreed to meet me at the hotel in an hour.

I found Mr You Ching Ren sitting patiently in the lobby and invited him to join me for a coffee. He was an extraordinary sort of chap. Although it was mid-July and excruciatingly hot and sticky outside, he was dressed in thick autumn tweeds and a colourful silk waistcoat. At one end of his body he wore, somewhat incongruously, a pair of scuffed trainers and, at the other, an ill-fitting honey-coloured wig. He presented a number of written testimonials that he had received over the years from seemingly satisfied clients, some were rather dog-eared and dated before I was born.

The man was extremely keen, the heavy suit was clearly designed to make me feel at ease, and his English was reasonable. It had been acquired, he reliably informed me, whilst working for a trading house in Shanghai before the revolution. He also volunteered that he had spent some time being 're-educated' after that, presumably in the virtues of a command economy and the teachings of Chairman Mao. He asked for ten dollars a day and so as not to offend him, I offered seven. He agreed.

We talked briefly about the reasons for my visit, and I explained that I was researching a book on wildlife and its use in traditional Chinese medicines, and that I would be interested to meet local pharmacists and buy samples. I also mentioned that in the course of my work I had met a number of traders and was always on the lookout for a lucrative business deal. I said that I was married to a Taiwanese and that my father-in-law dealt in all manner of exotic imports. He got the message. From my previous visit to China I had learned not to deviate too far from the truth although at times it was wise to bend it almost totally out of recognition. Mr You might well have had split loyalties, and be reporting my every movement to the State. His earlier unsolicited and almost anti-Communist remarks had struck me as somewhat insincere. If he was an informer, it was best that his reports were analogous to the official reason for my visit.

We agreed to go straight to work. I needed the bag-camera and told Mr You that I had to fetch something from my room. Fortunately I remembered my fax to Rebecca. It provided the most obvious excuse and three minutes later I returned clutching the paper and waved it triumphantly as I skipped down the stairs a little out of breath. The receptionist hardly looked up as I spoke to her. I repeated my request and asked her if she could send the fax. She merely cast a condescending glance at me as though I was the root cause of some personal annoyance.

Mr You appeared at my side. 'Can I help?'

'Yes, I have asked this young lady twice now if she would send

307

this urgent fax. It's to my wife. I should have sent it earlier but I forgot.'

He spoke to the girl who seemed to cut him off in mid-sentence as she snapped back at him.

'What did she say?' I asked him.

'Eh, something like, can't you see I'm busy,' he said matter-of-factly.

'I beg your pardon?'

'The girl can't send your fax because she is busy doing something else,' he said timidly.

'But she's reading a bloody magazine,' I said in utter disbelief.

Mr You spoke again to the girl, and this time her reply seemed less venomous.

'She says what's the rush?'

'What's the rush?' I couldn't believe it; Chengdu was never like this. 'I'll tell you what the rush is. I'm a guest in this hotel, a full-paying customer. She's on duty behind the reception desk, and it's her job to help me. I've asked her politely. I've a good mind to talk to the manager.'

The girl obviously recognised the word 'manager', and spat a torrent of abuse in our general direction.

'I'm afraid she says something like, go ahead and complain if you want to complain,' said Mr You apologetically.

I bit my lip. In another situation I would have lambasted the young woman with a few well-chosen expletives of my own. As it was, I thought it unwise to cause a scene. I did not wish to draw unnecessary attention to myself. This was China, a land where the customer is never right and certainly not king. It was not the girl's fault. The problem stemmed from over forty years of hard-line communism under which serving others is considered demeaning.

'Just give her the fax,' I said to Mr You. 'Tell her to send it as soon as possible.' We left her busy reading and stepped out of the hotel into the afternoon sunshine. Mr You did not seem to notice the leather shoulder-bag.

Whatever the Chinese State Council may have decreed six weeks earlier in Beijing, obviously hadn't filtered through to the town of Harbin. Or if it had, nobody was taking a blind bit of notice. We had no difficulty finding tiger-based products, and on the first attempt found several kilos of raw tiger bone.

The well-rounded pharmacist with the heavy black-rimmed spectacles took us into the back of his shop. With a deft sweep of his left arm he pushed aside a pile of abandoned plates and discarded food, and dropped a plastic carrier bag into the vacated space on the old wooden table with his right. I put the camera-bag down on a side shelf and twisted it carefully around so that the hidden lens could quietly record the scene.

He up-ended the bag and shook out the contents which fell on to the surface with a dull thud. I stared down at the tiger's leg, still wrapped in polythene. It was labelled in Chinese, but also the letters CMC and the date 92.11.10 were clearly visible. CMC, I thought, why those letters, what did they stand for? Chinese Medicine something; Council, Company, Corporation, Certificate? I made a mental note to find out.

I looked over at the shopkeeper, smiled and picked up the bag. It was heavy, about three kilos. There was a layer of rancid green mildew covering most of the thighbone. The lower shin was equally mouldy but it was tiger bone all right.

'How much?' I asked.

'Almost three and a half kilos,' translated Mr You.

'No, I meant how much does it cost?'

'10,000 *renmenbi* per kilo.'

About 1,700 dollars, I thought. Expensive.

'This piece here,' I said, indicating a broken joint with a blunt stump. 'How much?'

The man weighed it on a modern digital set of scales, tapped some numbers into an electronic calculator and turned the screen so that I could see it. The number 3328 stared back at me in phosphorescent green numerals.

'OK,' I said, 'I'll take it.'

I retrieved the shoulder-bag and we walked back into the shop and round to the front of the counter. I had no intention of parting with my money, and wondered just how far I could roll this charade.

The chubby pharmacist was quite cheerful now. He knew that he was charging an exorbitant price. I let him chortle away with Mr You for a while longer as he busily wrapped up my purchase in plain brown paper.

'Could I have a sales slip, please? My father-in-law doesn't altogether trust me as yet,' I explained politely.

With a shrug he produced a well-worn receipt-book and hastily scribbled a voucher, tore it off and tucked it underneath the neat package.

'Do you take American Express travellers cheques?' I enquired

309

innocently, knowing full well that they wouldn't.

Mr You looked at me in astonishment, and shook his head quietly from side to side in amazement. 'Cash only,' he murmured.

'I don't think I've got quite that much on me,' I said, heaving the shoulder-bag on to the counter beside the package. I rummaged elaborately around in the side pockets, edging the bag on to the narrow slip of paper.

'So sorry,' I said. 'No can do. I'll have to exchange some money at the hotel and come back later.'

Mr You translated and the shopkeeper grunted in acquiescence. He picked up the small parcel and turned slightly as I dragged the bag carefully away off the counter on to my flat outstretched palm. With one deft move I slipped the strap over my shoulder with one hand as I pocketed the receipt with the other.

'Come on, Mr You,' I said, 'time to go.' And with that we left the shop and jumped into a passing taxi. 'Do you know of anywhere else?' I asked him.

'Oh yes,' he replied, 'there are many in Harbin.'

By early evening we had been offered three complete skeletons and met with a fur trader that was in no doubt that he could deliver 'any amount' of tiger skins locally and from associates in Hebei Province just south of Beijing.

So much for the new law, I thought. It was time to go deeper. I asked Mr You if he could follow up some leads that I had for tiger-bone wine, and report back to me on the following Thursday. I gave him a twenty-dollar advance and he seemed content with the arrangement.

On Monday morning Professor Shi Shaoye met me as planned, albeit three hours later than arranged. With him was Mr Liu Xin Chen, the tiger breeding centre's director, and the deputy manager, Mr Yu Xiao Long. Somehow we all managed to squeeze into the back of an ancient and dilapidated jeep and we set off on the 290-kilometre journey south-east of the city toward the town of Dongning which separates China from the former Soviet Union.

It was a long hard drive. The road was badly pot-holed and the driver lunged the vehicle from side to side to avoid them. He was successful less than half of the time, presumably when there was something coming in the opposite direction. It was difficult for me to see. I was bent double most of the time bracing myself for the inevitable series of sharp sudden impacts, the dusty canvas top stubbornly obscuring all but a few cracks of light from my vision.

I find no shortage of skins for sale along the Thai–Burmese border (*Sophy Day*)

Scouting for any signs of 'the big boy', Khao Sok, 1990 (*Sophy Day*)

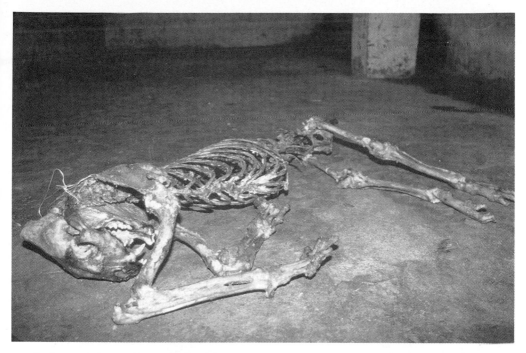

A tiger skeleton from the cold-storage room at the Heilongjiang breeding farm (*Michael Day*)

A Chinese girl feeds the tigers at the Heilongjiang farm (*Michael Day*)

Boon, our friend and tracker at Khao Sok (*Michael Day*)

Boonlerd Angsirijinda

Hard evidence: Korean mafia in Russia offers Steve Galster a tiger skin (*Tiger Trust Film Library*)

Hard evidence: a senior Russian customs official tries to sell Tiger Trust investigators a Siberian tiger skin (*Tiger Trust Film Library*)

Siberian tigers are bred for
the Chinese medicine trade in
Harbin, China (*Michael Day*)

Hard evidence: tiger bone
plasters illegally
manufactured in Harbin
(*Michael Day*)

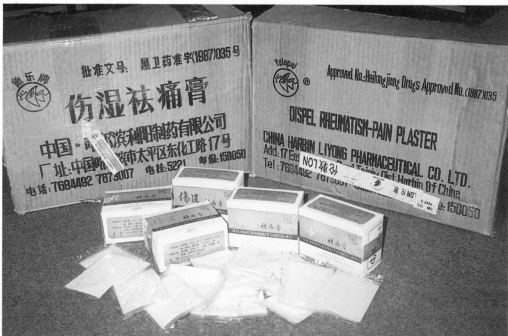

A Chinese official admits deceiving the United Nations CITES delegation, March 1994 (*Tiger Trust Film Library*)

Hard evidence: women packaging tiger bone plasters, Harbin, China, 1994 (*Tiger Trust Film Library*)

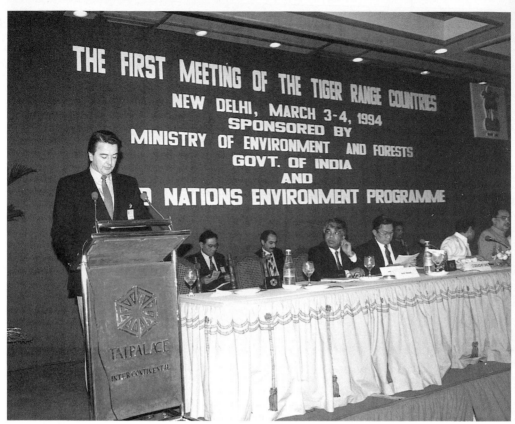

I addressed the global tiger forum in India, March 1994 (*Tiger Trust Film Library*)

Sophy and I being presented to the Princess of Wales, May 1995 (*Kent Messenger*)

We stopped three times, twice for food. My back was grateful for the respite and creaked loudly as I stretched my muscles. The third time we stopped was to change a tyre which had exploded abruptly as we were plunged into yet another highway crater only five miles from our destination.

We finally pulled into the gates of the compound shortly after sunset and Mr Liu insisted on giving me a quick tour of his facility. I could smell the tigers as I stepped out of the jeep on to the hard concrete ground, and I could hear their growls of discontent.

In the twilight we walked between rows of austere cages. Inside each one, a lonely tiger paced back and forth. The evening was their time. Thousands of years of evolution had equipped them to use this time of the day to stalk and hunt in the shadows of the undergrowth. The tiger's acute sense of sight and sound and awesome strength was instinctively known to all the creatures of the jungle. In the half light of dusk even the most sure-footed deer was always alert and on guard for the silent approach of a hungry tiger.

These wretched creatures instilled in me not a sense of fear but one of pity. It was quite obvious why they were there. The four-metre-square cages were designed for mass production. Each one could be interconnected with a common passageway which would allow a stud male to be introduced to any or all of the females. It reminded me of the Suffolk pig-breeding units, so familiar from my childhood in East Anglia. Everything about this place said farm. Factory farm.

As we walked around the complex, I noticed about a quarter of an acre of flat ground surrounded by a high chain-link fence. In one corner, a dozen pairs of young eyes stared back at me. As I approached, first one, then the whole group trotted timidly over to me and began rubbing their noses playfully up against the fence. The tigers were yearlings, barely half grown and they were going nowhere. I knew that in the wild a tigress keeps her cubs with her for at least two years. These young creatures had obviously been prematurely weaned and forever deprived of that crucial learning period, and had also lost their instinctive fear of humankind. If released into the wild they could not fend for themselves and hunger would drive them to desperate measures in the search of food. They could become man-eaters.

I left them as the last of the light faded from the night sky, and walked back to my sleeping quarters. There would be much to write up in my journal that night, I thought, and many questions to pose the next day.

We met for breakfast in the keepers' canteen: rice porridge, diced vegetables and a raw egg, followed by wafer biscuits washed down with sickly sweet coffee. The tea was undrinkable. My hosts were very perky and keen to talk. I had slept badly, my dreams invaded by sick and emaciated tigers pacing round in ever-decreasing circles. Sophy could normally decipher my dreams; these needed no further explanation.

Professor Shi Shaoye began by asking what specifically I needed to know about the centre's operations.

'Just about everything,' I replied. 'From how it was set up, where the tigers came from, how many have been successfully bred. Food, care and management. How much it all costs to run. Everything really.'

'Well, to answer your first question first, we began about seven years ago in 1986 with eight tigers, and the following year a further fourteen were added. These were all collected from zoos here in China.'

'And they were all pure Siberian tigers?' I enquired, knowing full well that from my experience of the Chengdu Zoo the officials hadn't a clue about the origin of their big cats.

'Oh yes, the zoo records were quite clear about that,' he responded with exaggerated sincerity. I let it pass.

'And when did you start to breed?'

'Later in the same year. Two litters were born, each of four cubs.'

'Remarkable,' I said. 'And what became of them?'

'Seven of them died.'

'I see. And how many have been born since that time?'

Mr Liu consulted a dog-eared exercise book and flicked through several worn and tea-stained pages, counting as he went.

'A further sixty-three,' said Professor Shi, hastily adding before I could interrupt, 'of which sixty-one survived.'

'An excellent record,' I said, trying to sound enthusiastic, busily taking notes as he spoke. Sixty-two cubs plus the original adult core stock of twenty-two . . .

'That makes a total of eighty-four tigers. But last night you told me that there were only sixty-nine,' I said directly to Mr Liu.

'A number have died of natural causes,' he replied.

'Fifteen, I presume?'

'Yes.'

'What did you do with the remains of these tigers?'

'They are kept in cold storage here at the centre.'

'Would it be possible for me to see them?' I asked hopefully.

'Yes, I think that can be arranged,' said Professor Shi nervously.

'Well, let's go,' I said quickly, standing up and grabbing my camera-bag.

We marched across a large courtyard toward a pair of tall wooden doors, heavily padlocked. Mr Liu produced a key and opened them to reveal a darkened empty room. Against the far wall was a rusted metal hatchway with a circular handle beside a protruding lever. It reminded me of the inside of a submarine, but I could see it was a walk-in freezer.

Mr Liu spoke rapidly to one of his assistants, who opened the door and disappeared inside.

'Do you mind if I take a picture?' I said, pulling out my Nikon camera. They just shrugged as I attached the flash. If I can get away with this, I thought, then the video shouldn't be too much of a problem.

Great billows of frosty air clung to the man as he stepped out of the enormous refrigerator with a massive frozen skeleton over his shoulder. He put the remains of the tiger on to the floor as I snapped away instinctively with my camera. He turned and walked back inside the icy chamber. I followed him.

The cold air caught in the back of my throat. A thick mist seemed to separate me from the man as he clambered over bulging sacks and wooden crates. He reached deep into one corner and tugged furiously at a particular bundle which eventually became separated from the pile. As he stepped out of the fog I could see that he was carrying a large skin. I shuddered, not from the cold but from the sudden realisation that I was standing amidst so much waste. Get a grip, I told myself. Record now, react later.

Outside, the man was unfolding the skin. It was well over two metres. The tail was missing.

I forced myself to say, 'It appears you have quite a stockpile in there. How many skins do you have?'

Mr Liu seemed ready for this question, and replied without hesitation, 'Twenty-six.'

'Are they all this large?' I asked, encouragingly.

'The smallest is about one and three-quarter metres.'

Very interesting, I thought. That means all twenty-six skins came from adults. It didn't make any sense. There were sixty-nine live

313

tigers plus the remains of twenty-six others, that totalled ninety-five. In addition, nine cubs were supposed to have also died, and yet according to the official records the grand total should be only eighty-four. Where did the other twenty come from, I wondered?

Mr Liu walked over to me as I panned over the gruesome remains with my video camera openly on view. There was no point in hiding it; they were bound to search my room at some stage and would certainly find it. There are times when it can be just as effective to film overtly and clown around inviting everyone to take part. This was one of them; there would be plenty of time for editing later. He showed me a contorted piece of frozen flesh, slightly pointed at one end with two vaguely spherical pouches at the other. I recognised the twisted organ. It was the tiger's penis.

'We have two,' volunteered the professor.

'Why only two?' I asked, thinking that they had probably sold the others.

'Because only two males have died,' he replied after a brief consultation with Mr Liu.

'How extraordinary. So the remains here are of twenty-four females, and only two males. Is that correct?'

'Yes.'

'Why so many dead females?' I asked, curious at the impossibly disparate mortality rate.

'They died of disease,' he replied, dodging my question and careful to translate Mr Liu's reply correctly. 'Eighteen died of disease, six of old age and two were culled because of growth abnormalities.'

Probably five legs, I thought. Professor Shi Shaoye was a self-confessed expert in bio-genetics and cloning. He had told me that he had a research laboratory on site somewhere; perhaps I would find more answers there.

'By the way,' I said, 'have there been any viral epidemics of any kind here?'

'No,' he replied. 'The diseases were mainly of an abdominal nature. In some cases requiring euthanasia.'

'Thank you, I think I understand now,' I said. Abdominal, I thought, very curious. Feline distemper or something more sinister, like botched embryo transplants? Maybe the lab would provide the answer.

For the next two days, the professor and Mr Liu remained guarded and considered all my questions carefully before replying.

314

They told me that the centre was now more or less privately owned by the Native Animal By-Product Import-Export Company which employed over 1,000 people and specialised in a number of other areas, most notably in the fur industry farming mink, racoon and silver fox. They confirmed that funding had been cut off following the State Council announcement banning the manufacture of tiger-bone medicines; the rest was easy to put together. They now hoped to blackmail the Chinese government into reversing the decision by threatening to starve the sixty-nine tigers to death.

We took the train back to Harbin. I still had a thousand unanswered questions in my head, and I was running out of time. There were five of us in the cramped compartment and I invited them all to join me in the restaurant car for lunch. I ordered copious amounts of beer, and after a while Mr Liu's face became flushed and his English miraculously improved.

In the space of an hour, before he fell asleep, he told me just about everything that I needed to know.

That evening I phoned Mr You, gave him the name of the Harbin Shiyitang Pharmaceutical Factory, and asked him to make an appointment for me the following day. On Friday morning he arrived at the hotel with an intermediary, a heavy-set but remark-ably agile man with a savage scar across his throat. He spoke as though the wound had punctured his larynx; his thin smile did little to relax me. The man was a thug.

We drove north out of town into the district of Daoli, passing convoys of three-wheeled Chinese tractors pulling carts piled high with red bricks fresh from the kiln. Dusty trees lined the road, some propped up precariously with rickety bamboo poles. Dark swarthy faces and cloth caps struggled to pedal ancient bicycles stacked high with wooden crates. Everywhere there were people on the move. Old men with bristly chins and grimy blue jackets, women with toothy smiles and drab cotton shawls bustled along the streets as we sped through the suburbs on our way to buy tiger-bone wine.

I was led into the boardroom of the large factory complex. The walls were lined with dark wood furniture curiously upholstered in clear plastic wrapping. Tea was served in delicate china cups, each with a matching porcelain lid. We sat at the highly polished table awaiting the arrival of the chief executive.

Mr Zhao Lu Yuan swept in to the fan-cooled room and took the empty seat between Mr You and the intermediary. He spoke rapidly through cigarette-stained teeth.

315

'You wish to buy tiger-bone wine?'

'Yes.'

'How much?'

'I understand you manufacture quarter-litre bottles; shall we say one thousand dozen as a trial order?'

He scratched his forehead and spoke briefly to a female colleague whom he summoned to his side with a brusque wave.

'This is a large quantity,' he began. 'There are many details to discuss. This product is very sensitive at the moment. The government have prohibited any further manufacture.'

'Yes, so I understand. But I am reliably informed that things can, how shall we say, be arranged?'

'It is possible. We still have some stocks, but not enough. We shall have to make more to fulfil your order. It could take time.'

'How long?'

'About one month.'

'That would be fine,' I said, wondering just how far I could push this charade. 'Would it be possible to inspect your manufacturing plant?'

He nodded and we all stood up. My bag-camera was on the floor beside my chair, and I picked it up.

'You can leave your things here. They will be quite safe,' said Mr Zhao.

Damn! I thought. Now what? There was nothing else for it but to come clean. I was outnumbered and in a remote part of China. If they caught me with the hidden camera, God knows what might have happened. At the very least they could hand me over to the authorities as an industrial spy. I doubted if the British Embassy in Beijing would have been sympathetic.

'Actually, I would rather like to take some pictures if I may,' I said, going for broke.

'I'm afraid that is not possible. Our manufacturing process is a closely guarded secret. Please leave your camera on the table,' he said.

There followed a rapid and heated discussion between the three men. My interpreter Mr You was clearly rattled by the exchange, anxiously wringing his hands as he spoke. I felt the situation was becoming unpleasant.

'Gentlemen,' I said, 'perhaps we might see the factory now?'

With that we left the boardroom and walked through the narrow corridor, down the steep wooden staircase and out into the open

316

courtyard. I was shown a high vaulted factory building containing a number of vats interconnected by pipes leading to three large cream-coloured pressure cylinders, each one with an impressive display of dials, valves and shining brass handles. This was the main processing room. It was here that the glutinous resin from the tiger bone was extracted by a system of heat and pressure. This was exactly what I had come to see, and yet my cameras were in another building. Without film evidence it would just be my word against theirs. Somehow I had to get proof.

We returned to the boardroom and drank foul-tasting tea whilst Mr Zhao tapped out figures on his pocket calculator. He began negotiations with a figure of US$3.50 per bottle; we finally settled at US$2.80.

'Perhaps you could confirm that in writing?' I said. 'And I would like a sample if that can be arranged.'

'Our warehouse is in the town centre,' replied Mr Zhao. 'I will have it sent to your hotel.'

'Excellent,' I said. 'I think that is everything. We should meet again on Monday to finalise the deal, and I shall arrange a cash deposit so that you can begin manufacture.'

Mr Zhao stood up and bowed slightly.

'Just one more thing,' I said. 'How am I to know that the product actually contains real tiger bone, there are so few of these animals now left in the wild?'

'We have a most reliable source of supply,' he replied.

'Oh really?'

'Yes, I understand that you have visited the facility quite recently.'

Got you, you bastard, I thought.

We drove back to the hotel. The thug sat up front next to the driver and occasionally leaned back across the seat to confront me with his rasping pidgin English. The scar on his throat stretched wide as he twisted his neck to face me. He saw me staring at it, and pointed to his damaged wind-pipe with a flick of his index finger.

'Knife!' he wheezed, and laughed madly. Threads of saliva ran from his blackened teeth. He was not the sort to meet late at night in a darkened alley.

It was Friday afternoon and there were still so many unanswered questions. There was now a definite link between the farm and the tiger-bone wine factory. Zhao had said as much, but I had no proof. I was convinced that the high female mortality was due to primitive genetic experimentation, and yet again I had no proof. I knew that the centre also bred silver fox, racoon and mink, and yet I had not been shown that side of their operation. Only the most naïve would believe that an organisation that bred and slaughtered animals for the fur trade would wince at the idea of farming highly lucrative tigers for the Chinese medicine racket. And then there was the stockpile of skins and bone in the cold-storage room. The numbers just didn't add up. Almost everything that I had witnessed so far was purely circumstantial. I would just have to go back.

Mr Liu was surprised when I called him at his office in town. He had already mentioned earlier that he was on duty that weekend, and would be returning to the centre on Friday evening.

'Unfortunately I was unable to complete all of my business today,' I said, 'and now I have to stay here until next week. I have nothing to do for the next two days and was wondering if I could come with you back to the centre?'

'But Professor Shi is busy.'

'Oh we don't need him, your English is fine. I would really love to see the tigers one more time before I leave,' I said.

Mercifully he agreed. I suspect he couldn't find the words to refuse gracefully, and therefore found it simpler to acquiesce. Whatever the case I met him at the central railway station at four-thirty, and we drank warm beer all the way back to the tiger farm. By the time we arrived we were old friends.

My head was still spinning as I crawled out of bed the next morning. It was five-thirty. I put the camcorder in a small back-pack together with spare video tape and batteries, and tiptoed quietly out of the room. Outside it was just beginning to get light as I moved silently across the courtyard, keeping to the shadows of the wall. I found the laboratory without difficulty: it was located opposite the cold-storage facility, inside a narrow portico roughly where I had imagined. I tried the door, but it was locked. I took out a credit card and fumbled around with the latch, but it wouldn't budge. I moved down the narrow hallway, past a window caked in filth and old cobwebs through which I could still make out the shapes of test-tube racks, retort-stands and glass beakers, until I found another door. I was now completely out of view and tried the handle. The door opened a few inches and then held fast. There was something blocking it on the other side. I put my weight against the flaky wooden panelling, and heaved gently. From behind the door I heard the dull creaking noise of heavy furniture scraping across the floor. There must be some sort of cabinet on the other side, I thought, as I continued to push. From behind the door a book fell to the floor with a loud thump. Damn.

I waited for at least five minutes. Nobody came. I pushed the door a few more inches and squeezed myself through the gap. The room was full of boxes and crates and books stacked high in uneven piles. There was a dank musty smell to the air. Slowly my eyes adjusted to the light. I closed the door quietly, replaced the cabinet tight up against it, and turned to survey the room. Beside the adjoining door to the laboratory there was another heavy wooden piece of furniture. On the cluttered surface were a number of tubular glass apothecary jars, each about eighteen inches high. I could see that they were full of liquid although I couldn't make out what was inside. Instinctively I reached into my bag, pulled out my camera and walked slowly toward them.

About ten feet away I stopped abruptly as my eyes finally registered the grisly nature of the contents. Submerged in what was almost certainly formalin were dozens of carefully preserved foetal tigers.

My hands shook uncontrollably as I tried to film the gruesome spectacle. Rage possessed me as I imagined the hideous experiments that had quite obviously gone disastrously wrong in this terrible place. Twenty-four female tigers had died, their skeletons strung up in cold storage. And then I remembered the text of the Chinese proposal to CITES the previous year. In the section devoted to 'Strategy for enlarging the population' were the words: 'to increase the pregnancy rate by using the techniques of transferring embryos.'

And this was some noble scheme to introduce tigers into the wild! The fucking bureaucrats were going to let them get away with it, I thought angrily. Somehow I had to get this film safely out of the country. I looked at my watch; it was five past six. With luck I could return to my room without being noticed.

Later that morning I staggered down to the canteen with an exaggerated hangover. Mr Liu looked bad, his eyes still bloodshot as he slurped his rice porridge noisily. Over coffee I lambasted him with more questions until finally he gave up and agreed to show me the mink farm. I should have guessed. The fur ranching and the tiger farm were all part of the same facility, and separated only by a ten-foot wall. In the afternoon, I climbed on to the roof of the administrative building, and panned my camera over from one side to the other.

There was now absolutely no doubt in my mind whatsoever. The Breeding Centre of Felid of Hengdaohezi (Heilongjiang) China was a scam to produce the maximum amount of tiger bone, and return the maximum amount of profit for its owners as possible. And I fully intended to expose it if only I could get to the airport and out of China.

The following afternoon we took the train back to Harbin. I stayed well clear of the beer. I had some packing to do.

The battle-scarred Bakelite telephone rattled angrily on the bedside table. It was 11 p.m. No-one would normally ring at this hour. Unless it was him again.

The man had phoned earlier that night demanding to know where I had been all weekend. It was none of his business. I fed him an elaborate saga involving a beautiful maiden and a hideaway love-nest in the mountains. His vile and wheezing voice had chortled salaciously into my ear. Reassured now, he arranged to meet me early the following morning in the downstairs lobby. I had no intention of being there. After that call, I went directly to the bar and swallowed a large scotch. Fifteen minutes later, having settled my account with the hotel cashier, I returned to the room to purge the evil of the past three days from my skin.

Turning off the bath taps, I stared impatiently at the steaming water. Damn the phone!

'Yes,' I growled, recognising the pidgin English of the late-night caller. 'Have you any idea what time it is?'

The wheezing voice was menacing now. 'Mister Mike, what are you playing at, why you check out of hotel?'

My brain catapulted into gear, searching for clues. Was he alone and *where* was he? How did he find out, and what the hell could I tell him?

'Oh, yes, but of course, I should have mentioned it before,' I struggled to sound convincing. 'My father-in-law is flying in from Taipei tomorrow and wants me to stay with him at the Excelsior.'

'Don't believe!' he bellowed. 'I think you are spy. People coming now to your room. We find out truth!' My hackles stood on end as he spat out the words.

The leather holdall lay open on the bed, and buried deep inside a

320

hidden pocket was the incriminating video tape. If I could only get this vital evidence safely out of the country, the world would finally know the truth. Counting seconds, I carefully turned on the bedside radio.

'Just a second, I think my bath water is overflowing, won't be a minute,' I stammered, setting the receiver down gently, an inch from the loudspeaker.

Stripping the towel from my waist, I made a frenzied dash for the bathroom and grabbed my clothes. Dressing in seconds, I threw the tiny cameras and video equipment from the bed unceremoniously into the bag and hurled myself toward the door. Outside, mercifully, the corridor was empty. I double-locked the room and fled.

I hid in the shadows of the stairwell, my pulse thundering inside my head. In the hall I heard the elevator stop and the sound of heavy feet running down the passage.

Slowly, one by one, I crept up the stairs away from the angry shouts and the loud banging at my door. Somehow I had to find a way out. If they found me, there would be no mercy.

I felt inside the leather bag, hoping against all odds that the sample bottles hadn't smashed. Miraculously they were both still intact. The tiger-bone wine had been waiting for me at reception along with the written quotation that I had requested. It was a vital piece of the jigsaw and material evidence. The farm and the factory were inextricably linked, I knew that now. I looked at my watch, less than five minutes had passed since the phone-call. What the hell do I do now, I thought?

If the thug broke down my door, it would take him five seconds flat to realise that I had fled. I scaled one flight of stairs and then another. Why was I climbing, I asked myself? Why is it instinctive to seek height when in danger. It was absurd. I should be on the ground running for my life.

On the tenth floor, I took a quick look through a gap in the partitioning door into the corridor. The concierge's desk was abandoned. I pulled open a drawer and grabbed a key, 1007, James Bond's room I thought, forcing myself to smile at the irony of the number that I had picked. I dashed down the hallway and tried the lock. There was no chain holding it on the other side. So far so good. I turned on the light briefly, the room was empty. I threw down my bag and locked myself in, pushed an armchair up against the door and waited.

The violent hammering of my heart inside my chest gradually

subsided and I began to think more clearly. After an hour or so, I stopped looking at my watch as the commotion downstairs finally died away. How the hell had they found out?

I should have guessed, when I first laid eyes on him in the car, that the cut-throat gangster would have had me watched. He must have suspected something all along and asked the hotel staff to keep an eye on me. He was clearly hostile when he had phoned earlier and yet I was sure that I had put him at ease. If he had guessed somewhere down the line that I had no intention of making the Monday morning meeting, then my sudden checkout must have convinced him. But why did he phone a second time? Had he and his thugs merely turned up outside my door, that would have been it. As it was, his impulsive nature had given me the opportunity to escape with only seconds to spare.

I sat down in the armchair and buried my head in my hands with relief. Later, when it was light and I was ready and armed with a wad of hard cash, I would head out to the airport and catch the first flight out of China, and never, ever come back.

At six o'clock I heard people moving around outside. The sounds were unhurried, normal, measured; early-morning-type sounds. At six-thirty I pulled the chair away from the door, looked through the spyhole and made a dash for it.

Lawrence McGinty, the science correspondent at the ITN newsroom on Grays Inn Road in London looked at the tapes. It was Friday afternoon. He spoke briefly into the telephone, then turned to me with a smile.

'I've spoken to my editor. We want to run the story tonight on the News at Ten. We'll need to speak to the Chinese Embassy, of course – for verification, comment, that sort of thing. Can you stick around? I'll need to do an interview with you. Yes, this looks good, very good,' he said, rubbing his hands.

That night, millions of television viewers across the country saw the whole sordid story of the tiger farm and the sample bottles of tiger-bone wine for themselves. The following day, the *Daily Mirror* carried the story under the banner headline, 'SCANDAL OF TIGERS TURNED INTO WINE', and The Tiger Trust quietly chalked up another victory.

That evening I swore to Sophy that I would never take such risks again as long as I lived. I lied.

CHAPTER TWENTY-SIX

Suffolk, England, September 1993

It was early September. The furore over the tiger farm had begun to subside. The Chinese Ambassador to the United Kingdom, Mr Ma Yuzen, had taken a personal interest and had written to me with assurances that the tigers at the Heilongjiang farm would be fed and well treated. There was little more that we could do for the time being, except make damn sure that it never ever happened again.

In the United States, the campaign to take sanctions against China and Taiwan under the terms of the Pelly Amendment was hotting up. The ITN news story had been taken up by the American networks, and it was all grist to the mill. The Secretary of the Interior, Bruce Babbitt, was planning to attend the CITES Standing Committee meeting in Brussels. The Chairman, Murray Hoskin, had once more given his assent to an informal presentation from the NGO community. Mr Babbitt would certainly be there and his presence would guarantee a full house. Nobody would be sneaking off to parties this time round, I thought, remembering the shoddy performance of the Thai delegation at the last meeting in Washington.

For days I worked on my speech. I was to be given just ten minutes. It's hard to say everything on such an important subject in such a small amount of time. It was the greatest opportunity that I would ever have to directly influence the bureaucrats and politicians in attendance, perhaps the last chance to force the plight of the tiger firmly on to the CITES agenda. I would leave nothing out. The tigers needed a voice, not a diplomat, and there was little room for compromise to my way of thinking.

There was only one thing for it. I would have to move my office temporarily to Brussels for the duration of the meeting, and so I loaded up my car with computer, photocopier, printer and files, and set off on the long drive via Dover and Calais to the Belgian capital.

I had hoped that my representations in Washington and the subsequent emergency resolution would have flushed out one or two tiger experts, people that I could compare notes with and share ideas. Once again I was utterly dismayed to find that there were no such people in attendance. As I stood up to address the meeting, I looked around the packed chamber and prayed that my words would not fall on deaf ears.

Mr Chairman, distinguished guests, delegates and observers, ladies and gentlemen.

Firstly, let me join my fellow NGO colleagues in thanking the Chair and indeed the CITES Secretariat for giving me the opportunity of addressing you this afternoon. This is now the second time in less than a year that NGO representatives have been allowed to address the Standing Committee, and it is my personal hope that this will become a tradition for many years to come.

Why?

CITES, Mr Chairman, is as important to us, working as we do within the NGO community, as I'm sure it is for you all. Many of us dedicate our lives, and by that I frequently mean our social lives as well as our working lives, to species conservation of one sort or another.

Some of us are what you might call the eyes and ears of the CITES Treaty. By *that* I mean that we spend a great deal of our working time investigating the trade *and* the implementation *and* the level of enforcement of this treaty, very often in parts of the world where, perhaps, environmental concern is a relatively new concept.

We gather information and wherever possible commit this information to camera and video film. Often at great personal risk. We then freely submit our findings as evidence for you all to consider, and we do this in the fervent belief that these findings will provide the basis for discussion, debate and, in some cases, decisive, severe and conclusive action.

Some of you here may never have had the opportunity to visit some of the world's 'trouble spots', or to have seen the rotting carcass of a dead tiger or handled a poached rhino horn . . . Those of us that have will all know that feeling of

324

utter waste and futility at the loss of these great creatures.

However, let mc tell you that much deeper than that is often the feeling of sheer overwhelming helplessness in terms of what, if anything, we can do to help.

It is in that spirit, ladies and gentlemen, that we freely share with you our findings because it is you and only you who have it in your power to make the necessary recommendations to ensure the effective enforcement of this treaty.

It will come as no surprise to any one of you here today that the tiger is in big trouble. By now you should have all received a copy of Mr Peter Jackson's report. On that let me make a few comments.

To my way of understanding, there seems to be a *slight* inference in the report that perhaps the tiger is in no worse shape now than it was twenty years ago. The reasoning behind this appears to be that the early successes of Project Tiger in India during the early 1970s compensate in some way for the decline of the rest of the subspecies more recently in other parts of Asia.

However, in all fairness, I should point out that Mr Jackson does mention in his report that should the results from this year's census in India show a significant decline on the last 1989 figures then this would provide substantial evidence to suggest, and I quote, 'a dramatic decline in tiger numbers in the past twenty years would be established'.

So what do we know about the current situation in India?

What we do know, quite categorically, is that last Monday the Indian authorities confiscated 287 kilos of poached tiger bone that was allegedly en route to China. The following day, a further 100 kilos were found. Ten days earlier 40 kilos were seized by the Nepalese authorities on the Indo-Nepalese border, and in the previous month an additional 100 kilos.

A staggering total of 527 kilos, ladies and gentlemen, or the equivalent of over fifty tigers!

Mr Valmik Thapar, the convenor of the IUCN Cat Specialist Group in India, reports that between 1988 and 1992, seventy-six tiger skins or skeletons were recovered.

So, what does this tell us? Simply this: we now know that in the last five years, the remains of at least 126 tigers have been confiscated by the authorities.

The next question we have to ask ourselves is what proportion of the trade does this figure represent? I refer again to Mr Jackson's report: 'The instances of poaching that come to light can be considered just the tip of the iceberg, which suggests that at least five or six times as many tigers are poached as instances known.'

Five or six times! That equates to between 630 and 880 poached tigers, from India alone in the last five years . . .

Let us try and put these figures into an up-to-date perspective. This year, and specifically in the last two months, 527 kilos of tiger bone have been confiscated by the Indian and Nepalese authorities, and from the report that I have here, ladies and gentlemen, it is *fresh* tiger bone.

Mr Valmik Thapar, who is also a much respected writer, photographer, tiger expert, and also a member of the Steering Committee of Project Tiger in India, states, and I quote, 'There are probably ten times this amount being poached in India every year.'

Over five tonnes of tiger bone! Over 500 tigers every year!

Can we believe him? Let's work the figures backwards for ourselves. 500 divided by Peter Jackson's iceberg-theory factor of five equals 100 tigers. And just how often does that iceberg turn over? We know that the illegal trade network works in hard cash. Common sense dictates that the traders do not wish to sit on their contraband for too long; they want to dispose of their stock as fast as possible. So shall we say once every six months, twice a year?

Et voilà! We are back to the figure of fifty tigers that we know have been seized in the last two months.

So why? And where is so much poached tiger bone going? The guilty party in last week's raid in Delhi, according to my report, clearly indicates China. For use in traditional medicines . . .

I was myself in China at the end of July, and most of you should by now have received a copy of my report. For those of you who have not, I have plenty of extra copies available. I visited China for two reasons:

1) to report on a captive-breeding operation for tigers in the north-eastern province of Heilongjiang, and,

2) to try to ascertain the continued existence, or otherwise, of tiger bone in commerce in that part of the world.

Within twenty-four hours of my arrival in the provincial capital

326

of Harbin, ladies and gentlemen, I had located the first secret cache of tiger bone, and within a week I had secured an appointment with a traditional pharmaceutical factory in an endeavour to place an order for 12,000 bottles of tiger-bone wine!

TRAFFIC has, in the past, documented one manufacturer alone in Taiwan that imported 2,000 kilos a year to brew 100,000 bottles of tiger-bone wine. On this basis, my bogus order would have required the equivalent of about 250 kilos of tiger bone, or about twenty-five dead tigers to fulfil!

I was shown around their factory, the extraction process was explained to me and I was shown tiger-bone samples. In answer to my question as to the source of the raw material, they told me that it could all be arranged.

Mr Chairman, the announcement made by the State Council in Beijing at the end of May this year states: 'The traditional Chinese medicines that have already been produced shall be sealed up and forbidden for sale within the duration of six months commencing from the date of this notice.'

And in addition, in case there is any doubt as to whether the product that I was offered actually contained any tiger bone, the State Council announcement goes on to say that 'any products marked with the words tiger bone shall be treated as containing tiger bone'.

I would like to now, if I may, turn your attention to the TRAFFIC report on South Korea, specifically page two. I quote: 'It is also interesting to note that, in 1991 and 1992, China supplanted Indonesia as South Korea's major supplier of tiger bone.' And the chart on the final page shows that in 1991, 600 kilos and the following year 1992, a further 252 kilos were imported into South Korea from the People's Republic of China. And China, if I'm not mistaken, Mr Chairman, has been a full member of CITES since 1981.

892 kilos of tiger bone, possibly ninety tigers, where did this come from? Captive breeding? Re-export? If it was so-called pre-convention, why did the exporting country in this case wait so long to sell it to the Koreans?

TRAFFIC's extremely valuable document shows that the Koreans have been actively buying tiger bone for several years, and quite significant amounts in the last five. Are we therefore honestly expected to believe that almost a tonne of highly lucrative tiger bone has been sitting in a warehouse gathering dust for the last ten years?

Let me finally move on to the most critical area of concern, the survival of the species, and in particular one very specific subspecies, the great Siberian tiger.

In the winter of 1992 to 1993 this, the world's largest cat, came under the most intense poaching pressure. Peter Jackson describes it, with numbers possibly as low as 250, 'as severely threatened by poaching'.

He goes on to refer to the report by Doctors Miquelle and Smirnov which state that 'at least sixty tigers were lost in Russia in 1992'. Adding from the accounts of the Russian biologist, Pikunov, that most products are sold abroad, notably to China. Anecdotal accounts indicate that in some cases sacks of tiger skin and bone have been bartered on the Sino-Russian border for automatic weapons and four-wheel-drive vehicles, *thereby making the poachers even more deadly and effective.*

Mr Chairman, in a few short weeks the first snow will begin to fall in the former Soviet Far East. The last remaining Siberian tigers will find it thus increasingly more difficult to hide from and elude the relentless pursuit of the poachers. *Panthera tigris altaica* can simply not withstand another onslaught of poaching pressure of the magnitude experienced last winter. With some estimates putting the figure as low as 250, poaching, even at last year's levels, would reduce numbers by almost 25 per cent. *It could well be more.*

By the time the CITES Standing Committee reconvenes in March next year, the Russian winter will be all but over, and the effects of our actions here this week will be known. If we are to avoid convening again in six months' time to the news that, as a direct result of massive, wide-scale poaching, the great Siberian tiger has been all but lost, we must send a message now, this week, before it is too late. A message that leaves the poachers, the middlemen and the entire illegal network in no doubt whatsoever that the market for tiger bone *is closed.* And that CITES, by using the full extent of its authority, has clearly demonstrated to the offending countries '*that it will not tolerate the loss and possible extinction of this most precious of living creatures*'.

Thank you, Mr Chairman.

For one terrible moment there was a deathly silence, and I thought

328

that I had gone too far. The hell with it: if this is my first and last CITES speech, I'm not about to pussyfoot around the issue and make the hideous reality of the tiger crisis more palatable for this bunch to digest. The facts were there to be seen; there was simply no avoiding the stark reality that China was guilty as hell. I glanced across at the Americans. Mr Babbitt was whispering something to a colleague. Suddenly a familiar face smiled back at me, and all at once the room erupted into applause.

As the noise subsided, the director of TRAFFIC waved his flag, and was given the floor by the presiding chairman.

'Thank you, Mr Chairman,' he began. 'TRAFFIC would like to concur with the sentiments of the representative of The Tiger Trust . . .'

There is a God, I thought.

The following morning, September 7th, 1993, US Secretary of the Interior, Bruce Babbitt, announced his government's decision to certify China and Taiwan under the terms of the Pelly Amendment. President Clinton now had sixty days to notify Congress on what action he intended to take and whether he would use his discretionary powers to impose limited trade sanctions against either country. The Tiger Trust and the entire NGO conservation community were one step closer to an historic victory.

Later that day, as I prepared to leave the characterless assembly halls, a tall, rather spindly-looking man in an immaculately tailored, pin-striped suit approached me.

'Ah, Mr Day,' he began, in an infuriatingly affected drawl, 'I wonder if I might have a word?'

Civil Service, probably Foreign Office, I thought, what the hell does he want. 'By all means.'

'You've been causing quite a stir, I hear.'

'Not really,' I said, 'and nothing that shouldn't have been said a very long time ago. I can't imagine why they have been allowed to get away with it for so long.'

'Quite. Eh, tell me, do you intend to pursue this matter further?'

'Why do you ask?'

'Well, I really think that you should now allow diplomacy to take its course.'

'I'm afraid I don't have too much faith in diplomacy, especially of the type employed in CITES matters. If the fate of the tiger was left entirely to diplomacy, we could all begin to write its epitaph today,' I said, already sick of this conversation.

'Nevertheless, there are those that feel a less, how shall we say, confrontational line should be taken from now on.'

'Is that so? Of course they might well have a point,' I said. 'On the other hand they might not.'

'Perhaps this is not quite the time to be rocking the boat with Beijing,' he continued.

So that was what this was all about, I thought. China gets upset, and the FO immediately think the whole Hong Kong pact is about to collapse. How utterly absurd.

'I'm afraid that rocking the boat and exposing hypocrisy is an essential part of our campaign. I don't especially enjoy doing it, but it has to be done.'

'Mr Day, I am required to tell you that certain people in Whitehall take a rather dim view of your rather brusque approach to this issue.'

'Do they now? And tell me, is this official?'

'Let us just say that it comes from on high,' he said pompously.

'Hmmm. I think the archaeologist Howard Carter coined the perfect response to that one,' I said.

'Oh really, and what was that precisely?'

'The only answer I can give, my dear sir, is spherical and in the plural.'

And with that I left him turning a peculiar shade of beetroot, and probably about to explode. I had other more important things on my mind. Like how I would explain to Sophy that I was going to Siberia.

There are all too few men and women involved in the perilous work of environmental espionage. Those that are seldom react well to arrogant and self-righteous political expediency. They live in a twilight world fraught with danger, where violence and even death is seldom far away. Somehow I found myself hopelessly caught up in that world, and determined that my endeavours should not be swamped by a tidal wave of complacency, indifference and virulent rhetoric. CITES was finally waking up to the tiger crisis, but all too slowly. The hidden agendas of all but a few of the delegates continued to hamper substantive progress. And the big cat was rapidly running out of time.

I left Brussels uneasy in the knowledge that, far from modifying my approach, I would have to delve even deeper to get at the truth. In order to do that, I was grateful to have with me a master of the trade.

Steve Galster had trained with the American security services and was proud of his country's commitment to wildlife conservation. He was familiar with the complexities of international conventions, and a frequent visitor to CITES. We had met eighteen months earlier in Kyoto and I was greatly impressed by his meticulous research into the illegal ivory trade. Since that time he had investigated the whale-meat underground in Japan, the wild-bird trade in Central America and, more recently, rhino-horn smuggling to China where he had uncovered an enormous stockpile, conveniently located not far from Hong Kong. His hidden-camera evidence had been seen by millions of people around the world. We had a great deal in common.

He was now heading home to his native Wisconsin for a well-deserved break, and I had offered him a lift to London. As we talked in the car, I began to sketch out a plan of attack for Russia.

The situation in the former USSR was critical. The reforms of *perestroika* had done little to help the people of the Russian Far East or their indigenous wildlife. There was wide-scale unemployment, lawlessness and political discontent. People's savings had been largely eroded by the plummeting value of the rouble on the world money markets, and spiralling inflation was driving the price of even the bare necessities of life out of reach of many of the nation's poorer individuals. Traditional values were being cast aside in the fight to survive. The corrupting influence of the Russian Mafia had permeated the entire system, their tentacles putting an unacceptable stranglehold on every aspect of trade and commerce. The police, the customs and even the armed forces were beginning to succumb to the pressure as more and more people resigned themselves to the philosophy of making hay while the sun shines. The country was in complete and utter disarray and its wildlife heritage was being plundered along with everything else.

Nowhere was the voice of reason or restraint more distant than in the vanishing wilderness of the Russian Far East. Gangs of marauding Chinese poachers would cross the expansive and largely unguarded border and take whatever they found: highly lucrative wild ginseng from the rich forest soil and Siberian tigers from the face of it. All to satisfy the insatiable appetites of the cash-rich consumers in Harbin, Beijing, Shanghai and beyond. What contraband failed to join the well-worn trade route across the border into China was smuggled out of the eastern seaboard bound for Japan, South Korea and Taiwan.

The Siberian tiger, the largest cat in the world, was disappearing fast, and Steve agreed to help me find a way to reverse that situation.

For the next six weeks, I coordinated operations from The Tiger Trust's base in Suffolk. I enlisted the help of Dr Bill Clark, the highly dedicated and passionate Israeli delegate to CITES, and the three of us agreed to rendezvous in Moscow in mid-November to discuss strategy with the Russian government before flying to Vladivostok to look at the situation for ourselves.

Three weeks before my departure, I took the train to London to meet up with a communications expert who worked out of a tiny office in Maida Vale. We had met before, and I was always fascinated by the extensive range of surveillance equipment that he had gathered from his various sources around the world. He stocked the most sophisticated UHF and VHF bugging devices, hand-made in Jerusalem, video cameras no larger than a credit card from a supplier in Tokyo; infra-red night-vision binoculars from Stuttgart; and microchip transmitters from a facility in Cheltenham. He was not cheap, but he was one of the best, and he knew my line of work. Over the next few days we put together a comprehensive kit that would dismantle and pass inspection upon arrival at Sheremetyevo airport in the Russian capital.

On November 18th, 1993 I boarded a British Airways flight at Heathrow and flew to Moscow to meet up with my colleagues who had already arrived and were stationed at the Budapest Hotel.

For two whole days we attended meetings with officials at the Ministry of Environmental Protection who seemed unable or unwilling to commit financial or tactical assistance to their colleagues seven time-zones away to the east. *Perestroika* had brought political reforms, although those reforms had brought virtual paralysis to the central administration in Moscow. The entire system was hopelessly bogged down in unutterably tedious and mind-boggling red tape. Economic uncertainty and the inevitable austerity drive had senior officials jostling for power, and nervous about involving themselves in anything other than the most critical issues of national interest. And although President Boris Yeltsin receives more letters about the Siberian tiger than any other animal on earth, wildlife conservation was a matter of irrelevant and trifling concern to all but a handful of his government servants.

Bill Clark, Steve Galster and myself had hoped to find strategic support in Moscow; instead we found cynicism and suspicion. The

Russian sceptics knew only too well the enormity of the task that we had taken upon ourselves, and resolved somewhat pessimistically that it probably couldn't be done. It was bitterly cold that week in Moscow, and it would have been so easy to turn tail and head for the warmth and security of home. Instead we boarded the most disreputable, jeopardous and unflightworthy aircraft I had ever seen and flew east across the permafrost of Siberia to the town of Khabarovsk.

CHAPTER TWENTY-SEVEN

Siberia, November 1993

The Central Hotel in Khabarovsk appeared, at first glance, to be an empty, austere and unloved monument to those heady days before *perestroika*. For Dr Clark, Steve and myself, and all those who bravely crossed its grey marble threshold in hope of finding shelter during that bitterly cold November *and* suffered the abuse of the receptionist hag who grudgingly dispensed room keys with the arrogant indifference of a lavatory attendant, it became a welcome sanctuary. And for the rest of the month we delved quietly behind the scenes into what many travellers have poetically referred to as the Wild East.

The hotel stood on the east side of a large characterless square, the drab exterior stretching northward to a lonely bronze statue that gazed down with lifeless eyes upon the unsuspecting visitor like some benign relic of a bygone age. The great man was still revered in Khabarovsk. Behind the crumbling façade there were unpainted walls, threadbare carpets and the most basic furniture. Cockroaches and mice mingled with visitors on every floor, perhaps more so on the fifth, where carelessly discarded titbits and other flotsam were more plentiful. The fifth floor, for some extraordinary reason, was especially reserved for foreign guests, and whilst inferior in every aspect to the rest of the hotel, the rooms were three times the price.

On the ground floor, the decaying dining salon, once a venue for wild evenings of laughter, song and vodka, was now a sad and hollow mausoleum, a silent epitaph to those carefree days before the dawn of *perestroika*.

I sat quietly at a corner table, sipping the last of the duty-free Courvoisier, the warm glow in my stomach a welcome contrast to the cold draught at my feet. I shuddered again at the memory of the previous night. The stifling dank and filthy interior of the poachers' truck kept invading my thoughts and the cognac wouldn't keep it at bay. I could still feel the horror, the reality, the death. Somehow it all still seemed so real, so vivid.

Just a few hours earlier, I had held in my hands the skin and bones of a creature that only a few short days before had roamed the frozen snow-swept forest, free and master of all he surveyed. A Siberian tiger.

It was Tuesday evening. Both Steve and I were feeling low and dispirited. Three times already that day, the middleman had failed to make contact. Our nerves were on edge. We waited until nine-thirty, then decided to abandon for the day our attempts to secretly film the merchants of death in this remote outpost of the illegal wildlife trade.

Carefully I removed the wires and cables that connected the hidden camera neatly hidden inside Steve's shirt. I folded the delicate mechanism gently and locked it away in the safety of a large trunk. We both needed a shower, a drink, and a chance to unwind, an opportunity to calm down, rethink strategy and plan for the coming days.

Looking much refreshed after a long hot shower, Steve returned to my room at ten o'clock. I was still catching up on my notes, so we agreed to rendezvous in the bar half an hour later and I returned to my desk. He could only have been gone a few minutes when there was a rapid and excited knock on my door.

'He's here, waiting outside, come on, let's go.' Steve hurriedly pushed his way into the room.

Automatically, and without thinking, I unlocked the trunk. This routine had been practised one hundred times before, eyes closed and in the dark. Steve tore off the clean button-down and slipped neatly into the old lumberjack's shirt with the secret eye innocently and almost inconspicuously sewn in behind a breast-pocket button. In less than three minutes the clandestine video was strapped and rigged to his body. We left the room together, and took the stairs rather than the elevator to meet our contact man in the hotel lobby.

Mr Lee was short, dark, bespectacled and thirty-something; much like many thousands of his fellow Korean countrymen. His unexceptional appearance belied a keen eye for business and a strong will to provide for his family. Steve had 'recruited' him one evening over several carafes of disgusting local wine in the hotel restaurant. Mr Lee traded in hand- and footwear and anything else where there was an easy profit to be made. He was a likeable chap and eager to please, and we exploited his gullibility unmercifully. He genuinely believed that both Steve and I were wildlife traders and eventually, after the wine had been supplanted by vodka, agreed to connect us with the Soviet-Korean Mafia. It was his own kinsmen in Khabarovsk who controlled the illegal tiger trade.

'He won't come inside,' said Mr Lee. 'He's frightened because last week someone tried to trick him and called the police. He'll only deal outside.'

In a dark corner of the parking lot, an old Japanese car belched exhaust fumes into the freezing night air. We had had no time to grab warm clothes, even less to think. There are times when an opportunity must be seized with both hands and caution thrown to the wind. This was one of them, and we stepped out into the night.

'Get in. The skin is not here, he will show you,' said Mr Lee.

I got in beside the three men already in the car. It was dark. I could not be sure, but they looked like Koreans.

'There's no room. I need the walk anyway,' said Steve, peering into the back of the car.

Steve was well over six feet tall. The cramped conditions inside the car, with the video camera strapped to the small of his back, would have been unbearable. Fortunately, nobody argued.

We drove around the front of the hotel under the silent shadow of the statue of Lenin. Mr Lee and Steve crossed quickly on foot and we met up in a narrow side-street at the far corner of the square. Parked away in the darkness was an old foresters' truck. The lights flashed briefly. A signal, all was well.

Two men got out of the cab, one Russian, the other of Korean descent. With a rough gesture we were ushered to the back of the lorry which the Russian laboriously unlocked, fumbling with the keys. A pungent haze of cheap vodka hit my nostrils. We climbed in. Inside the air was hot and sticky, and it stank. From the far corner and out from underneath a pile of firewood and broken boxes, an old sack was dragged into the dim light. I glanced over at Steve, nodded slightly. I prayed that the camera was on. All I could see was the tiny hole of the lens pointed directly at the sack.

Here we go, I thought. With clumsy, drunken hands, the sack was tipped unceremoniously on to the filthy wooden floor. Even before the contents were in full view I knew, I just felt that inside were the remains of a dead tiger.

One glance at the frozen, twisted, mangled skeleton was all it took to convince me. And yet somehow I was still unprepared for the horror of the sight of bones that were so obviously fresh. I picked up every one in turn and held them up to the light so that Steve could get a perfect view. Slowly and with great deliberation, I clinically examined each horrific piece. After fifteen minutes or so, Steve gestured that he'd seen enough, it was time to get out. I told Lee that we should return to the hotel to talk about money. He translated this to the poacher and the Koreans, and we all got out of the stinking truck into the cold night air.

The car sped us across the square and minutes later we were making our way to Lee's room. Once upstairs I told him that I needed to wash my hands. Steve took the hint. We said that we would be back in a minute.

I double-locked my bedroom door. Steve pulled frantically at the video recorder.

'Slow down, slow down,' I said. 'We've got plenty of time. Let the bastards wait.'

I connected up the tiny TV monitor in seconds. We had to be sure that we had filmed the whole grisly episode. I pushed the play button. Steve and I gazed at the empty screen in stunned silence. Nothing!

I rewound the tape. Images flashed before our eyes, the stairway, Lee in the hotel lobby, outside the bright glare of the street lamps as the automatic lens adjusted to the ambient light, the brisk walk across the square, the approach to the back of the poachers' truck, the back door opening, the inside, the pile of wood and boxes, the sack, the ascent into the truck, then nothing, a frazzled empty screen. Somehow the camera had shut itself off.

'Fuck it,' I screamed at that vacuous monitor, 'fuck, fuck, fuck!'

'We'll have to do it again,' said Steve finally.

'Are you out of your mind?' I snapped. 'The fucking camera's obviously playing up, there's no guarantee that it will work properly next time. The battery could be discharged. God knows why it's not working. How the hell could this happen? Fuck it!'

'It'll be OK. Work with me on this one, Mike, we can do it,' he said quietly.

'How can you be so fucking sure? How can you be so fucking calm? These people are killers.'

Steve was clutching at straws, we both knew it. In the past, in other parts of the world, both Steve and I had experienced the same nightmare. The soul-destroying anticlimax to the laborious process of winning the trust and confidence of the middlemen, the traders, the poachers. The wasted opportunity, the injustice of it engendered an almost suicidal despair.

Somehow we had to get back inside that truck again. I replaced the camera tightly in the small of Steve's back and we discussed, more rationally now, how it could be done.

'We'll have to demand to see the skin and the missing skull,' he said, 'it's the only way. Maybe we can convince them to go and get it.'

We returned to Mr Lee's room. The middlemen had grown impatient. I offered them some filthy Russian wine in cracked tea-cups to calm their pent-up aggression. I slugged straight from the bottle myself, took a deep breath and launched into my story.

'The situation is like this,' I began. 'My buyer in Hong Kong is only interested in perfect, whole specimens; they must be at least two metres from head to rump. The skeleton must be intact and if the skin is good, he will buy that too. In the truck it was impossible to see how big this tiger actually was. The market is very selective right now. There are new laws, buyers are very careful. Last year it was easier; I could buy almost anything. Now I have to be very cautious. Besides, there is a lot of merchandise around at the moment, prices are down, I can afford to be choosy. Show me the skin and the skull, and I will be better able to make a decision.' I sat back and waited for the translation.

A heated exchange began. Time after time, the Koreans glared at me with venomous eyes. Somehow I had to remain calm, impassive. It was imperative that I turn the initiative around. It was the only way we would ever be able to get back inside the truck for a second look.

Twice they demanded to know if I was serious. Did I have the cash? Would I definitely buy? Finally, disgruntled and very angry, they agreed to go and get the skin.

There was no mistaking the evil in the air as they left the room.

'Tell him we will be back in twenty minutes,' they said, and slammed the door.

Mr Lee suggested that we wait in our own room. He would call us when they came back. Steve and I returned to my room. I re-examined the camera, putting the battery on quick charge, testing the switches. Fifteen minutes later I was convinced that it was as good as it was ever likely to be. We sat down to wait.

Twenty minutes turned into almost an hour. We began to think that they would not show up again. Suddenly there was a rapid and excited knock at the door.

'This is Mr Lee. They are here,' came a quiet voice.

Downstairs in the hall we were met by the same three men, and taken outside to a waiting car. This time we did not return to the dark side-street but drove down the main town boulevard past three or four sets of lights before taking a sharp right. Down an icy hill we could see the poachers' truck cruising slowly, hugging the pavement. Again a flash of lights in recognition. They were obviously taking no chances this time; they wanted to be sure that they were not being tailed. We followed the truck into a small parking lot and pulled up beside it and got out. Behind us I noticed a green military-style jeep quietly come to a halt and douse its lights.

Mr Lee had refused to come with us this time, so I had to rely on gestures to ask about this extra vehicle.

'My friend,' whispered the Korean.

Knowing that Steve had to be last into the back of the truck, I motioned the others to get in. I followed, almost pushing them inside, leaving him to prepare the camera. Once inside, another bag quickly appeared. Rough hands pulled the contents out into the light of the cramped truck. There were seven of us in that confined space, I thought, and at least another three guarding outside in the parked jeep.

If any one of them had spotted the camera, without doubt we would both have ended up as dead as the wretched remains that were now on open view in front of us.

My hands trembled as I picked up the skin. Not so much from fear, but from sheer unadulterated anger at the futility and waste of such a precious creature. The tiger skin was heavy, thick with preserving salt. The hair was damp, probably clogged with snow from lying lifeless on the frozen ground long after it was trapped.

I was haunted by the feeling that the soul from this proud beast was somehow present in that dank room. Get a grip, I told myself angrily. Indifference is the key; hide behind indifference if you want to get out of here alive. I forced myself to look for the bullet hole. Somehow I had to hide my disgust at these cruel and evil men, had to make them believe that I was as dispassionate about this crumpled piece of fur as they were.

'Where was it shot?' I asked, folding my fingers into a gun and pointing at my head in mock, questioning surprise. The poacher understood, pulled down his lower lip, exposing blackened and decaying teeth, and pointed into his mouth.

I shuddered. He then gestured toward his left side, underneath the arm, with a dismissive wave of his hand. It was clear what he meant. And it was equally clear that it was him who must have fired the fatal shot. The tiger had been struck from in front and slightly above the mouth. The bullet had shattered the lower jaw and made a gaping exit wound through the upper chest, just behind the front leg. I looked in veiled horror at the fragmented jaw bone. The fucking bastards, I thought.

As I looked at the smashed skull, an idea came to me. With luck, I thought, if I played my cards very, very carefully indeed, Steve and I could both get out of the deal unscathed.

Bolder and more confident now, I asked two of the men to hold the skin up into the light to give Steve a better opportunity to capture the gruesome image on camera. After only two minutes he jerked his thumb at the back door and rubbed his index finger and thumb together, signalling that we should get out and talk about money. Money? What can have gone wrong this time, I thought.

We got out into the frozen night. We pretended to argue about cash while, quietly, his face torn in anguish, he whispered that he was not sure if the camera was still working.

'Shhh!' he demanded. 'Listen, can you hear it, is it on or off?'

It was impossible to say.

'Shut it down completely and turn it all back on again,' I said. 'Shhh! For Christ's sake, listen. Listen!'

Inside the truck I could hear the men talking angrily as they bundled the skin back inside a bag. There was the sound of something being dragged across the floor. I could only guess that they were hiding the incriminating evidence with bags of firewood and spare tyres. It was too late. They would never show us the skin again unless we showed them some money.

The door at the back of the truck was kicked violently open. The men stared menacingly at us as they jumped to the ground. With casual indifference I glanced inside. All trace of the dead tiger had been carefully hidden out of sight. It was time to move on to more secure ground. And quickly.

We zigzagged through the side-streets until we reached the familiar site of the characterless square. Several times I wondered if they would let us negotiate in the safety of our hotel. Once back inside we could be rid of these wretched thugs once and for all.

If only life could be that simple. The car skidded to a halt in the parking lot, and for a moment it seemed that they wanted to talk business right there and then.

'Mr Lee,' I said, pointing at the sanctuary of the lobby entrance. Reluctantly they opened the door and we all piled out. This time they were in no mood for polite conversation. We were shoved headlong down the corridor in the direction of Mr Lee's room.

He met us at the door, clearly surprised, toothbrush in hand. Getting ready for bed, I thought. He obviously wasn't expecting to see us again that night.

'Come in, come in then, quickly,' he said, coming straight to the point. 'Ok, what do you think, shall you make a deal?' he asked.

I had mentally rehearsed my speech in the car on the way back to the hotel. It had better be convincing, I thought.

'Two things, problems really,' I began. 'Firstly the skull is damaged, and you remember that I said that my buyer only wanted perfect goods. Secondly, the skin has not been properly cured. It could take up to three weeks to get to Hong Kong, and it would probably be useless and rotten by then. And another thing: the skeleton is not whole either; there were only six or seven loose ribs. My buyer specifically said that the bones must be intact. Last year I could sell any old rubbish, but now things are different; it's much harder to sell a bad specimen.'

'How can I tell him this?' asked Lee, clearly distressed.

'Wait, I tell you what I'll do, but there's no guarantee,' I said quickly. 'I'll phone my buyer in Hong Kong right away, see what he says. But I wouldn't be too surprised if he is pretty pissed off with me. He has already been waiting all day for me to call him. It's their fault. These guys didn't show up on time.'

'But this is your business,' responded Mr Lee. 'These men are not interested in your problem, they just want money, finish.'

'Tell them that I am only a middleman, just like them. I have to be sure that I can make a profit. There is a lot of merchandise around at the moment. There is someone down in Vladivostok who is desperately trying to off-load all of his stock. Tell them that they will have to be patient and trust me.' I prayed that I had sounded convincing as Mr Lee began the lengthy translation. Backwards and forwards they argued. For well over five minutes Mr Lee did his best to placate them.

Finally he said, 'Go make your call. I will try and help you.'

I got up and left the room. Outside in the corridor I shut my eyes and clenched my fists tightly. Keep control, I told myself, you can do it!

I went back to my room. On the window sill was a packet of Marlboro cigarettes that Steve had left behind. I had given up smoking years ago, but right there and then I wanted one desperately. I left the packet where it lay. In the bathroom I splashed cold water on my face and washed my hands. I went downstairs to the hotel lobby. On the wall was the only lifeline to sanity: a long-distance telephone. I picked up the receiver and for ten minutes had an elaborate argument with myself until I was ready to play my final card.

Somehow I now knew that I could pull this off. Back inside Mr Lee's room, I asked him to explain to the Koreans that my contact was not at home. That I had spoken with his wife who told me that he was very annoyed with me for not phoning earlier during the afternoon. That on no account should I buy anything until I had spoken with him first. I reinforced this argument by saying that I was using his money. And that last year I had decided to buy bear gall for over $12,000 in China. When I had smuggled it back to Hong Kong it turned out to be all fake. I was still paying back this debt.

'They want a deposit until tomorrow,' he said.

'How can I give them a deposit when I don't even know if I will be authorised to make the deal?' I replied angrily. 'I've already made it quite clear. If the specimen was perfect I would be prepared to take a chance. As it is, I cannot take that risk.'

'They don't believe you. They want $200 deposit right now, then everything OK,' he said, pleading with me, tears welling up inside his eyes.

'Listen,' I said, 'we'll do it this way. You don't leave for Seoul until tomorrow afternoon. I'll call my man first thing in the morning. Tell these people to contact you, say 11.30. That will give me enough time.'

By now the men were extremely angry. After a heated exchange one of them pointed at me, shouting madly and ran his index finger savagely across his throat. Lee refused to translate, but the threat was obvious.

They had made their point, and finally got up and left. Lee was tired and shaken. He was basically quite a nice guy. How he had got mixed up with these gangsters, I couldn't imagine. We said

343

goodnight, thanked him and rushed back to my room to check the camera.

I tore off the protective tape around the video recorder and popped open the cassette.

'Bingo!' I said. 'A lot of tape has been used. Let's see what we've got.'

I rewound the cassette and pressed the play button. With a large glass of cheap cognac each we huddled over the tiny screen and watched as the flickering images told their incriminating story.

'Got you, you bastards!' I said. 'Cheers to you, Steve.'

The following morning Steve came to my room to tell me that the Koreans would come by the hotel at 11.30. He wanted to set up the camera again.

'It's done,' I said. 'Let it go. If they come back, they will want either money or vengeance for being tricked. They are not going to get either. Instead we'll give them a message to take back to the entire illegal poaching network.' I explained my plan.

We borrowed a pair of tiger skulls from a friendly scientist with whom we were vaguely working and showed them to Mr Lee. Steve explained that we had just bought them at a knock-down price of $500 from a trader desperate to be rid of them. Steve told him that the bottom had suddenly dropped out of the tiger-bone market, and that dealers in Hong Kong, China and Taiwan were no longer paying high prices for tiger bone. There were tough new laws that were beginning to have effect. It was too risky. We had bought the skulls and that was enough.

Mr Lee looked absolutely shattered as he heard the news. His bottom lip quivered as he fought to control his emotion. He had no choice but to accept our story; the proof was right under his nose and the skulls established our credentials as bona fide traders. We left him to relay our message to the Korean thugs who in turn, we hoped, would pass the news further down the line that the value of tiger bone was plummeting and was no longer worth the risk. It was a shot in the dark, but worth a try.

Bill Clark had gone on ahead to Vladivostok and I was grateful that he was blissfully unaware of the risks Steve and I were taking. We were all there to help the Russians find ways to stamp out the tiger-poaching, not to spy on the Korean Mafia-driven underground trade. Nevertheless it was necessary to prove the existence of the smuggling network, and the ease with which it could be infiltrated and exposed. The formula was the same in Russia as it had been in Taiwan and China: if westerners could do it, then so could the local police authorities.

We took the overnight train to Vladivostok and for the next few days met with officials from the regional Ecology Committee. The men of the Russian Far East were proud of their tiger heritage. They needed only financial support, and together we mapped out a scheme to assist them. We named it 'Operation Amba' after the indigenous Udegi tribal name for the tiger which means 'great sovereign'.

Steve agreed to stay behind in Vladivostok and help get the programme off the ground. I returned home to arrange the funding. Both of us realised, however, that the single largest threat to the survival of the Siberian tiger was the continued underground trade into China. As long as that was allowed to persist, we would forever be fighting an impossible battle.

The Chinese town of Harbin was not far from the Russian border, and it was still the centre of the tiger-bone trade in that part of the world. I could never go back again. Steve had never been there, and as I said goodbye to him in the week before Christmas he agreed to go and have a quiet look at the town for himself.

CHAPTER TWENTY-EIGHT

England, March 1994

Steve Galster maintained regular contact by phone and fax as he
fought through the bitterly cold Siberian winter, carefully construct-
ing the essential framework of our anti-poaching initiative in the
Russian Far East. With the help of the Russian authorities, he
successfully recruited sixteen courageous men and coordinated a
comprehensive training programme. By the end of January, he had
organised the purchase of all the necessary vehicles and vital field
equipment to enable Operation Amba to go to work. At the same
time, Steve Galster kept his eyes and ears wide open on the lookout
for the ruthless Mafia-controlled smuggling gangs that were supplying the underground export trade with Russia's rapidly diminishing
supply of Siberian tigers. During the first ten weeks of 1994, he
helped uncover one of the most devastating and potentially catastrophic black-market networks in the region. Although I kept him
backed up with essential finance and supplies, all I could really do
was assist from afar.

The Tiger Trust was growing rapidly and it took all of my time
just to keep it afloat. The phone seemed never to stop ringing and
the postman would bring dozens of letters each day, sometimes
hundreds. The support of the great British public was overwhelming.

The fight for the tiger was, by now, in full swing, and the size of
the task often seemed quite terrifying. Despite China's and Taiwan's
much publicised claims to have cracked down on the tiger-bone
trade, coupled with pledges from other leading markets like Hong
Kong, Singapore and South Korea to follow suit, tiger populations
were still being decimated across Asia. Whatever we had achieved
so far, clearly wasn't enough.

In India, the Project Tiger reserves were under relentless attack from poachers. The famous Ranthambore National Park, featured in so many magnificent wildlife documentaries, had seen its complement of around forty-five tigers reduced to fewer than fifteen. That trend was being repeated throughout the entire subcontinent. The Indian authorities, while quietly admitting that there was no shortage of conservation funds, were short on political will and severely hampered by corruption and weak leadership. Our efforts to stamp out the illegal tiger trade were also being undermined by India's reluctance to police her own wildlife borders effectively. If thirty tigers could disappear from under the noses of the authorities at the world's foremost tiger reserve, then something was definitely very wrong indeed. Somehow we had to find out why the killing continued and what was happening to all those dead tigers. Clearly somebody, somewhere, was being less than sincere.

It didn't take long for us to establish that most trails still led eastward. Undercover operators in India reported that Nepalese and Tibetan middlemen continued to name China as the number one market for their contraband. Investigations in Singapore and Hong Kong convinced us that there was still considerable bilateral trade with Chinese dealers on the mainland. In Russia, we knew that at least fifty tigers had perished during the winter to supply markets over the border into north-eastern China. If that level of slaughter continued, the great Siberian tiger would be wiped out in less than five years.

Although he succeeded in penetrating one faction of the trade in Vladivostok, involving a senior customs' officer, Steve Galster would need help if he was seriously to infiltrate the Chinese black market. There was only one person to my mind that could help him succeed in doing that.

I telephoned Rebecca Chen.

At first she appeared reluctant to get involved; it had been over six months since she had been out in the field and she felt rusty and unprepared. She had recently got married and, although her priorities had shifted, I was pleased to discover that they had not changed altogether. Two weeks later, fully briefed and prepared for a long mission, she flew out to join Steve in Vladivostok and together they went to work.

I was becoming more of a spy-master than a spy, sending others into battle while I locked horns with the unutterably tedious bureaucracy of wildlife conservation. I hated the endless meetings, the false smiles and the tiresome rhetoric. I longed for the excitement of active combat. Nevertheless, I had to remain focused on pushing home our advantage internationally and establishing a place for The Tiger Trust in the vital decision-making political process.

And so, at the beginning of March, I flew off to New Delhi to attend a pan-Asian conference of representatives of the fourteen tiger range states. There was only one item on the agenda. The future survival of the tiger.

For two whole days, I listened to speakers from around the world, all of whom said approximately the same thing. The tiger was a magnificent wild creature, a source of wonder and inspiration since time immemorial, and it was being poached to within an inch of extinction. Few people had the guts to say why or dared point a finger at who might be responsible. Least of all at the main culprit, China, who had boycotted the meeting for fear of receiving the public censure that their continued appetite for tigers so justly deserved.

Once the assembled politicians and bureaucrats had had their say, the NGO representatives were given a turn at the podium and I was one of them. Once more I seized the opportunity to beg delegates to examine the reality so unmistakably documented before them. The tiger was in crisis, the main underlying reason was China's continued illegal import and consumption, and failure to recognise and act upon this stark reality would consign the tiger to extinction within a few short years, full stop. No fancy trimming, no crying wolf, the situation was as plain as it was inescapable. Energy, resource and commitment would have to be found immediately in order to coordinate an effective solution.

The politicians continued nonetheless to dance around the issue. Scared witless and unable to bite the bullet, they searched frantically for the path of least resistance.

The Americans, meanwhile, quietly monitored proceedings from the wings, hoping for a strong show of support for their threatened trade sanctions against Taiwan and China. They had the domestic legislation and political will to proceed and yet felt isolated without the support of the Asian countries whose tigers they had pledged to protect. These largely developing nations knew that to back the US initiative would infuriate the Chinese, who were already strong-arming them with threats of cancelled trade deals.

The tiger, the very animal at the heart of the original debate,

349

became sidelined as a sinister game of bluff poker was played out with China holding most of the aces.

The Global Tiger Forum in Delhi predictably produced nothing in the way of substantive proposals. At the end of four days of deliberations a statement was drawn up that made no mention of China. It was the usual type of document befitting such a meeting, full of rhetoric, expressing concern but providing no solutions. Although everyone at that assembly knew exactly what was going on, they failed to unite and send a strong message of condemnation to the guilty nations. Within days of the break-up of the meeting, it was business as usual for the poachers and middlemen. The tiger, of course, continued down the perilous slope toward extinction.

Meanwhile, back at my hotel, an important fax was waiting. It was from Steve and largely in code. He and Rebecca had crossed the border into northern China and made a remarkable breakthrough. They urgently needed backup and extra surveillance equipment. I faxed back telling him to get Rebecca on to a flight to London and I would meet her there in two days' time.

So much for India, and my opportunity to catch a glimpse of a Bengal tiger in the wild, I thought, as I dashed out to the airport and caught the first flight home.

The confinement of an aircraft cabin is an excellent place to do some serious thinking. There are few distractions. Unravelling the hidden message in his communiqué was the easy part. I now needed to find the answer to Steve's dilemma. The miniature camera in his shirt had been smashed. He needed a replacement and one that could be readily concealed. In my notebook I sketched out a man and gave him a wide-shouldered jacket, dark glasses and a brief-case. I was no artist and yet he looked like a Latin-American drug dealer. Good, I thought, I was on the right track! I examined the clothing and analysed each piece in turn, wondering where I could hide the tiny lens. A hat was too risky. I had tried that myself and knew the problems. A briefcase camera would certainly be easy to rig up but I had already decided to convert a handbag for Rebecca. There had to be another novel way to hide the camera and I began to focus my attention around the breast pocket of the blazer. And then the idea came to me.

'Can it be done?' I asked my enigmatic friend in London's Maida Vale, less than eight hours later.

'Oh yes. But it won't be easy. Would next week be all right?'

'I'm afraid not. My associate is flying in tonight and must leave again tomorrow. This is very urgent. We simply don't have too much time.'

'Well there might be a chance, if you can stay and help me.'

'Of course,' I said. 'Just tell me what I have to do.'

We worked until long after midnight. He was a wizard with electronics. With great precision he modified the miniature circuitry and realigned the lens so that it was barely visible. I stripped away the lining of a dark blue double-breasted jacket and together we positioned the tiny camera behind the breast pocket and cut a small hole through the fabric. Across the front we tacked an elaborate club badge through which we bored a tiny hole. With delicate cable stitching I sewed the emblem to the navy brass-buttoned blazer. The result was quite incredible: the lens was almost completely invisible!

For the next hour or so, we tested the hidden camera until we were satisfied that it would film and record every detail within a thirty-foot range. Finally, at about three o'clock in the morning, I called a cab and returned to my hotel room on Edgware Road. Shortly after nine o'clock, Rebecca arrived to collect the new equipment, some emergency cash and flew back to China.

For the next four days, I hardly ate or slept a wink. I was able to alert contacts in both Beijing and Hong Kong that two of our people were treading on thin ice up north, but that was about all. They agreed to provide a safety net in case something went terribly wrong. There was nothing more that I could do but wait. Steve and Rebecca were on their own.

By Tuesday of that week they were in position and poised to infiltrate the very same tiger-bone wine factory that I had visited the year before. This time, with hidden cameras. Despite repeated claims by the authorities in China that this and every other tiger-bone medicine facility had been shut down, Steve had discovered that it, and several more just like it, were still very much in business.

Two months earlier, in January, the Chinese government had hosted a top-level delegation of CITES officials. Their job was to examine and report upon China's recent measures to stem the illegal tiger-bone trade, a process that I had helped to engineer less than a year earlier, at the Standing Committee meeting in Washington. The officials were manifestly impressed. They were shown around empty factories and surveyed sacks of bone neatly fastened with extravagant lead seals; they were even treated to a bonfire party where several hundred kilos of 'tiger bone' were ceremoniously

351

torched. The local and international press were invited to view the spectacle and the Associated Press agency put out the following wire story:

ASSOCIATED PRESS. Jan. 13, 1994

Beijing. (AP). About 1100lbs of tiger bones, an important ingredient in traditional medicines, were burned by Chinese officials enforcing a ban on their use. China, under pressure from environmental groups, last year prohibited trading in rhinoceros horn and tiger bone to protect the animals. The tiger bones were burned Wednesday in the north-eastern town of Harbin, the State-run *China Daily* reported today. They were confiscated in September by law-enforcement officials it said.

And, as the hapless CITES officials were being ushered out the front door in a blaze of pomp and officialdom, Steve and Rebecca were quietly letting themselves in the back door and discovered a quite different story. It had taken them nearly two months finally to run down, but Steve was a tower of tenacity and strength and Rebecca was a relentless bloodhound. Together they slowly got closer to the truth and as I waited for news back at our Suffolk base during that fateful week in March, I prayed to the Almighty for their safe deliverance.

On Friday, I received an urgent call from Rebecca's sister in Taiwan. Her voice was faltering and yet there was no hiding the excitement of the message it conveyed. I was to get down to Heathrow Airport by mid-afternoon. They were coming home.

A great surge of adrenaline thundered through my veins as I finally caught sight of them both, wearily emerging from behind the sliding perspex doors into the arrivals lounge. Steve's huge smile was as welcome as any that I have ever known and Rebecca looked radiant despite the discomfort of the long flight. Their mission had been a huge success and strapped to the inside of Steve's elastic body belt was the vital evidence to prove it.

For the next two days we reviewed the extraordinary undercover video film in a darkened studio in the heart of Berkshire, cutting and editing until we had pieced together the whole story. By late Sunday afternoon we had put together a fifteen-minute compilation tape and as we ran through the final edited version, I watched in utter amazement as the stunning images unfurled before my eyes.

In one scene, Steve and Rebecca were being shown around the Chinese medicine factory's manufacturing plant. I could recognise three huge vats that extracted the glutinous tiger-bone resin. A man wearing a heavy dark-blue overcoat was explaining the production process in great detail. The hidden lens panned around the room and came to rest on a number of khaki-coloured hessian sacks, piled up on the floor.

'Raw tiger bone,' explained Rebecca.

The images swirled in and out of focus as the tiny camera adjusted to the new light of another room. I could see dozens of women sitting at a long table busily bundling small blue cellophane packages into cardboard cartons. Beside them, a fully automated machine clanked loudly as its rotating mechanism churned out hundreds of compressed fabric squares, each about half the size of a postcard.

'Tiger-bone plasters,' said Steve quietly. 'The Chinese believe they help relieve the discomfort of rheumatism and arthritis. Actually, it's the deep-heat effect of the essential oils combined with the camphor, menthol and eucalyptus liniments contained in the embrocation that has the effect. The bone is inert, so God knows why they put it in. Its all hocus-pocus, crazy superstition, but there's a huge market. These guys can produce one and a half million plasters every day and the profit is phenomenal, all the way down the line.'

'How phenomenal?' I asked.

'Well over 1,000 per cent from factory to consumer, so there's your incentive right there. They didn't say how much *they* were making, but you can bet it's massive by any standards. This *is* a highly lucrative business.'

'Like printing your own money?' I said.

'Yeah, pretty much,' he said. 'And you know what, this is just one factory. The director told me that he controls another thirty just like it!'

'Jesus Christ,' I said softly. 'Did they say where they were getting the bone?'

'Just about anywhere that they can get their hands on it. Russia, of course; a lot comes over the border by both road and rail. Then from India either via Tibet or through Burma into South-east China. He also mentioned a very interesting route from Sumatra through Singapore. That checks out with the rumours we've been hearing that Korea gets much of its bone this way, with the Chinese transshipping it up from Shanghai. And, of course, from somewhere

353

else that you're very familiar with, Mike,' he said.

'Where's that?' I said, as the answer suddenly hit me like a bullet.

'The tiger farm,' he said, without emotion.

'Are you sure?' I asked, knowing that he was.

'Oh yeah, I'm sure,' he said. 'It's all in the tapes. See that stuffed tiger in the glass cabinet?'

The film had now cut to inside the medicine factory's boardroom, the same one that I had visited nine months earlier, although there was no elaborate centrepiece when I was there.

'That room look familiar?' enquired Steve. 'It should do, 'cos they mentioned you a lot. You see to begin with, they were very much on their guard, they told us about an "English spy" that had caused them all sorts of embarrassment last year! At one point they even asked Rebecca if she was a little spy as well. She just smiled and told them no, that in fact she was a big spy! Everyone laughed it off and relaxed. Anyway, the stuffed tiger was a gift to the so-called tiger breeding centre from the Russian government. It was a pure, wild-caught Siberian male. The Chinese reckoned it was infertile so they killed and ate it and stuffed what was left, presumably as a permanent reminder of Russian gullibility.'

'The bastards,' I said angrily.

'Just wait until you hear the next part,' he said.

Across the smoky room, a man lounged on a large sofa whom I recognised as the factory's chief executive, puffing away on a stream of Marlboro cigarettes. Beside him was the Chinese government official instructed to collect and burn the tiger-bone stockpile for the benefit of the press and the visiting CITES dignitaries two months earlier. They obviously had no idea that they were being secretly filmed. They were discussing with Rebecca a deal to buy medicinal products containing tiger bone. The conversation had been meticulously translated and the studio technicians had managed to caption the film with the following words:

REBECCA: If we want to order a big quantity, how much can you supply monthly?
OFFICIAL: We can provide as much as you want.
REBECCA: But CITES wanted you to burn your stockpile. They said you burned it all.
OFFICIAL: Why should I burn it?
REBECCA: But you burned it in front of people.
OFFICIAL: That was fake.

354

REBECCA: How much did you burn?

OFFICIAL: I did not burn any at all, why should I?

REBECCA: I heard that some people came to take photos of the burning.

OFFICIAL: The photos they took were of the fake bones being burned.

REBECCA: It was fake bones you burned?

OFFICIAL: Yes, all fake!

I rewound the tape and watched the sequence over and over again; that brief statement had said it all. In a few short words, this official summed up the Chinese total disregard for endangered wildlife. There was absolutely no doubt now. The Chinese had been consistently and blatantly lying; not only to the international community but they had suckered the visiting CITES officials into the bargain. It was men like this who were responsible for the epidemic tiger slaughter across the Indian subcontinent, the Russian Far East and throughout the rest of Asia.

The evidence was there for all the world to see. I now had to somehow make that happen. I was short on time. The CITES Standing Committee met in Geneva for their biannual meeting the very next day.

That evening, after I had dropped Steve off at his hotel, I drove back home to Suffolk. It was raining, and the rhythmic beat of the windscreen wipers helped me to relax and think clearly. I needed to plan my strategy very carefully. I was in possession of some of the most damning evidence imaginable against the Chinese; essentially more than enough proof for the Americans to pull out the stops and impose their much-threatened trade sanctions. In Washington, Sam LaBudde was already mounting a tireless media campaign inviting the American people to phone the White House and urge tough action from President Clinton. The tactic was paying off; nobody could dispute the jammed phone-lines. And yet the President was still sitting on the fence, trying to balance all the arguments, unsure which way to go. The climate was perfect, I thought; it was now time to give him a gentle push.

I arrived home at about 10 p.m.; it was late, but not too late to call my friend Lawrence McGinty from Independent Television News. We set up a meeting for the following morning at their Grays Inn Road studios.

Physically exhausted but mentally very much awake I tried to get some sleep. It was impossible. So many things were going through my mind. I had come such a long way since that fateful encounter with 'the big boy' just over four years earlier, and yet there was still so much left to do. How many more times would it be necessary to risk life and limb in order to prove to the world the obscene reality of the illegal wildlife trade, I wondered? Somehow, I had to make this latest evidence tell the whole sickening story. I could not go back to China, and now neither could Steve or Rebecca. There were very few others who either knew the issue or were prepared to take the risk. I had no choice but to hurl this evidence into the international arena with all the force and strength at my disposal.

On Monday morning, I hastily packed a few items of clothing, grabbed a spare suit from the wardrobe and left poor Sophy wondering whether I had finally taken leave of my senses.

'I have a meeting with ITN at ten o'clock and then an early-afternoon flight to Geneva. I'm meeting Steve at the airport,' I said as I kissed her goodbye.

'Be careful,' was all she could say, and I was gone.

I telephoned Nick Nuttal from *The Times* and agreed to rendez-vous with him at ITN headquarters in London. I now knew exactly what I had to do and I was in no mood to pull any punches.

Lawrence McGinty had been called away urgently on another assignment by the time I arrived and I was met by his colleague Eric MacInnes. He wasted no time at all in finding a free studio and playing the tape.

'This is dynamite,' he said. 'When did you get this?'

'Five days ago, last Wednesday,' I replied.

'Forgive me, but I have to ask, is it genuine?'

'Every last frame of it,' I said quietly. 'The translation is as good as we could get, but I'm sure you have access to someone that can double-check it.'

'That's no problem,' he said. 'Can I do a quick interview with you now; I want to get this out on the lunch-time news.'

'Now that is a problem,' I said. 'I'm going to have to ask you to sit on it until this evening. You have my word that this is exclusive, but I must make a formal presentation to the CITES delegates later this afternoon in Switzerland.'

He looked at me for a few brief moments before saying, 'OK.'

While he was organising a cameraman and sound recordist, I gave a full interview to Nick Nuttal. He listened intently to what I had to say, saying little and making copious notes in shorthand. By noon I was on my way out to the airport leaving the time-bomb gently ticking away in the studios of ITN.

At exactly five o'clock that evening, I walked into the conference hall in Geneva, took my seat at the top table reserved for speakers at the meeting, and awaited my turn to address the delegates. By now I was familiar with most of the faces in the room, some of whom smiled while others merely glared back at me with thinly disguised contempt. For them, I was a trouble maker, a thorn in the side of their nefarious schemes further to undermine the credibility of CITES and legalise all trade in endangered wildlife, irrespective of the consequences. I smiled back at one of them, a balding, bearded individual; you're not going to like this, I thought, as I was called to the podium to speak, you won't like this at all:

Mr Chairman, distinguished delegates, observers, ladies and gentlemen.

The Tiger Trust has been monitoring the illegal trade in tiger products for over three years. We have documented the poaching of tigers in Thailand and Indo-China, Sumatra, India and most recently in the Russian Far East. In my address to the Standing Committee last September in Brussels, I spoke of the active work of many NGOs in hands-on conservation work and the importance of a strong cooperation with the CITES secretariat and government organisations around the world. I also spoke about perhaps the most valuable role of investigative NGOs like ourselves in that we are often the very eyes and ears of this Convention. These days, with hidden cameras, sound recording equipment, solid intelligence information and a good deal of guts and commitment, undercover investigators can delve deep into the sordid, dangerous underworld of the gangsters involved in endangered species smuggling and follow that trail wherever it leads. Frequently, that trail leads us down paths that many would prefer us not to travel and sometimes it leads to corruption at the highest levels. The film evidence that you are about to see was recorded less than one week ago. I invite you to view it with an open mind and ask yourselves the following questions:

1) Just how sincere are the Chinese when they tell us that

357

the entire tiger-bone trade has been shut down?

2) Was the wool pulled over the eyes of the distinguished delegation that visited this part of the world just over two months ago?

I signalled to Steve and the lights were dimmed. Behind me, a massive audio-visual screen crackled into life. There really is no turning back now, I thought.

EPILOGUE

Suffolk, England, July 1995

Our evidence was just too much for the assembled delegates to handle. They had come to Geneva to discuss the fate of the tiger, and yet they came with closed minds.

Our undercover information, categoric proof of the continued illegal trade in tiger body parts, obtained at great personal risk to my investigative team, was dismissed with contempt by all but a handful of people at the meeting. The reason was as simple as it was outrageous – Sinophobia!

By the time I delivered my damning address, the CITES Secretariat had already circulated their own confidential report based on the top-level visit to China earlier that year. It was a done deal. The delegates had no stomach for a fight with Beijing and their diffidence was quite obviously reflected in the subsequent resolution, adopted later by the meeting which noted '. . . *with satisfaction the progress demonstrated by China in meeting certain criteria designed to halt the continued illegal trade in tiger parts and derivatives*'.

The final document, a masterpiece of United Nations rhetoric, offered no clues whatsoever on how to halt the tiger's perilous nose-dive towards extinction. Instead, and incredulous as it may seem, CITES buckled under the political pressure from the Chinese and actually gave them an almighty pat on the back thereby slamming the door in the face of the American initiative to sanction them for flagrant CITES violations into the bargain.

The fate of the tiger was thus demoted to a process in which decisions were based, not on the prevailing plight of the species, but upon matters analogous to both political and diplomatic expediency. And once again both the world's press and the pro-active

359

NGO conservation community were locked out of the entire debating procedure. It was a disgrace.

Fortunately for the tiger, a time bomb was still ticking quietly in the studios of ITN back in London. Five hours after my presentation in Geneva, our undercover story was aired on the News at Ten. It was one of the top five news stories of the day. Whether CITES liked it or not the big cat was finally out of the bag.

Within minutes of the transmission, I received a call from an executive in World Television News asking for permission to air the piece internationally; I couldn't say yes fast enough! All through the night and well into that week, the story of China's duplicity was beamed down into the homes of millions of people around the planet. CITES might have dismissed our findings, but the world was finally beginning to wake up to the crisis affecting the tiger.

Despite the bitter disappointment of the Geneva meeting, Steve and I flew on to the United States and submitted our findings to a packed press conference hastily arranged on our behalf by Diane MacEachern and her wonderful team at Vanguard Communications in Washington. That night, one day after my forty-first birthday, our story ran on the American TV networks and the call for action to the President of the United States grew louder.

Less than four weeks later, in arguably one of the most historic acts of his entire administration, President William Jefferson Clinton authorised limited trade sanctions against The Republic of China on Taiwan, and in so doing, joined the ranks of the growing army of people around the world ready to roll up their sleeves and fight for the tiger.

There can be no doubt that the decision to single out Taiwan, at the expense of the entire Chinese mainland, was a bold and calculated risk designed to send an unequivocal message to the entire tiger consuming countries of the Far East. The threat of trade sanctions is only as strong as the political will to follow through with decisive action. In the face of intense international opposition, the United States had the guts to stand firm on the issue; although, I am ashamed to say, they received little or no support from Westminster for their courage. The British government's prevailing policy on international CITES matters is shamefully to hide behind the apron of so-called European unity. Where once our statesmen would have been proud to stand up to the bullying of the underdog third-world by the massive economic might of nations like China and Japan, now they cower like rabbits, conveniently caught in the headlights of the blinding Eurocratic red tape from Brussels. Last year, in November, the United Kingdom was handed the Chair of the CITES Standing Committee on a silver plate. Nevertheless, in an arrogant and stupefying error of judgement, they allowed it to be finessed from their flimsy grasp by the masterly artifice of the political strategists from Tokyo. Japan remains to this day one of the last countries in Asia freely to allow the abominable trade in tiger products, an irony seemingly lost on our elected representatives in both this country and in Europe.

Most of us have, at some stage of our lives, been consumed by a feeling of utter helplessness over what, if anything, we can do to redress the grave injustice so often inflicted by our fellow man upon our common world. For some, the issue is human suffering, whether it be famine in the Horn of Africa or the refugee crisis in the former Yugoslavia. For others, it is environmental degradation, deforestation and pollution. For me, it has been the plight of one of the most easily recognised of all living creatures and yet one that remains under the most calamitous threat of extinction in the wild.

I have been fortunate. Circumstances somehow contrived to allow me a greater insight into the immediate threat to the species and permitted me the opportunity to assemble a damning case against those responsible. I do not have a death wish and yet I can not sit idly by and watch the animal kingdom sink deeper into the quagmire without trying to stop it. Change invariably comes only in the wake of a crisis, a context in which a new ideology can emerge, and if you believe strongly enough in a cause you put your mind and effort into it, irrespective of the personal danger. Whether I have been successful in reversing a precipitous trend only time will tell, but by joining the fray, I hope that I have added some weight to international pressure and a growing public awareness of the problem.

It is not too late, the plight of the tiger is not without hope, the war against continued illegal consumption and political apathy is winnable, of that I have no doubt. We are all constituents of this planet, each with a voice and at some time in our lives, a vote. We must not be afraid to use either.

King George VI once said, '*The wildlife of today is not ours to dispose of as we please. We have it in trust, we must account for it to those that come after.*' Those words must surely be as true now as they have ever been.

List of Organisations

CIA   – Central Intelligence Agency
CITES   – Convention on International Trade in Endangered Species
EGAT   – Electrical Generating Authority of Thailand
EIA   – Environmental Investigation Agency
IFAW   – International Fund for Animal Welfare
ITN   – Independent Television News
IUCN   – International Union for the Conservation of Nature
KNT   – Kuomintang
MTR   – Mass Transit Rail System (Singapore)
NGOs   – Non Governmental Organisations
RFD   – Royal Forestry Department (Thailand)
TRAFFIC   – Trade Records Analysis of Flora and Fauna In Commerce
WWF   – Worldwide Fund for Nature/World Wildlife Fund

The Tiger Trust, founded by Michael and Sophy Day, is the only organisation in the world exclusively working on the issue of wild tiger conservation. It has successfully combined the use of covert investigative material with political lobbying at the highest level to fight the illegal trade in tiger derivatives and secure a greater public awareness of the critical plight of the species. The Tiger Trust devised the highly successful 'Operation Amba', a unique anti-poaching programme in the Russian Far East that is fighting to save the last 180 Siberian tigers from extinction in the wild. The Tiger Trust has built the largest natural habitat sanctuary in Asia for tigers rescued from the illegal trade and continues to campaign for an end to the abominable commerce in tiger genitalia and other body parts throughout the world.

Membership of The Tiger Trust costs only £15 per year. For further information, or to make an immediate donation please write to:

The Tiger Trust
Chevington
Bury St Edmunds
Suffolk IP29 5RG
United Kingdom

Registered Charity Number 1014670

Index

Family relationships to the author are given in brackets